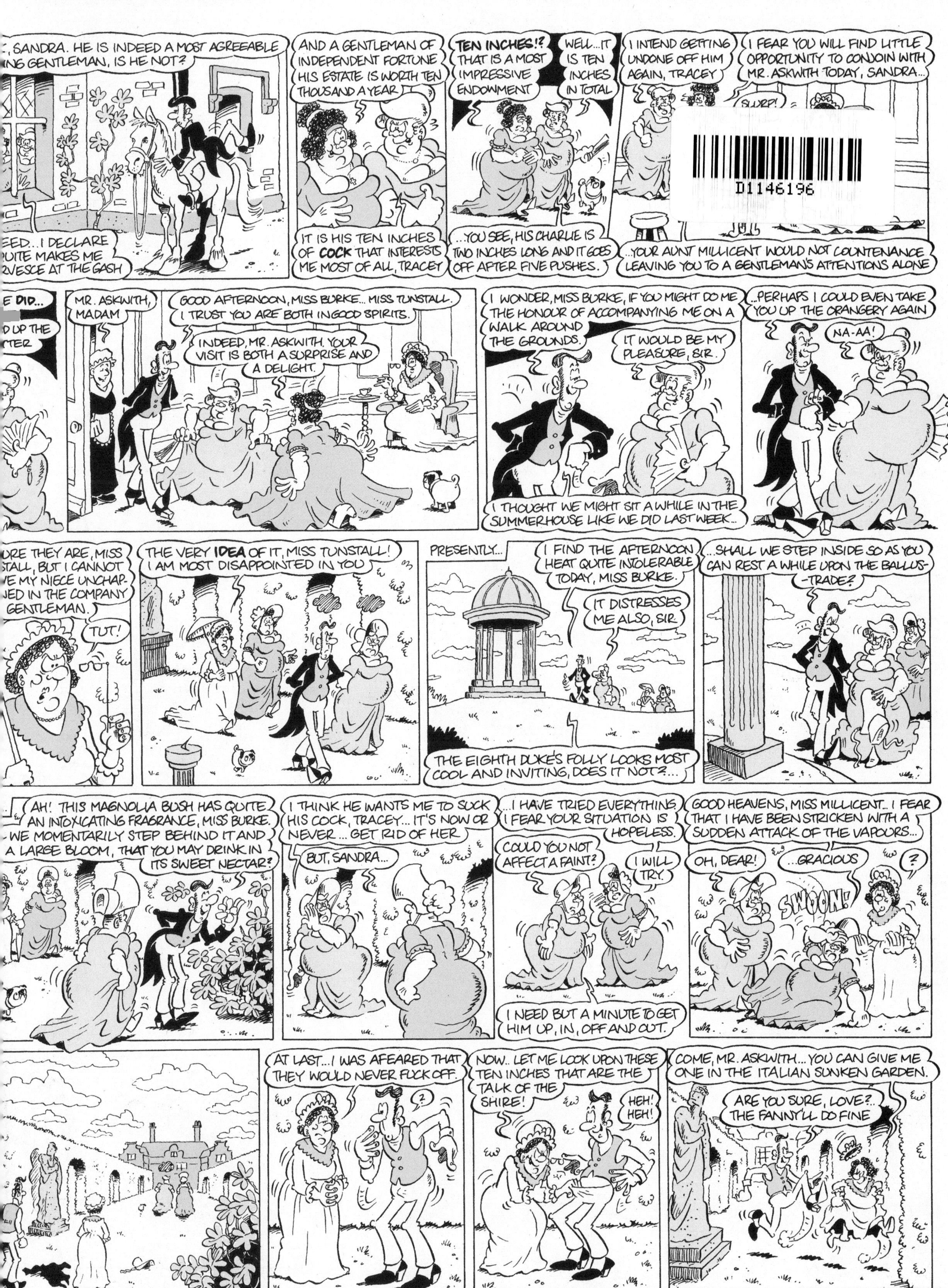

C, SANDRA. HE IS INDEED A MOST AGREEABLE
NG GENTLEMAN, IS HE NOT?
EED... I DECLARE
UITE MAKES ME
RVESCE AT THE GASH
AND A GENTLEMAN OF INDEPENDENT FORTUNE HIS ESTATE IS WORTH TEN THOUSAND A YEAR
IT IS HIS TEN INCHES OF COCK THAT INTERESTS ME MOST OF ALL, TRACEY
TEN INCHES!? THAT IS A MOST IMPRESSIVE ENDOWMENT
WELL...IT IS TEN INCHES IN TOTAL
...YOU SEE, HIS CHARLIE IS TWO INCHES LONG AND IT GOES OFF AFTER FIVE PUSHES.
I INTEND GETTING UNDONE OFF HIM AGAIN, TRACEY
I FEAR YOU WILL FIND LITTLE OPPORTUNITY TO CONJOIN WITH MR. ASKWITH TODAY, SANDRA...
SLURP!
...YOUR AUNT MILLICENT WOULD NOT COUNTENANCE LEAVING YOU TO A GENTLEMAN'S ATTENTIONS ALONE
E DID...
D UP THE
TTER
MR. ASKWITH, MADAM
GOOD AFTERNOON, MISS BURKE... MISS TUNSTALL. I TRUST YOU ARE BOTH IN GOOD SPIRITS.
INDEED, MR. ASKWITH. YOUR VISIT IS BOTH A SURPRISE AND A DELIGHT.
I WONDER, MISS BURKE, IF YOU MIGHT DO ME THE HONOUR OF ACCOMPANYING ME ON A WALK AROUND THE GROUNDS.
IT WOULD BE MY PLEASURE, SIR.
I THOUGHT WE MIGHT SIT A WHILE IN THE SUMMERHOUSE LIKE WE DID LAST WEEK...
...PERHAPS I COULD EVEN TAKE YOU UP THE ORANGERY AGAIN
NA-AA!
ORE THEY ARE, MISS
STALL, BUT I CANNOT
VE MY NIECE UNCHAP-
NED IN THE COMPANY
GENTLEMAN.
TUT!
THE VERY IDEA OF IT, MISS TUNSTALL! I AM MOST DISAPPOINTED IN YOU
PRESENTLY...
I FIND THE AFTERNOON HEAT QUITE INTOLERABLE TODAY, MISS BURKE.
IT DISTRESSES ME ALSO, SIR.
THE EIGHTH DUKE'S FOLLY LOOKS MOST COOL AND INVITING, DOES IT NOT?...
...SHALL WE STEP INSIDE SO AS YOU CAN REST A WHILE UPON THE BALLUS--TRADE?
AH! THIS MAGNOLIA BUSH HAS QUITE AN INTOXICATING FRAGRANCE, MISS BURKE.
WE MOMENTARILY STEP BEHIND IT AND A LARGE BLOOM, THAT YOU MAY DRINK IN ITS SWEET NECTAR?
I THINK HE WANTS ME TO SUCK HIS COCK, TRACEY... IT'S NOW OR NEVER ... GET RID OF HER
BUT, SANDRA...
...I HAVE TRIED EVERYTHING. I FEAR YOUR SITUATION IS HOPELESS.
COULD YOU NOT AFFECT A FAINT?
I WILL TRY.
I NEED BUT A MINUTE TO GET HIM UP, IN, OFF AND OUT.
GOOD HEAVENS, MISS MILLICENT... I FEAR THAT I HAVE BEEN STRICKEN WITH A SUDDEN ATTACK OF THE VAPOURS...
OH, DEAR!
SWOON!
...GRACIOUS
?
AT LAST... I WAS AFEARED THAT THEY WOULD NEVER FUCK OFF.
?
NOW.. LET ME LOOK UPON THESE TEN INCHES THAT ARE THE TALK OF THE SHIRE!
HEH! HEH!
COME, MR. ASKWITH... YOU CAN GIVE ME ONE IN THE ITALIAN SUNKEN GARDEN.
ARE YOU SURE, LOVE?.. THE FANNY'LL DO FINE

NONE OF THIS IS PUBLIC, GEORGE
WELL, YOUR EX-WIFE'S MEMOIRS WOULD BE A CLEAR INVASION OF YOUR RIGHT TO PRIVACY, ROGER...

READ OUR LIPS!

THE CAMEL'S TOE

A Blind Man's Buffet loaded with choice snatches from issues 202 - 211

Lawrence of a labias
Graham Dury, Davey Jones and Simon Thorp

Knicker sausages
Mark Bates, James Blyth, Julian Boffin, Alex Collier, Simon Ecob, Tom Ellen, Barney Farmer, Jason Hazeley, Lee Healey, Hobnob, Alex Morris, Joel Morris, Paul Palmer, Terry Stickney, Lew Stringer, Cat Sullivan, Kent Tayler, Biscuit Tin and Nick Tolson

Pigs' trotters
Russell Blackman and Stephen Catherall

Published by Dennis Publishing Ltd
30 Cleveland Street, London W1T 4JD

ISBN 9781781062456
First Printing Autumn 2013

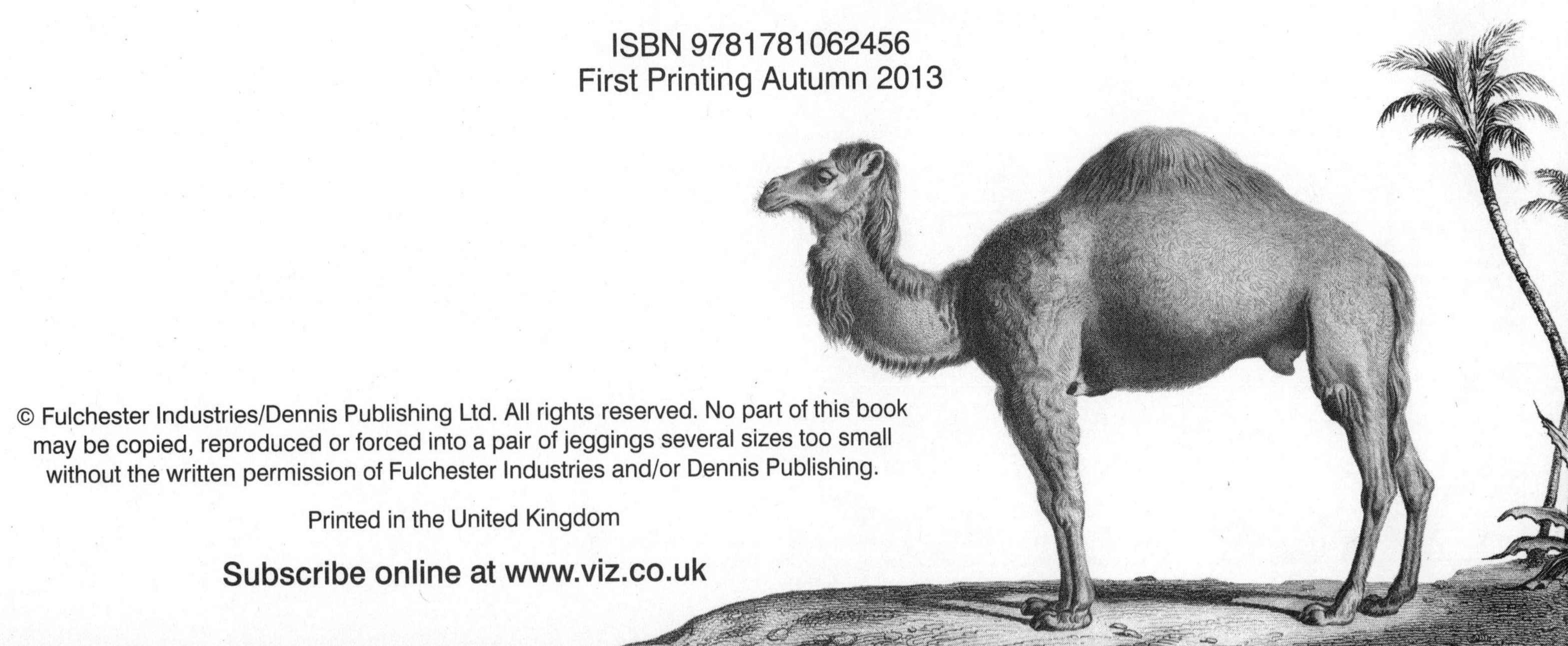

Printed in the United Kingdom

FRU T' BUNN
The MASTER BAKER & HIS GINGERBREAD SEX DOLLS

6.00 am CHRISTMAS MORNING...
TING!
BUNN the BAKER

ACROSS TOWN...
CLICK!

HEH-HEH! YOU'RE A SLY FOX, FRUBERT T. BUNN... SETTING THE OVERNIGHT TIMER ON YOUR BAKERY OVEN..!

...THAT HORNY LITTLE GINGERBREAD CRACKER IN SEXY SANTA ICING THAT YOU PREPARED YESTERDAY WILL BE READY BY THE TIME YOU GET TO THE SHOP... READY TO GIVE YOU YOUR CHRISTMAS "BOX"!
DROOL!

...EVEN BETTER... YOU'LL BE THERE AND BACK WITH EMPTY NUTS BEFORE THE MISSUS AND WOTSERNAME EVEN WAKE UP..!

...THEY'LL NEVER SUSPECT A TH–
DADDY! DADDY! HAS HE BEEN..?!
FUCK MY LUCK.

NO HE HASN'T, CHELSEA. SO COME ON – BACK TO BED. IF SANTA KNOWS YOU'RE UP SO EARLY, HE'LL BE VERY ANGRY AND HE'LL TAKE ALL YOUR TOYS AWAY ...AND BURN THEM!
ERP!

GOODNESS ME! YOU TWO ARE UP EARLY! SHALL WE GO AND SEE IF SANTA'S LEFT YOU ANY PRESENTS UNDER THE TREE, CHELSEA..?
SHITE! THE WIFE!

COME ON, FRUBERT... LET'S WATCH LITTLE CHELSEA OPEN HER PRESENTS..!
...ERM...NO... I CAN'T, YOU SEE DEAR... I'VE GOT TO GO TO THE BAKERY...

BUT IT'S CHRISTMAS DAY, LOVE! YOU CAN'T GO TO THE BAKERY ON CHRISTMAS DAY!

MUMMY! MUMMY! DADDY! DADDY! HE'S BEEN!
...BUT I THINK I MIGHT HAVE LEFT THE MIXER ON...

...IT'LL SHORT-CIRCUIT AND BURN THE BAKERY DOWN..! IS THAT WHAT YOU WANT TO HAPPEN..?
OH, FRUBERT, IT'LL BE FINE. LET'S JUST WATCH CHELSEA OPEN HER PRESSIES.

GO AND GET THE CAMERA, LOVE. I WANT YOU TO CAPTURE THIS MAGIC MOMENT..!
MUMBLE! GRUMBLE!

BAH! THAT SEXY LITTLE BISCUIT BITCH AT THE BAKERY WILL BE COOLING DOWN..! I OUGHT TO BE THERE HAVING A BIT OF FESTIVE COOKIE NOOKIE, BUT INSTEAD I'M STUCK HERE WATCHING SOME BRAT OPEN A FUCKING BARBIE DOLL..!

...BARBIE! BARBIE! BARBIE! BARBIE..!
CLICK
TCHOH

...AND HERE'S A LITTLE SOMETHING FROM ME TO YOU, FRU...
EH..?!
...I'VE BEEN SAVING UP THE FAMILY ALLOWANCE ALL YEAR... I HOPE YOU LIKE IT..!

YES, WELL... I'LL OPEN IT LATER... LOOK, IS THAT ENOUGH PHOTOS..? ONLY I'VE REALLY GOT TO GO TO THE BAKERY... I THINK I'VE LEFT THE BATH RUNNING...
BATH!? THERE ISN'T A BATH AT THE BAKERY!
ERM... ER...

...BATH BUNS! I MEANT BATH BUNS!
...BATH BUNS?!..YOU LEFT SOME BATH BUNS RUNNING!?... WHAT DOES THAT EVEN MEAN..?

YOU'VE GOT A BLOODY ANSWER FOR EVERYTHING, HAVEN'T YOU..!? DID YOU SPEND TWO YEARS AT BAKING COLLEGE? NO, I DON'T THINK YOU DID, DID YOU..?!

THERE-THERE FRUBERT DEAR... YOU WORK SO HARD ALL YEAR. YOU DESERVE A NICE DAY AT HOME WITH YOUR LOVED ONES.

MUMMY! MUMMY! SANTA'S BROUGHT ME A COLOURING BOOK!
BIP! BIP! BIP! ...BLIDDIP!... BIP...

DRRINGG! DRRINGG!
OH, I WONDER WHO THAT CAN BE, RINGING US UP AT TEN-PAST-SIX ON CHRISTMAS MORNING...

SHOVE!
I'LL GET IT!
!?

HELLO..? OH HELLO YOUR MAJESTY... WHAT'S THAT..? YOU NEED FOUR FRUIT SCONES URGENTLY..?
?

YES... OKAY, YOUR MAJESTY... I'LL GET OVER TO THE BAKERY RIGHT AWAY...
...GOODBYE.

WELL I'VE DEFINITELY GOT TO GO INTO WORK NOW. THAT WAS THE QUEEN. APPARENTLY THE DUKE OF EDINBURGH WANTS SOME SCONES...
TSK. SOMEONE'S HAVING YOU ON, LOVE...!

...NOW LOOK - IT'S CHRISTMAS DAY... TIME TO BE WITH YOUR FAMILY. YOU ARE NOT GOING TO THAT BAKERY TODAY, AND THAT IS FINAL!
...BUT I'M A BAKER! I'M ONLY HAPPY WHEN I'M STOOD IN FRONT OF AN OVEN!

WELL I'LL TELL YOU WHAT... IF YOU'RE SO DESPERATE TO COOK SOMETHING, WHY DON'T YOU DO THE THE CHRISTMAS DINNER..?
WHA..?! NO, I DIDN'T MEAN...

EVERYTHING YOU NEED IS IN THE FRIDGE, FRUBERT... TURKEY, SPROUTS, POTATOES, SAUSAGES, YORKSHIRE PUDDINGS... AND A BIG PLUM DUFF...

6 HOURS LATER...
...MMM! THERE'S SOME DELICIOUS SMELLS COMING FROM THE KITCHEN, AREN'T THERE, CHELSEA..? WE'RE LUCKY TO HAVE SUCH A CLEVER DADDY, AREN'T WE..?
DADDY! DADDY!

DINNER IS SERVED!
SMASHING! WE'RE STARVING!
DINNER! DINNER! DINNER!

EH!? POT NOODLES?
...ER... YES, DEAR... I'M AFRAID I BURNT EVERYTHING.
?

YOU BURNT THE WHOLE DINNER?
YES. I HAD A SLIGHT MISCALCULATION, I'M AFRAID...
COULD NOTHING BE SAVED..?
NO...

...IT'S ALL GONE... THAT 20lb TURKEY... THE MASH... CHIPPOLATAS... SPROUTS... ALL BURNT TO A CINDER!
WHAT A SHAME.
SIGH!

ANYWAY, DON'T WAIT FOR ME... YOU TWO TUCK INTO YOUR POT NOODLES...
...I'LL JUST GO AND... ERM... TIDY UP IN THE KITCHEN.

OH WELL, NEVER MIND... COME ON, CHELSEA, LOVE. EAT UP.

OH LOOK - WE HAVEN'T GOT ANY SPOONS. I'LL JUST GO INTO THE KITCHEN AND FETCH SOME...!

...YOU LOVE IT UP YOU, DON'T YOU, YOU FESTIVE LITTLE SLUT! AND DON'T YOU COMPLAIN... YOU LED ME ON... WITH THOSE COME-TO-BED SPROUTS OF YOURS...!
...UGH-UGH... UGH-UGH... UGH-UGH-UGH... UUUUUGH!

LetterBocks

VIZ COMIC, PO Box 841, Whitley Bay, NE26 9EQ | e-mail: letters@viz.co.uk

I RECENTLY read on Wikipedia the other day that lumpy-faced Victorian The Elephant Man had to have his corpse formally identified by his uncle. Can any other readers think of a bigger bureaucratic waste of time?

Robert Rowcliffe, e-mail

I WORK in a theme park on the rides. Could I ask that all female visitors ensure they wear loose fitting tops so their jugs fall out? It makes for excellent viewing on dull days.

Rob Crawford, e-mail

I FEEL really sorry for the poor drummer out of Chas 'n' Dave. He drums his little heart out and he never even gets a mention.

Ross Maxfield, e-mail

STAR LETTER

I SEE the Royal Navy are to build a new aircraft carrier called *'The Prince Of Wales'* in 2011. I don't see why those horse-faced bluebloods should have ruddy great battleships named after them when royalty doesn't even commission the construction of British vessels of war anymore. It's the poor bloody taxpayer that does that, out of his wages every bloody Friday. I reckon the new gunboat should be called *'The Barry From Stoke'* instead.

Barry, Stoke

'THERE'S no place like home', they say. Unless of course you own a second home.

Christina Martin, e-mail

THE other evening I was enjoying a particularly long, drawn out and sensational sunset from my balcony. It was extremely relaxing. My neighbours, however, seemed to be finding it extremely exciting. Imagine my surprise when I realised I was facing east and their house was on fire.

Gordon, Perth, Australia

I'D LOVE to be a judge on *Masterchef*. All you have to do is poke your head around a kitchen making a face like one of the chefs has farted.

Sandy Waxchuff, e-mail

WHY didn't those scientists at CERN build a Small Hadron Collider first, to see if it worked?

Steve Stenslie, e-mail

I LIKE the fact that Nick Clegg always wears a yellow tie. It clearly demonstrates his independent liberal voice while he sits quietly nodding along with whatever welfare cuts the Prime Minister is announcing.

Mark Pogson, e-mail

ACCORDING to the public information film, in the event of a car crash, an unrestrained rear-seat passenger moves forward with the force of an elephant. This is particularly worrying for me as I regularly drive a circus van with an elephant in the back who refuses to put his seat belt on. How hard is HE going to clout me in the back of the head if I have a prang?

Billy Smart, Muddyfield

I WOULD like to ask why, at the early-morning summer swimming for boarders at my prep school in the 70s, all boys had to swim naked while the supervising master jingled his change and chain-smoked feverishly. Would the boys donning trunks have made it less character-building, I wonder? I know there's a rational, innocent explanantion, I'm just still trying to identify it.

Sammy "Edward" Willetts, e-mail

I WAS very nervous about a forthcoming job interview until my mate gave me a great piece of advice. "Just imagine the interviewer sitting there in his underwear," he said. Sure enough, the mental image made me feel a lot more confident. However, when I entered the interviewer's office, he was indeed sat there in his underwear. I must admit I felt even more nervous than I did before.

Paul Solomons, e-mail

It Nearly Happened to Me!

EACH issue, the writer of the best letter about something that almost happened to them wins a £300,000 DREAM COTTAGE in the county of their choice...

Send your letter to: It Nearly Happened to Me, Viz Comic, PO Box 841, Whitley Bay, NE26 9EQ. Don't forget to state which county you would like your £300,000 dream cottage to be in.

*__DURING__ the recent cold snap I walked to my local corner shop to buy a loaf. On the way back, I slipped on some ice and almost fell over. Fortunately, I managed to regain my balance.

Edna Bolero, Norfolk

HOW about a picture of Adam West as Batman sitting on a baby elephant?

Wings Hauser, e-mail

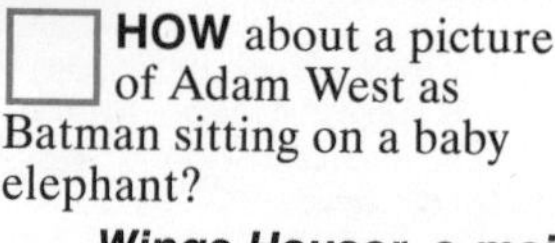

* *No problem, Mr Hauser.*

I WAS wondering if any of your readers had the home address of the man who wrote the 'We buy any car' jingle, only I wish to congratulate him in person on the catchiness of the tune. My three-year-old son has been singing it incessantly for over six weeks now.

Mad Bob, e-mail

UP THE ARSE CORNER

Sender: *Oliver Kayly (or Bough)*

Paul Daniels' WORLD of WOE

ON THE 14th of July 1928, a party of 500 blind orphans set sail across the English Channel on their way to Lourdes to be cured. Halfway across, their ship collided with a boat carrying 300 labrador puppies. Both boats caught fire, and to avoid the flames the terrified orphans and puppies jumped overboard where they were either drowned or eaten by sharks. Only one orphan managed to make it to safety, finally staggering onto the shore in Dieppe where he was ran over by a steamroller.

...Now THAT'S Tragic!

TOP TIPS

CHEESE eaters. Instead of eating a large piece of mild cheese, save time and money by eating a much smaller piece of extra mature cheese.

Shenkin Arsecandle, e-mail

CLOSET gays trapped in straight marriage. Sellotape a pair of glasses just above your wife's pubes. Vaginal sex will then look like you are getting a blower off a man with a beard.

Pete Howies, e-mail

NEW mothers. Estimate the size your child will be when fully grown and christen them Small, Medium, Large or Extra Large accordingly. When they are older, they will automatically have their name sewn into their clothing.

Peter Cooke, e-mail

CHEER yourself up at the next funeral you go to by hiding a tenner in the pocket of your black suit today.

Big Shug, e-mail

ACTION heroes. Save money on guns by not throwing them on the floor the moment they run out of ammunition.

Adam Gatward, e-mail

VACUUM cleaner manufacturers. Install headphone ports into your products, then only the user will have to put up with the noise.

Malcolm Alcock, e-mail

REPLACEMENT clothes line too long? Measure it to find the extra length, then simply knock your house down and rebuild it the requisite distance from your linen post.

Paul Arger, e-mail

DUE TO a faulty toilet door lock, I once walked in on 50's rocker Marty Wilde (Kim's dad) doing a poo. Has anyone else ever seen any C-list celebrities in the act of pinching one off?

Jamal McTaggart, e-mail

IF WOMEN could grow beards would they be more inclined to embark on Arctic, Antarctic and Everest type expeditions, do you think? You never see many of them doing this type of thing. Would any lady *Viz* readers care to comment?

Mr Bowen, e-mail

I DON'T know how anybody manages to join the mile high club. At 5280 feet the plane is either ascending or descending and the 'fasten seatbelt' lights are still on.

Peter Dantic, e-mail

Desert Island WHISKS

A famous celebrity chooses what type of whisk they would most like to be stranded on a desert island with.

No. 855

Fading cocksmith
BEN DOVER
(real name Linseed Honeypot), 73

NEXT WEEK: United Nations frontman **BANKSY MOON**

IS THIS the first time you have been written to from West Wittering in Sussex?

Rob Ryan, Oxford

** That's a tricky one, Rob. Perhaps our readers can help. Have YOU ever written to Viz from West Wittering? Write and tell us whether or not you have.*

HOLLYWOOD directors. If the action jumps to Paris, have an onscreen caption saying 'Paris, France' over an establishing shot of the Eiffel Tower just in case the audience think you mean some other fucking Paris.

Carlos, e-mail

RATIONAL thinkers. Test your self-control by listening to *Thought for the Day* on Radio 4, while trying to refrain from laughing out loud or shouting 'bullshit' at the radio.

Mike Tatham, e-mail

CRICKET fans. Save yourself some cash by fashioning a pair of cricket gloves from a pack of iced finger buns, sticking one one each of your fingers. Not only do they look like the real thing but you can eat them once you're done playing.

Electric Eric, e-mail

KEEP your hands warm in the cold weather by cutting the finger tips off a pair of woolly gloves. These can be used as little warm 'hats' for each of your fingers.

Steven Ireland, Manchester

WEATHER reporters Avoid overuse of the word 'treacherous' in your reports during snowy spells by investing in a bloody Thesaurus.

Brian Patrick, e-mail

AUDIOPHILES. Eating 'space dust' while listening to your MP3 player adds that authentic crackly vinyl sound to your music.

Chaddy McChad, e-mail

HUSBANDS. Prevent accusations of being impolite or discourtious in the bedroom by simply saying "excuse me love, would you mind passing me the fanny," to your wife. It works everytime.

Steve Bates, e-mail

AS FAR as I'm concerned, there are not enough men being attacked by old ladies with umbrellas in the high street these days.

Richard Emery, e-mail

WHEN spoffing on your bird's tits for the first time, it's best not shouting "Bang, and the dirt is gone." I find it really kills the mood.

John Bagger, e-mail

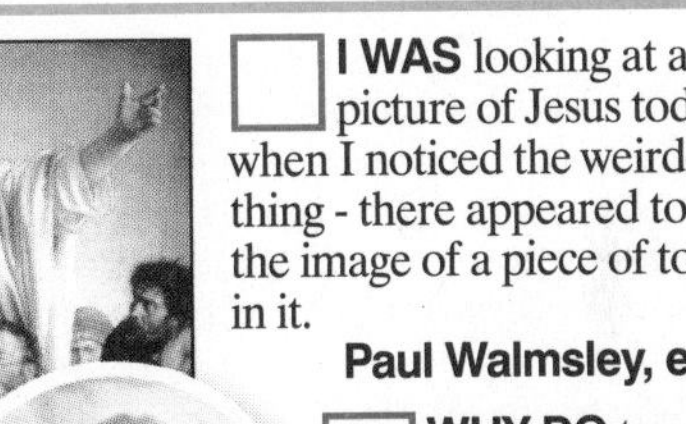

I WAS looking at a picture of Jesus today when I noticed the weirdest thing - there appeared to be the image of a piece of toast in it.

Paul Walmsley, e-mail

WHY DO travellers always complain when they get moved on? They're travellers for heaven's sake.

Janey, e-mail

SIMPLY RED RAW

IN an interview with the *Guardian*, Simply Red frontman Mick Hucknall claimed to have slept with more than 1000 women a year at the height of his fame. Is this something of which he should be proud or ashamed? Is the ruby-toothed minstral a hunky stud or a filthy beast? We went on the streets to see what YOU thought...

...A THOUSAND women a year means that Hucknall had sex with an average of three different women a day. Three a *DAY!* I can just about manage to get my leg over one bird a *MONTH* tops, and that's if I'm not being too choosy. I can only assume that Mr Hucknall has extremely low standards when it comes to picking his sexual partners.

Rev. J Foucault, Truro

...WHAT I want to know is, when Mick Hucknall was laid up with diarrhoea or a Winter vomiting bug for a week and wasn't out on the pull, did he then have to go out and fuck six women a day when he was better, just to keep his averages up?

Frank Hurley, Frinton

...IT'S QUITE obvious that Mr Hucknall didn't suffer from piles while he was banging all them women. I've got septic haemorrhoids at the moment, and I have barely been able to stand up or sit down for a fortnight. I'm only really comfortable in a half-crouch, leaning against a wall with my knees bent. The last thing I feel like doing is pushing my arse backwards and forwards for ten minutes, three times a day.

T Medford, Surbiton

...I AM Emeritus Professor of Statistics at Oxford University. I have been analysing Mick Hucknall's claims and have come to some quite interesting conclusions. If we start from the quite reasonable position that Mr Hucknall was sexually active at his claimed rate of three different women a day between 1984 and 1993 - the period of his band's greatest success - then we reach a figure of 10,950 conquests (or 10,959 including leap years). Let us further assume that Mick had intercourse with women who were between 18 and 19 years-old in 1984. We can get a rough estimate of the total number of women in this group by taking the current UK female population (say 30 million), and dividing the result by 85 (roughly approximating that the female population is divided into equal portions throughout the median age-range). This gives us a working figure of 352,941 women who were born in 1966. Of this group, we must discount 10% who are lesbians and wouldn't go with a man, leaving us with 317,647 heterosexual women of a suitable age. Of this group, at least half can further be excluded from consideration due to being right pigs and boilers who Mr Hucknall wouldn't even touch with yours, which gives us a final subset containing 158,823 potential sexual partners for the Simply Red frontman throughout the period under consideration. Dividing this total by the original stated tally of 10,959 women, we are left with the inescapable conclusion that, if your wife is 45 now and was half decent looking when she was 18, there's a one-in-fifteen chance that she has been banged off Mick Hucknall.

Prof Ralph Hoffenheimer, Oxford

A balanced portfolio of the songs YOU love,
performed by Britain's favourite singing pension experts...

Includes: *Unchained Melody * If You Leave me Now * Love is All Around * Everything I Do (I Do for You) * The Power of Love * Hello (Is it Me You're Looking For?) * Total Eclipse of the Heart... & many more!*

Also available: Their brand new EP
The Value of Love can go Down as Well as Up
out now on FIMBRA RECORDS

Stop Gear!

It's time to put brakes on telly show, says sacked toilet cleaner

MILLIONS tune in each week to watch *Top Gear.* The motoring show's high octane mix of fast cars, bloke-ish banter and political incorrectness has made it BBC2's top-rated programme.

Petrolhead presenters Jeremy Clarkson, Richard Hammond and James May have won a legion of fans with mad-cap adventures such as driving to the North Pole, racing across Europe in £1million supercars and crossing the desert in second hand bangers.

Meanwhile the identity of the show's mystery racing driver - known as "The Stig" - has been kept a closely-guarded secret, only having been revealed twice during the show's nine-year run.

show

We welcome them into our homes each Sunday, and we think we know them. But what are the *Top Gear* presenters **REALLY** like when the cameras are turned off? No-one really knows, but one man who does is **RAMPTON BELLEND**, who spent three years working behind the scenes on the show.

"I saw the side of *Top Gear* the public never sees," lavatory attendant Bellend told us. "And the things the presenters get up to would turn your hair white, I can tell you."

And now, following his dismissal for stealing 48 bottles of Toilet Duck, 52-year-old Rampton feels the time is right to lift the lid on the show's backstage scandals. And in his new book, he gives us a glimpse of the presenters' true characters.

kiss

In his no-holds-barred account, Bellend paints a lurid picture of life on the *Top Gear* set, where it would come as no surprise to encounter scenes such as:

**** JEREMY CLARKSON snorting a million pounds of cocaine off the breasts of a well-known royal***

**** JAMES MAY goose-stepping across the set in a Nazi uniform, giving Heil Hitler salutes***

**** Grave-robber RICHARD HAMMOND making himself an Ed Gein-style skin suit***

"I never saw any of those things actually happening, but it wouldn't have particularly surprised me if I had, frankly, what with the way they carried on," Bellend told us.

letter

And he made this plea to BBC bosses: ***"It's time to pull the plug on this show before it's too late. Clarkson, May and Hammond are dangerously out of control and I've got hard evidence to back up my claims."***

SKID PAN MAN: Toilet cleaner Rampton Bellend (main pic) had brush with *Top Gear* crew (below).

Clarkson's Prostitute Orgy Shame was Open Secret

ON SCREEN, JEREMY CLARKSON makes sexist comments, jokes about lorry drivers murdering prostitutes and is always poking fun at lady drivers. But according to Bellend, once the cameras stopped rolling his behaviour deteriorated even more.

"After filming finished for the day, Clarkson would send a runner into nearby Guildford to bring back a load of good time girls so he could have an orgy in his trailer. The orgies would last all week, with more and more hookers being bussed in round the clock to replace the ones he'd worn out."

"It's always been an open secret in TV circles that Jezza likes his women top-heavy. If any prostitutes didn't measure up, Clarkson had a Harley Street plastic surgeon available round the clock to give them breast enhancement surgery in the room next door before he satisfied his perverted lusts on them."

"And if you think Clarkson drives hard, you should see the way he parties. His post-show sex marathons were so vigorous that his trailer would regularly fall to pieces and have to be replaced. He would destroy two or three top-of-the-range Winnebagos per orgy, which would have to be replaced at a cost quarter of a million pounds each."

"That was licence payers' money, but unfortunately I can't prove this because the expense will have been cleverly hidden in the *Top Gear* accounts. But the public needs to know the lengths to which the BBC will go in order to keep their big stars happy."

Captain Slow was Slave of Satan

ACCORDING TO Bellend, it wasn't merely financial mismanagement that was covered up in the *Top Gear* office. For co-presenter JAMES MAY was also hiding a dark secret, and one that his fans would never guess from his avuncular on-screen persona.

"You wouldn't think it to see him on the telly, but mild-mannered May is a diabolist. He worships Beelzebub as his master and is obsessed with black magic. Nobody is allowed inside his dressing room, where he spends all the time between takes chanting Latin incantations in honour of his Satanic overlord."

"The only time I ever went in this trailer was to change the disinfectant block in his lavatory pan. I'd often wondered why May's caravan sat so low on its suspension, but now the reason became clear. He had ripped out the typical dressing room vanity unit, and replaced it with a two-ton granite altar, carved with mystic runes. On the top was an inverted crucifix."

"Standing before the altar was May, but instead of his trademark flowery shirt he was wearing the black, hooded cowl of a disciple of Lucifer. As I watched, he cut the throats of several goats and chickens, using their blood to daub pentagrams on the walls and floors. It was like he was in a trance, and instead of eyes he had red, burning coals. Needless to say, I was out of there as quickly as possible. I've never changed a Brobat Blue as fast in my life!"

"Sacrificing farm animals was one thing, but a couple of days after that May's behaviour took an even more sinister turn. He phoned up the Top Gear canteen and asked for a ham sandwich and some crisps to be delivered to his trailer. Not an unusual request in itself, except he specified that the girl who brought them had to be a virgin. Looking back, this should have set alarm bells ringing, but at the time nobody thought any more of it."

"However, the pretty young intern who was despatched with May's lunchtime snack was never seen again. Now I'm not suggesting that James May slit her throat, drank her still-warm blood out of a ram's skull chalice and then plucked out and devoured her heart as part of some attempt to summon the Lord of Hades from the netherworld, because I simply don't have any evidence to back up the facts. I'll leave my readers to draw their own conclusions on that score."

"But I gave Captain Slow's caravan a wide berth from that moment on, let me tell you."

Stig's Multiple Identity

OVER THE years, the identity of *Top Gear*'s tame racing driver has been kept a closely-guarded secret. Many names have been suggested, and there has even been speculation that there may be more than one STIG hiding inside the trademark white helmet and fireproof overalls. However, the truth, says Bellend, is even more unbelievable.

"My suspicions were first aroused when I noticed that my stocks of disinfectant were running low. It was as if someone was letting themselves into my storeroom in the night and helping themselves to Toilet Duck. I didn't know what to make of it. But when I finally discovered what it was being used for, my blood ran cold, I can tell you."

"It turned out that the Top Gear presenters had been driving round derelict areas of London in a van, looking for tramps and offering them a warm bed for the night. Once they got them back to the studios, they were injecting bleach into their heads to destroy the parts of their brains that felt fear, and turning them into emotionless automotons that simply did Jeremy Clarkson's bidding."

"These hapless zombies were then dressed up in Stig outfits and forced to drive racing cars round the track at ridiculous speeds. If they were lucky, they'd make it round in one piece, but more often than not they'd spin off the track and perish in a horrific fireball. Clarkson, May and Hammond couldn't have cared less. The charred tramp bodies were simply pulled out of the twisted wreckage and buried in the grass in the middle; then another Stig was brought out and strapped into the next car."

"After nine years, the death toll must run into hundreds if not thousands. But the crashes are simply edited out for the final brodcast. This is the face of *Top Gear* the public never gets to see."

Hamster Hammond's Sordid Double Life

ACCORDING TO Bellend, there were also regular deliveries of livestock to RICHARD HAMMOND's trailer. But unlike his colleague, the Hamster wasn't sacrificing them; he had a completely different kind of interest in our four-legged friends.

"Unknown to his legions of fans, the Hamster was a practising beastialist, who got his kicks performing sordid sex acts on animals. I first found out about his secret double life when I accidentally went in his locker in the *Top Gear* production office. On the inside of the door, where any normal red-blooded bloke would have pin-ups of Page-3 girls, Hammond had hardcore photographs of cows, sheep and pigs in explicit poses."

"Later, on top of the wardrobe in his dressing room, I found pornographic horse magazines. They had been extremely well-thumbed, clearly by very small hands."

"But Hammond's worst act of depravity occurred when he was supposed to be test-driving a new Ferrari. I had my suspicions that he was up to no good, so I hid in the boot to keep an eye on him. We drove for hours, and when he finally pulled up, I peeked out of the boot and realised we were in the car park at Aintree race-course."

"I got out and followed Hammond, who was heading towards the restricted area behind the stands. Taking advantage of his diminutive stature, he had disguised himself as a jockey, and easily snook into the stables. Interested to see what he was up to, I followed him."

"I couldn't believe my eyes as he went from stall to stall and orally pleasured the manhoods of each and every one of the forty-two horses running in that day's Grand National. Luckily, I'd remembered to bring my camera along, and from my hiding place behind a haybale I snapped away, capturing the entire sordid episode on film as evidence."

"By the time Hammond had worked his way through all the racehorses, he must have swallowed gallons of equine semen and he looked pretty green around the gills. He got back in the Ferrari and drove to the local hospital, where he had his stomach pumped."

"Sadly, I'd forgotten to take the lens cap off my camera, so none of the pictures came out. And the doctors who syphoned all those buckets full of horse sperm out of him will probably be bound by patient confidentiality, so the vile truth about Hammond will remain a secret forever."

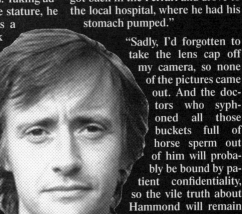

Bellend had no qualms about going public with his shocking story. "They're not going to gag me. I know what I know, and even though I can't prove any of it, and in fact have no evidence whatsoever to back up a single one of my accusations, they know I'm telling the truth," he told us.

And he was adamant that taking a stand against the scandalous goings-on at the BBC2 show had cost him his job. "I was set up, pure and simple. Those boxes of bleach were planted in my shed. Then the BBC special effects department made up someone to look like me and try to sell it at my local British Legion. It's the oldest trick in the book."

"They knew that being accused of workplace theft was my Achilles heel, as I had been dismissed from six previous jobs for stealing janitorial supplies."

"It's typical of the *Top Gear* management to use that against me in order to keep me quiet," he added.

***You Bunch of Cunts - My Life Behind the Scenes at Top Gear* by Rampton Bellend is available to borrow from the author's table just next to the fruity in the snug of Flexford British Legion every day from 11am till closing.**

Mrs Brady Old Lady
DOLLY'S ROUND FOR TEA...
HOW'S YOUR SISTER EDNA, DOLLY..?
NOT SO GOOD, ADA. SHE'S BACKED UP DOWN BELOW ON ACCOUNT OF A SURFEIT OF EGGS.
OH DEAR. HAS IT BROUGHT ON HER OLD SPASTIC ANUS, DOLLY?
I JUST DON'T KNOW, ADA, BUT SHE WERE IN THE YOU-KNOW-WHAT ALL YESTERDAY TRYING AND NOT A DICKY BIRD.
SLOOP
IT'S ODD, BECAUSE SHE'S NOT USUALLY CONSTIPATED. SHE TENDS MORE TOWARDS A LOOSE MOTION, ADA. ORDINARILY, SHE DARESN'T TRUMP FOR FEAR OF AN INADVERTANT SOILAGE...
EEH.
...CAN'T HANG HER SMALLS OUT ON THE LINE, YOU KNOW. THE NEIGHBOURS'D HAVE A FIELD DAY WITH 'EM, ADA.
EEH. A DIRTY BOWEL IS A TERRIBLE THING, ISN'T IT, DOLLY..?
IT IS.
OF COURSE, IN THE END, EDNA'S 'BACK BODY' SUCCEEDED IN DRIVING A WEDGE BETWEEN HER AND HER LATE HUSBAND...
ALBERT?
AYE.
NEVER SAID ANYTHING, OF COURSE. BUT YOU COULD TELL FROM HIS EXPRESSION HE DIDN'T LIKE THE SMELL. SPENT A LOT OF TIME IN HIS SHED, DID ALBERT, TINKERING WITH AN OLD ARIEL SQUARE FOUR.
EEH. I NEVER...
WAS THAT WHY HE LEFT HER FOR EUNICE PLAYTON..?
AYE. WELL, THAT AND THE FACT THAT IN THIRTY YEARS OF MARRIAGE, SHE NEVER ONCE ACCEDED TO HIS CONJUGAL DEMANDS...
...WHEREAS EUNICE PLAYTON WOULD SUCK HIM OFF AT THE DROP OF A HAT.
EEH...
OF COURSE, SHE HAD THE ADVANTAGE OVER EDNA, HAVING LOST HER GAG REFLEX FOLLOWING RADIUM TREATMENT FOR AN OVER-EXCITABLE THYROID.
AYE, WELL THAT WOULD EXPLAIN IT, DOLLY.
'APPEN, ADA.
ANYWAY, AS I WAS SAYING, EDNA'S NOT PASSED A STOOL TO SPEAK OF FOR CLOSE ON A FORTNIGHT NOW.
A FORTNIGHT?! EEEEH!
YES ADA, AND I WOULDN'T MIND ONLY IT'S MAKING HER BURP... AND HER BURPS SMELL A BIT LIKE FEESHUS.
B-FOOF!
I MEAN, THAT'S NOT GOOD IS IT, ADA..?
NO DOLLY, IT'S NOT...
...TO BE HONEST, I'D BEEN BLAMING IT ON THE CAT'S TRAY.
HERE YOU ARE, EDNA LOVE, HAVE A PEPPERMINT...
BETTER THAN THAT, DOLLY... I JUST REMEMBERED I'VE GOT HALF A TIN OF PRUNES IN THE FRIDGE... THEY'LL SHARP GET HER MOVING AGAIN.
EEH. CHAMPION.
HERE THEY ARE. I'LL PUT THEM IN A BOWL FOR HER...
OOH, YOU SURE THEY'RE ALRIGHT, ADA..? THEY LOOK A BIT MOULDY TO ME, THEM...
THEY'RE FINE, DOLLY...
...I ONLY OPENED 'EM YESTERDAY. SIDNEY HAD 'EM FOR HIS TEA.
...BUT ADA, SIDNEY'S BEEN DEAD FOR YEARS...
HE HAS, DOLLY. 26 YEAR COME TUESDAY WEEK. AND THERE'S NOT A DAY GOES BY WHEN I DON'T THINK ABOUT HIM.

OH SIDNEY ≡SNIFF≡ WHY DID YOU HAVE TO LEAVE ME..?
THERE-THERE, ADA. TRY NOT TO UPSET YOURSELF, LOVE.

MIND, I'M A BIT WORRIED BY THEM PRUNES, THOUGH ADA. 'APPEN THEY'VE GONE PAST THEIR BEST BEFORE..
GIVE 'EM A SNIFF IF YOU'RE NOT SURE, DOLLY.
≡M-PWWWF!≡

WELL I WOULD DO, ADA, ONLY I CAN'T SMELL OWT AT THE MOMENT ON ACCOUNT OF EDNA'S SHITTY BURPS.
TRUST ME, DOLLY. THEY'RE FINE.

THERE YOU GO, EDNA LOVE. THEY'LL GET YOUR FOULAGE MOVING AGAIN.

≡CHOMP≡ ≡CHOMP≡ ≡CHOMP≡
EEH, YOU'RE ENJOYING THEM PRUNES, AREN'T YOU EDNA..? I SAY.. YOU'RE ENJOYING THEM PRUNES..!
SHE'LL NOT HEAR YOU, ADA.

SHE WENT TO THE HAIRDRESSERS FOR A SET LAST WEEK AND HER POPPITS MELTED UNDER THE DRIER.
EEH! NEVER!
AYE...

...THE MOLTEN PLASTIC RAN DOWN INTO HER INNER EAR. DOCTOR CHAKRABORTY SAYS TO ME, HE SAYS, MRS EARNSHAW, HE SAYS, I'M AFRAID IT'S SET SOLID ROUND HER ANCHOR AND STIRRUPS, HE SAYS.
EEEH!

IS THERE OWT THEY CAN DO, DOLLY?
NO, ADA. YOU'VE JUST GOT TO GET ON WITH IT, HAVEN'T YOU..?
YOU HAVE.

EEH ADA, LOOK AT THAT! SHE'S POLISHED 'EM OFF, THE WHOLE TIN...!
WELL, IF ALL THEM PRUNES DON'T SHIFT HER EXCRETA, NOTHING WILL, DOLLY...

HOLD UP, ADA. I DON'T THINK THESE WAS EVEN PRUNES, YOU KNOW...

...IT WERE POTTED HASLET.
EEH! YOU'RE RIGHT, DOLLY, IT WERE! I DID IT SIDNEY ON TOAST YESTERDAY FOR HIS TEA..!
EMPI BRAND 4d
PIG LIVER HASLET

WELL, WE'VE HAD A LOVELY AFTERNOON, ADA... BUT IT'S TIME ME AND EDNA WAS GETTING BACK, LOVE...

SHE'S GOT THE MOBILE CHIROPODIST COMING OVER TO DRAIN HER BUNIONS AT SIX.
THAT'S NICE, DOLLY.

BYE THEN.
NOW DON'T FORGET, YOU'RE COMING ROUND TO MINE FOR TEA TOMORROW, ADA. I'VE BOILED A TONGUE.
OOH, SMASHING. I'VE GOT QUITE A PENCHANT FOR A BIT OF TONGUE, ME.

BUT I DON'T THINK SIDNEY'LL BE COMING WITH ME, DOLLY. HE'S GOT SUMMAT ON AT THE LEGION TOMORROW...
SIDNEY'S DEAD, ADA LOVE...

I KNOW, DOLLY. 26 YEAR COME TUESDAY WEEK... AND THERE'S NOT A DAY GOES BY WHEN I DON'T THINK ABOUT HIM...

OH SIDNEY ≡SNIFF≡ WHY DID YOU HAVE TO LEAVE ME..?
SEE YOU FOR TEA TOMORROW THEN, ADA..!

CONTINUED OVER

NEXT DAY...
...EEH, YOU BOIL A LOVELY TONGUE, DOLLY.
THANK-YOU ADA. IT'S ME MAM'S RECIPE - 8 HOURS IN THE PAN.
SPEAKING OF WHICH, THEM PRUNES FROM YESTERDAY SEEM TO HAVE OF SORTED OUT EDNA'S CONSTIPATION.
I THOUGHT THEY WOULD, DOLLY. PRUNES ARE GOOD.
...BIT TOO GOOD ACTUALLY, ADA... THEY'VE HAD A DRAMATIC EFFECT ON HER BOWELS. SHE'S BEEN SAT ON THAT POT ALL NIGHT... BETWEEN YOU AND ME, SHE'S NOT BEEN ABLE TO STOP STOOLING SINCE SHE GOT IN.
IT WERE LIKE SOMEONE'D TURNED ON A TAP, ADA. WE ONLY JUST MANAGED TO MAKE IT HOME BEFORE THE FLOODGATES OPENED.
OH DEAR.
STILL, SHE MUST'VE HAD A LOT OF BACKED-UP FEESHUS TO SHIFT, THOUGH...
AYE, ADA. BUT HER SPHINCTER'S NOT CLOSED SINCE! LIKE A MAGICIAN'S RUDDY HANKIE, IT'S BEEN. I JUST DON'T KNOW WHERE IT'S ALL COMING FROM...
EEH.
...MUST BE LIKE THE BLACK HOLE OF CALCUTTA, HER CAECUM... ISN'T THAT RIGHT, EDNA..?!
...SHE CAN'T HEAR ME.
I SAY, EDNA... YOU CAN'T HEAR ME, CAN YOU..!?
SHE CAN'T HEAR YOU, DOLLY.
SHE CAN'T HEAR ME.
I THINK SHE NEEDS SUMMAT TO BIND HER UP BEFORE SHE PROLAPSES, ADA.
EEH...
...I WISH YOU'D TOLD ME BEFORE I COME OVER, DOLLY...
...ONLY I'VE A FRIDGE FULL OF LEFT-OVER HARD-BOILED EGGS I DID SIDNEY ON TOAST FOR HIS TEA YESTERDAY...
SLOOP!
...THEY'D SEE HER RIGHT.
SQUOOOOOK!

JOKERS WILD!

Angry Comics Who Can't See the Funny Side

WE SEE THEM on our televisions every night, cracking jokes and making us laugh. However, our favourite TV comics seem to suffer a complete sense of humour bypass when the joke's on them. For a small band of funnymen off the box, things aren't so funny when the boot's on the other foot.

We decided to test the take-a-joke-ability of our favourite telly jesters, and the results are set to shock you. It's time to name and shame the top 5 laughter-merchants who failed to crack a smile when we turned the tables on them.

HARRY ENFIELD

LOADSAMONEY star Enfield has made a fortune tickling the nation's ribs for the past 25 years. So we thought we'd return the favour by ringing him up at 3 in the morning every day for a month and making farting noises down the receiver. For the first fortnight, instead of joining in the fun, misery-guts Harry simply put down the phone. Then he began to get abusive, finally ending up shouting angrily and threatening to call the police. *Enfield should take a leaf out of his own "Scouse" character's book, who would no doubt tell him: "Alright, alright, calm down, calm down"!*

TAKE-A-JOKE-ABILITY: 5 out of 10

JIMMY CARR

JIMMY fills theatres up and down the land with his own brand of humour. But when we ordered a gravestone bearing the inscription "Jimmy Carr 1972-2011" and had it delivered to his house, the *10 O'Clock Live* star failed to see the funny side. Whilst anyone else would have been crying with mirth at such a bonkers stunt, Carr's face remained stonier than the 4cwt granite slab propped up against his garden wall. *It's a safe bet that 8 out of 10 cats would have laughed their socks off, but not misery-guts Jimmy, who seemed more interested in comforting his weeping girlfriend than doubling up with laughter.*

TAKE-A-JOKE-ABILITY: 1 out of 10

EDDIE LARGE

FUNNYMAN Eddie hasn't had a great deal to laugh about recently, after suffering several cardiac arrests and undergoing a heart transplant in 2006. So we thought we'd cheer him up with a couple of light-hearted practical jokes. We followed him to the car park of Papworth Hospital, and whilst he was inside having a check-up, we cheekily let down the tyres on his Ford Focus and sprayed the words "Fat Bastard" in shaving foam across the bonnet. When he came out of the hospital two hours later, instead of doubling up with laughter at our pranks, Large had a face like thunder. *He didn't once crack a smile during the fifty minutes it took him to pump his tyres back up and wipe down his motor.*

TAKE-A-JOKE-ABILITY: 4 out of 10

PAUL MERTON

PAUL Merton's topical quips are the highlight of *Have I Got News For You*, but here's a scoop he won't be featuring on the hit BBC2 programme - he can't take a joke. Every day for a week, we smeared the door handle of Paul's swish North London home with dog excrement for a bit of harmless fun. But oh dear, the deadpan comic's face was even straighter than usual when he discovered our jape. So much so that on the fourth day, the humourless grump even called in Notting Hill police, who finger-printed the door. *Perhaps Paul could fill in the missing word in this headline - "Lighten Up, You Miserable _______!"*

TAKE-A-JOKE-ABILITY: 3 out of 10

PHILL JUPITUS

JUDGING by his performances on *Never Mind the Buzzcocks*, you'd think that roly poly comic Phill loves a laugh. But when we pulled his chair away for a slapstick laugh as he sat down in a Brighton seafront cafe, a different side to his personality came out. After hilariously hitting the deck like a sack of spuds, Jupitus didn't seem the slightest bit amused, screwing up his face, clutching the base of his spine, groaning like a curmudgeon and accusing us of being "f***ing cunts". *It seems that foul-mouthed Phill's quite happy to dish out the laughs on the long-running pop quiz, but it's quite a different story once the cameras are off.*

TAKE-A-JOKE-ABILITY: 2 out of 10

The way you eat your Christmas lunch reveals your secret vices, say

Christmas SINNERS

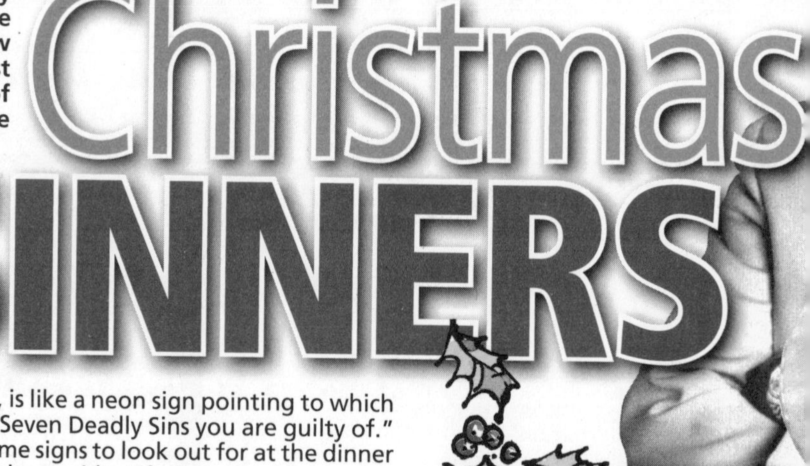

WHETHER we want to admit it or not, we all occasionally fall foul of one of the Seven Deadly Sins. Whether we feel envy when a neighbour rolls up in his brand new car, anger when he lights his bonfire when we've just hung the washing out, or lust when we climb onto the top of the wardrobe to watch his wife soaping her ample breasts in the shower, each of us is guilty of sinning in one way or another.

We like to think that we cover our tracks, and that no-one around us suspects our secret transgressions. But as we enjoy the festive season we should think again, for according to discredited telly shrink DR RAJ PERSAUD, the way we eat our Christmas dinner reveals more about the sins we're prone to commit than we realise.

"When you sit down on December 25th to tuck into a plate piled high with turkey and all the trimmings, you will be laying bare your innermost vices," Dr Persaud told us. "To a psychologist like me, everything you do during that meal, from how you hold your knife and fork to whether you put gravy on your spuds, is like a neon sign pointing to which one of the Seven Deadly Sins you are guilty of."

Here's some signs to look out for at the dinner table, to help you identify the moral trespasses of your fellow dinner guests.

AVARICE

AVARICE is the all-consuming desire for material wealth or gain, and a sure sign that one of your fellow diners is guilty of this Deadly Sin is if they pull their cracker as soon as they sit down at the table - even before the meal is served. Their desperate desire to get their hands on the gift within - whether it's a small plastic magnifying glass, a pair of tweezers or a miniature pack of playing cards - is all consuming. And chances are, plastic trinkets from a Christmas cracker are merely the tip of an avaricious iceberg. This guest will never be happy, spending all their waking hours stockpiling expensive cars, million pound homes around the world, valuable oil paintings and Ming vases.

CELEBRITY EXAMPLES: Sting, Elton John, Jonathan Ross, Noel Edmonds.

GLUTTONY

YOU MIGHT think that a person committing the Deadly Sin of Gluttony would be easy to spot as they pile their plate high with more than their fair share of food at the Christmas dinner table, but nothing could be further from the truth. A true glutton will have very little on their plate: a single sprout, perhaps half a Yorkshire pudding, and one or two peas. That's because they're saving themselves for a blowout at pudding time. They may try to subconsciously disguise their secret vice by refusing puddings and after-dinner mints, but that's merely a ruse to leave enough space so they can stuff themselves sick with a monster teatime spread of leftover turkey, sausage rolls, trifle and all the icing off the Christmas cake.

CELEBRITY EXAMPLES: Kate Moss, Patrick Moore, Delia Smith, Sir Mervyn King

PRIDE

AT EVERY Christmas dinner, someone sitting round the table will loftily announce that they don't want any sprouts. To the untrained eye, it might appear that they simply dislike the taste, but to a highly-qualified day-time telly psychiatrist like I used to be, such behaviour is a sure sign that the Deadly Sin of Pride is being committed. For whilst the sprout denier knows what havoc the tiny brassicas can play on the human digestive system, they believe themselves too hoity-toity to break wind. As the old saying goes; pride comes before a fall, and such people usually die young, as they are too proud to ask for help when they fall ill, in a canal or down a cliff.

CELEBRITY EXAMPLES: Penelope Keith, Posh Spice, Tara Para-Tonkinson, Rod Hull

ENVY

AT ANY large Christmas gathering, there are never enough proper chairs to go around, so someone always ends up sitting on an unsuitable folding seat or piano stool. Look closely at the person who agrees to sit on this chair, for he is guilty of the Deadly Sin of Envy. On this occasion, he will be resentful of all the other diners whose chairs are more or less the right height for the table. And it's not only what everyone else is sitting on that he'll be envious of; in his mind he'll be coveting their expensive watches, their suits and even their wives, fantasising about taking them to his king-size bed and exploring every nook and cranny of their supple bodies with his jealous hands.

CELEBRITY EXAMPLES: Huw Edwards, Chris Kamara, Jeremy Clarkson, Esther Rantzen

ANGER

THERE'S usually one person who sits themselves at the head of the Christmas dinner table and insists on carving the turkey. These people are guilty of the Deadly Sin of Anger, and are sublimating their furious rage by attacking and dismembering an innocent animal with a sharp knife. Like Jack the Ripper, they vent their violent impulses as they carefully carve slice after slice of delicious turkey onto the serving dish, smiling all the while. But remember, just like an iceberg, 90% of their fury is boiling beneath their deceptively cool exterior, so be careful when asking for seconds. The red mist could descend at any moment, and you may well end up as their next victim, lying dead on a mortuary slab.

CELEBRITY EXAMPLES: Fred West, Dame Vera Lynn, Joe Pesci, Richard Briers

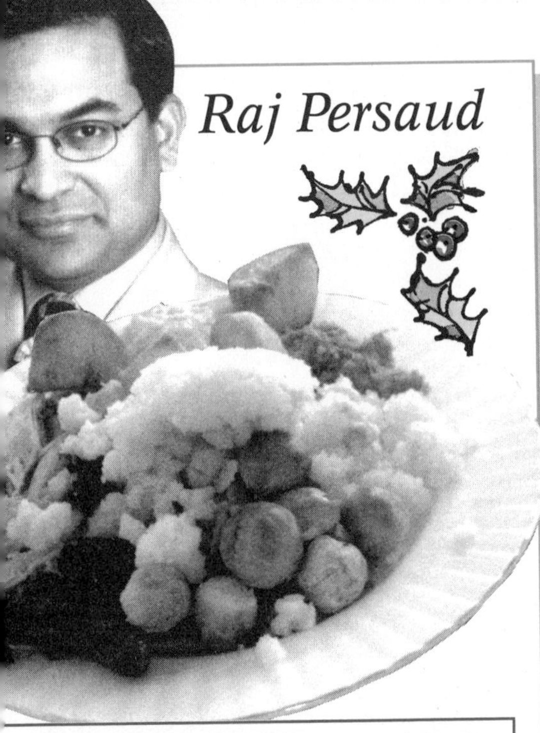

Raj Persaud

SLOTH

THE DEADLY Sin of Sloth manifests itself as extreme lethargy and laziness, characteristics exhibited by the animal of the same name. The slothful Christmas dinner guest is too idle to eat quickly and will take time to eat their meal, chewing slowly through the various courses and often being the last to finish their pudding while everyone else is waiting to light the indoor fireworks. But remember, as well as being lethargic and unenergetic, sloths are also very crafty, and may try to disguise their sluggish indolence by helping to clear the table, doing the washing-up and organising energetic party games for their fellow guests late into the evening.

CELEBRITY EXAMPLES: Hans Blix, Sebastian Coe, Tracy Emin, Lenny Kravitz

LUST

YOU MAY suspect that a guest who uses his knife and fork to pile mashed potato into two round mounds, each one topped with half a sprout with a pea on it, before pushing a cocktail sausage backwards and forwards between them, may be guilty of the Deadly Sin of Lust - an inordinate craving for the pleasures of the flesh. However, you would be wrong, because the signals are actually much more subtle than that. Beware the diner who pours brandy over his pudding instead of round it, for chances are he's fantasising about stripping to his socks, donning a small facemask and participating in a filthy bukkake session, masturbating himself to orgasm and ejaculating onto the face of the nearest woman.

CELEBRITY EXAMPLES: Melvyn Bragg, Leslie Grantham, Una Stubbs, Dappy

HELP! MY HOUSE IS GAUNTED!

HOME OF FEAR: Polworth Lintlaw says his house (inset) is infested by Sun columnist.

A DAGENHAM council tenant is demanding to be re-homed after *Sun* columnist JON GAUNT materialised in his house.

Polwarth Lintlaw told his local paper *The Barking Clarinet*: "It's absolutely terrifying. We never know when he's going to turn up next. My wife won't go in the sitting room any more in case he appears on the sofa, spouting his shit."

semi

The low-brow tabloid hack first materialised in the modest suburban semi several months ago. "We were woken in the middle of the night by overweight, reactionary noises," said Lintlaw. "At the time, we put it down to faulty plumbing and went back to sleep."

In the morning the Lintlaws found that furniture had been moved in the living room, plates had been broken in the kitchen and there was a wet patch on the sofa.

The disturbances continued the next night. "I went to investigate," said Lintlaw. "It was dark, but I could just make out the silhouette of a pig ignorant gobshite on the landing."

half a teacake

"As my eyes became accustomed to the light, I recognised him as Jon Gaunt from the *Sun*. He was all sweaty and red-faced and holding forth about political correctness and health & safety legislation."

"There was a strong smell of beer, urine and chips."

Mr Lintlaw ran back into his bedroom and bolted the door. "We didn't sleep for the rest of the night," he continued. "We could hear him out there, getting louder and louder as he delivered an alliteration-filled tirade about barmy Brussels bureaucrats and bent bananas. My wife was in tears."

"We had the local vicar round in an attempt to rid the house of his presence. Gaunt finally appeared after midnight, just after chucking-out time. He staggered through the front door, all bright purple and shouting angrily about dole scroungers and so-called asylum seekers," said Mr Lintlaw.

TWAT: *Gaunt yesterday.*

"As Gaunt passed him in the hallway, the vicar flicked him with holy water and commanded him to leave in the name of God, but it didn't seem to have any effect," he continued.

"He just went in the front room, put the telly on and started shouting in an eerily high-pitched voice about John Terry's marriage, teenage mums and gay plotlines in *Coronation Street*."

half a sixpence

A housing department spokesman confirmed that there had been several recent sightings of the right wing bollocks-spouter in Dagenham Council properties, but insisted the columnist was harmless.

"Residents should not be worried," he told the paper. "Jon Gaunt lives in a neighbouring street and occasionally enters the wrong house when returning from the pub all pissed up."

And he had this advice for anyone who finds the poor man's Richard Littlejohn manifesting in their property: "Simply coax him towards the door with a brush, whilst repeating the following words: 'Go back to your own realm. You are not welcome here.'"

little white bull

"And if that doesn't work, just call the police," he added. "They'll shift the fat cunt."

Drunken bakers

GILBERT RATCHET

MILLIE TANT

MAY 1st...
... COME ON, JANE. LET'S RECLAIM THE PARK FOR WIMMIN. FOR TOO LONG HAVE THE SISTERHOOD LIVED IN TERROR OF OPEN SPACES... OF MEN LURKING IN THE SHADOWS...
THE PARK

... LUST-CRAZED PRIAPIC BEASTS! UNABLE TO RISE ABOVE THEIR BASE PRIMEVAL URGES... MAKING THE PARK A NO-GO AREA FOR US VULNERABLE FEMALES..!

I NEVER ENTER HERE WITHOUT MY 300 DECIBEL RAPE ALARM ABOUT MY PERSON!
MILLIE... LOOK AT THIS!

EH..?!
TOMORROW! *MAY-DAY* BANK HOLIDAY CELEBRATION FEATURING THE FULCHESTER MORRIS-MEN & their BIG MAYPOLE!

SHALL WE GO? IT SOUNDS LIKE FUN!
SOUNDS LIKE FUN, DOES IT!? WATCHING A BUNCH OF PATRI-ARCHAL TESTOSTOCRATS ERECT A GIANT, TUMESCENT PENIS IN CELEBRATION OF THEIR POWER TO DEFLOWER LESBIANS..!?

OH, MILLIE! I THINK YOU'RE READING A LITTLE TOO MUCH INTO...
... DANCING AROUND IT... SKIPPING... LEAPING TO THE MUSIC OF AN ACCORDION... ITS BELLOWS GOING IN, OUT... IN, OUT...!

... IN, OUT!... IN, OUT! FASTER AND FASTER...! AND DEEPER AND HARDER...!

...THE RIBBONS BURSTING FORTH FROM THE TOP OF THE POLE...! SQUIRTING OUT INTO THE SKY IN ENORMOUS GREAT HOT GOBS OF STICKY...
MILLIE... MILLIE!

CALM DOWN, MILLIE. IT'S JUST A MAYPOLE.
I'VE GOT TO STOP THEM, JANE. FOR THE SAKE OF WIMMIN EVERYWHERE!

SO...
BANG! BANG! SAW! SAW!
MILLIE'S SHED
NO MEN
BANG! BANG!

NEXT DAY...

SUDDENLY...
SISTERS! SISTERS! COME AND CELEBRATE THE SPRING WITH ME INSTEAD - BY DANCING AROUND MY MAY VAGINA!
?

YOUR MAY WHAT?
MY MAY VAGINA!
WELCOME

...THE TRUE SYMBOL OF FERTILITY AND THE BRINGER-FORTH OF ALL LIFE!
HMM... WELL, IT DON'T LOOK MUCH LIKE A FANNY TO ME, LOVE.

TYPICAL! YOU DISMISS IT SIMPLY BECAUSE IT DOESN'T CONFORM TO YOUR UNREALISTIC PORNOGRAPHY-FUELLED, MALE MASTURBATORY IMAGE OF A VAGINA!
EH!?

THESE RED RIBBONS REPRESENT THE MENSTRUAL BLOOD, SHED BY SUFFERING, UNCOMPLAINING WIMMINKIND FOR MILLENNIA..!

...THESE TWO DOORMATS REPRESENT THE LUXURIANT PUBIC HAIR, LEFT UNTRAMMELLED, GROWING FREE AS MOTHER NATURE INTENDED... NOT WAXED AND SHAVED AT YOUR WHIM...!

FELIX and his AMAZING UNDERPANTS

LetterBocks

VIZ COMIC, PO Box 841, Whitley Bay, NE26 9EQ | e-mail: letters@viz.co.uk

WHY is it that space aliens always give their planets a name *and* a number, like Metabilis-3? Surely there can't be two other planets in their solar system called Metabilis. And if there are, why didn't they call them somthing else instead, like Zargon, or Kargol?

Arthur Pewtey, Cheam

STAR LETTER

YOU CAN set your watch by South West Trains. Provided you remember your watch will be about ten minutes behind.

Christina Martin, e-mail

THEY say that with 80% of the cost of a packet of cigarettes being duty, smokers buying black market fags are effectively stealing from the government. But what about the people who have never smoked? They have never paid a penny in tobacco tax. They are the *real* thieves.

Brentford Nylon, Luton

SO CAMILLA Parker-Bowles was poked by a protester during the tuition fee riots. Could Christina Martin do the punchline to this letter, then at least the bloody thing will get printed?

Hank Droppings, e-mail

KIDS really do say the funniest things. My son came out with an absolute corker the other day, but I was busy trying to find a parking space, so wasn't really listening, but it sounded funny. Do I win £5?

Ashley Newman, e-mail

WHEN my wife found out that I have been sleeping with her sister for the last five years, she started crying her eyes out. When she finally calmed down she asked me, "How could you keep something like this a secret?" I had to laugh as it seems pretty obvious. I simply didn't tell anybody.

Lorenzo Vincenzo, e-mail

WHILST on holiday recently in Zakopane, I spotted Jimmy Hill running for the Polish parliament. Is there no end to the man's talents?

Lee Pouncey, e-mail

I WAS recently investigating my family tree after my wife told me there would be no history in my feckless side of the family. So imagine my surprise on discovering that my great, great grandfather was actually a Victorian! I can't wait to tell the missus. She might stop calling me a lazy cunt and telling me to get a job.

M Greeny, e-mail

DOES anyone know the correct dishwasher setting to get dried egg off a World Cup?

Ada Iniesta, Barcelona

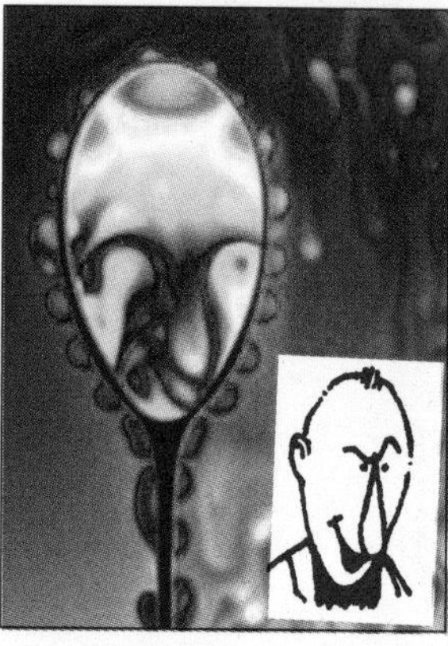

I REALISE that this is several years too late and that many of your readers won't have a clue who I'm talking about, but doesn't this soap film look like Paul Whicker?

Nookieball, Australia

I DON'T believe in conspiracy theories but I have been taking another look at the shooting of JFK. The Warren Commission, named after Earl Warren who headed it, said that there was only one shooter in Dallas on that fateful day. However I have done some research and found out that there is no aristocracy in the US, so Mr Warren could not have been an earl. Do I win a grassy knoll?

Alan Heath, e-mail

MY fucking cat has ripped the bobble off my favorite hat and torn it to shreds. He hasn't even got anything good that I can break.

Ben Fetch, e-mail

MY MATE reckons that when Mick Hucknall dies *The Sun* is going to run the headline 'RIP Hucknall', whereas I'm certain they will go with 'Simply Dead'. So if you're reading this Mick, could you speed it up? I've got £5 riding on this.

Rob Frazer, e-mail

You Ask, I Spout Some Utter Bollocks

with The Archbishop of Canterbury

Dr. Rowan Williams

Dear A B of C,

I SAW on a recent news report that the trapped Chilean miners said they prayed to God to be rescued and God answered their prayers. But if God was going answer their prayers and allow them to be rescued, wouldn't it have been better if he hadn't gone to the trouble of trapping them in the first place? I can't help thinking God wasted his own time a little there.

Edna Barrageballoon, London

The A B of C says...

THAT IS a very interesting question, Mrs Barrageballoon. But what you have to remember is that the concept of wasted time is unique to mortal man. We all have a limited amount of time upon this earth and so every minute is precious. None of us would spend all Sunday washing a car that we were going to take to the scrapyard on Monday. God, however has no concept of wasted time. He is immortal and has infinite time to do anything he wants, even if he's going to undo it later. So trapping 30 miners underground is neither here nor there to him.

† † † † † † † † † † † † † † †

Dear A B of C,

I ALSO saw the same news report as Mrs. Barrageballoon, and I couldn't help wondering how God heard the trapped miners' prayers being so deep underground. Surely their prayers couldn't have gone through 700m of solid rock?

Doris Rabbit, Totnes

The A B of C says...

YOU ARE absolutely right, Mrs Rabbit. Prayers can travel through the air and through clouds, but not through half a mile of granite! That would be ridiculous. I would imagine that God was answering the prayers of the miners' families on the surface rather than those of the miners themselves. Either that, or the miners may have sat directly beneath the small borehole that the rescuers had drilled and prayed up it in between sending letters and newspapers down.

† † † † † † † † † † † † † † †

Dear A B of C,

I LIVE on the third floor of a 24 storey tower block, and I am a little concerned that my prayers may not be reaching God. Are the 21 floors above me blocking my prayers like the rock did with the miners? They're not solid granite, but there must be a fair few tons of concrete in them. I wouldn't normally worry, but I prayed to Him to let me win at the Bingo this weekend, and I spent £35 and I didn't even get 4 corners.

Mavis Doodlebug, Croyden

The A B of C says...

I'M NOT a chemist, so I don't know how the structure of concrete differs from granite. I imagine that it is not as dense, and there is certainly not 700m of it, so I assume that your block of flats would not be as impenetrable to prayers as a Chilean mountain. But just to be on the safe side, why not go up onto the roof next time you pray to win the bingo, or perhaps lean out of your window?

† † † † † † † † † † † † † † †

Dear A B of C,

WHY does God let Nazi War criminals die peacefully in their homes in South America at the age of 98, yet he gives my 25-year-old brother cancer of the brain, and he didn't kill 6 million Jews?

Ada Saturn, Crewe

The A B of C says...

I'M SORRY, Mrs Saturn, I was about to give you a really convincing answer to that, but my secretary's just come in and told me I've got to go and take the Eucharist.

IS SOME ASPECT of religious or spiritual life confusing you? Perhaps you're wondering why God professes his love for us but half the world starves. Maybe you can't believe how he can visit catastrophic natural disasters on his children. Or perhaps you can't understand why a caring God could allow Russell Brand win an Outstanding Contribution to Comedy Award. Write to: *The (former) Archbishop of Canterbury, Viz Comic, PO Box 841, Whitley Bay, NE26 9EQ.*

SURNAME Castle? Christen your son Warwick and save a fortune on personalised gifts buy buying all his presents from the souvenir shop at Warwick Castle.

Greg Jackson, e-mail

DIP the tops of leftover Yorkshire puddings into melted chocolate, then wait for it to harden and fill it with Angel Delight for a delicious council house eclair.

Cora Flange, e-mail

PORNSTARS. Save money on anal bleaching and bum wad by wiping your arse with disposable toilet cleaning wipes.

Ishta the Relaxed, e-mail

SHOPPERS. Avoid having to queue for stuff in shops by ordering online and queuing down at the sorting office instead.

Barak Obamford, e-mail

A SMALL bird tied by the leg to your ear with a short piece of string makes an ideal fan in warmer climates than this bloody shithole.

M Coppereno, e-mail

SAVE money on correcting uneven floors at home by wearing orthopaedic shoes.

Ed O'Meara, e-mail

BRITAIN'S 2.5m jobless. Why not retrain as Premier League football managers? Vacancies are always cropping up.

Alan Mac, London

CHOCOLATE hundreds and thousands make ideal 'casualty' ants for ant action movie film directors.

Sanny Sutherland, e-mail

A RECENT advert for Emirates Airlines claims that 'There's Nothing Like Australia.' I always thought New Zealand would be pretty similar.

L Dowds, Rugby

WHY is it that darts players are allowed to wear glasses? Is this not cheating in the same way as an athlete who takes steroids?

Dominic Booth, e-mail

I WAS at Heathrow the other day and I saw this Quantas plane land and it was full of Australians coming to our country. Now I know that everyone deserves a second chance and bygones should be bygones but didn't we ship off all our criminals there? And before letting them back into the country is there anyone checking to see if their sentences are up?

Alan Heath, e-mail

COULD the BBC please stop using licence payers' money phoning up religious nut-job Stephen Green to ask him what he thinks about things? From same sex marriage to mosques being built in London, it's obvious what he thinks about everything and nobody gives a fuck anyway. The money they save could be spent making some good programmes, like a lively cop drama with plenty of sex scenes.

M Cheesemonger, Tring

HAS anyone else noticed the remarkable similarities between sharks and vampires? They both have the ability to sense blood and they both have big pointy teeth.

Chris Higson, e-mail

WELL done to the Lakeland Bakery Shop in Durham for this amazing offer in the January Sales. Can any of your readers beat this reduction of 0.4%?

David Milner, Durham

* *Well, readers. Have you spotted any shop keepers really pushing the boat out to help cash-strapped shoppers in austerity Britain?*

TO THE gentleman in the end cubicle in South Mimms Services toilets: Your fake coughing, no matter how well-timed, does not hide the gargantuan plopping noises coming from your cubicle.

Randy Lahey, Sunnydale Park

I WONDER if any readers can settle an argument. I reckon the word 'unlimited' means unlimited. However my mate, Sir Richard Branson, reckons that when used in sentences like 'Virgin Mobile gives you unlimited internet access' it means 1GB and not a kB more. Who is correct?

Alan Heath, e-mail

I DON'T know why local councils don't just use ordinary gloss paint when renewing road markings. Several years ago my neighbour painted a large erect penis on our road using some gloss he had left over from doing his bathroom. He did it just after the council had renewed the road markings. The giant penis is still clearly visible but the white lines faded away a long time ago.

Ian Ferguson, e-mail

I HAVE just opened a packet of 'Salt or not' crisps to find that *not* is the the operative word. If anyone finds that they have two sachets of salt in their crisp packet, then please let me know via the pages of *Viz*, as I think one of them is mine.

Ronny Pew, Redruth

Paul Weller's STYLE COUNCIL

IF there is one issue that is guaranteed to make rock stars' blood boil when they are having a ridiculous haircut, it's anecdotal evidence of loony wheelie bin policies by barmy local authorities.

This week we put your half-baked and unsubstantiated refuse collection gripes to **Paul Weller** as he sits and gets his hair done in that style he has. Will Paul be able to offer any advice to our readers before his stupid haircut is finished?

Hi Paul,

THE LID of my blue bin was damaged last month when the binmen were emptying it. Now they are refusing to empty it because they say the lid isn't shut properly when I leave it out. What can I do?

Judith, Runcorn

Paul says...

Sorry, who the fuck are you? I'm trying to get my hair cut in that style I have. I couldn't give a flying fuck about your frigging wheelie bin. If they don't get them pointy bits done right at the sides you'll be getting the twatting bill.

Hi Paul,

I LIVE in West Yorkshire and my council have significantly reduced the size of my household waste bin. I have 5 children and a fat husband. We tried putting the excess food waste in a blender, freezing it and then painting it to look like cardboad but council snoopers caught us at it. What can we do?

Margerie, Keighley

Paul says...

Jesus fucking Christ! I'm trying to concentrate on making sure I get that bit at the top stuck up! Do you people not listen? I have no interest in your petty, domestic household waste quibbles! Fuck you. And fuck your cunting bins.

Hi Paul,

I'M A mod and have one of them haircuts. I can't park my scooter round the back of my house because of all the wheelie bins I have - there is simply no room for all the massive wing mirrors. It makes me want to shout to the top.

Ace Face, Brighton

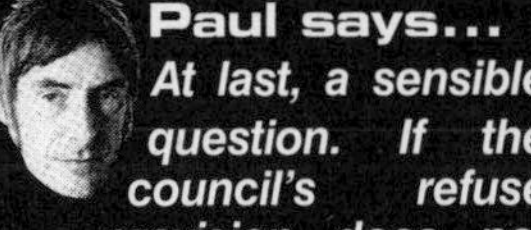

Paul says...

At last, a sensible question. If the council's refuse provision does not make allowances for personal transportation storage, then you could be entitled to make a claim. Take photographic evidence of your scooter being impeded and also of your fucking daft haircut as well. Right, that's me done... short fringe, long bits at side and a spiky bit on top. I'm off for a shit.

NEXT WEEK

Stone Roses frontman **IAN BROWN** reluctantly tries to answer your pressure selling complaints while having that haircut he has.

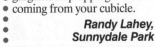

COULD I SEE THE DOCTOR PLEASE?
I'M SORRY. HE'S ON HIS LUNCH.

YOU CAN FORGET pop stars, footballers and Hollywood hunks, because these days a girl's more likely to have a poster of a boffin pinned up on her bedroom wall. And it's a scientific certainty that the object of her affections will be hunky TV egghead DR BRIAN COX.

With his boyish good looks, tight jeans and brown hair, particle physicist Cox has got all the ladies' atoms in a state of excitement. But how much do you really know about this sexy scientist with his Cosmos-wide smile? Just like the Periodic Table, you can find out all about his unique elements by studying the letters in his name...

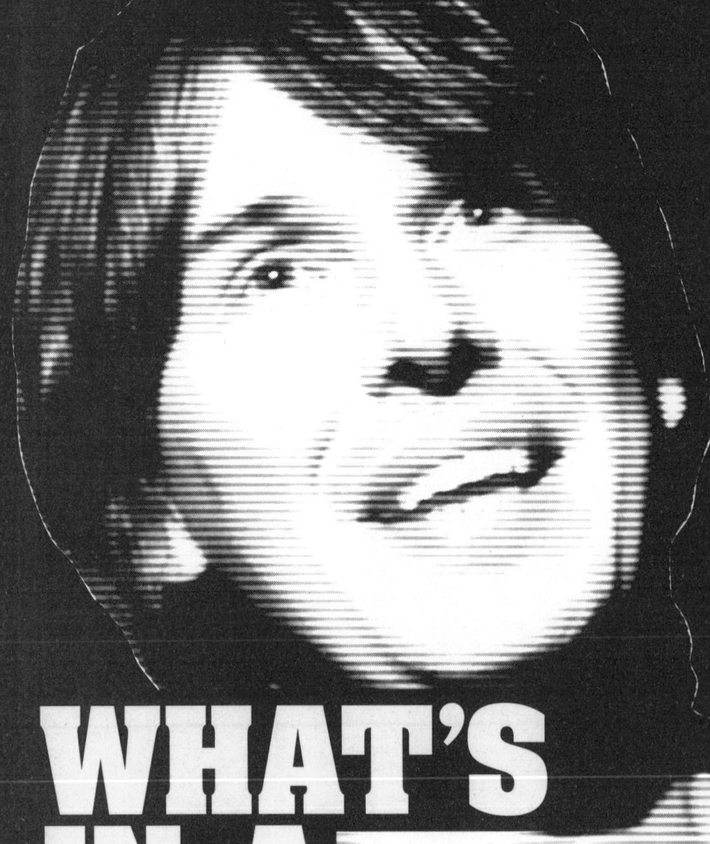

WHAT'S IN A NAME?

D is for a D IN MATHS Super-intelligent Brian wasn't always a genius. In fact, whilst at school he flunked his Maths A-level. "I could never remember what seven eights was," he told the *Worcester Yellow Ads* paper. "And just my luck, it came up in the exam!" But in the words of the song later made famous by his band D:Ream, things could only of got better, and in Brian's case they did. These days, he could do seven eights backwards, and at his desk in CERN's Large Hadron Collider Brian now does sums using numbers of up to a million or more.

R is for ROCKY 2 Cox's favourite film is *Rocky 2*, starring Sylvester Stallone. He is such a fan that he has even had the 1979 film's principle characters Rocky Balboa and Apollo Creed tattooed on his buttocks, squaring up to each other across the cleft. As his party piece at the Manchester University Physics Department Christmas bash, the Professor drops his trousers and recreates the movie's climactic fight scene by twitching his gluteus maximusses, making the two heavyweights slug it out for eight rounds. Finally he bends over and Burgess Meredith, whom he has tattooed on his taint, steps in to stop the bout.

B is for BUDGERIGAR Brian is allergic to budgerigars, and the slightest bite from one of the pint-sized parrots could prove fatal. In fact, the telly boffin nearly died at the age of fifteen, when he went round to the home of former Olympic shot-putter Geoff Capes, who had advertised a pair of his old football boots for sale in the local paper. Whilst waiting for Capes to bring them down from the loft, Cox inadvertently sat down on a sleeping budgie, which pecked him on the scrotum, causing it swell up like a balloon.

R is for ROBOTS Like most scientists, Brian's ultimate aim is to build a realistic sex robot. His solar-powered Sex-Bot 3000 is still at the drawing board stage, but he expects to have a working prototype - complete with computerised tits, a remote control fanny and gripping hands - up and running by the end of the year. "I probably won't use it a great deal, because I'm happily married," he told the *Oldham Autotrader*. "I'd probably only have a go on it if my wife's away on holiday with her friends, visiting her sister for the weekend or when she nips to the shops."

I is for INFINITY Brian's favourite number isn't 3, 7 or 9 like most people's. It's not even pie or 100. It's infinity - and it's the largest number that there is! "Imagine the biggest number you can," says Cox. "Infinity is that number plus a million. Then timesed by a hundred. Plus a billion billion billion." It's a difficult concept to grasp, so the hunky egghead puts it into perspective. "Imagine all the grains of sand on all the beaches on earth. If each of those grains of sand was a planet with beaches, then all the grains of sand on all those planets would add up to infinity. Well, a bit less. About three quarters of infinity, actually."

A is for ATOMS People think atoms are the smallest things in the world. Except, that is, for Professor Cox. For the ex-D:Ream ivory tinkler believes that atoms are in fact made of smaller things, such as quarks, leptons, pulsars and hardons. "There are lots of these little bits inside every atom in the world, and when you split the atom into these bits you get a mushroom-shaped bomb," he told *Loot* magazine. But as to what these tinier particles are mode of, Cox confesses that he is in the dark. "I really haven't got a clue," he admitted. "They are probably made of some kind of waves or string theories."

N is for NUDE Sexy cosmologist Cox was recently offered half a million pounds to reveal his heavenly body in *Playboy* magazine. But after serious consideration, he declined the offer to bare all for cash. "The thought of all those readers looking at my body would be a turn on, I must admit," he told Lorne Spicer of TV's *Car Booty* programme. "But at the end of the day, I'm more than a piece of meat. I'm a professor of particle physics at Manchester University, and I want to be appreciated for my intellect and not just my curves."

C is for COLLIDER Most people love to see big things smashing into each other and bursting into flames, for example Formula 1 racing cars, air display planes or railway trains. But Cox gets his kicks from watching TINY objects crash - and the tinier, the better. To this end he has built himself a Large Hadron Collider, which fires microscopic particles no bigger than a salt into each other at the speed of light. "The particles go round the 27km long circular collider 11,000 times per second. However, the impacts take place in a silent vacuum, so I have to make the skidding and explosion noises with my mouth," he says.

O is for OCTOPII Brian has gone on record as saying that octopii are the animals that he envies the most. "I really, really love doing physics, and If I had eight arms like an octopus I could do four times as many experiments all at the same time," he told the *Whitley Bay Advertiser*. "Or I could do three times as many experiments and use my last pair of tentacles to play the keyboards in D:Ream," he added. Brian also likes other animals beginning with the letter O, such as ospreys, ocelots, otters, ostriches and owls. But not orang-utans. "I can't wait for them to go extinct, the big, orange twats," he added.

X is for XEROPHTHALMIA Xerophthalmia is a particularly debilitating inflammation of the mucous membrane around the eye. The sufferer experiences recurrent bouts of painful irritation which, if left untreated, could lead to permanent eye damage. Contracting this disease is every scientist's worst nightmare, as they need their eyes to look through microscopes and telescopes. "I'm pleased to report that I have never suffered from xerophthalmia," Cox told *Exchange & Mart*. "But I do get some right proper gyp off my piles."

Next Week's WHAT'S IN A NAME?: Jeremy Cunting Kyle

SMACK! BLAM! CLANG! THUD! SMASH! BANG! CRACK! THUNK!

OH, LORDY!... IT'S THE
FAT SLAGS
...AN' IT WEREN'T TILL HE GOT 'OME THAT NIGHT AN' LOOKED IN THE MIRROR THAT HE SEEN IT...
THIS PUB FOR LEASE SEE LANDLORD
DOG & HAMMER
WOODY WAS HERE
... A BIG RING O' DRIED BLOOD ROUND 'IS GOB... LOOKED LIKE RONALD McDONALD
HE'D BEEN AT WORK ALL DAY AN' ALL... SEEN PATIENTS, DONE FILLIN'S THE LOT
NAA-AAA!
OOH! 'ERE COMES DAVE
CHRIST... HE LOOKS WHITE AS A SHEET.
WOT'S UP, DAVE?.. 'AVE Y' SEEN A GHOST?
NO, I AIN'T... BUT I MIGHT BE ONE TOMORROW... I GOT WRONG OFF A GYPSY
EH?
...I'VE GOT T'AVE A BARE KNUCKLE FIGHT WI' THE BASTARD TONIGHT
I FOUND A LOAD O' MEAT IN THE BINS BEHIND THE BUTCHERS, AN' I SOLD IT T' MAD MICKEY O'FISTS
SO WHY IS HE GOIN' T' FIGHT YER?
...WELL, IT GIVE HIM TERRIBLE SHITS AN' KILLED ONE OF 'IS DOGS
MAD MICKEY O'FISTS?... HEY, Y' DON'T WANT T' GET ON THE WRONG SIDE OF 'IM, DAVE. HE'S A FUCKIN' ANIMAL, THAT ONE
TOO LATE NOW
WOT SORT O' MEAT WAS IT?
SIRLOIN STEAK... OR PORK...
HARD T' SAY... IT LOOKED A BIT GREY IN THE BIN BAG... AN' THERE WERE TONS O' FLIES BUZZIN' ROUND
...IT SMELT ALRIGHT, THOUGH. HE COULDN'T OF COOKED IT PROPER....
I GIVE 'IM 'IS MONEY BACK, BUT HE SAYS HE WANTS REVENGE... SAYS HE WANTS TO FLATTEN ME
AYE, WELL THAT'S THE GYPSY CODE OF HONOUR, THAT, DAVE
YOU'RE A BIT TASTY WI' YER FISTS, THOUGH, DAVE... YOU LAID THAT BLOKE OUT WI' ONE PUNCH LAST WEEK, REMEMBER?..
... Y'KNOW... HIM QUEUING FOR 'IS PENSION... THAT MIDGET.
OH, AYE... BUT THIS FELLA'S A 'ARDER NUT T' CRACK ON ACCOUNT OF WOT HE DOES FORRA LIVIN'...
WOT DOES HE DO?
HE'S A PROFESSIONAL BARE KNUCKLE FIGHTER, TRAY
I SEE Y' PROBLEM THERE, DAVE
COULD GIVE 'IM AN EDGE, THAT.
CAN I 'OLD THE BOARDS UP BETWEEN ROUNDS LIKE THEY DO ON THE TELLY?
WELL, Y' CAN DO IT F' ROUND ONE IF Y' LIKE... THERE WON'T BE A ROUND TWO.
WELL, AT LEAST IT'LL BE OVER QUICK, DAVE
AYE
ONE PUNCH AN IT'LL ALL BE DONE FOR YER.
NO!.. I'VE SEEN MAD MICKEY O'FISTS IN ACTION... HE DON'T STOP JUST 'CAUSE YER ON THE FUCKIN' DECK!
DON'T HE?
HE FUCKIN' DON'T!
HE JUST KEEPS PUNCHIN' AN' PUNCHIN' AN' PUNCHIN' AN' PUNCHIN' AN' PUNCHIN' AN' PUNCHIN' TILL THERE'S NOWT LEFT!
EEH, I'M EXCITED... I'VE ALWAYS WANTED T' BE ONE O' THEM ROUND GIRLS
I'M SAYIN' NOWT
COME ON, TRAY... I'M GOIN' T' GET A SEXY NEW BIKINI FOR ME BIG MOMENT

CONTINUED OVER

TEN MINUTES LATER...
NO PUSHING, NOW... LET THE KIDDIES TO THE FRONT SO THEY CAN SEE
BIG FIGHT TONITE IN THE BEER GARDEN DAVE "BINMAN" BOOTHBY V MAD MICKEY O'FISTS
THIS PUB FOR LEASE
FIGHT NIGHT SPECIAL A PINT, A PIE AND A FAGGA
DOG & HAMMER
ROUND 1
HE'LL BE HERE ANY MINUTE, DAVE... 'OW ARE Y' FEELIN'?
LIKE A DEAD MAN WALKIN', BAZ
I'VE LEARNT ME LESSON... I'LL NEVER SELL RANCID MEAT TO A GYPSY AGAIN. I'LL TAKE IT DOWN THE CARE HOME NEXT TIME
'ERE HE COMES!
ANY CHANCE OF A LITTLE SIT DOWN BEFORE DE FOIGHT?.. ONLY ME BACK IS FUCKED AN' ME LEGS HAVE TORNED TO JELLY, SO DAY HAVE
?
NO FUCKIN' CHANCE, MR. O'FISTS... LET'S GET ON WI' IT!
SECONDS OUT!.. ROUND ONE!
ROUND 1
WOBBLE!
FLOOOF!
DANCE!!
PRANCE!
OOF!
FEEBLE TAP!
F=ma
F = 0.25kg x 0.5ms⁻¹
F = 0.13N
CRASH!!
AN' THE WINNER BY A KNOCKOUT... DAVE 'BIN MAN' BOOTHBY!
WELL DONE DAVE!
ROUND 1
NEXT DAY...
DID Y'SEE IT?.. I GIVE 'IM THE OLD BOOTHBY 1-2... A RIGHT HOOK SQUARE ON THE KISSER. WALLOP! ONE PUNCH, DOWN HE WENT LIKE A SACK O' SPUDS... DID Y'SEE IT, EH?
AYE!.. WE WAS THERE... WE SAW IT
OUT FER THE COUNT, HE WERE... DIDN'T KNOW WAT FUCKIN' DAY IT WAS... DID Y'SEE IT?
HMM!
WHEN Y' GET HIT BY ME, YOU STAY HIT, TRAY, KNOW WHAT I MEAN?.. THE POOR BASTARD...
DON'T KNOW ME OWN STRENGTH, THAT'S MY TROUBLE... IT MUST BE...
"... LIFTIN' BINS ALL DAY" AYE, DAVE, Y'VE SAID
OOH...
... 'ERE'S BAZ!
WOT'S UP, BAZ? 'AVE Y' SEEN A GHOST?
NO... BUT I MIGHT BE ONE TOMORROW
EH? WOT'S 'APPENED?
I'LL TELL Y' WOT'S 'APPENED...
... I BET SCOTCH JIMMY TWO 'UNDRED QUID THAT IRONFIST BOOTHBY 'ERE WOULD GET FLATTENED IN THE FIRST FUCKIN' ROUND...
?
... TWO 'UNDRED QUID THAT I 'AVEN'T GOT BY THE WAY...
NOW HE'S GOIN' T' PUNCH ME FUCKIN' LIGHTS OUT LATER ON TONIGHT
SCOTCH JIMMY FROM THE SCRAPYARD?.. THE GIANT?
THAT'S 'IM!
10 MINS LATER...
'ERE, JIMMY... DO YOU FANCY 'AVIN A FEW HIGHLAND FLINGS WI' US BEFORE Y' PUNCH BAZ'S LIGHTS OUT?
EH?..
... I THOUGHT WE WAS GOIN' T' FUCK 'IM, TRAY

GILBERT RATCHET

NEW McGANN FOUND

Boffins uncover fifth Scouse actor brother

THE LIVERPUDLIAN light entertainment world was reeling last night after scientists in Canada announced the discovery of a new McGann brother.

Conventional thinking has long had it that there are only four of the Merseyside thespian siblings in existence. However, a research team from Vancouver University blew that theory out of the water yesterday when they unveiled proof of an entirely unique fifth brother at a press conference in Calgary.

The new McGann, whom the eggheads have dubbed MG206, reportedly stands 5'10" and has the same curly brown hair as his most successful relative, Paul.

discovery

"This is an unprecedented discovery," said Dr Henry Sternbaum. "In the same way we now struggle to believe we ever thought the earth was flat, we will one day look back in amazement at the fact we considered Joe, Paul, Mark and Stephen to be the only McGann brothers."

The Canadian brainboxes claim to have stumbled upon their astonishing find whilst watching an old episode of *Inspector Morse* one lunchtime.

"There was a scene with this lorry driver who was humourously chastising Lewis for the quality of his parking," said Sternbaum. "My colleagues thought it was definitely Stephen McGann playing this bloke, but I thought it looked more like a young Joe," he continued.

"But a quick IMDb search revealed that neither Stephen nor Joe had ever been in Morse – only Mark had. And it definitely wasn't Mark because I remember the one he was in. It was where Morse had to work out who shot this woman who was having an affair with an Oxford don."

bid-up.tv

Intrigued, the team immediately rented the DVD containing the episode in question and took it straight to their lab for testing. Detailed genetic scans over every scene with the lorry driver indicated that he was indeed being played by a McGann brother never previously encountered.

A quick phone call to the *Inspector Morse* producer confirmed the existence of a new addition to the Wirral-born stage brethren.

"The producer told me he was sure he had cast Paul McGann in that part," said Sternbaum. "But his Wikipedia entry showed clearly that he was doing a two-episode stint in Heartbeat at the time, so he couldn't have done."

He added, "It's incredible to think that the cast and crew of Morse had an entirely new McGann right under their noses that whole time, but didn't realise it."

babestation

Further investigation by the Canadian scientists uncovered several more brief appearances by MG206 in other mediocre British TV programmes, including masquerading as a concussed builder in an episode of *Casualty* and delivering the line "Does anyone know the Heimlich Manoeuvre?" in a cafe scene from an early *Jonathan Creek*.

And Sternbaum insisted that this is only the beginning. "We're confident that, with the right level of funding, we can trace this new McGann right up to the present day – and maybe even discover his current whereabouts," he said.

This is not the first time a group of Canadian scientists has uncovered a secret sibling in a family of UK television personalities. In 1998, physicists from Quebec found a third Dimbleby brother asleep under an ITV news desk.

SIBLING REVELRY: **Canadian scientists are celebrating discovery of fifth McGann brother.**

MICKEY'S
MINIATURE
GRANDPA
ADVENTURE WAS NEVER FAR AWAY FOR YOUNG MICKEY MARSTON – FOR HIS GRANDFATHER WAS CONVINCED THAT A GYPSY'S CURSE HAD SHRUNK HIM TO AN INCREDIBLE TWO INCHES IN HEIGHT!

THE WORLD CAN BE A DANGEROUS PLACE WHEN YOU'RE ONLY TWO INCHES TALL, MICKEY!
SO I'VE MADE MYSELF THIS MINIATURE SUIT OF ARMOUR MADE OUT OF TWO HALVES OF A WALNUT SHELL, AND A THIMBLE FOR A HELMET!

UH-OH! MY SUIT OF ARMOUR WON'T PROTECT ME AGAINST THAT BIG DOG!
THE ENORMOUS BRUTE COULD EASILY SWALLOW ME WHOLE!

I'D BETTER HOP ONTO YOUR HAND SO YOU CAN LIFT ME UP OUT OF HARM'S WAY, MICKEY!
OW! GET OFF, GRANDPA!
CRUNCH!
YOU'RE CRUSHING MY FINGERS!

I'LL BE SAFER PERCHED UP HERE ON YOUR SHOULDER, MICKEY. WOW! BUT IT'S A LONG WAY DOWN TO THE GROUND FOR A LITTLE FELLOW LIKE ME!
GRANDPA, GET OFF! MUM! HELP!

GOLLY! I HOPE A SPARROWHAWK DOESN'T SWOOP DOWN AND CARRY ME AWAY!
OH DEAR!
TELL HIM TO GET OFF ME, MUM – HIS TROUSERS SMELL OF STALE WEE.

COME ALONG, DAD. I THINK MICKEY JUST WANTS TO READ NOW, OK?
HMPH!
WHY DON'T YOU COME THROUGH INTO THE KITCHEN?

SHORTLY
WHOOPEE! COME AND WATCH THIS, MICKEY – I'VE MADE A PINT-SIZED SEE-SAW OUT OF A LOLLY STICK AND AN OLD COTTON REEL
ME AND YOUR TOY SOLDIER ARE HAVING TERRIFIC FUN! SEE-SAW, MARJORIE DAW...

THAT'S THE DUSTING FINISHED, DAD. AND I'VE RINSED OUT YOUR PLASTIC PANTS.
GASP!
CLOTHES PEGS
I'LL JUST POP THEM ON THE WASHING LINE TO DRY.

LOOK OUT, MICKEY! THAT MYSTERIOUS GYPSY WOMAN WHO SHRUNK ME TO MIDGET SIZE HAS COME BACK TO GET ME!
NO DAD, IT'S ME, FLOSSIE. I'M YOUR DAUGHTER, REMEMBER?

GULP! I'VE GOT TO GET AWAY BEFORE SHE PUTS ANOTHER GYPSY CURSE ON ME!
I'LL MAKE MY ESCAPE THROUGH THE CAT-FLAP – SHE'LL NOT BE ABLE TO FOLLOW ME THROUGH THERE!

HNNNGGH! THIS CAT-FLAP IS THE PERFECT SIZE FOR SOMEONE OF MY MINISCULE STATURE!
I CAN – HNNGGH – SLIP THROUGH IT EASILY!

DAD, WILL YOU PLEASE STOP IT. YOU'LL HURT YOURSELF.
WHY DON'T YOU COME AND WATCH COUNTRYFILE WITH JULIA BRADBURY AND MATT BAKER? THAT ALWAYS CALMS YOU DOWN.

SHE'S CAST ANOTHER ONE OF HER SHRINKING SPELLS ON ME, MICKEY! NOW I'M REDUCED TO THE SIZE OF AN ANT!
AND I'M GETTING SMALLER AND SMALLER BY THE SECOND!

NOW I'M SO TINY, I'M BARELY VISIBLE TO THE NAKED EYE!
MICKEY! MICKEY! I'M DOWN HERE ON THE CARPET! DON'T TREAD ON ME, MICKEY!

HELP! HELP! I'M SHRINKING DOWN SMALLER THAN AN ATOM! I'M HURTLING THROUGH THE VAST EMPTY SPACES THAT LIE BETWEEN SUB-ATOMIC PARTICLES!
YES, I'D LIKE TO SPEAK TO THE DOCTOR...

LATER
WE'VE PUT YOUR FATHER UNDER SEDATION, MRS MARSTON...
FULCHESTER GENERAL HOSPITAL
AND HERE ARE THE RESULTS OF THE C.A.T. SCAN WHICH WE DID ON HIS BRAIN...

THEY SHOW THE DEVELOPMENT OF A SMALL BLOOD CLOT HERE IN HIS BRAIN, WHICH WOULD ACCOUNT FOR THESE DELUSIONS OF HIS.
CAN YOU DO ANYTHING TO HELP HIM, DOCTOR?

WELL, THE BLOOD CLOT IS IN AN AWKWARD PLACE, AND REMOVING IT WOULD BE A VERY TRICKY OPERATION – ALMOST IMPOSSIBLE FOR ANY ORDINARY SURGEON.
FORTUNATELY, HOWEVER, I AM NOT AN ORDINARY SURGEON...

AS I AM ONLY A FRACTION OF A MILLIMETRE IN HEIGHT, I CAN BE INJECTED DIRECTLY INTO YOUR FATHER'S BLOODSTREAM, SWIM UP THROUGH HIS VEINS AND REMOVE THE CLOT WITH MY MINIATURE HAMMER AND CHISEL!
NURSE, HOLD THE SYRINGE STEADY WHILST I CLAMBER IN!

FINBARR SAUNDERS AND HIS DOUBLE ENTENDRES
FNARR! FNARR!

...THUMP-THUD! THUMPITTY-THUMP!
?
KITCHEN
DO NOT DISTURB

MR. GIMLET - WHATEVER ARE YOU DOING IN THERE?
I'M BEATING MY MEAT WHILST WATCHING NIGELLA MRS SAUNDERS.
FNARR! FNARR!
YIP! YIP!
KWOUK! KWOUK!
ROFL! ROFL!

...I BEG YOUR PARDON.
I SAID, I'M JUST PUMMELING MY PORK.
K-YAK! K-YAK!
SNIB! SNIB!
HAT! HAT!

AS YOU CAN SEE, I'M FOLLOWING A RECIPE WHILST WHACKING A CHOP REPEATEDLY WITH THIS STOUT TENDERIZING MALLET.
GOODNESS GRACIOUS. I'VE NOT SEEN ONE OF THOSE BEFORE.

...IT'S AN INVALUABLE KITCHEN AID WHICH IS AVAILABLE IN EITHER TIMBER OR METAL FORM. I'VE GOT WOOD.
PLEWB! PLEWB!
NOP! NOP!
CHUD! CHUD!

WHEN I WAS FIRST MARRIED, I VISITED THE LOCAL BUTCHER EVERY DAY TO PICK UP A TASTY CUT OF SOMETHING FOR MRS GIMLET'S TEA. SADLY, THOUGH, SHE HAS RECENTLY DECIDED TO BECOME A STRICT VEGETARIAN.

THESE DAYS, MY WIFE RESOLUTELY REFUSES TO SWALLOW MY MEAT.
FLAMP! FLAMP!
K-SWIP! K-SWIP!
HOON! HOON!
POB! POB!

SHE WON'T EVEN PREPARE IT FOR ME. I CAN'T REMEMBER THE LAST TIME I GOT HOME AND SHE GAVE ME A NICE HAM-SHANK.
YARM! YARM!
CHURB! CHURB!
NOP! NOP!
HIMP! HIMP!
F-NUK! F-NUK!

WHAT ABOUT FISH, THOUGH MR. GIMLET..? I UNDERSTAND THAT MANY VEGETARIANS STILL EAT FISH.

ALAS NO, MRS. SAUNDERS. SHE'S BECOME 100% HERBIVOROUS. IT'S A SHAME, AS SHE USED TO HAVE QUITE A PENCHANT FOR SEAFOOD OF ALL VARIETIES.

SHE'D OFTEN COME BACK FROM AN EARLY MORNING TRIP TO THE DOCKS WITH A FRESH CASE OF CRABS.
K-WUFF! K-WUFF!
PROOB! PROOB!
SNIT! SNIT!
TARF! TARF!
YUNT! YUNT!

...OR SHE'D SURPRISE ME BY UNWRAPPING HER KIPPER ON THE KITCHEN TABLE AND GETTING ME TO FILLET.
F-LARP! F-LARP!
CHONT! CHONT!
NOIK! NOIK!
LIMP! LIMP!
SPAG! SPAG!

WAS SHE LIKEWISE PARTIAL TO A BIT OF GAME, MR. GIMLET..?
INDEED SHE WAS. SHE HAD A PARTICULARLY APPETISING RECIPE FOR A PASTRY-TOPPED MAIN COURSE DISH MADE USING THE FLESH OF THE EASTERN JACKRABBIT.
GLEET! GLEET!

...YES. THE PROSPECT OF FILLING MY FACE WITH MRS. GIMLET'S HARE PIE USED TO MAKE MY MOUTH WATER.
GLAP! GLAP!
INSP! INSP!
WIKI! WIKI!

SHE USED TO SPEND A LOT OF TIME EXAMINING THE WARES AT THE MEAT COUNTER OF OUR NEIGHBOURHOOD FARM SHOP.

SHE WAS VERY IMPRESSED BY THE SIZE OF THE LOCAL FARMERS' SAUSAGES. THEY USED TO GET HER SPECIAL BEEF DRIPPING.
YURT! YURT!
F-NOO! F-NOO!
WURP! WURP!
HEB! HEB!
K-NOG! K-NOG!

IT WAS DELICIOUS STUFF, THAT DRIPPING. IT WAS IMPORTED FROM DOUGLAS ON THE ISLE OF MAN...
...I USED TO LOVE BASTING MY WIFE'S MASSIVE BANGERS IN HOT MAN FAT.
BROMP! BROMP!
SNIBBIT! SNIBBIT!
PONK! PONK!
CHOO! CHOO!
SPAD! SPAD!

...ERM...TALKING OF MEAT, MRS. SAUNDERS, I WAS JUST WONDERING...DO YOU FANCY A BIT OF TONGUE..?
OOH YES! I'D LOVE A BIT!
ERM...COULD YOU EXCUSE YOUR MOTHER AND I FOR A FEW MINUTES, PLEASE FINBARR..?
YES. RUN ALONG NOW, THERE'S A GOOD LAD...

AND...
OOH YES! MR. GIMLET! JUST THERE!... UP A BIT..! YES..! OOOH! OOOH! OOOH! YES! OOOH GOD! OH GOD! YES..! JUST THERE..! OOH!!
MMF! MMF! SLURP!
KITCHEN
DO NOT DIST...
EAR PLUGS XXXXL ELEPHANT STRENGTH
THAT'S IT MR. GIMLET! RIGHT ON ME CLIT.

Scandal shame of toilet grin mag as Viz finally

WE'VE HACKED THE TV PUPPETS

THE NEWS OF THE WORLD recently paid the price for abusing the public's trust after hacking into more than 4,000 voicemail messages. The tabloid, published each Sunday since 1868, found itself summarily axed when owner Rupert Murdoch found out what his so-called journalists had been doing.

EXCLUSIVE

The list of allegations against the paper gets longer and more shocking each day, as new targets of its disgusting dirty tricks are identified.

gutter

But now evidence is beginning to emerge that such underhand news-gathering techniques are not confined to the gutter press.

For even your big-hearted Viz has become embroiled in the scandal, after letting its usual high standards slip.

A private investigator working for this magazine yesterday admitted:

- **HACKING the voicemail of TV puppets such as Sooty, Orville and Lamb Chop**
- **BLAGGING their personal and confidential medical records**
- **ACCESSING their online bank accounts and stealing secret passwords**
- **BRIBING the police to access puppets' ex-directory telephone numbers**

Blake Muir was paid £300,000 a year for his services, which involved using illegal methods to gather personal information about television puppets.

Muir worked at Viz for twenty years until his retirement, when he was presented with a gold clock by mag bosses.

Shocked editor Hampton Doubleday issued a statement expressing profound regret that journalistic practices at Viz had got out of hand.

"There is no denying that there was a culture of dishonesty which flourished at Viz during my editorship," he told us.

soffit

"However, I have to stress that I was personally completely unaware of what was going on due to being on holiday or on the toilet whenever any questionable or illegal activity was taking place.

PARADE of SHAME
Some of the Viz stories obtained by underhand means
THE VIZ
PLAY TIT BINGO
BUNGLE'S EXPLICIT SEX TEXTS TO ROD, JANE & FREDDY
THE VIZ
GO TO FRANCE FOR A PENCE
WORLD EXCLUSIVE
LORD CHARLES: MY SECRET WOOD-WORM AGONY

"Nevertheless, as the editor, I must take full and complete responsibility for what has happened. Viz must draw a line under the past, and look to the future, and that is why I have decided to sack a few rogue members of staff who carried out these despicable acts whilst acting under my direct instructions."

drainpipe

Doubleday also ordered what he called a "root and branch clean-up" of editorial practices at the magazine.

To this end, millions of documents were last night being shredded and set on fire in the grounds of the secure Viz compound on a Whitley Bay industrial estate.

Meanwhile, teams of executives were working round the clock, smashing computers with sledgehammers in a bid to destroy incriminating emails.

Detectives from Fulchester police are presently working their way a list of hacked puppets believed to run into many thousands of names.

boot-cut

When told that his voicemail messages may have been listened to by private investigators working for this magazine, Bernie Clifton's comedy ostrich ran around in circles, whilst its short and floppy-legged owner sat on its back with an alarmed expression.

Another potential victim is Sooty, whose tax returns are thought to have been compromised.

A spokesman for the tiny, magic bear said: "What's that Sooty? You're disgusted by this? What's that? You think the editor should resign immediately?"

"What's that? You think that, in order to guarantee transparency there should be a judge-led public enquiry?" he added.

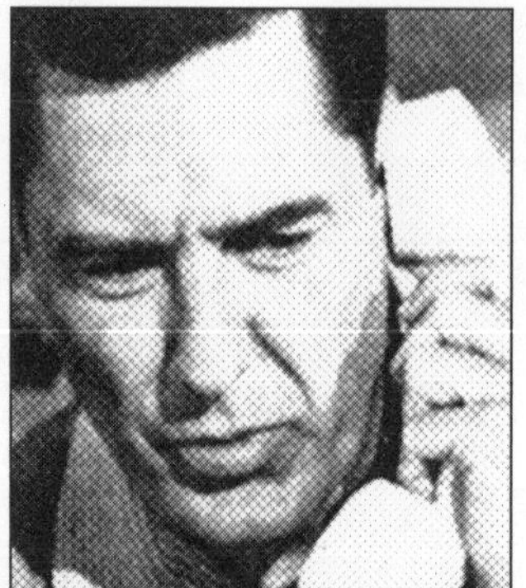

PRIVATE EAR: *Investigator Muir listened into puppet phone calls.*

...nes clean and admits...

CLEAN SWEEP: *Viz vows root & branch purge of rogue practices following puppet scandal.*

OUR APOLOGY TO YOU: THE VIZ READER

VIZ has always prided itself on its high standards of journalism. Recent events have shown that these standards have, on occasion, slipped. The disgraceful hacking of television puppets is an episode that has brought shame to a proud, British paper. We've let ourselves down, but more importantly than that, we've let **YOU**, our dozens of readers down, and for this we apologise unreservedly.

We're **SORRY** that we allowed our hunger for a sensational story to override our principles. We're **SORRY** that we used underhand means to access private information. And we're **SORRY** that our actions caused distress to innocent glove puppets, marionettes and ventriloquists' dummies. But most of all, we're **SORRY** that we've been found out.

MEDDLESOME RATBAG

Mr LOGIC

HE'S AN ACUTE LOCALISED SMART IN THE RECTAL AREA

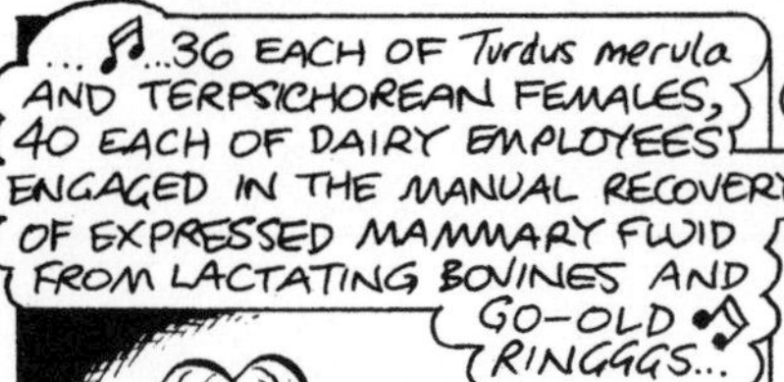

IVAN JELICAL

in

"Down South!"

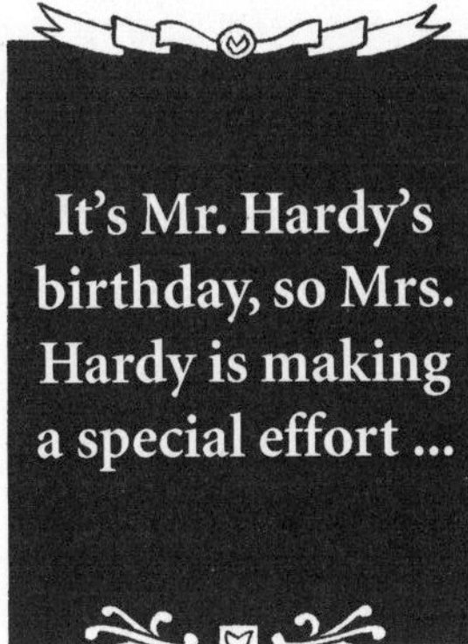

STEAK THIS THICK, SWEET POTATOES AND HOMEMADE APPLE PIE AND ICE CREAM.
YUM!
GOOD! WELL YOU CAN HELP ME CLEAR UP.

TOP TIPS

KRAFT cheese slices can be used to make an attractive patchwork shoulder bag, sewn together using cheesestrings. Use it for carrying cheese!

Edna Prolapse, Mickleover

OFFSET the carbon footprint of your daily car trip to work by driving home in reverse.

Bjorn Smorgesbord, Sweden

MODEL Railway Enthusiasts. Recreate the excitement of a "Dastardly Whiplash"-style villain leaving a woman in peril chained to the railway tracks by exchanging your driver's cap for a top hat and cape and tying your tiny 'screaming lady' cock to a 2mm Standard gauge turnout track.

Christian Frank Billingham

LOOK at text upside down in a mirror. Hey presto! It looks like Russian writing, or something.

Phil Wadsworth. e-mail

CAT owners. Encourage your moggy to live a more active life by telling it that it died peacefully 8 times in its sleep.

Martyn Green, e-mail

DENTISTS. Save time telling patients to "open wide", by simply showing really scary movies on a TV glued to the ceiling.

James Eadon, e-mail

GIVE Monday mornings that Friday feeling by not turning up to work on Tuesday.

James Bailey, e-mail

DON'T want to move out of your favourite armchair to make your dinner? Simply put the ingredients in a slow cooker tied to the back of a tortoise and leave a trail of lettuce leaves from the kitchen to your chair. In 6 hours time your meal will be ready and delivered to your feet.

Dave Wombat, Hull

Letterbocks

...viz Comic, PO Box 841, Whitley Bay, NE26 9EQ ...e-mail letters@viz.co.uk

STAR LETTER

I WAS dismayed the other week to discover than my credit card had been fraudulently used to pay for some flights. But I was somewhat relieved when the bank informed me that it was darts flights that had been purchased. However, my relief was short-lived when I realised that it was the members of 1970s pop group Darts who had all bought first class tickets to Australia.

Slim Shandy, Croydon

IN THE TV show *The Avengers*, what is it they are supposed to be avenging? And in *The New Avengers*, were they still trying to avenge the same thing as the original Avengers or was there some fresh grievance? You'd think that after twenty years they would have avenged whatever it was they were avenging in the first place.

Geoff Dennis, e-mail

"FE-FI-FO-FUM, I smell the blood of an Englishman," said the giant in Jack and the Beanstalk. Surely "Fe-fi-fo-fan" would have made a better rhyme. It's not as if the giant had to come up with a real word, after all. And they wonder why you never hear giants on Radio 4's *Poetry Please*.

Paul Solomons, e-mail

HERE you go. Perhaps a shot of Winston Zeddemore from *Ghostbusters* bumming himself will finally make you happy.

Alex Ferris, e-mail

I ALSO sent the above picture in.

Paula, Blaydon

IF SNOW reflects the sun's heat due to its whiteness, why don't we leave all our white litter, like yoghurt pots, carrier bags and newspapers, lying around outside in gutters and hedges? They would work like tiny ice-caps, bouncing the deadly cosmic rays back into space and reducing global warming.

Mark Hayden, Durham

WHAT IS IT with funeral directors driving at 1 mph? Their passengers are dead. They're not going to wake them up, and I've got to get to the shops before they shut.

Javier, e-mail

WHILST masturbating over an episode of *Emmerdale* today, I realised that some of the actors on there were actually men, and that I might have a slight gay tendency. I think future episodes should only contain slim, nubile women soaping their breasts up with shower gel whilst blowing kisses to the camera and sucking on lollypops. This would avoid causing any unnecessary confusion to male viewers who may be uncertain as to their true sexual proclivities.

Floyd Bowelsyndrome e-mail

I WONDER if your readers know the meaning of the phrase "at no extra cost"? I was under the impression that it meant at no extra cost, but when used by Virgin Broadband in the phrase "Upgrade from 20Mb to 30Mb at no extra cost", it appears to mean an extra £1.53 per month.

Hampton Plywood Harpenden

I THOUGHT of a great new competition ~ Soft Toy Soap Stars. I'll get things started with EastEnders 'hard men' Grant and Phil Mitchell. Can I have a fiver or something?

Roger Clark, e-mail

I'M SURPRISED Apple haven't moved into the lucrative pirate market and created an i-Patch. Thank you very much, I'm here all week.

Christina Martin, e-mail

IN ANSWER to the question on the back of the supermarket delivery lorry that tore the wing off my friend's 3-week-old car before driving off without exchanging insurance details: Your driving is utter shit, thanks for asking.

Joe da Vighi, e-mail

FACEBOOK isn't working today so I was wondering if you could let me use your letterbocks page to tell my 213 friends that "Cheese on toast with brown sauce rules - LOL". Thanks in advance, it's important that they know these things.

Ben Morling, Rochester

UP THE ARSE

Madeleine Brettingham, e-mail

Simon Harrington, e-mail

CORNER

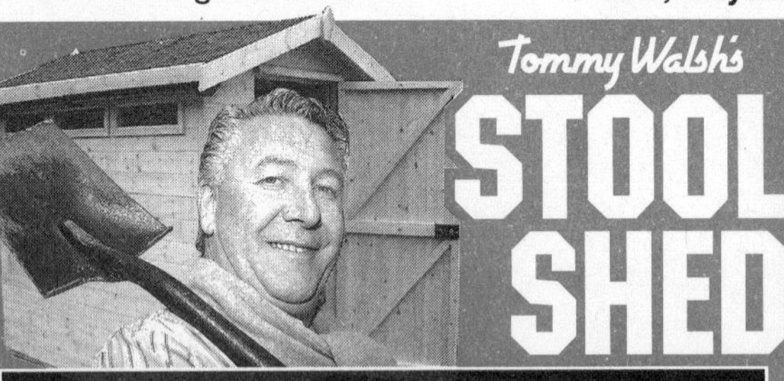

Your letters about faeces with TV handyman Tommy Walsh

IN CASE any of your readers were wondering, I can confirm that no good whatsoever comes from a violent mid-piss sneezing fit, unless of course you're filming a low budget German porn flick. Which I wasn't.

Ben Jamin, Medway

WHAT goes around, comes around, or so they say. Well, yesterday I had two sausages for my lunch. Later on, during my evening dump, I did two perfectly formed sausage-shaped shits.

Vladimir Pooinatin, e-mail

DO ANY of your readers think if one was to eat uncooked penne pasta without chewing it would whistle on the way out?

Matthew Black, Parramatta

Send your turd-related missives to: Tommy Walsh's Stool Shed, PO Box 841, Whitley Bay, NE26 9EQ

I THINK Prince William should have got married to someone with bigger tits.

Steve Chambers, e-mail

I RECENTLY won a dining table, a crockery set and a canteen of cutlery on the TV show *Family Fortunes*, and to celebrate I threw an open invitation dinner party at my house. Imagine my disappointment when my guests turned out to be the local karate club, some Greek tourists and Uri Geller.

Grant B Warner
New Zealand

IF BEES like jam so much, why do they make themselves honey to eat?

Dr M Butcher, Tintwhistle

HOW HARD can it be for the Highways Agency to build a giant robot arm that picks up the car of anyone who cuts me up on the inside lane and throws them into the sky? I pay my taxes.

Julia Raeside, London

HOW about a picture of Idi Amin playing the accordian?

Spud, Luton

* *NO problem, Mr Spud.*

I'M AN optician, and a man came into my shop the other day to buy a pair of reading glasses. I showed him a selection of spectacles with lenses suitable for close-up use. I had to laugh when he explained that he was a hot air balloonist about to go on a tour of Berkshire, and he wanted a pair of glasses for looking at the town of "Reading" from a height of 10,000 feet.

Japheth Garritty
Wakefield

I'D LIKE to use the pages of your magazine to publicly thank the makers of my washing machine for reminding me to take my cock and balls out of my trousers before I wash them.

Dr N Brodie, e-mail

Don't tell him, Pyke!

ARTHUR LOWE interrupts Dr MAGNUS PYKE before he gets to answer science questions from PHILIP MADOC............

"HOW do magnets work?" *Philip Madoc, Tenby*

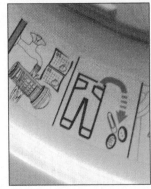

"To explain how the concept of magnetism, one must first understand the p… idual indu… nd hysteresis. A magnet… ce of i… h the two are … tact … f m… x) which co… t m… h and south) … utually attracted and … ch other with … varies inversely with … distance betw… he behaviour of a m… may best be un… considering its perme… d hysteresis loo… les a balanced comp… lative increase i… duction, p… of H for w… terials, H(… induction … simply, magn… of

Don't tell him, Pyke!

NEXT WEEK: CAPTAIN MAINWARING interrups Dr MAGNUS PYKE before he gets the chance to explain cold fusion to PHILIP MADOC

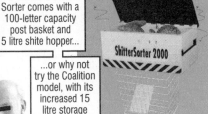

WHATEVER happened to good old-fashioned Arctic explorers who got frostbite, had to eat their dogs and then died halfway to the Pole? These modern so-called explorers, with their thick anoraks, GPS systems and fancy walkie-talkies, just get to drive there in a car with big wheels and then they're back home in time for tea. What a load of rubbish. It's no wonder this country's going to Hell in a handcart.

Expat Bob
Marbella

POLITICIANS! Are you fed up with constituents pushing turds through your letterbox, fouling up your letters with dog dirt?... Now you can keep the post and the poops separate with the

ShitterSorter 2000

It's the revolutionary new invention that automatically sorts the mutts' mess from the mail

NEW from RonTel

No mess! No fuss!*

*Some smell

ShitterSorter 2000

A basket for letters and parcels. A hygienic bin for the dog eggs.

The RonTel ShitterSorter utilises state-of-the-art computerised electronics to detect what's being pushed through your door by disgruntled voters, before automatically directing it to the right place.

Just empty it once a day!

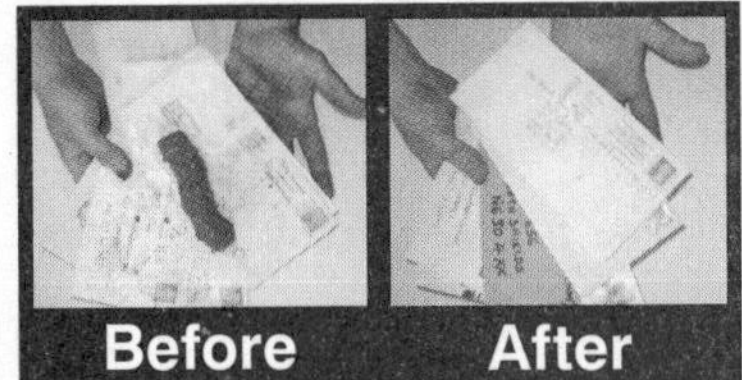

The standard ShitterSorter comes with a 100-letter capacity post basket and 5 litre shite hopper...

...or why not try the Coalition model, with its increased 15 litre storage capacity?

"I was spending up to 3 hours a day scraping canine excrement off my letters. Thanks to the Ronco ShitterSorter, that's a thing of the past."

Rt Hon NC MP, Sheffield Hallam

"I wiped my arse on my principles and accepted a cabinet post. Now I couldn't manage without my Ronco ShitterSorter. I simply have to empty it three or four times a day."

Rt Hon VC MP, Twickenham

PLACE chairs alongside the touchline at football matches so that if a mouse runs onto the pitch during the game, the female linesman can jump on one and scream her fucking head off.

Simon Picklewank
e-mail

FARMERS. Instead of injecting your animals with hormones, improve the taste of the meat by injecting them with sauces, ie, mint for lambs and gravy for cows.

Blarney O'Shite, e-mail

SAVE the price of one of those blankets with arms in by putting your dressing gown on backwards.

Mark O'Kane, e-mail

CHARITABLE People. Instead of buying the *Big Issue*, simply give the seller a house brick, roof tile or door handle, which can form the basis of a home-build project.

John Laing, e-mail

MEN who are insecure about their sexuality. Cut bananas into little discs before eating them to prevent any unwanted thoughts.

Tom Dowling, e-mail

DOG owners. Convince your pet that he or she is hard of hearing by silently mouthing the words 'walkies' and 'fetch.'

Stewart Ferris, e-mail

ENVIRONMENTALISTS. Halve your carbon dioxide emissions by only breathing out once for every two intakes of breath.

Dan Purvis, e-mail

USE PAPER underwear but don't throw it away after use. Simply use a rubber to remove skid marks.

Graham Castle, e-mail

CREATE fun pub beer garden umbrellas for ants by pressing a few coloured drawing pins into a piece of plywood.

Darren Burke, e-mail

+++ VOX POP +++ VOX POP +++ VOX POP +++ VOX POP +++ VOX POP +++ VOX POP +++ VOX

Have Your Say!

LIBERAL DEMOCRAT leader NICK CLEGG admitted that, as a 16-year-old schoolboy, he and a friend set fire to two greenhouses full of cacti whilst on an exchange visit to Munich, Germany. Now deputy Prime Minister, Clegg says he looks back on the episode as deeply regrettable and embarrassing. But charges of hypocrisy have been levelled at him after he criticised the looters and arsonists in the recent London riots, with many people saying that their behaviour was not so dissimilar to his own. So should we forgive Clegg for past mistakes, putting it down to the high spirits of a drunken public schoolboy? Or should he be held to account for his criminal act of burning some spiky plants and forced to step down from his position? We went on the streets to find out what YOU think...

...AS A child I fell into a patch of prickly pear cactuses whilst on holiday in Cyprus. I was in agony and my parents spent the whole week pulling tiny spines out of my back and buttocks with tweezers. I hate these vicious plants and in setting fire to a load of them, Nick Clegg has assured himself of my political support.

Frank Radar, bricklayer

...FIRE is not always a bad thing for plants, and in fact many Eucalyptus species are dependent on fire for their survival as the flames cause them to release their seeds. Perhaps Clegg was merely trying to help propagate the plants in this way, and his only crime was in misidentifying the species.

Edgar Wattle, roadsweeper

...I'M in charge of the cactus house at Kew Gardens and I would insist that Clegg left any matches or cigarette lighters at the door before allowing him in to look at the specimens. I understand that the incident took place a long time ago, but a leopard doesn't change its spots.

Ernest Balthazar, botanist

...I KNOW that Nick Clegg promised never to set fire to any more cactuses, but he also promised to oppose any rise in tuition fees, and we all know what happened there. I think that anyone with a valuable cactus collection should be wary.

Morgan Freemantle, costermonger

...THERE is a world of difference between setting fire to a mattress shop in London and setting fire to some cactus plants in Munich, and anyone trying to equate the two is being ridiculous. One is a potentially lethal act of vandalism perpetrated by lower class scum, the other is an absolutely cracking schoolboy wheeze pulled off by a couple of jolly fellows.

B Johnson, Lord Mayor

BURNING ISSUE: Does ex-arsonist Clegg have moral high ground over modern-day rioters?

...I UNDERSTAND that the German professor of botany who owned the greenhouses had spent his entire life gathering specimens from around the world to create this collection. But for heaven's sake, Clegg and his mate were only have a laugh. Take a chill pill, Professor Fritz.

Stu Gasper, fishmonger

...MY grandad flew bombers during the war and he was given a medal for setting half of Germany alight. In burning a load of cactuses in a German greenhouse, Nick Clegg perhaps thought he was doing his patriotic duty, and his only crime was being about 40 years too late.

Bjorn Harbottle, cabbie

...I THINK Clegg should be made to wear an orange boiler suit with 'Cacti Arsonist' written on the back every day for a year. Perhaps then he wouldn't smile quite so smugly as he sat in the House of Commons nodding at everything David Cameron said. And whenever he got up to say anything himself, all the other members of the house would be reminded of the kind of man he is.

Rosemary Flatbread, traffic warden

...THE question that no one seems to be asking is, what does a German professor want with two greenhouses full of cacti anyway? The man was obviously up to no good. I daresay this mad German professor was working on creating monster plants with spines to use as weapons for when they eventually kick off world war three, which they will sooner or later, you mark my words.

Frank Melchior, window dresser

...SINCE our deputy Prime Minister set fire to a couple of greenhouses in Germany, I think the most decent thing we could do is invite the German Vice Chancellor Philipp Rösler to come to London and torch the palm house at Kew Gardens. An eye for an eye and a tooth for a tooth, that's what the Bible says.

Arnold Paintbrush, carpenter

...FIRST Boris Johnson and David Cameron smashing up a restaurant in the Bullingdon club. Then Nick Clegg burning down Germany's most important cactus collection. What is it with our political leaders? If they like wrecking things so much why didn't they go into the demolition industry when they left school and leave the running of the country to normal people?

Henry Crosscut-Saw, painter

...ALTHOUGH Clegg regrets what happened, he attempts to explain away his behaviour by saying that he was drunk. This is no excuse at all. I get rolling drunk most Fridays and Saturdays, and I have yet to set fire to one greenhouse full of cactuses, let alone two.

Nigel Apollo, chicken farmer

...I THINK that too much is being made of this incident. After all, cacti are utter rubbish as plants. They are all roughly the same shape, they haven't got any leaves and their flowers are only ever shades of red. Had he burnt down a collection of orchids on the other hand, which show tremendous variation in form and colour, he should ought to of rightly been thoroughly ashamed of himself.

Stanley Chainmail, optician

...CACTI have incredibly sharp spines that could easily stick in the eye of a small child visiting the greenhouse. In putting these dangerous plants to the torch, our deputy prime minister has possibly prevented a nasty accident. If I were the Chancellor of Germany Angela Merkel, I would throw a state dinner in his honour and give him the freedom of the city of Munich.

Ada Hedgefund, OAP

the
REAL ALE TWATS
FRIDAY EVENING
ALL ABOARD THE SKYLARK, CASKETEERS!
62 CITY CENTRE
LOVELY CHEESE
THE HOSTELRY AWAITS, AND THOSE ALES WON'T QUAFF THEMSELVES
THE CITY CENTRE PLEASE DRIVER, AND DON'T SPARE THE HORSES!
I AND MY CONFRÈRES ARE CHAMPING AT THE BIT TO SINK A BEVVY OR THREE!
ONE SIXTY.
TUT TUT AND THRICE TUT!
METRO
BRITAIN BOOZE SHAME
DEARIE ME, THIS WON'T DO AT ALL!
ONCE AGAIN THE REPUTATION OF REAL ALE DRINKERS HAS BEEN BESMIRCHED BY THE PRINTED MEDIA!
TAKE A LOOK AT THIS ARTICLE CONCERNING THE RISING TIDE OF ALCOHOL-RELATED VIOLENCE...
IT IS ILLUSTRATED WITH A PHOTOGRAPH OF WHAT IS QUITE CLEARLY A PINT OF OWLD SCOUTMASTER'S DOWNRIGHT PECULIAR...
BOOZE BRITANNIA
SHOCK REPORT
DRUNKEN YOBS TERRORISE OUR TOWNS
...A DARK, FRUITY BEER FROM THE WEST COUNTRY, WITH A MALTY TANG AND A LONG, BITTER FINISH. 5.3% ABV.
WHAT OUTRAGEOUS CALUMNY! HOW DARE THEY ASSOCIATE THE DRINKING OF REAL ALE WITH ANTI-SOCIAL BEHAVIOUR!
IT IS NOT WE WHO ARE RESPONSIBLE FOR THE DRUNKEN THUGGERY WHICH BLIGHTS OUR CITY CENTRES ON A FRIDAY NIGHT!
NO, THE PERPETRATORS OF TROUBLE ARE INVARIABLY IMBIBERS OF GASSY LAGER AND THE SO-CALLED "ALCOPOP"...
Lager Lager
HAPPY HOUR 6-7
... IGNORANT NEANDERTHALS WHO WOULDN'T RECOGNISE A DECENT BEER IF IT WERE CASK-CONDITIONED RIGHT UNDER THEIR NOSES!
THEIR TINY BRAINS ARE INFLAMED BY SUCH MASS-PRODUCED HORRORS AS "FOSTERS" AND "CARLSBERG"...
PLIX BAR
AND THEY ARE FURTHER DRIVEN TO BARBARISM BY THE INCESSANT "DOOMF! DOOMF! DOOMF!" OF WHAT PASSES FOR MUSIC IN THEIR HELLISH BOOZING DENS!
THE BEARD AND PUGGLE
GOOD FOOD
REAL ALES
CAMRA APPROVED
BUT DO NOT DESPAIR, CASKOPHILES!
FOR SANCTUARY IS AT HAND!
BEHOLD! AN OASIS OF CIVILISED DRINKING!
GUEST BEERS
FRRP!
ALE 'N' HEARTY
YOU'LL WITNESS NO ROWDINESS OR LAGER-LOUTERY HERE!
HERE IS A HAVEN WHERE WE HAPPY BREED OF HOP AFICIONADOS MAY GATHER TO MAKE MERRY...
..TO SUP WITH FRIENDS AND ENGAGE IN JOVIAL REPARTEE.
EVENING, GENTS. ANYONE CARE FOR A FREE SAMPLE OF SINGLE MALT WHISKY?
IT'S A PROMOTION PUT ON BY A SMALL LOCAL DISTILLARY.
WHISKY, EH? I RARELY INDULGE IN THE OLD "HARD STUFF" MYSELF...
BUT I'M ALWAYS WILLING TO SUPPORT THE EFFORTS OF A LOCAL ENTERPRISE.
ONE SNIFTER LATER...
...AND THEN THAT FUCKING LANDLORD OF THE CASK AND SPIGOT IN ROSS-ON-WYE TRIED TO TELL ME THAT BRITISH RAIL DIDN'T COMMISSION THE CLASS FIFTY FIVE DELTIC LOCOMOTIVE UNTIL 1963...
GUEST BEERS
WRONG! IT WAS IN 1961, YOU FUCKING IGNORAMUS!
THE BASTARD'S NAME WAS ROGER, AND I'M GOING TO GO BACK THERE AND KILL HIM!
ALE 'N' HEARTY

Feline Lingerie Range Hits Catwalk

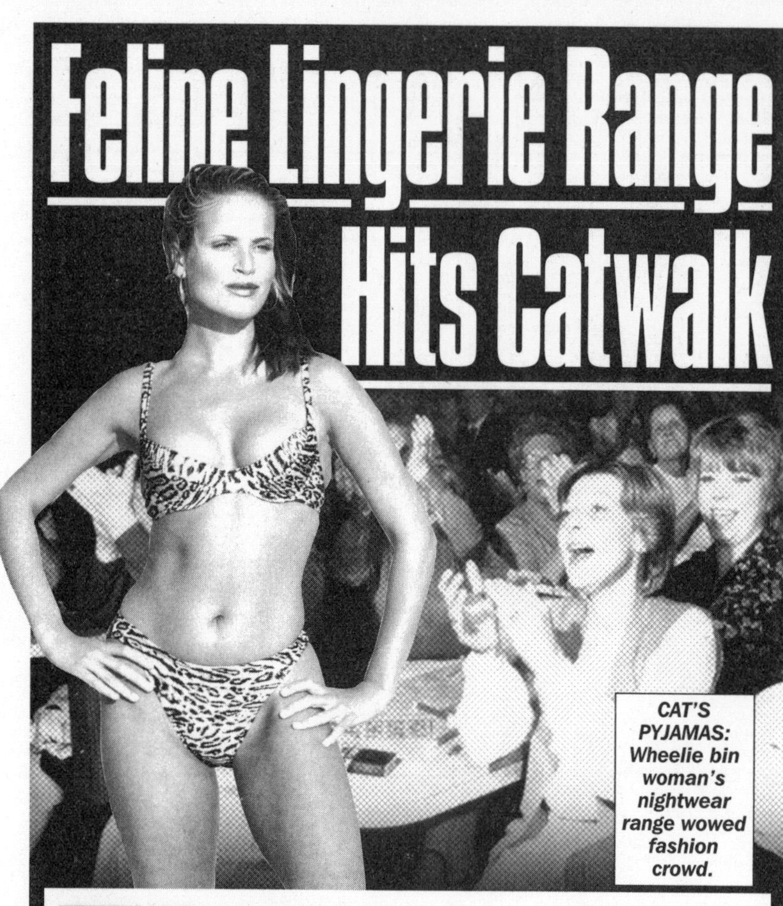

CAT'S PYJAMAS: Wheelie bin woman's nightwear range wowed fashion crowd.

THAT woman who put a cat in a wheelie bin has chosen LONDON FASHION WEEK to launch her new collection of stunning lingerie.

The range, including bras, camisoles, basques and bustieres was revealed to an invited audience of fashionistas at an exclusive catwalk preview at The Grosvenor House Hotel.

DREAM

Speaking to Vogue magazine, that woman who put a cat in a wheelie bin said that the opportunity to design a range of intimate apparel was a dream come true.

"I've always wanted to put my name to an exclusive line of exciting underwear," she said. "But working in a bank or whatever it was I did, I never got the chance."

PAINT

"Then I put that cat in a wheelie bin and my YouTube video became a global sensation."

"My new-found fame allowed me to explore other avenues, one of which was turning myself into a premium lingerie brand," she added.

And early signs were that her new collection - 'Felinique - by that woman who put a cat in a wheelie bin' was set for success.

"It's a stunning debut, and an exciting range," said fashion godfather Karl Lagerfeld. "It's sexy, but not slutty. And that is right on trend for 2011."

TOOTH

And veteran Paris couturier Coco Chanel agreed. "It's the most stunning line I've seen in years. It's really sleazy without being sexy. And that's what's going to be big this year," he said.

But exclusive underwear isn't the only avenue that that woman who put a cat in a wheelie bin is exploring. She recently signed a £3million 5-book deal to write a series of children's stories about a wheelie bin whose best friend is a cat.

She is also in negotiations with several Hollywood studios who are said to be bidding for the rights to bring her story to the big screen.

BASIL

Industry gossip says Scarlet Johanssen is already being lined up to star as that woman who put a cat in a wheelie bin, with Morgan Freeman as the voice of the cat.

SEMI-SKILLED MINK
...YEAH. THE TILING'LL TAKE ME A COUPLE OF DAYS. BUT YOU'LL HAVE TO GET SOMEONE ELSE IN FOR THE PLUMBING...
... AND I DON'T DO ELECTRICS.

New Film Releases for Summer

Reviewed by Mark Commode

Eggbound in Brooklyn

Dir: Spiro Theocropolis
1hr 27mins (PG)

Fast-paced yarn with a twist

★★★

CITY trader Renton Gilhooley (Wesley Snipes) has eaten five triple-decker egg mayonnaise sandwiches on white bread. Now he's got just 24 hours to find a lavatory before he becomes constipated. To complicate matters, he's also embroiled in a custody battle against his egg farm heiress ex-wife Shirley (Meg Ryan), who has left him for omelette chef Dwight (Liam Neeson). On the way to court, Renton's search for a gents becomes more frantic as time runs out. In a boiled egg cafe, he meets toilet attendant Jake (Danny de Vito), on his last day at work before retiring, and the two men form an unusual bond.

Laces

Dir: Henry Winkleheimer
1hr 52mins (15)

Vietnam feelgood movie staring Jack Nicholson

★★★★

VIETNAM veteran Frank (Jack Nicholson) had his shoelaces tied together whilst held prisoner by the Vietcong. Now back on civvy street, he must face a future where he can only only take very short steps. Life becomes a constant battle that costs him his wife (Shelley Duvall), his kids (Gary Coleman, Macauley Culkin, Wee Jimmy Krankie)... and very nearly costs him his mind. After hitting rock bottom, Frank resolves to take on the might of the Pentagon, whom he holds responsible for the state of his shoelaces. It's a personal war that he fights not just for himself, but for every soldier who had their shoelaces tied together in 'Nam.

Microbes

Dir: Satoru Nakajima
1hr 20mins (PG)

Family film with voice of Woody Allen

★★★★

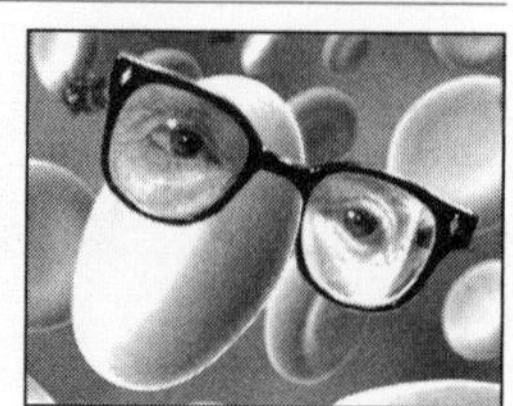

IN THIS latest CGI offering from Pixar Studios, Luke the white blood cell (voiced by Woody Allen) must work with his fellow microbes to defeat an army of syphilis germs led by sarcastic bacterium General Gleet (Bill Nighy). During his adventure, Luke is joined by wise-cracking Pete the platelet (Eddie Murphy or Chris Rock) and a ramshackle band of antibody pals. Romantic interest is provided by Erin the erythrocyte (Winona Ryder), who is kidnapped by General Gleet and held hostage in the urethra. Will Luke rescue Erin and live happily ever after? This is a Pixar movie - what do you think?

Le Peinture Sécherant

Dir: Claude Parapluie
23hr 4min (15)

Challenging French psychodrama

★★★★★

A BLEAK examination of alienation and loss, directed by Claude Parapluie (*Le Mort et la Chaise, Le Velo Malhereux, Le Plombier qui a Pleuré*). On a Normandy beach, suicidal architect Michel (Jean Luc Putain) and drug-dependant cellist Isabel (Francoise Escargot) come together in an abandoned pill-box where they take shelter from persistent drizzle. Over the next twenty-two hours they contemplate their own mortality, stare at the walls whilst smoking Gitanes and alternately laugh, scream or burst into tears for no apparent reason. Filmed in black & white in one continuous take on a hand-held camera.

SHITTY DICK

TODAY IS A VERY SOMBRE DAY – IT'S MY GREAT-UNCLE CEDRIC'S FUNERAL.
DONG! DONG! DONG!
CAW! CAW! CAW!
HE WAS A HIGHLY-RESPECTED VICAR OF THE LOCAL PARISH.

OH NO! I'VE DONE A GIGANTIC SHIT RIGHT NEXT TO GREAT-UNCLE CEDRIC'S GRAVE...
...AND HERE COME ALL HIS FELLOW VICARS WITH THE COFFIN FOR BURIAL!

GOT TO WORK QUICKLY!
PAT PAT
I'LL BEND OVER MY TURD LIKE THIS, THEN SMOOTH DOWN THE FRONT...

AH, GOOD! I SEE THAT DEAR CEDRIC'S GRAVESTONE HAS BEEN INSTALLED ALREADY.
RIP CEDRIC RICHARDS
~AHEM~
REST

~SNIFF SNIFF~ GOOD GRACIOUS! WHERE ON EARTH IS THAT DREADFUL SMELL COMING FROM?
MING
OO-ER! ERM...

ERM.. I EXPECT THAT'S GREAT-UNCLE CEDRIC'S BODY STARTING TO PUTREFY...
THE UNDERTAKER PROBABLY USED ONE OF THOSE CHEAP BOGOF BRANDS OF EMBALMING FLUID

OH GOOD! HERE COMES THE BISHOP OF FULCHESTER TO OFFICIATE THE FUNERAL SERVICE!
PHEW! I THINK I GOT AWAY WITH THAT ONE!

LET US COMMENCE WITH THE BURIAL OF OUR DEARLY DEPARTED...?!
WAIT A MINUTE – WHAT'S THAT?!

CRIPES! I'VE BEEN AND GONE AND DONE ANOTHER MASSIVE CRAP...
...RIGHT SLAP DAB ON TOP OF GREAT-UNCLE CEDRIC'S COFFIN!

ERM – THAT'S JUST A LARGE HANDFUL OF SOIL I THREW ONTO THE COFFIN AS A MARK OF RESPECT.
LET ME JUST REMOVE IT WITH THAT MECHANICAL DIGGER!

THERE, GOT IT! NOW I'LL DUMP IT BEHIND SOME BUSHES.
SCOOP

HELLO – WHAT'S THIS DANGLING FROM THE REAR-VIEW MIRROR?
WHY! IT'S A LITTLE TOY NOVELTY VICAR...

WAH! WOULD YOU BELIEVE IT?!
I'VE EVEN MANAGED TO DISGRACE MYSELF BY CRIMPING OFF A LENGTH IN FRONT OF A PLASTIC VICAR!

HELP! THE DIGGER'S OUT OF CONTROL!
I CAN'T REACH THE BRAKE PEDAL, PERCHED UP ON TOP OF THIS GINORMOUS DOUGLAS HURD!

CRASH!
YARGH!

DEAD

COO! THERE'S THE PEARLY GATES!
I MUST BE GOING TO HEAVEN!

WELL, THAT'S FOR ME TO DECIDE, MR RICHARDS. FIRST I MUST JUDGE WHETHER OR NOT YOU ARE WORTHY.
HUNH? WHO ARE YOU?

I AM SAINT PETER, THE SYMBOLIC KEYSTONE OF THE CHRISTIAN CHURCH. OUR LORD JESUS CALLED ME "THE ROCK UPON WHICH THE CHURCH IS FOUNDED."
ESSENTIALLY, I COULD BE DESCRIBED AS THE ULTIMATE VICAR, IF YOU WILL.
HMM.

NOW THEN. LET'S SEE IF YOU HAVE EVER COMMITTED ANY IMPURE OR DISGUSTING ACTS WHICH WOULD PREVENT YOU FROM GETTING INTO HEAVEN...
ETHEREAL STENCH
OO-ER!

+++ RESORT GEARS UP FOR SIMIAN TAKEOVER +++ RES... GE

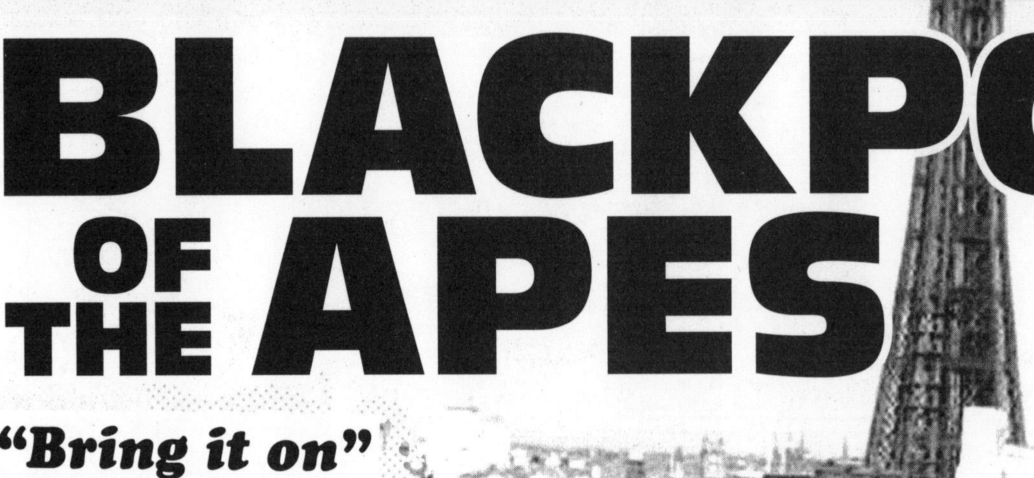

BLACKPO... OF THE APES

THE RELEASE of summer blockbuster *The Rise of the Planet of the Apes* highlighted a new threat that is facing the world: *MONKEYGEDDON.*

EXCLUSIVE!

In the movie, scientists inject chimpanzees with an experimental Alzheimer's antidote, causing them to become superintelligent. The apes then use their new-found brainpower to rise up against their human masters, with mankind becoming slaves to their brutal simian overlords.

According to boffins, it's a terrifying scenario that could all too easily come true. And it's a threat which is being taken seriously by the mayor of Blackpool, Ivan Lewis.

resort

But Coucillor Lewis had this message for any apes planning to seize control of the popular seaside resort: "There'll be no monkey business on the streets of Blackpool. Our visitors want chip shops not chimp shops, and that's what they're going to get."

Speaking to the Blackpool & Fleetwood Clarion, Councillor Lewis said that the prospect of an apocalyptic showdown between humans and monkeys was only too real. "After years of living in our zoos, circuses and laboratories, chimpanzees have become angry and resentful," he said.

bus

"Were they to somehow escape, they might join together in some sort of primitive society and declare war on the hated humans."

GORILLA TACTICS: Council employees could be forced into monkey slavery.

"Bring it on" says Mayor

MONKEY NUTS: Blackpool is unde... threat from mad apes, just like in t... movie, says mayo...

"Although they are less technically advanced than us, they are ten times as strong and could easily subjugate our species by sheer force and aggression," he added.

At an emergency planning meeting last night, Blackpool Council finalised a 10-point plan to deal with any attempted simian revolution. Some of the measures announced included

"There'll be no monkey business in Blackpool. Our visitors want chip shops not chimp shops."

- ***A TEMPORARY** by-law preventing greengrocers from displaying bananas for sale on the street, in order to cut-off the monkeys' primary source of sustenance.*
- ***A CLOSE-DOWN** of the Lucky Sheriff Rifle Range on the Golden Mile, as well as a withdrawal of the beach donkey rides concession. This is to prevent armed gorillas from riding about the town, rounding up terrified tourists to use as slaves.*
- ***BARBED WIRE** rings to be placed around the legs of Blackpool Tower approximately ten feet from the ground to hinder monkey attempts to climb to the top and throw excrement at holidaymakers.*
- ***THE MAYORAL** chain, hat and robes of office to be kept in a locked safe to prevent an orang-utan from crowning himself Lord Mayor of Blackpool and Lytham St Annes.*
- ***THE MAN** who stands at the end of the South Pier selling cigarette lighters three for a pound to be requested to move on in order to prevent monkey insurgents from discovering the secret of man's red fire.*
- ***WORKING** on the assumption that approximately half the borough's Refuse Department employees will be captured as slaves and forced to wear chamois leather pants, bins will be collected on a fortnightly rather than a weekly basis. Following a Bank Holiday, if your bin day is normally Monday to Thursday, and the Bank Holiday falls on a Monday, your refuse will be collected a day later than usual (ie., Tuesday to Friday), or Saturday if the Bank Holiday falls on a Friday. In the second week of a collection cycle, bin collections will be unaffected. Please note that bins must not be put out before 7pm on the day before collection, and must be brought in within 6 hours of being emptied. Further details are available on the council website www.blackpooludc.gov.uk/monkeyuprising/bins.pdf*

UP FOR SIMIAN TAKEOVER+++

OL

At the meeting, Councillor Marjorie Grimbledeston (Squiresgate) was appointed Chair of the Humans for Freedom Ape Resistance Committee by a majority of 8 votes to 3, with 2 abstentions. She told councillors: "I am very excited to be heading this group and leading the fightback against our putative monkey oppressors."

orders

"And I've got a very simple message for any baboons, gibbons or chimpanzees thinking of trying to take over this municipal district: Take your stinking paws off Blackpool, you damn dirty apes," she added.

Councillor Grimbledeston announced that work has already begun on digging a 10 foot deep water-filled moat around the Town Hall in Corporation Street. She explained: "Although monkeys can swim, they don't know that they can."

supper

"This moat will protect the levers of local authority power from monkey hands and ensure that angry primates are unable to gain control of essential council services, such as Parks & Recreation, Transport & Tourism or Allotments & Libraries," she said.

Mrs Grimbledeston is also liaising with the Kwik-Fit branch on Preston New Road. "The management have kindly offered to donate 600 used tyres, which we will be hanging from trees in Stanley Park," she said.

of the Mohicans

"We're hoping that the monkeys will forget about trying to overthrow and enslave the human race, and just swing about in those whilst picking fleas out of each other and scratching their arses," she added.

Shock as U2 star declares monkey allegiance

"I'm with the Apes" ~ BONO

PINT-SIZE pop twat *BONO* shocked U2 fans yesterday when he vowed to fight *ALONGSIDE* the apes in any future human/monkey conflict.

"Monkeys can't make a bigger mess of this planet than mankind already has," the taxophobic bell-end told reporters at Heathrow Airport.

bananas

"They live in harmony with the nature, so they do, so they do," the 4'6" cock continued. "They don't drive gas-guzzling SUVs, use disposable nappies or leave their televisions on standby when they're not watching them."

"They just sit in the trees eating bananas, bejasus."

The sunglasses-in-the-house-wearing arsehole angrily rejected accusations that he was a traitor to his species.

"My loyalty lies with this planet," he said. "To me, there's no difference between a worm, a blade of grass, an elephant and a mountain."

"As far as I'm concerned, we all belong to the same species - Earthius habitus, and unless we act now, time is running out for us all."

"We're standing on the edge of the abyss and staring into the void, and all and all," the short-arsed twat continued.

sleeper

"The real traitors are those who are raping mother earth, with their 60 watt lightbulbs, antiperspirant aerosols and plastic carrier bags," the complete and utter fuck-witted knob-yanker, who was waiting in the VIP lounge at Terminal 4 for a jumbo jet containing his hat, added.

MAJOR MISUNDERSTANDING

The Osama Bin Laden Story — Part 1

Tora Bora Hospital, 1957...

At school, Osama wasn't interested in any of his lessons...

Ali Baba. Maths is boring. I want to kill thousands of infidels and bring the decadent West to its knees.

And 44 years later, his dream came true...

Next Week: Osama hides for ten years and then gets shot through the eye.

SID THE SEXIST
TITS OOT!

LUNCHTIME PINTS...
...SO, THEN SHE STANDS UP, AND SHE'S ONLY WRITTEN THE WORDS 'BUM-BOY ON HIS CHEST INSTEAD!
HA HA HA!
EH? SO... HOW'S SHE HOLDING THE PEN AGAIN?

AFTERNOON LADS... YEEZ REMEMBER ME BROTHER ALAN...
HOW LADS
HOW ALAN
AFTANOON KIDDA

LONG TIME NO SEE, BONNY LAD.
AYE SID. I'VE BEEN AWAY FROM THE TOON FORRA BIT
ALAN'S COMPANY MADE HIM A TRAVELLING SALESMAN, LIKE.

WHEY, 'TRAVELLING FANNY RATTLER' IS MORE LIKE ME OFFICIAL TITLE, MIND.
REALLY?
AYE JOE. I HAD TO LEAVE THE TOON COS I'D FUCKIN' NAILED IT DRY

OH AYE. THIS JOB TAKES US TO AAL THE FAWA CORNERS. I GET TO BANG A DIFFERENT BIT O' EXOTIC FLAP EVERY NEET, MAN. RHYL. LUTON. HULL. FUCKIN' EVERYWHERE

FREQUENT FLYER...? FREQUENT HAIRY-FUCKIN-PIE-ER, MORE LIKE!
HA HA HA HA!
EH?

ARE YUH BACK TO GIVE YER COCK A REST, THEN?
I WISH SID! NAR, IT'S THE OFFICE CHRISTMAS PARTY, MAN. I HAVE TO BANG HALF THE LASSES AT THE MAIN BRANCH
EH?

AYE. THESE OFFICE BIRDS HAVE BEEN WAITING AAL YEAR FORRIT, MAN. THEY SPEND TWELVE MONTH BEING AAL REPRESSED, SO COME CHRISTMAS THEY'RE FUCKIN' RAMPANT...
...LIKE A PACK O' RANDY FUCKIN' DOGS, SID MAN.

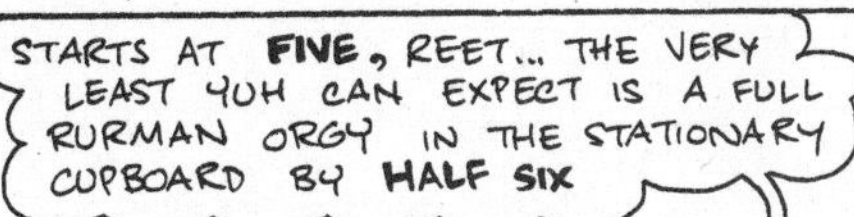
STARTS AT FIVE, REET... THE VERY LEAST YUH CAN EXPECT IS A FULL RURMAN ORGY IN THE STATIONARY CUPBOARD BY HALF SIX

...AND THEY CANNAT SACK YUH, COS IT'S CHRISTMAS. IT'S LIKE, AN UNWRITTEN RULE. IN FACT, IT'S ENCOURAGED, MAN.

WELL LADS, I'M OFF TO ME MAMS TO GET SOME REST BEFORE THE FUCKIN' ORDEAL BEGINS
SEE YUH ALAN
AYE, SEE YUH BONNY LAD

FUCK ME! DID YE HEAR THAT, SID? A FUCKIN' OFFICE FULL OF PENT UP, SEXUALLY FRUSTRATED LASSES PURELY FROTHING AT THE GASH. THE LUCKY BASTARD!

SID...?

HOO, I'M RINGING UP ABOOT THE OFFICE TEMP VACANCY IN THE CHRONICLE...
JOBS

THANKS FOR COMING OVER AT SUCH SHORT NOTICE MR SMUTT. IT'S GOOD TO KNOW YOU'RE SO KEEN
OH AYE PET. I'M CANNY KEEN LIKE. KEEN TO GET STUCK IN

BASICALLY, I'VE GOT A POSITION FOR YOU AT THE BOTTOM, IF YOU'RE PREPARED FOR THAT
AYE, WHATEVER PET. SOONDS CANNY.
SALES

OBVIOUSLY IT'S DOWN TO YOU TO WORK UP FROM THERE
AYE. LIKE, UP TO FEEL YER TITS AND THAT PET.
SID'S CV

WELL, WE CAN GET STARTED STRAIGHT AWAY, IF YOU LIKE... ANY QUESTIONS?
ERM... GULP! AYE... WHERE'S THE STATIONARY CUPBOARD?

SO...
HERE WE ARE MR SMUTT. FOLLOW ME...
HERE WE GAN!

SCREAM!
STATIONARY CUPBOARD

SOMEONE'S COMING OVER TO RETRIEVE THE STAPLER FROM OUT OF YOUR ARSE NOW. IF WE CAN JUST GO OVER THE DETAILS OF THE INCIDENT ONE MORE TIME, MR SMUTT...
GUMPH!
LOST
WANTED
HAVE YOU SEEN THIS MAN?

8
ACE

DOCTOR

PUSH, MRS ACE..!
GNNN..!
OOH! ME FUCKIN' FANNEH!

POP! ...WAH! WAH! WAH! WAH!
PTSCHFT!

PTSCHFT!

AYUP LUV... 'AVE YER JUSST 'AD ANUTHEH F-FFUCKIN' BABBEH..?
AYE, EIGHT. IT'S A FUCKIN' BOY.
WAH! WAH! WAH! WAH! WAH!

WOT'S IT F-FFUCKIN' SKRIKIN' FOH..?
IT'S 'UNGREH, EIGHT...
WAH!

D'YER WANT US TER F-FFUCKIN' BRAY IT?
NO. IT WANTS FED.
OH.

'AN'T YER GORRA F-FFUCKIN' DUMMEH..?
AYE, EIGHT... A 'AVE... IT'S YOO, YER USELESS FUCKIN' BASTOD. YOO KNAW FUCKIN' NOWT ABAHT BABBEHS, YOO...

YER CAN'T GIVE A FUCKIN' NEW-BORN BABBEH A FUCKIN' DUMMEH...! NOW GET DAHN TER'T PRECINCT AN FETCH IT SUM FUCKIN' PASTEHS.
WAH! WAH! WAH! W-W-W-WAAH! WAH! WAH! WAH! WAH! WAH! WAH! W-W-W-W-WAAAH! WAH! WAH! WAH! WAH!

'ERE'S SUM MUNNEH FOH PASTEHS... BAKERY'S GORREM ON FOH THREE FER ONE FORTEH NINE. AN' 'URREH BACK WI' 'EM... A'VE GOT 'EALTH VISITOH CUMMIN' ROUND IN AN 'OUR AN' SHE'LL PLAY 'ELL WI' US IF IT'S STILL FUCKIN' ROARIN'.

AN' DUN'T GO SPEND THIS PASTEH MUNNEH ON ACE, EIGHT... A KNOW WOT YER LIKE.
AS IF... AS F-FFUCKIN' IF!

A MAY OF DUN WRONG IN TH' F-FFUCKIN' PAST, A ADMIT IT... F-FFUCKIN' F-FF-FFAIR E-F-FFUCKIN'-NUFF...

...A MAY OF VEREH OCCASIONALLY INDULGED IN EIGHT F-FFUCKIN' TIN OF ACE WHEN, IN 'INDSIGHT, A F-FFUCKIN' SHOULDN'T OF...

...BUT DUN'T TAR ME WI' THE SAME F-FFUCKIN' BRUSH AS MESELF. A DUN'T DRINK NO MORE... A'M COMPLETELEH ACE-TOTAL... A'VE CAST THAT F-FF-F-FFUCKIN' PISS ASIDE!

OH AYE..? SINCE WHEN?
JUSST NOW... JUSST BEFORE... JUSST THEN.

THESE EIGHT TIN 'ERE WAS THE LAST F-FFINAL F-FFUCKIN' ACE A'LL EVEH F-FFUCKIN' SWIG. NOT ANOTHEH DROP WILL PASS ME LIPS... ON THAT F-FF FFUCKIN' BABBEH'S LIFE.
WAH! WAH!

ACTUALLEH... THEH'S A BIT LEFT IN THIS 'UN...

GLUG!
WAH! WAH! WAH! WAH! WAH!

...A'VE GOT TER F-FFUCKIN' MAN UP... STARTIN' REYT F-FFUCKIN' NOW! THAT BABBEH NEEDS F-FFUCKIN' FED AN' A'M TH' PASTEH-WINNEH IN THIS FAMBLEH!

GERRIT A COUPLE OF STEAK BAKES AN' MEBBE A CHICKEN AN' MUSHROOM. NOWT TOO SPICEH.

REY'T. CUMM ON, EIGHT. YOO CAN F-FFUCKIN' DO THIS... PASTEHS FOH TH' BABBEH... NOT ACE..!

PASTEHS NOT ACE... NOT ACE... PASTEHS NOT ACE.. PASTEHS... NOT ACE...

...PASTEHS NOT ACE... ...PASTEHS NOT ACE... F-FFUCKIN' PASTEHS!
SMEGG
SPECIAL OFFER 3 PASTIES ONLY £1.49!
OPEN

PASTEHS PASTEHS PASTEHS...

...ACE.. ACE.. ACE...

WAK-WAARK!
PATEL'S 24 HOUR NANOMART
PATE
8 ACE £1.49

EIGHT ACE.
ONE FORTY-NINE.

SO WOT..? GLUG
...S-SSO F-FFUCKIN' WOT!?

THEZ NOWT WRONG WI' WETTIN' TH' F-FFUCKIN' BABBEH'S F-FFUCKIN' 'EAD..!

SHE F-FFUCKIN' JUDGES ME JUSST 'COS A LIKE AN OCCASIONAL CAN OF F-FFUCKIN' ACE...

...ACTUALLEH... THISSUN'S A BIT GASSEH... MBBFF ... MMBBBBFFF! ... ...HUP-HUP-HUP-HNNN... HNBBBBRRRGH..!
!?

BLOOAARGH!

CKKKAH! JESUS!... YAK! HOCK! GAKK! PTHWA!

SHE'D DENY ME THE ONE F-FFUCKIN' PLEASURE A'VE GOT LEFT IN ME LIFE... THE F-FF-FFUCKIN' B-BB-BBB...

COW!

SHORTLY...
...WELL, MRS ACE, HE SEEMS TO BE SLEEPING WELL.
AYE. 'E WOH CRYIN' BEFORE, BUT IT WOH JUST 'COS 'E'D SHIT 'ISSELF.

...AND WHAT ABOUT THE BABY..?
IT'S STILL IN TH' OUSE, SKRIKIN' FER A PASTEH.

HAVE YOU THOUGHT OF A NAME FOR YOUR BABY YET, MRS. ACE?
AYE. A'M GOIN' TER CALL IT AFTEH ME 'USBAND.

6 WEEKS LATER...
...IN THE NAME OF THE FATHER, THE SON AND THE HOLY GHOST, I BAPTIZE THIS CHILD FUCKING USELESS FUCKING CUNT.
WAH! WAH! WAH! WAH! WAH! WAH!

Mr Logic of the Lamp

OH WOE IS ME! MY WICKED UNCLE ALI BONGO HAS KIDNAPPED ME FROM MY HOME AND IMPRISONED ME IN THIS DARK CAVE!
HOW I WISH I WAS SAFELY BACK IN MY BED!

I SHALL LIGHT THIS DUSTY OLD LAMP TO GIVE ME SOME LIGHT IN MY FINAL HOURS.

WHOOSH!
GREETINGS, O MASTER! I AM THE LOGICAL GENIE OF THE LAMP, AND I CAN GRANT YOU ONE WISH..! SUBJECT TO THE FOLLOWING PROVISO...

...to wit, THAT SAID WISH DOES NOT GAINSAY THE PREMISE OF THE ORIGINAL VERBAL CONTRACT AS HERETOFORE ESTABLISHED.
RIGHT... SO I COULDN'T WISH FOR ANOTHER HUNDRED WISHES, FOR EXAMPLE...
EXACTLY.

...OR WISH THAT ALL MY FUTURE WISHES CAME TRUE?
INDEED, O MASTER. IT IS A STANDARD GENIE CLAUSE TO PREVENT AN INFINITE REGRESSION FEEDBACK LOOP OF WISHES.

SO WHAT SHALL IT BE, O MASTER? NAME YOUR DEAREST DESIRE AND IT SHALL COME TO PASS!
THAT'S EASY, O LOGICAL GENIE OF THE LAMP..!

...I WISH I WAS BACK IN MY BED RIGHT NOW!
SO SHALL IT BE, O MASTER! LOGICAZAM! LOGICAZOO!
PUFF!

RATS' COCKS.

THE BACONS

HOO BIFFA, D'YA WANT TO SMELL MY FLOO-AH?

EH?

PISS OFF MAN MUTHA. THAT'S JUST A PLASTIC SQUORTY FLOO-AH! DIVVUNT BE SUR CHILDISH!
ALREET, ALREET. I WUZ AANLY HEVIN' A BIT FUN.

EEH FATHA, I WUZ AANLY TRYIN' TO HEV A BIRRAVA LAUGH AN' A JOKE
TEK NEE NURTICE OF THAT MISERABLE TWAT, MUTHA - HE'S GOT NEE SENSE OF HUMOUR.
HOWAY, Y'CAN DEE YA FLOO-AH TRICK ON ME, INSTEAD.

ALREET FATHA. D'YA WANT TO SMELL ME FLOO-AH?
AYE MUTHA THAT'S A CANNY LOOKIN' FLOO-AH, THAT!
:SNIFF SNIFF: THAT'S FUNNY - I CANNAT SMELL ANYTHING

HA HA! GOT YOU FATHA!
EEEH, MUTHA! Y'VE SQUORTED US WITH WATTA!
SQUIRT
HOO HOO!
HA HA!
HO HO!

HA HA HA! Y'GORRUS THERE, MUTHA!
HO HO HO! AYE, I DID AN' ALL
EEH, Y'SHOULD'VE SEEN YOUR FACE, FATHA!
HA HA, AYE! HEY, WE HAVE A REET LAUGH, US TWO!

HOWAY MUTHA, TRY IT ON ME NOW!
EH? WHY WOULD I DEE THAT, BIFFA? Y'DIVVUNT FIND IT FUNNY.
AYE SON. YA THINK JOKES ARE CHILDISH.

AH HOWAY YEEZ TWO! LERRUZ JOIN IN AAL THE FUN AN' LAUGHTER!
WELL...
ALREET THEN

WOULD Y'LIKE TO SMELL MY FLOO-AH, BIFFA?
WHY AYE, MUTHA!
:SNIFF SNIFF: THAT'S FUNNY! (SNIGGER) I CANNAT SMELL ANYTHING!

CRACK!
THAT'S CUZ I'VE JUST BUST Y'FUCKIN' NURS, SON!
HEH! HEH!
Y'DAFT CUNT!
OOF!

"We haven't got a fucking clue"

Police no closer to catching 'Mr X' murderer

SCOTLAND Yard last night admitted they were no closer to arresting a serial killer believed to be responsible for over 30 deaths in London.

The murderer, dubbed "Mr X" by Chief Constable Sir Orde Wingate, has so far evaded attempts at detection throughout a six-month killing spree.

At a press conference last night, the Metropolitan Police boss made the embarrassing admission that his detectives had so far failed to unearth a single piece of evidence as to the multiple killer's identity.

clue

Sir Orde told reporters: "He could be young, old, black, white or pink with yellow spots for all we know. We literally haven't got a fucking clue."

And he asked members of the public with any suspicions of who the murderer might be to come forward. "If you think you know who Mr X is, please let us know," he said.

"Any name will do, because quite frankly we're standing around with our hands in our fucking pockets on this one."

Li

The Chief Constable admitted that his force's performance on the case had fallen short of the standard that might have been expected.

"You'd think that with a new murder every six days for half a year, we might have picked up a few clues here and there, but we still know fuck all about the perpetrator of this terrible spate of crimes," he said.

"For example, I say Mr X. It could be Mrs X, Dr X, the Duke and fucking Duchess of X for all we know," he added.

Lu

And Sir Orde had this plea for the mystery assassin: "Come on, mate, throw us a fucking bone. Next time you murder someone, leave us a clue for fuck's sake."

"A glove, a footprint, anything. We're like headless fucking chickens at the moment," he said.

A Scotland Yard spokesman confirmed that the detectives still had no description of Mr X.

Dil

"The killer's got two arms, two legs and a head, probably," he told us. "But even that's a fucking guess."

"You might as well ask the fucking station cat," he added.

NOT EASY PC: Cops are finding it hard to identify multiple killer.

LETTERBOCKS

APPARENTLY it costs £95,000 a year to keep a prisoner. What the hell are these people thinking of? I've got a cat, which is much cheaper and is yet to murder me.

Stuart Gardener, e-mail

HAVE any of your readers been to a driving theory test centre recently, and also spent time in a Category B prison? I was wondering in which environment individuals were treated with more respect and dignity. My money's on the nick.

David, e-mail

STAR LETTER

MY GRANDAD never talks about his time in the war. He was shot by a German sniper in Belgium in 1943 and killed instantly.

David Harris, e-mail

CALL ME uncharitable, but I find the Comic Relief segments where they present footage of landmine victims and starving children less harrowing to watch than the bit where the newsreaders all dance.

Brendan Canavan, e-mail

Viz Comic
PO Box 841
Whitley Bay
NE26 9EQ
letters@viz.co.uk

WHILST reading *Viz* on the train, it occurred to me that you should print adverts for expensive household items or well-paid jobs on one side of each page. That way, the tidy bit of crumpet sitting opposite would think I'm all posh and that, instead of being the sort of riff-raff who reads your magazine.

S.C. Unthorpe, e-mail

SO MUCH for BMW's 'new' stop/start technology. The wifey's Y-reg Focus has been cutting out at the lights for over four years.

Henry Ford, Granada

I RECENTLY passed an escalator which had a mural painted on the wall next to it. Making a rough estimate of the amount of time the mural would have taken to complete, I calculated that the poor artist must have walked up approximately 28,800 steps whilst painting it.

Craig Renneberg, e-mail

SCIENCE tells us that when water freezes and turns to ice, it expands. This is how mountain ranges and crevices were created millions of years ago during the ice age, and the same process causes water pipes to burst in the cold weather. Logic therefore dictates that when there is a thaw, the water molecules must contract. And yet scientists would have us believe that the melting of the Polar ice caps causes flooding and sea levels to rise. Come on you boffins, you can't have it both ways.

T. O'Neill, e-mail

THREE cheers for Burger King! Whilst visiting central London I popped into one of their fast food outlets and ordered a meal. Inspired by their advertising slogan 'Burger King – Have it your way', I asked the assistant if I could have my burger on a rubbish-strewn table next to a sleeping tramp who had blood all over his forehead. And I have to say, they really delivered the goods.

Ed Surname, e-mail

WOULDN'T it be more appropriate if glamour models were called tit models? As I am yet to see a glamour model do something glamorous but I always see them with their tits out.

Tom Bishop, Nottingham

YOU OFTEN hear it said that "the truest things are said in jest". Well the other day my mate John told me a joke about a talking monkey going into a bar, and frankly I don't believe a word of it.

Paul Connell, e-mail

I'VE JUST read that Comic Relief spends £50 for each bicycle they send to Africa. Surely if they send unicycles they could send twice as many for the same price.

Tim Rusling, e-mail

ON *Time Team* they usually dig a site until they hit Anglo Saxon stuff, then they dig deeper to find Roman stuff. Then they usually call it a day. When are the lazy cunts going to dig even deeper until they find ancient Egyptian stuff? Might make it worth watching for a change.

M Ramsden, Bradford

I DON'T think we should buy Trident nuclear missiles until we've used up used up the ones we've already got.

AC Linton Blair, e-mail

Have Your Say

Tutan-Cabbie!

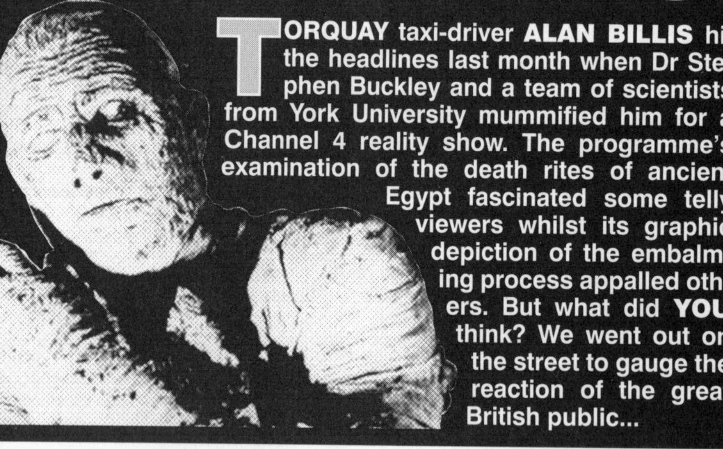

TORQUAY taxi-driver **ALAN BILLIS** hit the headlines last month when Dr Stephen Buckley and a team of scientists from York University mummified him for a Channel 4 reality show. The programme's examination of the death rites of ancient Egypt fascinated some telly viewers whilst its graphic depiction of the embalming process appalled others. But what did **YOU** think? We went out on the street to gauge the reaction of the great British public...

...I THOUGHT it was a bad documentary because it didn't have enough peril in it. The programme makers should have given the boffins just 3 hours to make the mummy. Either that or they should have got the man who does the voiceover on Come Dine With Me to do a sarcastic commentary, and make fun of them when they ran out of bandages half way through.

Penny Black, pubic hairdresser

...WHO'S Alan Billis when he's at home? I've never heard of him, and I don't watch reality shows unless they've got celebrities in them. Channel 4 should have got the scientists to mummify Lembit Opik or someone out of Steps or Hollyoaks.

Tommy Gun, corn plasterer

...APPARENTLY, the scientists intend to keep the mummy in their laboratory and unwrap him from time to time to examine the progress of their experiment, but mummies are famous for getting angry when their eternal rest is disturbed. It will serve them right if Mr Billis comes back to life and chases them round their lab, lumbering after them with outstretched arms.

Wendy House, neighbourhood watchmaker

...WHAT a shame the boffins decided to bind Mr Billis's legs together with bandages. If his mummy does come back to life and wants to chase people round, now it will be forced to hop like someone in a sack-race or shuffle along on its bottom in an undignified manner.

Stanley Knife, static electrician

...ALAN Billis is a rubbish name for a mummy. Before he died, he should have changed his name by deed poll to Alan Hotep, Alan Khamun or Ramesses IV Billis.

Terry Towelling, Victoria plumber

...WELL I loved the show. A good sequel would be if Professor Stephen Buckley got all bits of dead bodies and sewed them together to make a "Frankenstein" taxi driver, which he then brought to life by harnessing the power of an electrical storm. Instead of rising up to destroy his creator, the taxi driver could merely talk to Dr Buckley about immigration whilst driving him back from the pub, and then over-charge him for his fare.

Bill Hook, coconut milkman

...WHAT an utter waste of perfectly good bandages. They could have been used to treat genuinely ill people, such as old men with gout, or been tied round the heads of toothache sufferers. No wonder the Health Service is up the Swanee.

Sandy Beach, mustard gasfitter

...FURTHER to the previous commenters, Mr Billis's mummy would have an advantage over the scientists when chasing them, because as an ex-cabby he would have "the knowledge". But only if he was chasing them around Torquay.

Pete Bog, Tuesday welder

...FOLLOWING on from Mr Bog's comments (above), if the scientists did find themselves being pursued around the Torquay area by Mr Billis, they could escape from him by taking the direct route to their destination. By force of habit, a taxi-driver's mummy would probably go round the houses a bit.

Paddy Field, electric fireman

What would the Celebrity Cuntbubbles do if they were...

BLUE for a DAY?

IMAGINE waking up in the morning and discovering you have of went blue in the night. We asked the celebrities what they would do if it was them who had went blue.

NOEL EDMONDS
Tidy-bearded cuntbubble

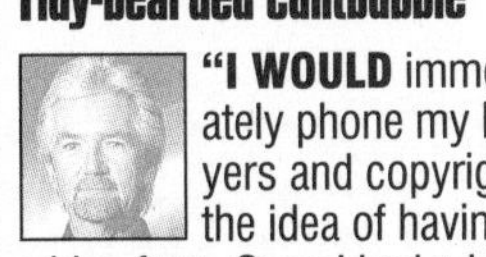

"I WOULD immediately phone my lawyers and copyright the idea of having a blue face. Once I had added the intellectual property to my portfolio, I could issue writs against anyone else who went blue - perhaps whilst having a heart attack or choking on a boiled sweet, and seize the contents of their bank accounts."

JIM DAVIDSON
Bigoted cuntbubble

"I'VE always been a bit of a blue comic, but if I actually went blue I imagine that I might suffer discrimination on account of the colour of my skin. It wouldn't surprise me if certain black comedians, such as Lenny Henry and Charlie Williams, started doing racist jokes about me, perhaps inventing a character called "Chalkie Blue" who speaks with a ridiculously exaggerated blue accent."

BONO
Gobshite cuntbubble

"I'D change the name of my group from "U2" to "Blue2", so I would, and give all the profits from that day's album sales to blue charities, such as Save the Blue Whales, and many others. After tax of course, to be sure to be sure. And reasonable expenses. And disbursements. And the cost of having my hat's private Jumbo Jet painted blue to match my face, begorrah bejasus."

JEFFREY ARCHER
Lying cuntbubble

"TO a storyteller like me, the idea of waking up having changed colour is a fascinating one. I would immediately sit down and write a short story about suddenly becoming blue. That is, if I can find one that somebody else has written that I can copy out word for word, like the thieving, blue-faced, spotty-backed whore-banging little shit that I am."

TOP TIPS

SOUTH Cambridgeshire bin men. Behind the hedge on the side of the road between Barrington and Haslingfield would be a great place to take a discreet shit if there were leaves on the hedge at the time.
Taig Knut, e-mail

GEORGE Osborne. Don't get too depressed about your inability to function as Chancellor. Give it ten years and you'll be laughing about how you sold out to the banks and forced further millions into poverty on *Have I Got News For You*.
Jacksie, e-mail

REBELLIOUS Arabs. Increase your chances of overthrowing a well-armed military dictatorship by not firing half your ammo into the sky every time you drive past a BBC camera crew.
Gaz Daffy, e-mail

RECREATE a visit to the homeopath by simply drinking some tap water and throwing £50 out of the window.
Oli, e-mail

COMMUTERS. If you read the manual, you will find that your mobile phone was designed to REPLACE shouting.
Andy Mac, e-mail

WHEN hosting sophisticated dinner parties, make all your guests drink out of the same glass, thus confusing CSI-style forensic teams in the event of someone being murdered.
Luke , e-mail

ELECTRIC toothbrush manufacturers. Render your product totally useless by utilising the most sensitive of on/off switches, so that following any reasonable period of travel your £60 electric toothbrush will have slowly turned into a £60 manual toothbrush by the time you've arrived and unpacked.
Bill Drummond, e-mail

MAKE fancy American root beer for your Fourth of July party by simply squirting Deep Heat into a bottle of Coke.
James O'Carroll, e-mail

AN OLD plastic chicken packaging tray from Tesco can be placed upside down in your back yard to make an ideal 'eyesore civic building' for the ant community.
Emma Ness, e-mail

CAPRI-SUN drinks make excellent 'blood transfusion' bags for Jehovah's Witnesses.
Simon Ullyatt, e-mail

FAT people. Save money on expensive 'skinny jeans' by just buying jeans.
Mable Syrup, e-mail

MOTORISTS. Avoid costly road tax by simply fitting a skirt and a large fan to your car to convert it to a hovercraft. Ensure you never stop on a journey or park on the road and you won't have to pay as your 'car' never touches the road.
Terry Dactill, e-mail

TELL friends you've got access to Narnia by storing your Christmas tree in the back of your wardrobe.
Garreth Drummond, e-mail

LONDON Zoo. Attract more visitors by putting some animals in the cages.
Mickey Sparkle, e-mail

BEAR Grylls. When taking a helicopter trip, try sitting inside instead of out on the rails. It will be safer, much more comfortable and you won't have to shout.
Swiss Gary, e-mail

REBOTTLED Smarties make ideal medication for hypochondriacs.
Sanny Sutherland, e-mail

POO ARE THE REF

With Level 2 FA Proctologist Dr HOWARD WEBBSTER

Q AN indirect free kick is awarded to an attacking team inside their opponents' half. The defending team form a wall, but the player on the right complains of abdominal spasms. He alerts the linesman to the fact that during the morning, he has had several trips to the lavatory, where his stools have been small, black and hard. As the kick is taken, the player moves forward and the shot is saved by the keeper. What action do you take?

A: As the player moved forward, you would insist that the kick was re-taken. The player who moved forward would be shown the yellow card for having insufficient fibre in his diet.

Q YOU are about to blow the whistle to start the second half of a match when you notice that one team has only ten players. The manager informs you that his goalkeeper has done a particularly sticky motion that is taking a lot of wiping. He requests that you delay the restart until the player in question has drawn an ace. What should you do?

A: The period between halves is fifteen minutes, and is not subject to change unless by prior agreement of the two managers and yourself. To allow play to resume straight away, you would ask the manager to put another player in goal, although he would have to change his shirt. When the original keeper eventually finishes wiping his bottom and has washed his hands, he will be allowed back onto the pitch at a suitable break in play.

Q DURING active play, your linesman brings to your attention the fact that a defending player is moving his bowels by the corner flag. The player claims that he is suffering from food poisoning after eating a prawn sandwich that was past its sell-by date. How do you react?

A: Provided the player hasn't left the field of play, he has committed no offence. The FA allows the evacuation of the nose on the field of play, and there are no rules stating that the bowels may not be evacuated in the same way. However, the defending team's manager would be required to remove the excreta from the pitch. The game should be restarted with a dropped ball.

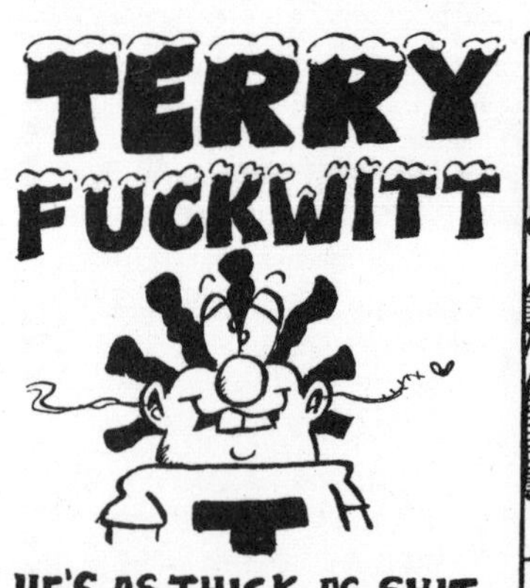
TERRY FUCKWITT
HE'S AS THICK AS SHIT

I'M HAVING GREAT FUN AT THIS NEW YEAR'S EVE FANCY DRESS PARTY, READERS!
POP!
WHOOPEE! HA HA! HAPPY NEW YEAR, EVERYONE!

PSST, TERRY! THIS ISN'T A FANCY DRESS PARTY - IT'S A HOSPICE FOR TERMINALLY ILL NATIVE AMERICANS
SITTING BULL MEMORIAL HOSPICE
OH!
SNIFF SOB
SNIFF
AND I DON'T THINK THIS FAMILY OF GRIEVING CHEROKEES APPRECIATES YOU CAVORTING MERRILY AT THE DEATHBED OF THEIR JUST-DECEASED ELDERLY MOTHER

GOD, I NEVER FAIL TO PUT MY FOOT IN IT, DO I? I'M SUCH A NINNY!
FUCKWITTED PALEFACE GOT UM HEAP BUFFALO SHIT FOR BRAINS.

TERRY, WHAT THE HELL ARE YOU PLAYING AT?
HUSH, DAD! SHOW SOME RESPECT - THIS IS A HOSPICE, YOU KNOW.

NO IT'S NOT - THIS IS OUR HOME, WHERE YOUR MOTHER AND I ARE ATTEMPTING TO HOLD A NEW YEAR'S EVE PARTY
HAPPY NEW YEAR!
SITTING BULL MEMORIAL HOSPICE
AND THESE DEAD BODIES, NURSES AND GRIEVING RED INDIANS OF YOURS ARE SPOILING THE PARTY ATMOSPHERE!

GO ON, GET OUT OF MY HOUSE!
HOSPICES FOR TERMINALLY ILL NATIVE AMERICANS INDEED! HONESTLY TERRY, I DON'T KNOW WHERE YOU FIND THESE PEOPLE

HERE, MAKE YOURSELF USEFUL SON - YOU CAN BE 'FIRST FOOTER' AT OUR NEW YEAR'S PARTY.
GO OUTSIDE, THEN ON THE STROKE OF TWELVE COME BACK IN WITH THIS LUMP OF COAL, FOR LUCK.

RIGHT! GO OUTSIDE... THEN COME BACK IN AGAIN.
EVEN A USELESS CUNT LIKE ME CAN'T MAKE A PIG'S EAR OF THAT

WAH!
FOR GOODNESS SAKE TERRY! HOW MANY TIMES DO I HAVE TO REMIND YOU THAT WE LIVE IN AN AEROPLANE?!

ALVIN'S ANVILS
ANVILTASTIC BARGAINS!
FUCK ME!
CLANG!

AND
WHEE-OO-EE!
HOSPITAL
ANVIL INJURIES
AMBULANCE

SHORTLY, AT HOSPITAL
I'M AFRAID THERE WAS NOTHING WE COULD DO. THE PATIENT IS COMPLETELY BRAIN DEAD.
BEEEEE EEEE EEP
THERE ARE NO SIGNS OF NEUROLOGICAL ACTIVITY WHATSOEVER.

SO, NO ILL-EFFECTS FROM MY ACCIDENT THEN, DOCTOR?
BEEEE EEEE EEP
THAT'S RIGHT TERRY. IT'S PRETTY MUCH "BUSINESS AS USUAL" FOR YOU - YOU CAN LEAVE THE HOSPITAL STRAIGHT AWAY.

WOW! IT'S FOUR MINUTES TO MIDNIGHT!
HOSPITAL MAIN ENTRANCE
I'LL HAVE TO HURRY IF I'M GOING TO GET TO A PARTY WHERE I CAN SEE IN THE NEW YEAR!

AND
TEN!.. NINE!... EIGHT!.. SEVEN!... SIX!...
PHEW! I JUST MANAGED TO FIND A PARTY IN TIME - HERE COME THE CHIMES!

FIVE!.. FOUR!.. THREE!.. TWO!... ONE!
ERM...
DANGER KEEP OUT DEMOLITION BLASTING IN PROGRES
DYNAMITE
ACTUALLY, READERS - I THINK I MAY HAVE MADE ANOTHER BOO-BOO!

FUCK...
BOOM!
...ME!

Fanny Batter's HOLLYWOOD gossip

ALL THE BUZZ FROM SUNSET STRIP TO TINSELTOWN... *AND BACK!*

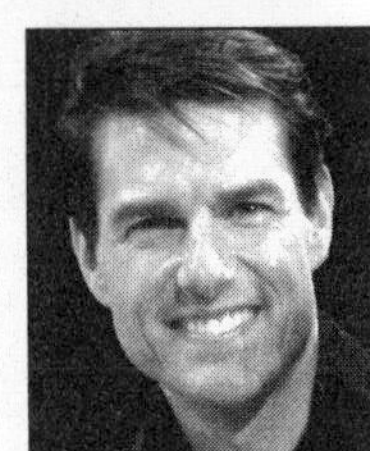

TINY *Top Gun* **TOM CRUISE** was caught even shorter than usual the other day when he ran out of bathroom tissue. Word is, the 4-foot Scientologist faced a ***Mission Impossible*** after doing a big number two in the lavatory at pal **KEITH CHEGWIN**'s Miami Beach condo. Speaking on ***Oprah***, the inch-high ***Last Samurai*** actor relived the moment when he discovered there was no paper left to wipe his pint-sized sphincter. "I had no choice," said Tom, 49. "I had to rip up the cardboard roll and try to use that." The ***Days of Thunder*** star broke down as he recounted what happened next. "I tried wiping it as usual, but the card just spread it around. In the end I was forced to use an edge of it as a scraper." Pals say Cruise may find it hard to forgive former ***Swap-Shop*** host Cheggers for the WC oversight, but ex-sauce-addict Keith lays the blame firmly at Tom's door. "He must have had his eyes wide shut when he went in the bog not to see that there was no paper on the roll," he is believed to have said. Meanwhile, an informer tells me Cruise left all the bits of cardboard floating in the pan, meaning that Chegwin's walk-in-bath-ad wife **MAGGIE PHILBIN** had to fish them out with a swing-bin bag on her arm.

COMEDY legend **EDDIE LARGE** has demonstrated an appetite to match his gargantuan name ... after he ATE the **HARLEM GLOBETROTTERS**! The roly-poly funnyman was sharing a plane with the New York-based basketball team, en route to a gig supporting **VAN HALEN** at Paraguay's Montevideo Stadium, when his private jet crash-landed in the remote Andes. 30-stone Eddie weighed up the situation, and within ten minutes had tucked into 6' 8" point-guard **MEADOWLARK LEMON**, polishing him off before wolfing down 7'11" short forward **FRED "CURLY" NEAL** for pudding. When he was found by rescuers eight hours later, sole survivor Large had already chomped his way through the entire team ... as well as manager **CLYDE SINCLAIR** and head coach **LOU DUNBAR**! Word on the street is that the tubby entertainer, 69, has now developed an insatiable craving for human flesh ... so watch out if he invites you round for dinner!

OMG! The internet is buzzing with rumours that a new sex-tape featuring raunchy hotel heiress **PARIS HILTON** is doing the rounds. And according to those who've seen it, the horny webflick features Hilton in a no-holds-barred romp with veteran TV astronomer **PATRICK MOORE**! Talk about heavenly bodies! Boggle-eyed xylophonist Moore was last night remaining tight-lipped about the XXX-rated vid. "He's in his observatory and he doesn't want to talk to anybody," said his latest squeeze **CHRISTINA AGUILERA**. Betcha he's polishing his 8" reflector!

"See you next time, Goss-fans!"

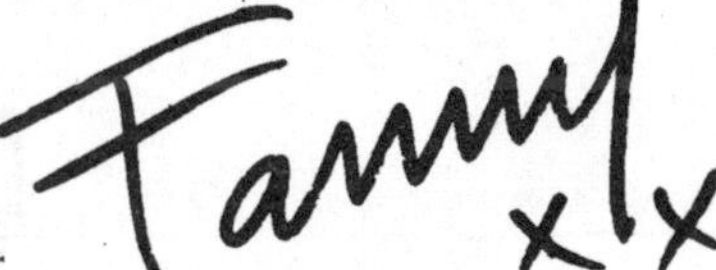

TIPTON BLOOD BATH!

Guthrie's guards shoot demonstrators

A WEST Midlands town was last night teetering on the brink of anarchy after a council leader ordered his guards to shoot protesting ratepayers.

Hugo Guthrie, Mayor of Tipton, gave the command to open fire on about fifty residents who had gathered in front of the town hall to demonstrate about changes to Bank Holiday bin collection services. Details are still sketchy, but it is believed that up to fifteen protestors may have been killed, and at least as many again taken to hospital with serious gunshot wounds.

civic

Guthrie, 62, has been in charge of Tipton since 1992. It is thought that he now fears his grip on the reins of power may be loosening, and his violent response to civic unrest is an attempt to stamp his authority back on the Black Country borough.

Over the years, Guthrie's controversial autocratic style has earned him notoriety in local government circles. He reacts badly to criticism, and any challenges to his authority are dealt with swiftly and mercilessly .

In 1996, the Tipton Tourism & Recreation Committee approved plans to re-locate several litter bins in the vicinity of the flower clock in Steve Bull Park. Guthrie was enraged that he hadn't been consulted before the plan was mooted at the monthly council planning meeting, and had the entire committee of six councillors frogmarched from the Town Hall chamber and hanged in the Arndale Centre.

prelude

Guthrie is one of the few civic leaders in the West Midlands to maintain a personal band of heavily-armed mercenary bodyguards - the so-called "Municipal Brigade". This crack group of ruthless fighters are recruited from the Foreign Legion and Special Forces, and are trained in urban warfare, as well as the use of machine guns, rocket launchers and chemical weapons.

Growing resentment about his heavy-handed style of local government administration has left the mayor increasingly isolated in the Town Hall. Guthrie has not been seen out in public since December 2009, when a local newspaper printed pictures of him judging a snowman competition at a local primary school, surrounded by flak-jacketed gunmen.

VOCAL AUTHORITY: Guthrie's word is law.

Last night Guthrie made a rambling 7-hour speech on local radio, setting out his intention to stay in charge of his council "to the bitter end". Speaking on Tipton Gold 1051, the embattled Chief Executive claimed that he would never surrender.

accord

"Tipton is Hugo Guthrie and Hugo Guthrie is Tipton," he told listeners. "I will not bow to the forces of chaos, the drug takers, the anarchists and the squeaking rats with their wheelie bins and bus timetables."

"Those who rise up against Hugo Guthrie will be squashed like ladybirds. They will be scraped off the bottom of Hugo Guthrie's shoe like dog dirt into the gutter," he continued.

"I will not relinquish my mayoral chain until the last drop of blood has been spilled in the streets of Tipton," he added.

However, despite the rhetoric it is rumoured that the increasingly embattled council leader may be making preparations to flee before his overthrow becomes inevitable. A convoy of cars believed to be carrying his wife and children was recently seen speeding along the A459, heading for the relative safety of nearby Wombourne. It is expected that Guthrie may soon follow suit, taking with him treasures looted from Tipton Museum and a personal fortune estimated at more than £1300.

COMMUNITY BATON CHARGE: A demonstrating ratepayer is rounded up by riot cops yesterday.

CHRIST THE REDEEMER

BEEP!
BEEP!
BEEP!
9

OK. THAT'S £19.65. HAVE YOU GOT A LOYALTY CARD?
PAT! PAT!!
ER... YES. SOMEWHERE!

BLIP!
YOU'VE GOT £2.50 TO COME OFF THAT IF YOU WANT.

OH. YES PLEASE!
TAP!
£17.15 PLEASE.

SEEDY PIGG
Teecher is a sleazy Perv.
PORN
SUMS

DROOL! THE DINNER LADY HAS COME TO SCHOOL BY BICYCLE THIS MORNING!
I BET THE SADDLE IS ALL WARM AND MOIST FROM HER BOTTOM!

I'LL NIP INTO THE BIKE SHEDS AND HAVE A RIGHT GOOD SNIFF OF THAT SADDLE
SCHOOL BIKES
SLAVER! SNUDGE CITY, HERE I COME!

I WONDER WHERE MR PIGG IS — I HAVE A FAVOUR TO ASK HIM.
SNURDLE! BARUMPH!
HEAD
EH? HERE COMES THE HEADMASTER!

BAH! HE'S PROBABLY GOING TO ASK ME TO TAKE HIS THIRD FORM'S HISTORY LESSON.
WHY SHOULD I WASTE MY TIME TEACHING WHEN I CAN BE GETTING MY SEEDY CHEAPIES?

I'LL TAKE THE DINNER LADY'S BIKE ROUND THE BACK OF THE TOILET BLOCK AND CONTINUE MY QUUMFING THERE.
THE AROMA OF STALE URINE WILL PROVIDE A SUITABLY SQUALID BACKDROP TO A SPOT OF GARBOONING.

MEANWHILE
HOORAY! WE'VE DISCOVERED MR PIGG'S SECRET STASH OF SORDID PORN MAGS BEHIND THE TOILET CISTERN!
TOILETS
LET'S GO AND OGLE THEM LASCIVIOUSLY

JUST ROUND THIS CORNER...
OOPS!
TOILETS
I'VE DROPPED ONE!

SKID
WAH!
CRUMBS! PIGGY HAS SLIPPED ON THAT GLOSSY DANISH SPANK RAG!

CRASH!
YOW!
I'VE JAMMED MY NOSE IN THE BICYCLE SPOKES!

DON'T WORRY MR PIGG — WE'LL SOON GET YOUR NOSE SOME MEDICAL ATTENTION
NURSES TRAINING COLLEGE
LUCKY THING THERE'S A NURSES' TRAINING COLLEGE NEXT DOOR TO THE SCHOOL
DAW! GED ID OFF!

AND
THERE YOU GO MR PIGG — BUT I'M AFRAID YOU WON'T BE ABLE TO USE YOUR NOSE FOR A WHILE.
FIRST AID ROOM
MATRON
HEAD
OH! THAT'S A SHAME...

THE MATRON HAD ASKED US TO DO A FAVOUR FOR HER TRAINEE NURSES. I THOUGHT IT MIGHT BE RIGHT UP YOUR STREET — BUT NOW YOU WON'T BE ABLE TO HELP.
MATRON
FAVOUR? WHAT KIND OF FAVOUR?

MY TRAINEE NURSES HAVE GOT ALL THEIR BICYCLES MIXED UP, AND THEY DON'T KNOW WHICH ONE BELONGS TO WHOM.
MATRON
HEAD
I WAS HOPING YOU'D HELP SORT THEM OUT BY SNIFFING ALL THE BICYCLE SEATS, AND TRYING TO MATCH THE SCENT OF EACH ONE TO MY NURSES' PANTIES.

BUT WITH YOUR NOSE OUT OF ACTION, THE HEADMASTER WILL HAVE TO DO IT ALL BY HIMSELF.
MATRON
RIGHT, MAY I SNIFF THE PANTIES OF THE FIRST TRAINEE NURSE, PLEASE?

HO HO! PIGGY IS "RALEIGH" UPSET THAT THE HEADMASTER HAS BEEN "SADDLED" WITH DOING ALL THE SNURGLING!
GURR!
SNUFT! MOOMPH! PRINGLE!

ROGER MELLIE
THE MAN ON THE TELLY
ROGER HAS BEEN CALLED INTO TOM'S OFFICE...
F.T.V.
F.T.V.

AH, ROGER... THANKS FOR...
HEY, TOM. I'VE HAD A GREAT IDEA FOR A SHOW...

CELEBRITY PIG WANK!
WE GET A LOAD OF CELEBS ON A FARM, AND THEY HAVE TO WANK OFF THE PIGS...
IT'S BEEN DONE, ROGER. THE FARM... CHANNEL 4
EH?..

HAS IT!?.. FUCKING HELL!... I WAS ONLY JOKING AN'ALL, TOM.
JESUS...
...I'M GOING TO HAVE TO UP MY GAME, I CAN SEE.

ANYWAY, WHAT DID YOU CALL ME IN FOR, TOM?
I'VE HAD THE SUN ON THE PHONE ROGER

OH? WANT ME TO FRONT THEIR FUCKING BINGO AGAIN, I SUPPOSE
WELL, TELL 'EM TO DOUBLE WHAT THEY GAVE ME LAST TIME AND STICK A NOUGHT ON THE END FOR LUCK...

I WANT TWO PAGE 3 BIRDS SENT ROUND EVERY NIGHT AND A DOUBLE PAGE PLUG FOR MY AUTOBIOG, TOM... AND TELL 'EM WE CAN CHEW OVER THE DETAILS AT SPEAR-MINT RHINO ON THEIR FUCKING TAB!

NO, ROGER...

...THEY CALLED TO SAY THAT THEY'VE GOT SOME PHOTOS OF YOU.
PHOTOS?
YES... DOGGING, ROGER...

...IN THE LOCAL PARK. APPARENTLY THEY SHOW YOU HAVING SEX WITH A WOMAN ON THE BONNET OF YOUR CAR
EH?..
OH, THANK CHRIST FOR THAT, TOM.

PHEW! YOU HAD ME GOING FOR A SECOND THERE... I THOUGHT THEY'D DUG SOME REAL DIRT UP
YOU KNOW, I THOUGHT I SAW A FLASH GO OFF IN THE BUSHES

I WISH I'D HAVE KNOWN, TOM. I'D HAVE PROPPED A COPY OF MY BOOK UP AGAINST HER ARSE... IT WOULD HAVE BEEN A NICE BIT OF FREE PUBLICITY, THAT.
WHAT!?!... NO IT WOULDN'T, ROGER...
THERE'S A GANG OF MEN IN THE PICTURE WATCHING YOU AND WANKING...
THAT'S NOT GOOD PUBLICITY HOWEVER YOU LOOK AT IT.
BUT I'M A MAN'S MAN, TOM. EVERYONE KNOWS THAT. IT'LL DO MY REPUTATION THE WORLD OF GOOD

MAYBE IN THE PAST, ROGER. BUT AREN'T YOU FORGETTING SOMETHING?
DON'T KNOW TOM... AM I?

YOUR NEW SHOW ON CEEBEEBIES
UNCLE ROGER'S HAPPY PARK?..
WHAT ABOUT IT?

WELL, YOU PLAY A PARK KEEPER IN A SHOW FOR TODDLERS! IT'S THE MOST POPULAR PRE-SCHOOL SHOW SINCE THE TELETUBBIES

I CAN SEE THE HEADLINES NOW, ROGER... THE BEEB WON'T BE ABLE TO SACK YOU QUICK ENOUGH WHEN THOSE PHOTOS COME OUT
F.T.V.

THAT JOB IS WORTH £250K A YEAR, ROGER. YOU CAN KISS **THAT** GOODBYE... PLUS ALL THE MERCHANDISE SPIN-OFFS THAT GO WITH IT...
FUCK!

...THE UNCLE ROGER ACTION FIGURES, THE HAPPY PARK DVDS, PENCIL CASES, JIGSAW PUZZLES, LUNCHBOXES...
FUCK!
...T-SHIRTS, PYJAMAS, SOCKS, BOARD GAME, INTERACTIVE CD...

YOU'RE ON 10% OF THE NET OF THAT LOT... WELL, YOU WOULD HAVE BEEN.
FUCK!

THIS COULD FINISH YOU, ROGER. YOU'LL BE LUCKY TO GET THE ARSE END OF THE HORSE IN NEXT YEAR'S PANTO
FUCK!
WHAT AM I GOING TO DO?

YOU'LL HAVE TO PHONE THEM UP, ROGER... CUT SOME SORT OF DEAL
LEAVE IT TO ME, TOM
OKAY... JUST MAKE SURE THOSE PHOTOS NEVER SEE THE LIGHT OF DAY.

HELLO!? IS THAT THE SUN NEWS DESK?..

NEXT DAY...
AH, ROGER... I SEE YOU MANAGED TO SWING IT WITH THE SUN
SURE DID, TOM
...WE DID SOME STRAIGHT TALKING

THEY SAID THEY WOULDN'T REFER TO ME BY NAME AND THEY'D BLACK MY UGLY MUG OUT...
YES... THE ARTICLE REFERS TO "AN UN-NAMED TV PRESENTER"

EH!?.. CHEEKY **BASTARDS!**... STAR WE AGREED ON... T.V. **STAR!!**
BASTARDS!
HEY, THEY DRIVE A FUCKING HARD BARGAIN, AN' ALL, TOM...

I'VE GOT TO BE THE FACE OF THEIR BINGO SCRATCHCARDS AND DO ALL THEIR TELLY ADVERTS THIS YEAR... ALL FOR FREE, TOM
FREE!..
...CAN YOU FUCKING BELIEVE IT?

NOT ONLY THAT, I'VE GOT TO WEAR A 'SUN' T-SHIRT WHENEVER I GO OUT THE HOUSE...
...AND I'VE GOT TO DRESS UP AS SANTA FUCKING CLAUS AT NEXT YEAR'S NEWS INTERNATIONAL CHRISTMAS PARTY

STILL, AS LONG AS THEY KEPT THEIR SIDE OF THE BARGAIN AND BLACKED MY FACE OUT, EH TOM?
OH, YES, ROGER...
THEY BLACKED IT OUT ALRIGHT. YOU'RE COMPLETELY UNRECOGNISABLE

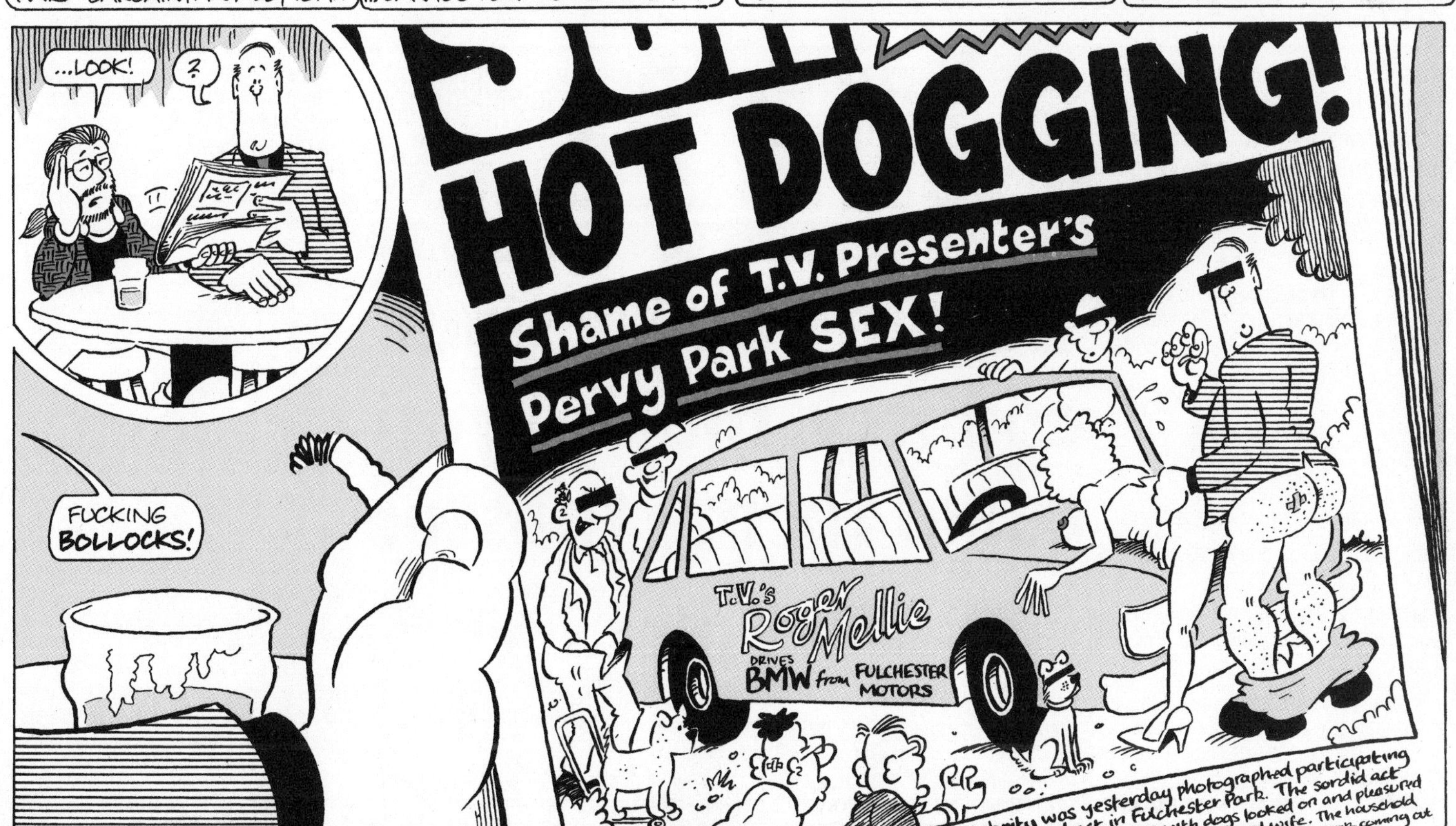
...LOOK!
?
HOT DOGGING!
Shame of T.V. Presenter's
Pervy Park SEX!
T.V.'s Roger Mellie
DRIVES BMW from FULCHESTER MOTORS
FUCKING **BOLLOCKS!**
lebrity was yesterday photographed participating
ual act in Fulchester Park. The sordid act
men with dogs looked on and pleasured
second wife. The household
all spunk coming out

Mad Man Escapes

MEMBERS of the public were warned to be on their guard last night after a dangerous lunatic escaped from Russ Abbot's madhouse.

ABBOT & LOST FELLOW: Cannibal lunatic escaped from funnyman Russ's private asylum.

It is believed that the man - a 6' 8" psychopath who was sectioned after murdering and eating his parents - made his way over an electrified fence after bludgeoning security staff with a chair-leg and stabbing a warder through the eye with the handle of a sharpened toothbrush.

hammers

The man later broke into a shed in the grounds of the madhouse, where he is believed to have armed himself with a sickle, a chainsaw, several hammers and an axe.

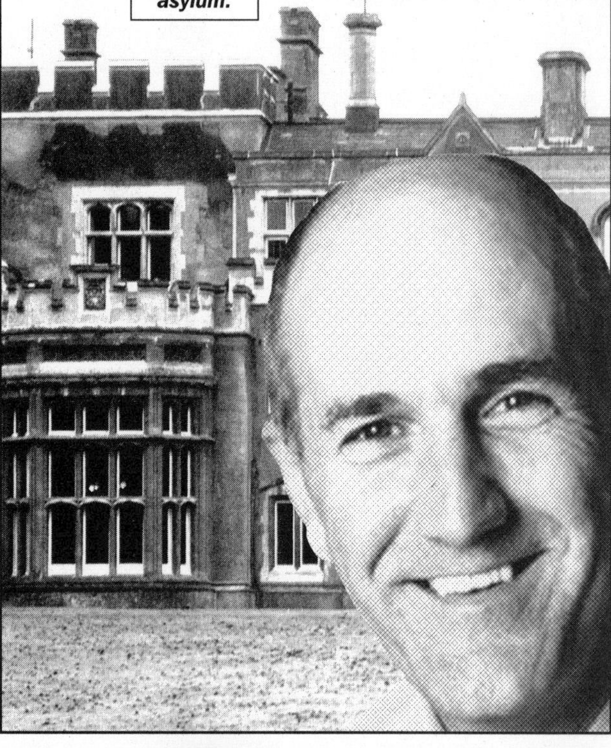

The controversial asylum, which is situated in the outskirts of Chester, was set up by the popular comedian with the proceeds of his 1984 hit I Love a Party (with an Atmosphere). It houses over a thousand of the country's most dangerous and violent lunatics.

cobblers

Russ Abbot said local residents should on no account attempt to tackle the fugitive, who he described as an "extremely ferocious, blood-thirsty cannibal with the strength of ten men".

"People living within a hundred-mile radius of my madhouse should lock their doors and bolt their windows, or get out of the area until he is safely back under lock and key," he warned. "This lunatic is completely unpredictable and very violent indeed."

bollocks

"If he sees you, he will kill you. It's as simple as that," Mr Abbot added.

The MAN in the PUB

SOLVES YOUR LEGAL PROBLEMS

MY NEIGHBOUR'S got some pigeons, and every morning when he lets them out they fly straight over onto my house and shit on the roof. I've told him to stop them landing on my house, but he says it's a free country and they can land where they like and he's got no control over where they shit.

WHAT IT IS, right, your neighbour is talking out his arse. You see, you own the air above your house, right. It's yours right up into space, all the clouds and aeroplanes over your house, they belong to you while they're there, and that's the law. Like if he's got a tree and the apples are hanging over your fence, you can have them. And it's the same with his pigeons, they're the same as apples as far as a judge is concerned. They're your property when they're on your fucking roof, so you can shoot them if they shit on it, it's up to you. And he can't do a thing to stop you.

I WAS driving home from the pub the other night and I was lighting a fag when I went up the kerb and through a fence. The police arrived and breathalysed me. I was well over, and now it looks like I'm going to lose my licence.

FIRST THING to remember is it's NOT illegal to be pissed up in a car, right. As long as you're not in charge of the vehicle, they can't touch you. So the first thing you should of done, right, is turn the engine off and got in the back seat. And left the keys in the ignition. If the keys are in your pocket, the law says you're in charge of the vehicle. If you're on private land, there's nothing they can do to stop you drink driving, like Jeremy Clarkson when he went to the Artic. Your car was off the Queen's Highway, right, as long as all four wheels was off the road the police have no jurisdiction to breathalyse you. You tell the coppers that, and if they try to arrest you, just knock their hats off. If they're not wearing their hats, they're out of uniform and they have no powers of arrest. It's true, that. Go on then, I'll have a pint if you're bending my arm.

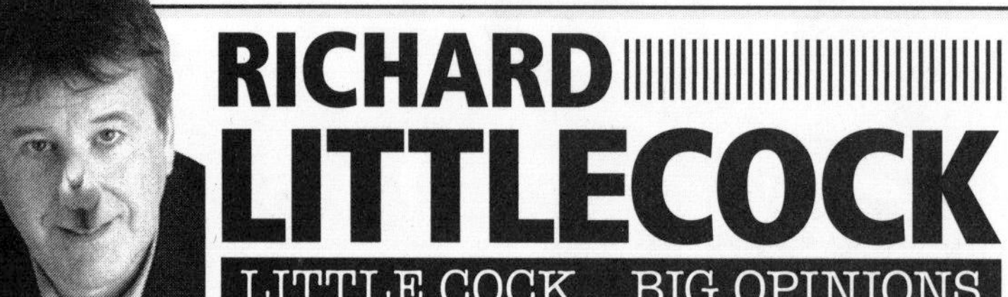

RICHARD LITTLECOCK

LITTLE COCK... BIG OPINIONS

Before you fix your country, maybe you could fix my toaster

I HAVE to say, recent pictures from the Far East have been shocking: disaster and human misery like something from out of the Old Testament or the Bible.

Millions of hardworking British pounds have poured into the Red Cross disaster fund, and football fans from Land's End to John O'Groats joined in two minutes' silence.

It seems everyone wants to honour the dead in that faraway, mysterious land of the Geisha and the gong.

But I won't be joining anyone in mourning the loss of life in Japan.

And you'd understand how I feel, if you had my toaster.

My toaster was made by Matsui. I think they're Korean, but it's the same thing.

It doesn't matter whether you put it on 1 or 6. It doesn't matter if you press the 'reheat' button. It takes two minutes then the bread pops out warm and soft. That's not toast. That's an abomination.

And I blame the Japanese.

Just because they like their fish uncooked, doesn't mean I want my toast the same way.

As they rush around proudly picking up the pieces of their shattered nation in their beautiful, noble, nimble hands, I wonder if any of them have given a chopstick's thought to my breakfast. And the fact that no amount of bowing is going to fix the real problem.

And that's soft toast.

It wouldn't have been that way in the good old days.

My old dad wouldn't recognise this new Soft Toast Britain.

He wouldn't have understood why thousands wept in the streets at the deaths of Princess Diana or Fred Titmus. He wouldn't have understood why newsreaders wear burqas, or why schoolchildren are fed environmental lies about "global roundness".

But he would have understood about my toaster. And why I can't forgive the Land Of The Rising Sun.

He loved toast, my old dad. Brown toast, or white toast. He didn't mind. He didn't need the *Guardian* Stasi telling him not to build a toast golliwog to understand that it's not what colour your toast is, it's what you spread on it.

But he didn't like it soft. And that's what my inscrutable toaster makes.

Say what you like about the Japanese, they are efficient. They took just six days to rebuild a motorway that had been broken into pieces like it had been bashed by a Godzilla. Six days. That's something they could teach our workmen, if we could only understand their charming ning-nong language!

But if they can rebuild a highway in six days, why can't they fix my toaster?

RAFFLES
The Gentleman Thug

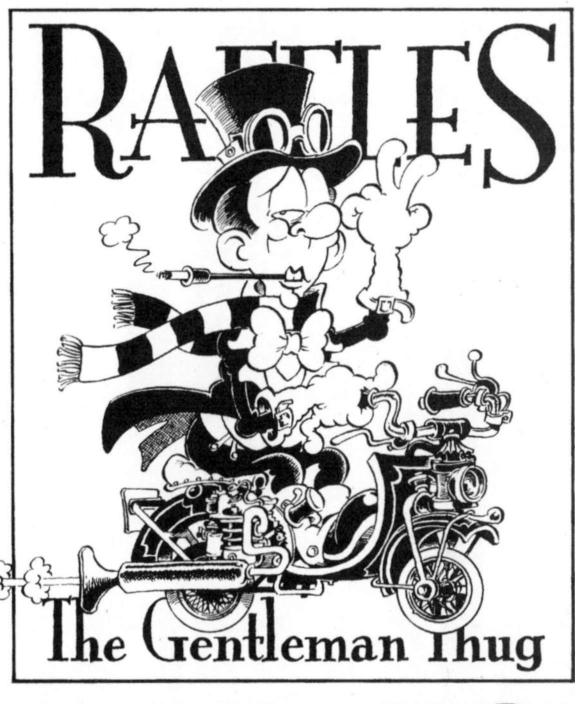

I'VE HAD AN ELEGANT SUFFICIENCY OF PERAMBULATION, BUNNY. MAINTAIN A STATE OF WATCHFULNESS WHILST I ENDEAVOUR TO HOT-WIRE THIS MOTORISED VELOCIPEDE.
THE BULL INN

HURRY ALONG, RAFFLES! THE OWNER MAY RETURN WITHOUT NOTICE!
OH, DO PARTAKE OF A REFRIGERATIVE TINCTURE, BUNNY. I'M NEARLY DONE.

COUGH! SPLUT! VROOM!
EGAD!
MY MOTORBICYCLE!

VROOM! V-V-V-VROOM!
I SAY! YOU SIR! DESIST AT ONCE.!
COME, BUNNY. LET US DEPART FORTHWITH.

YOU SCOUNDRELS! RETURN MY PROPERTY THIS INSTANT..! DO YOU HEAR..?!
PUT-PUT-PUT..!
CONSUME MY PULVERULENCE, CUNT-BUBBLE.

I'M NOT STANDING FOR THAT!
THE BULL INN
A TELEPHONE IS AVAILABLE ON THESE PREMISES

...HELLO!? IS THAT THE POLICE..? GOOD. NOW LISTEN HERE, I WANT TO REPORT THE THEFT OF MY MOTOR-BICYCLE BY A GENTLEMAN RUFFIAN AND HIS ACCOMPLICE..!

I'VE NOTIFIED THE AUTHORITIES! YOU'LL NOT GET FAR!
PUT-PUT..! K-POP!

5 MILES DOWN THE ROAD...
STEP IT UP, BUNNY OLD BEAN..! I WANT TO SEE WHAT THIS COPULATOR CAN DO!
VERY WELL, RAFFLES.

HALT, SIR..! IN THE NAME OF THE KING!
FORNICATE MY FORTUNE. IT'S THE PIGS.

ARE YOU THE REGISTERED KEEPER OF THIS MOTORBICYCLE, SIR? ONLY WE'VE RECEIVED A REPORT THAT A VERY SIMILAR ONE'S BEEN STOLEN NEARBY.
I AM INDEED, OFFICER.

THEN WOULD YOU BE SO GOOD AS TO FURNISH ME WITH THE DEEDS OF OWNERSHIP..?
CERTAINLY...

I HAVE THAT WHICH YOU ARE ASKING FOR HERE, SAFELY ENSCONCED WITHIN THE INTERIOR POCKET OF MY MACKINAW.

SPANG!
EMBROIDER THAT, TIT-HEAD.

PHEEEP!
LET US ABSQUATULATE, BUNNY. WITH THE UTMOST POSSIBLE ALACRITY.
I AVER THE VAGINA IS SUMMONING REINFORCEMENTS!

YOU THERE! STOP IN THE NAME OF THE LAW!
QUICKER, BUNNY! THEY'RE CATCHING UP!
PUFF! PANT!

I SAY, RAFFLES! I FEAR I CANNOT MAINTAIN THIS PACE FOR MUCH LONGER!
THAT IS WHAT YOUR MATERFAMILIAS VOUCHSAFED, BUNNY.

A WEEK LATER...
...THIS TEMERARIOUS FELLOW THOUGHT HE COULD OUT-PACE A CHARABANC FULL OF HIS MAJESTY'S FINEST ON A STOLEN MOTOR-BICYCLE...

...NOTWITHSTANDING THAT HE GAVE THEM A SPLENDID RUN FOR THEIR MONEY, HIS FELONIOUS CAPER WAS BROUGHT TO A SWIFT CONCLUSION WHEN HIS FLAG-MAN LOST THE SOLE OF HIS SHOE ON A VELOCITOUS BEND IN THE ROAD..!
Mr. ICHABOD STEWART Esq. presents his SPLENDID diversion...
Constabulary, Magic Lantern...Action!

Airport baggage handler lifts the

Something to Declare!

WE ALL love our favourite stars, but we're only really familiar with the face they choose to show to the public. The intimate details of their private lives remain locked firmly behind the doors of their mansions.

But one man knows them better than most. For airport baggage handler FRANK ARSE has been granted privileged access to their most intimate secrets... the ones that they keep tightly locked away in their suitcases. In a career spanning thirty years behind the scenes at one of Britain's busiest airports, the personal luggage of a glittering array of stars has passed through his hands.

After three blameless decades working at the airport, Frank was recently sacked following an allegation that he had been interfering with personal property. Now retired to a luxury static caravan overlooking Redcar Sands, he has decided it's finally time to tell the world some of the celebrity secrets he uncovered during his three decades at Teesside Airport.

"As long ago as I can remember, I wanted to work in the airline industry. When I was a small child, I would look up into the sky and dream about being a pilot, flying above the clouds to exotic locations around the globe. Unfortunately, they wouldn't let me train as a pilot as I was colour blind and suffer from blackouts and nervous twitches. Also, following a misunderstanding in some bushes near a primary school, I was on the sex offenders' register. I put my dream of flying on hold and decided to get a job on the ground.

A vacancy came up as a baggage handler at my local airport just outside Middlesbrough. I applied, and got the job. Even though I wasn't at the controls, I knew I was still responsible for the safety of all the passengers on each plane on the runway. It was my duty to make sure there were no bombs getting smuggled onto any of the flights.

Teesside Airport is a glamorous working environment. I found myself constantly rubbing shoulders with the jet set. Any star travelling from Hollywood via Heathrow to the Teesside/Cleveland area had to pass through my turf, and the list of baggage I handled reads like a *Who's Who* of Tinseltown A-listers.

And although I never uncovered a single bomb during my thirty year career, some of the stuff I found whilst searching the stars' suitcases was even more explosive!"

As an example, Frank cites an occasion when a famous US personality's bag turned out to contain far more than met the eye.

"One day, a rumour ran through the canteen that 'it-girl' **PARIS HILTON** was about to land at Teesside. Apparently, the blonde socialite's plane from LAX had been diverted following a diesel spill on the runway at Stansted.

Hilton's reputation for partying preceded her. I knew she had several drug convictions to her name, so I was keen to check her luggage to make sure she wasn't trying to smuggle any contraband into the country. I recognised her suitcase the moment it appeared on my carousel. It was a kid-leather Louis Vuitton valise, with her initials picked out on the top in 24-carat diamonds.

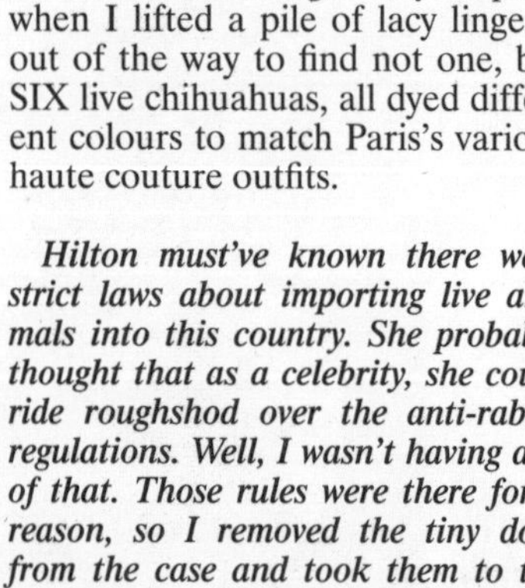

Within seconds I had prised the locks off it with a screwdriver, and was rummaging through the contents. As I expected, there was a lot of designer underwear in there; bras, skimpy undies and thongs - the sort of stuff she was wearing in her video. But imagine my surprise when I lifted a pile of lacy lingerie out of the way to find not one, but SIX live chihuahuas, all dyed different colours to match Paris's various haute couture outfits.

Hilton must've known there were strict laws about importing live animals into this country. She probably thought that as a celebrity, she could ride roughshod over the anti-rabies regulations. Well, I wasn't having any of that. Those rules were there for a reason, so I removed the tiny dogs from the case and took them to the quarantine department. They were very thirsty and desperate for a shit after their long flight.

Then I slapped a sticker reading "Opened for security purposes" on the lid of the case, closed it as best I could and sent it on its way on the conveyor. As it vanished from sight, I realised that I had forgotten to repack a pair of Hilton's knickers, so I popped them in my pocket and made a mental note to drop them off at Lost Property at the end of my shift."

Sometimes Frank found that a random check could throw up interesting results. And that was certainly the case when a certain A-list couple tried to pull the wool over his eyes.

"On any flight leaving or arriving at Teesside airport, a number of bags were picked at random to be searched. The rule was, every tenth bag was opened to make sure the owners weren't trying to slip anything dodgy past customs.

I remember one particular day, picking a suitcase off the carousel and being surprised to see the names **ANGELINA JOLIE** and **BRAD PITT** written on the luggage label. The movie star couple had apparently been flying first class from Hol-

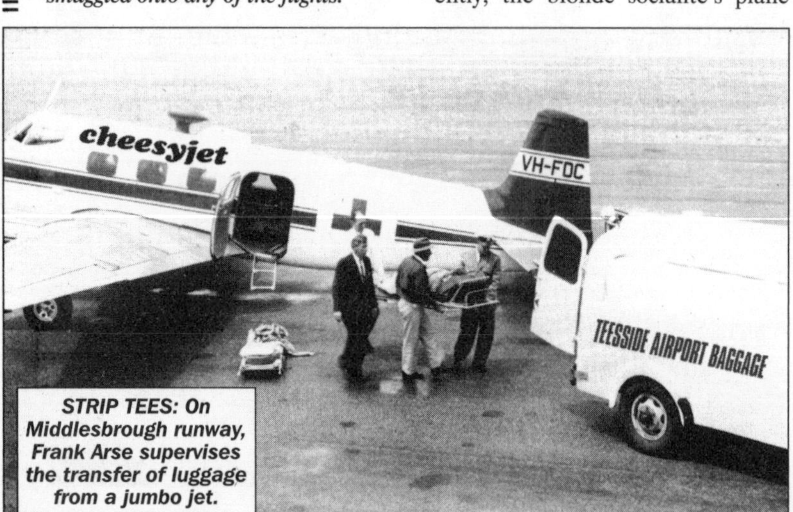

***STRIP TEES:** On Middlesbrough runway, Frank Arse supervises the transfer of luggage from a jumbo jet.*

se lid on sordid celebrity secrets

lywood to Cannes for the film festival, but had made a special detour in order to go to Middlesbrough for a look at the world famous Tees Transporter Bridge.

But Brangelina's celebrity status didn't cut any ice with me. As far as I was concerned, one piece of luggage was just like another and they weren't going to receive any special treatment from me just because they were famous. Their case had a fancy combination lock, but baggage handlers have a special tool a bit like a hammer for getting past such security measures. I soon got inside, and as it turned out it was a good job I did.

For there, nestling among Angelina's underwear and Brad's shirts, were 2000 Benny Hedges. Now Jolie and Pitt were seasoned travellers - they must have known they were strictly limited to bringing a thousand cigarettes into the country. I had no option but to confiscate half their stash of smokes.

Since the catches weren't lining up any more, I stuck the lid back down with gaffer tape. Unfortunately, I can't have done a particularly good job, because as it made its way along the conveyor a matching pair of his'n'hers Rolex watches fell out, along with a few pairs of Angelina's knickers. And a bra. I popped them in my pocket and made a mental note to drop them off at Lost Property at the end of my shift. ”

Baggage handlers often need a sixth sense to spot when something's amiss. But it was one of Frank's five other senses that alerted him to what was going on in one star's luggage.

“ Often when I open someone's bag, it's not because I have suspicions about the contents but because I'm doing the owner a favour. That was what happened one day when a large Samsonite case belonging to superstar singer **MADONNA** came past on the conveyor. She'd been spending the week with her new beau **A-ROD** at Primrose Valley near Filey, and was jetting out to New York on the next plane.

I could hear a buzzing noise coming from inside the bag. It was a sound I'd heard any number of times before, and I knew exactly what was making it: an electric toothbrush. I've been in this business thirty years, and you'd be surprised how many times electric toothbrushes are inadvertently switched on as luggage gets bumped about at airports. I knew I had to act fast. It was a seven-hour flight to the Big Apple, and if I didn't switch Madonna's toothbrush off for her, by the time she landed at JFK the batteries would be as flat as a plate of piss.

It was a particularly secure case, built to withstand the rough and tumble of jet-set international travel, so I had to use bolt-cutters on the hinges to get it open. Once inside, I sorted through the *Like a Virgin* singer's personal possessions to get to her toilet bag. Like a good Samaritan, I switched off the toothbrush.

The suitcase lid didn't fit back down any more, so I bundled it into an official airport plastic bag. It was all part of the service. However, seconds after I lobbed the case back onto the conveyor, I realised that as well as a couple of pairs of her knickers and one of her pointy bras, I had accidentally forgotten to re-pack an expensive looking digital camera too. I popped the lingerie items in my pocket and made a mental note to drop them off at Lost Property at the end of my shift.

Obviously, I wanted to post the camera back to its famous owner, so later, while I was having my mid-morning toilet visit, I looked through the photos on the memory card in case one of them contained a clue as to where I could send it. Sadly there was no sign of Madonna's home address amongst the pics. Instead, there was shot after shot of her and her famous boyfriend on their holidays.

I won't say what they were getting up to in the pics, because those photographs were private and confidential, and I was looking at them in my professional capacity. Suffice it to say, they were dynamite. If the prints I made off that memory card were to fall into the wrong hands, the papers would pay a fortune for them. But Madonna can rest assured that I will never sell them, because that would be a breach of the passenger/baggage handler relationship. ”

After thirty years at the sharp end of the airline business, Frank was used to acting on a hunch. But this time, his intuition was to cost him his job.

FRANKIE SAYS: ***Baggage handler Arse has written tell-all memoir.***

“ It was the height of the summer holidays, and I was sparking up a lunchtime Benny Henny one day at the back door of the baggage handling shed. I had a good view of the departure lounge, where I was surprised to recognise the familiar figure of **POSH SPICE** queueing up at the RyanAir desk for a package tour to Benidorm. Spotting the Spice Girls star at Teesside airport with a budget airline ticket in her hand struck me as unusual to say the least. You see, I knew for a fact she'd been through the airport about three months previously, jetting off for a short break in Lanzarote.

Nobody can afford to take two holidays in a year, so I started wondering if Posh might possibly be supplementing her pop earnings by muling drugs for a South American narcotics cartel. Even though I was on my dinner, I waited for her suitcase to come past on the conveyor and cracked it open.

On the surface, there was nothing out of the ordinary amongst Posh's luggage; it was mainly expensive designer lingerie, such as black satin knickers, lacy basques, see-through bras and the like. But drugs mules are well known for hiding their illicit cargos amongst clothing, so I decided to look through it all very carefully, closely examining each and every item for evidence.

Unfortunately, I was eating my lunch at the time, and I accidentally spilled a couple of teaspoons of yoghurt into the suitcase. I thought nothing about it at the time. After all, I didn't think anyone would make a fuss over a bit of harmless yoghurt. But apparently Posh kicked up a stink when she found it and complained to the authorities. To cut a long story short, there must have been some saliva on the spoon or something, because they managed to DNA test the yoghurt and trace it back to me. ”

Frank was suspended from his job, and when airport bosses searched his locker they found more than a thousand pairs of women's knickers, as well as dozens of bras.

"All I was guilty of was bad timing," says Frank. "I was going to take all those knickers and bras to Lost Property that very afternoon."

Frank Arse's book: **Man in a Suitcase - On & Off the Baggage Carousel of Life** *(Branflake Books, £1.99)* is available from the site shop at Sunnydale Caravan Park, Redcar.

ARE YOU BEING SERVED
AT THE CENTRE OF THE EARTH

DATELINE: THE FUTURE. AND THE CITIZENS OF LONDON ARE BEING MENACED BY AN INFESTATION OF GIANT ANTS.
LONDON BUS

IN THE OFFICE OF THE PRIME MINISTER OF ENGLAND
THESE GIANT ANTS ARE AN ABSOLUTE NUISANCE
THEY KEEP CRAWLING ALL OVER LANDMARK BUILDINGS AND BITING PEOPLE.

WE HAVE A SERIOUS SITUATION HERE, PRIME MINISTER
TOMORROW, THE ARCHBISHOP OF CANTERBURY WILL BE HOLDING A GARDEN FETE TO RAISE MONEY FOR THE WESTMINSTER ABBEY STEEPLE FUND.

WITH THOSE GIANT ANTS CRAWLING ALL OVER THE HOME-MADE CAKE STALL AND GETTING IN THE CANDY FLOSS, THE WHOLE EVENT COULD BE RUINED.
MY GOD! THOSE FORMIC MONSTERS MUST BE STOPPED!

PROFESSOR SIDGWICK, THE COUNTRY'S TOP ANT EXPERT, STEPPED FORWARD
THE GIANT MUTANT ANTS APPEAR TO BE COMING UP THROUGH A CRACKED PAVING STONE IN TRAFALGER SQUARE.
WE BELIEVE THAT THEIR NEST IS MANY THOUSANDS OF FEET BENEATH THE GROUND — AT THE EARTH'S CORE!

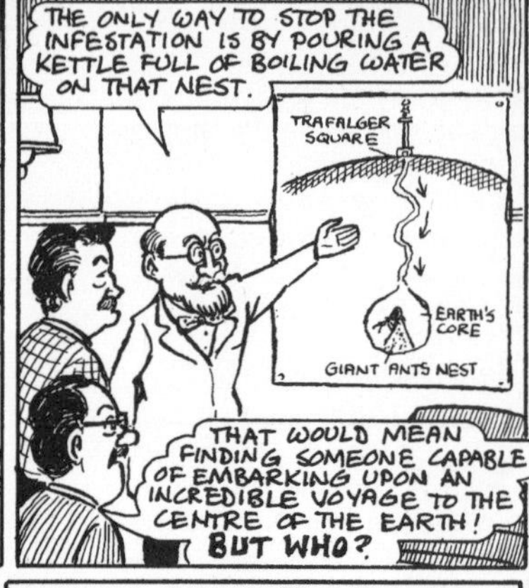

THE ONLY WAY TO STOP THE INFESTATION IS BY POURING A KETTLE FULL OF BOILING WATER ON THAT NEST.
TRAFALGER SQUARE
EARTH'S CORE
GIANT ANTS NEST
THAT WOULD MEAN FINDING SOMEONE CAPABLE OF EMBARKING UPON AN INCREDIBLE VOYAGE TO THE CENTRE OF THE EARTH! BUT WHO?

THE PRIME MINISTER DIDN'T HESITATE
CALL THE CAST OF THE MUCH-LOVED BBC SITCOM 'ARE YOU BEING SERVED?'!
TELL THEM TO MEET US AT TRAFALGER SQUARE IN PRECISELY ONE HOUR'S TIME!

AND SO
IT'S UP TO YOU TO SAVE THE ARCHBISHOP OF CANTERBURY'S GARDEN FETE, ARE YOU BEING SERVED!
TRAFALGER SQUARE
HERE IS YOUR KETTLE OF BOILING WATER.

LOWER GROUND FLOOR, EARTH'S CORE AND GIANT ANT'S NEST — GOING DOWN!
AND THE BEST OF BRITISH LUCK TO YOU, ARE YOU BEING SERVED!

THE STAFF OF GRACE BROS. BEGAN THEIR REMARKABLE SUBTERRANEAN JOURNEY
MIND YOU DON'T SPILL THAT BOILING WATER, CAPTAIN PEACOCK!
I DON'T WANT YOU TO SCALD MY PUSSY

DEEPER AND DEEPER THEY DESCENDED
THERE'S A FALLEN STALACTITE ACROSS THE PATH, MR LUCAS — I NEED YOUR HELP WITH GETTING A LEG OVER.
THAT'S THE BEST OFFER I'VE HAD ALL DAY, MISS BRAHMS!

WE MUST BE APPROACHING THE EARTH'S CORE, MRS SLOCOMBE — THE TEMPERATURE IS RISING.
YES CAPTAIN PEACOCK, MY PUSSY IS GETTING QUITE OVERHEATED!

SUDDENLY
MR HUMPHRIES, LOOK OUT! THAT GIANT ANT IS ABOUT TO TAKE YOU FROM BEHIND!
IS HE, NOW?
WELL THAT'S A BIT FORWARD OF HIM, I MUST SAY!

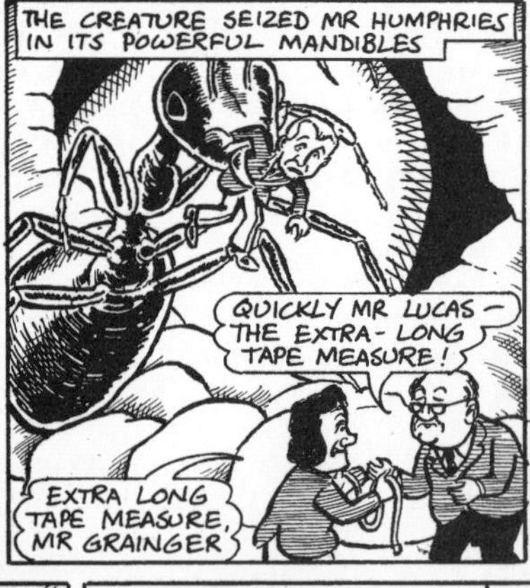

THE CREATURE SEIZED MR HUMPHRIES IN ITS POWERFUL MANDIBLES
QUICKLY MR LUCAS — THE EXTRA-LONG TAPE MEASURE!
EXTRA LONG TAPE MEASURE, MR GRAINGER

MR GRAINGER SWIFTLY TIED THE MEASURING TAPE AROUND THE ANT'S LEG
GET READY TO HEAVE, MR LUCAS!
READY TO HEAVE, MR GRAINGER!

CRASH! THE BEAST LOST ITS FOOTING AND FELL TO THE FLOOR, RELEASING ITS CAPTIVE.
ARE YOU FREE, MR HUMPHRIES?
I'M FREE, CAPTAIN PEACOCK!

EVENTUALLY
HERE WE ARE, AT THE EARTH'S CORE!
AND LOOK DOWN BELOW — IT'S THE GIANT ANTS' NEST!

CAPTAIN PEACOCK TIPPED THE BOILING WATER ONTO THE NEST
HOORAY! THE ARCHBISHOP OF CANTERBURY'S GARDEN FETE HAS BEEN SAVED!

AND, THE NEXT DAY
WESTMINSTER ABBEY GRAND FETE
GOOD WORK, ARE YOU BEING SERVED — YOU'VE ALL DONE VERY WELL!
THANK YOU, YOUR GRACE!

NEXT ISSUE: IT AIN'T HALF HOT MUM'S VOYAGE TO THE BOTTOM OF THE SEA.

FRY 'T.' BUNN
THE MASTER BAKER AND HIS GINGERBREAD SEX DOLLS

KNOCK-KNOCK!
HELLO..? MR. BUNN..? I'D LIKE TO BUY A BAP...
BUNN THE BAKER
CLOSED
MR. BUNN..?

HEH-HEH! THE SHOP'S CLOSED FOR THE HOLIDAYS, BUT I'VE GOT SOMETHING IN THE BACK ROOM THAT'S OPEN...!

...MY LATEST GINGERBREAD BIRD'S LEGS!

I MADE HER WITH FLOUR FROM ESSEX, SO SHE'S A RIGHT DIRTY COW! I DON'T KNOW WHICH SHE DROPS QUICKER - HER KNICKERS OR HER CONSONANTS!

WHAT'S THAT YOU SAY..? YOU'VE VAJAZZLED YOUR DOUGH NAY-NAY..? ...WITH HUNDREDS & THOUSANDS..?
PHWOOAR!!

...MR. BUNN! MR. BUNN!
CLOSED
...ARE YOU IN..?

I'M "IN" ALRIGHT! ALL 4 5/16 INCHES OF ME...! HEH-HEH!
FLOUR

...UH-UH-UH-UH-UH-UH-UH-UH-UH-UH-UH-UH-UH-UH-UH..! HANG ON...I'VE SLIPPED OUT...
FLOUR
...UH-UH-UH-UH- .....UH-OH...

NO... IT'S NO GOOD... I'M GOING SOFT..! WHAT'S THAT YOU SAY..? I'M NOT TO WORRY AND IT'S NOT MY FAULT..?

I KNOW IT'S NOT MY FAULT... IT'S YOURS. YOUR MERINGUE KNOCKERS SIMPLY AREN'T BIG ENOUGH FOR ME TO MAINTAIN TURGIDITY.

WHAT!? YOU'VE BEEN TOYING WITH THE IDEA OF GETTING THEM ENLARGED..? UP TO A DOUBLE-G MIXING BOWL...!? WELL, WHY DIDN'T YOU SAY?!

OSTRICH FARM
EGGS FOR SALE

SHORTLY...
TING!
AH! SHE'S DONE!
BAKERY KEEP OUT

GAW! LOOK AT THE SIZE OF THOSE MERINGUES! THEY'RE COMPLETELY OUT OF PROPORTION! I'M GETTING HALF A TEACAKE JUST LOOKING AT 'EM!

SLAVER! YOU'D LOOK EVEN SEXIER WITH A TAN... WHAT'S THAT..? WHY DON'T I TAKE YOU ON HOLIDAY..? JUST WAIT TILL THE OTHER FELLAS GET A LOAD OF YOU ON THE BEACH, YOU SAY..?

DROOL! THEIR EYES WILL BE OUT ON STALKS!

HELLO... NOREEN?... LISTEN - I'M AFRAID YOUR WEEK IN IBIZA HAS BEEN CANCELLED... YES, YOU AND LITTLE CHELSEA TOO... SOME SORT OF MIX-UP WITH THE TICKETS.

NEXT DAY...
...WELCOME ABOARD THIS SQUEEZYJET FLIGHT TO IBIZA...

...WE ARE PRESENTLY CRUISING AT A HEIGHT OF 35,000 FEET...
POP!
POP!

FUCKING RATS' COCKS.

Letterbocks

PO Box 841, Whitley Bay, NE26 9EQ

STAR LETTER

I THINK it's a ruddy disgrace that the Queen didn't bother shaking the hands of everybody who turned up outside the Palace for the Royal Wedding. Princess Diana would have done.

Edna Flabbybottom, e-mail

MY mate Mez is still owed £5 by Vernon Kay for watching the Tyson/Bruno fight in 1989 on pay per view at his house. He appealed a number of years ago in *Viz* for Vernon to pay his dues but with no joy. Please can I win £5 for this letter so I can give it to Mez and pretend it is off Vernon and we can finally put this matter to bed.

John, Salford

IT'S very nice of the Warwickshire Air Ambulance pilots to keep posting free bin-liners through my letterbox, but I can't help thinking they should be saving their money to buy bandages, and petrol for their helicopter.

Mark Glover, Coventry

ON a recent family holiday to Amsterdam my wife agreed to me going out for a couple of hours on my own 'for a walk'. I can't work out if she's really gullible or if she's burying her head in the sand for the sake of the kids. What do your readers reckon?

Sedgewick Wankel, e-mail

I'M FED up with sudoko and word puzzles. If it hasn't already been done, hows about a nice join-the-dots picture of that bloke kissing that bird's arse with her arse being the main focal point!

Denis, e-mail

* *No problem. Here you go, Denis.*

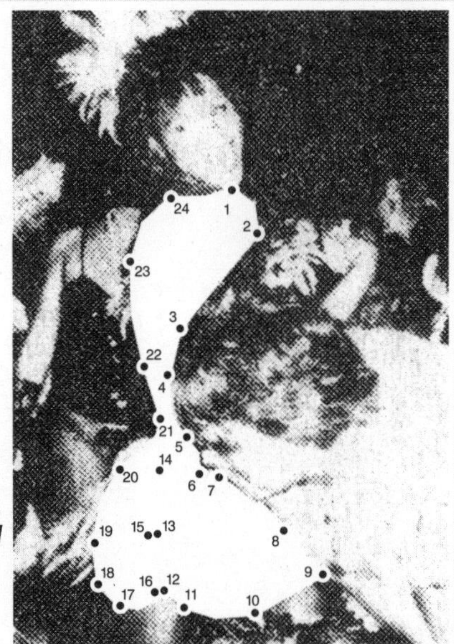

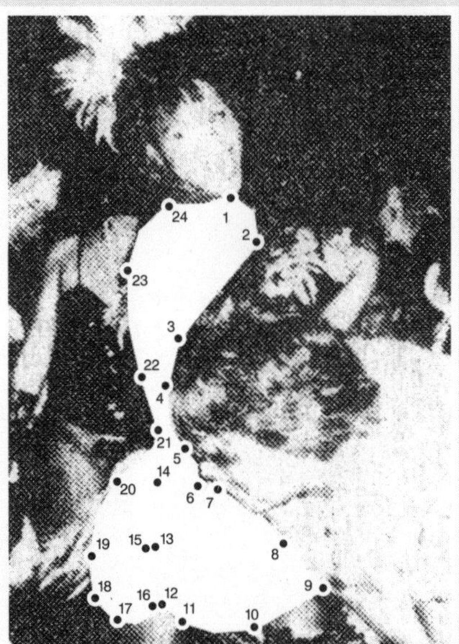

I KEEP geting Andrew Lansley, the Health Secretary, and Angela Lansbury out of *Murder She Wrote* mixed up. Do any readers know of a short verse that will allow me to discern the differential qualities of these two personalities?

D Cooper, e-mail

WITH reference to Mr Cooper's letter (*above*) my grandfather used to tell me this little rhyme which I have remembered for years.

The first does act in Murder She Wrote,
The next a man who wants your vote,
The first called Angela Lans-bury,
The latter Andrew Lansley be.

Tarquin Ballcock, e-mail

WHY is it there aren't any revolving boards on gameshows these days? When I was a kid every show on telly had a revolving board, now it's just shit computer graphics and clever 'media' stuff. Ted Rogers and Dusty Bin would be turning in their graves, it genuinely makes me sick.

Gavin Millar, e-mail

WHEN your wife says "there's so much housework to do I don't know where to begin?" your suggestion that she starts the laundry first and then cleans up the kitchen while the washing machine is running its cycle may make complete sense from the perspective of logical time-management, but it is not necessarily in your best interests to answer this question in such a literally correct fashion. Women, eh?

Paul Bradshaw, e-mail

HOW about a picture of rostrum cameraman Ken Morse? He spends so much time behind his rostrum camera, that it would be nice to see him this side of it for once.

Terry Handley, e-mail

* *Here you go, Terry.*

I WAS disappointed that *Newsnight* chose presenter Gavin Essler to question Nick Clegg about the government's plan to stop people using family connections to get their children into prestigious workplaces. When dealing with such a serious issue as institutional nepotism, surely

the Deputy Prime Minister should have been grilled by one of the BBC's more heavyweight employees, such as Mike Sergeant, Sally Magnusson, Dan Snow or one of the Dimbleby boys.

Spud, Luton

GOOD SAMARITAN OF THE WEEK

MY HUSBAND is very forgetful. I sometimes think he'd forget his own head if it wasn't screwed on! The other day, he was doing his first parachute jump for charity, and would you believe it, he forgot to take his parachute with him when he jumped out of the plane. Fortunately, half way down he met a man who had a spare one, and he said my husband could borrow it until he reached the ground. So a big thank-you to him, whoever he was, for his kind gesture.

Mrs Lark, Nene

A HUGE thank-you to the kind lady who went in the local off-licence and bought my 13-year-old son some cigarettes, glue and cider when he was really rattling the other day. We read a lot in the papers about bad behaviour on our streets, but this lady's generous offer to help a youngster in his hour of need proves that there really are some genuinely good people about.

Mrs Dunnock, Falkirk

TOP TIPS

FOOL friends into thinking you have a passion for swimming by combing watered down bleach through your hair, and complaining of verrucas.

Fat Asp, e-mail

A GREYHOUND racing video, a picture of Basil Brush stuck to the telly and a kazoo makes an ideal fox-hunting kit for poor people.

Lenin G Radd, e-mail

A DAIRYLEA triangle coated with Tippex makes perfect 'funsize' Brie.

Chris Francis, e-mail

WANT to know the time? Simply go to Argos and buy yourself a cheap watch. Hey presto! You should find the time printed on the till receipt.

Tomas Crauch, e-mail

SWAMIS. Avoid getting your feet blistered or burnt when fire-walking, by replacing your hot coals with Tesco Instant Light Charcoal Briquettes.

Spud, Luton

DOGS. Forgotten which year you were born in? Simply take your age in dog years and divide it by seven, then subtract this number from the present year.

Jeffrey Dharma, e-mail

AN EMPTY egg carton makes an ideal training bra for dogs.

Rob, e-mail

JAZZ pianists. Screw up your eyes and face and shake your head about like you're Stevie fucking Wonder so everybody can see how amazing it all is.

Adam Gatward, e-mail

MOTORISTS. Find out the price of petrol everywhere else by driving to a BP garage and deducting 4p from their displayed price.

Geoff, e-mail

COMMUTERS. Instead of walking around with scalding hot buckets of watered-down coffee which you drink out of a tiny hole in a plastic lid costing you at least £2.50, I suggest you buy a kettle and wake up one minute earlier than normal and have a coffee at home like most normal people.

Javier, e-mail

I WATCHED the recent Royal Wedding and was captivated by the pomp and pageantry. The golden coach and horses, the uniformed soldiers and the crowned heads of Europe in their finery made it a spectacle to behold. But by far the finest sight of the day was Pippa Middleton's arse. I wonder if you had a picture of it without anything on.

Herbert Rudd, Croydon

** Here you go, Mr Rudd. We've used a special X-ray camera and image enhancing software to produce a picture of the future queen's sister climbing the steps of Westminster Abbey with her arse in all its regal glory.*

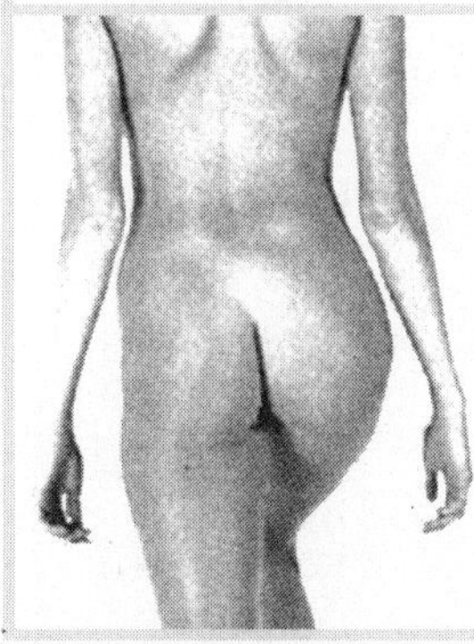

AS FAR as the Royal Wedding goes, I think a couple of quick snogs on the balcony of Buckingham Palace is selling us a bit short, to be honest. Given the vast sums of public money squandered on Will and Kate, they should have at least treated us to a Boston Pancake, or even Arabian Goggles. And Teabagging.

Mark Jay Smith, e-mail

I AM an airline pilot, and the other day I was flying through the Bermuda Triangle when I suddenly spotted a large, cigar-shaped object hovering directly in front of me. I reported what I had seen to air traffic control, but they said that there was nothing on the radar. Image how foolish I felt when I remembered that I was smoking a big cigar.

Capt. H Trubshaw, Surrey

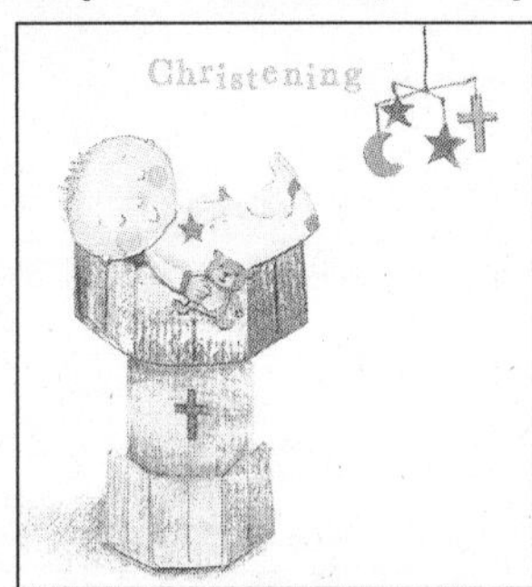

I DON'T think it takes much imagination to see that the mobile hanging from the ceiling spells out the word: "CUNT." How very jolly.

Tim Wain, e-mail

HAVE any of your readers ever seen a more uninspiring table of raffle prices. The DVDs I'm told are signed by someone dead. Great!

Simon Hinks, e-mail

IF you fancy your best mate's wife just go ahead and sleep with her. If he really is your best mate he won't mind, and if he does then he's obviously not a real mate.

Tomas Crauch, e-mail

DO ANY of your readers happen to know if Margaret Thatcher is dead yet? It's just that the champagne is good for a few more years but these fireworks go out of date in January.

A Scraghill, e-mail

I'LL tell you something about Jimmy Carr's hair - he has it dyed, like a girl. And what's more, he pays extra to have it done in a private room so that he can't be seen. Oh yes.

Denise Parkes, e-mail

Perfect Pippa wows crowds at wedding of the century

WEDDING BELLE

IT MAY have been Kate and Wills's big day, but the real stars of the Royal Wedding were PIPPA MIDDLETON and her buttocks. We mingled with the crowds of royal well-wishers outside St Paul's to gauge their reaction to Pippa and her superlicious booty.

...JUST think of all the millions of pounds that have been wasted on all the pomp and ceremony of this royal wedding. They could have saved the lot and just pointed a camera at Pippa's fartclappers all afternoon. I'd have tuned in, I can tell you.

Huw Edwards, commentator

...I THOUGHT that this lovely day couldn't get any better, but when I saw Pippa's lovely bum-cheeks as she got out of the carriage, it did just that.

Jim Foucault, vicar

...I WAS so taken with Pippa and her bottom, that I have written a poem about it. Oh Pippa, how I like a lot / That sexy little bot you've got. / I'd like to mash your buttock cheeks / For weeks and weeks and weeks and weeks.

Tom Paulin, ex-poet

...I'VE been sitting outside the cathedral since eight o'clock yesterday morning, but the moment I caught sight of Pippa's dirt-box, all the waiting was worthwhile.

Kirby Fairoak, butcher

...IT'S certainly one-in-the-eye for the Anti-Royal brigade. If they had their way, we'd be having to ogle Tony Benn's flabby old arse. No thank-you!

Kelsey Redbourne candlestick maker

...I'M AN American, over here for the Royal wedding, and when I commented loudly about what a cute fanny the bride's sister had, I was booed by the crowd. Their boos turned to cheers when I explained that in the States, fanny means ass, not pussy.

Hymen T Oysterburger III clambake organiser

...I THOUGHT Pippa looked absolutely radiant. She even outshone the bride. I'd love to do her up the shitter, and I mean that in the most respectful way.

Fishwick Dalkeith spoon straightener

...I'M MORE of a breast man myself. Arses do very little for me, to be frank, so I'd rather Prince William had decided to marry someone whose sister had a decent set of top bollocks on her. I pay my taxes too.

Aisby Barkwit, airline pilot

...I THINK Pippa's a real stunner. And with that super behind she's got, she's pretty enough to be a model. I think she should make some anal porn videos. It would be a real boost for the ailing UK gonzo industry and show the monarchy in a thoroughly modern light.

Linseed Honeysuckle, actor

...PIPPA'S such a naughty girl, teasing all the billions of male viewers across the globe with her pert, peach-like derriere on display in that cheeky, figure-hugging dress. I'd like to put her across my knee, lift that skirt up and give her bare bottom a spanking she'd never forget, the dirty little minx.

Rowan Williams, Archbishop

SHOPKEEPERS. When selling booze, say to your customers "It's Friday, it's 5 to 5..." and if they reply "and it's Crackerjack" you don't have to check ID.

Pat Pending, e-mail

A McCOY'S crisp, painted silver, makes a realistic washboard for your Victorian dolls house.

Nisbet Crawford, e-mail

GUINNESS World Record Fans. Don't bother shoving Smarties under your foreskin as apparently they will not accept this as a world record.

Gareth D, e-mail

AMERICAN pastors, instead of burning expensive Korans, simply download the e-book from the internet for free and delete it from your hard-drive.

Peter Wardrobe, e-mail

CAMPERS. Inflatable airbeds make ideal ground-sheets 10 fucking minutes after blowing the fuckers up.

Carey Hunt, e-mail

FITNESS Instructors - help fat people do sit-ups by gluing Scotch eggs to the tops of their shoes.

Stu Mandry, e-mail

SAVE money on parrots by instead buying a brightly-coloured dictaphone with a voice-activated replay function.

Monkey Boy, Nintendo-on-Sea

LADY drivers, think of your car headlights as mood lighting rather than essential safety equipment. You may then switch them on.

Miggy, e-mail

GEEKS. When talking to someone face-to-face, simulate the shapes of emot icons using your facial muscles.

Stu, e-mail

VICARS. Increase the size of your congregation by substituting sour cream & chive Pringles at Holy Communion instead of the outdated unleavened bread wafers. I'm sure Jesus wont mind.

Joderell Blank, e-mail

George Bestial

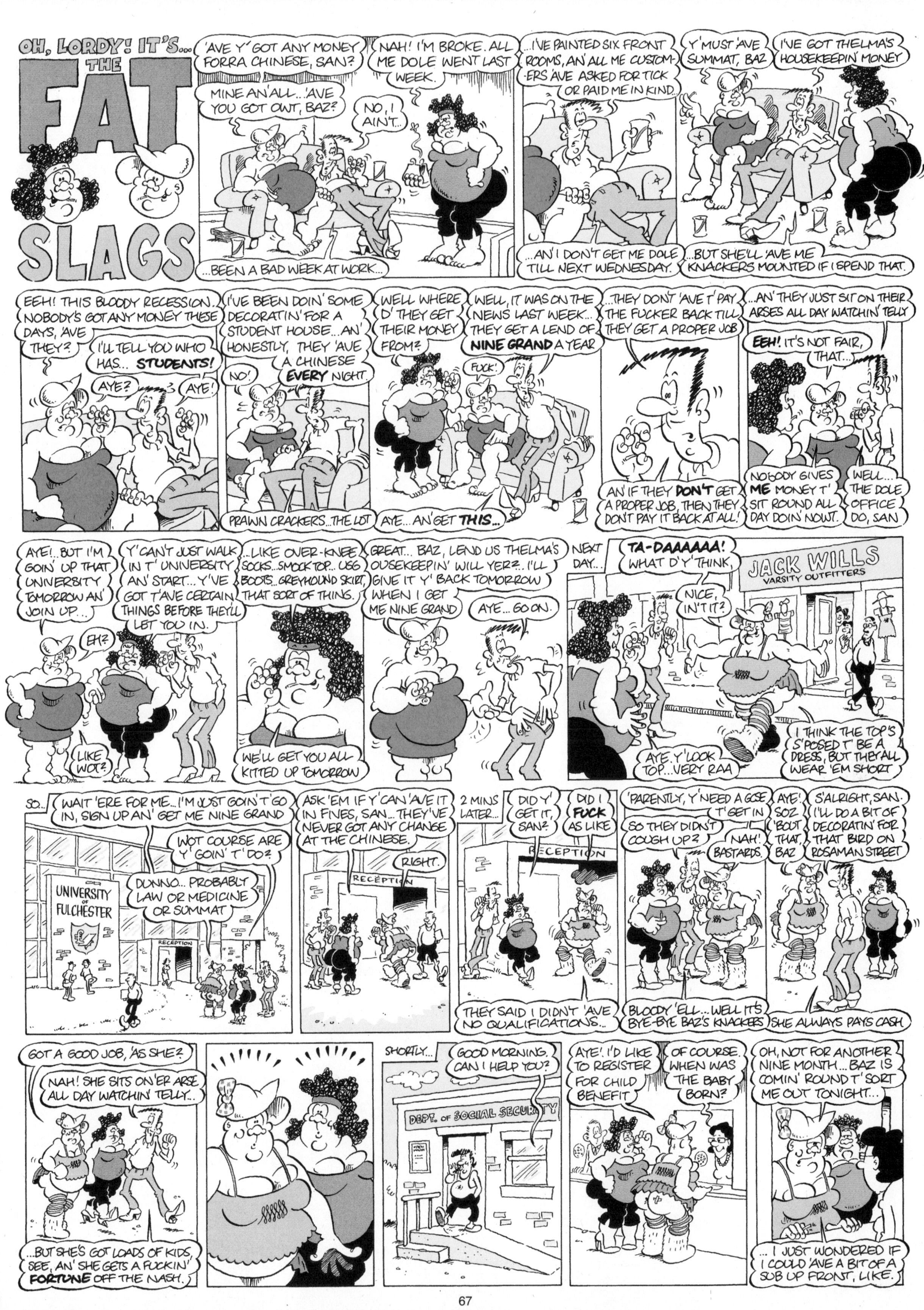

OH, LORDY! IT'S...
THE FAT SLAGS
'AVE Y' GOT ANY MONEY FORRA CHINESE, SAN?
MINE AN'ALL... 'AVE YOU GOT OWT, BAZ?
NAH! I'M BROKE. ALL ME DOLE WENT LAST WEEK.
NO, I AIN'T...
...BEEN A BAD WEEK AT WORK...
...I'VE PAINTED SIX FRONT ROOMS, AN' ALL ME CUSTOM-ERS 'AVE ASKED FOR TICK OR PAID ME IN KIND...
...AN' I DON'T GET ME DOLE TILL NEXT WEDNESDAY.
Y' MUST 'AVE SUMMAT, BAZ
I'VE GOT THELMA'S HOUSEKEEPIN' MONEY
...BUT SHE'LL 'AVE ME KNACKERS MOUNTED IF I SPEND THAT.
EEH! THIS BLOODY RECESSION... NOBODY'S GOT ANY MONEY THESE DAYS, 'AVE THEY?
I'LL TELL YOU WHO HAS... STUDENTS!
AYE?
AYE!
I'VE BEEN DOIN' SOME DECORATIN' FOR A STUDENT HOUSE... AN' HONESTLY, THEY 'AVE A CHINESE EVERY NIGHT.
NO!
PRAWN CRACKERS... THE LOT
WELL WHERE D' THEY GET THEIR MONEY FROM?
WELL, IT WAS ON THE NEWS LAST WEEK... THEY GET A LEND OF NINE GRAND A YEAR
FUCK!
AYE... AN' GET THIS...
...THEY DON'T 'AVE T' PAY THE FUCKER BACK TILL THEY GET A PROPER JOB
AN' IF THEY DON'T GET A PROPER JOB, THEN THEY DON'T PAY IT BACK AT ALL!
...AN' THEY JUST SIT ON THEIR ARSES ALL DAY WATCHIN' TELLY
EEH! IT'S NOT FAIR, THAT...
NOBODY GIVES ME MONEY T' SIT ROUND ALL DAY DOIN' NOWT.
WELL... THE DOLE OFFICE DO, SAN
AYE! ...BUT I'M GOIN' UP THAT UNIVERSITY TOMORROW AN' JOIN UP...
EH?
Y' CAN'T JUST WALK IN T' UNIVERSITY AN' START... Y'VE GOT T' 'AVE CERTAIN THINGS BEFORE THEY'LL LET YOU IN.
LIKE WOT?
...LIKE OVER-KNEE SOCKS... SMOCK TOP... UGG BOOTS... GREYHOUND SKIRT, THAT SORT OF THING.
WE'LL GET YOU ALL KITTED UP TOMORROW
GREAT... BAZ, LEND US THELMA'S 'OUSEKEEPIN' WILL YER?... I'LL GIVE IT Y' BACK TOMORROW WHEN I GET ME NINE GRAND
AYE... GO ON.
NEXT DAY...
TA-DAAAAAA! WHAT D'Y' THINK
JACK WILLS
VARSITY OUTFITTERS
NICE, IN'T IT?
AYE, Y' LOOK TOP... VERY RAA
I THINK THE TOP'S S'POSED T' BE A DRESS, BUT THEY ALL WEAR 'EM SHORT
SO...
WAIT 'ERE FOR ME... I'M JUST GOIN' T' GO IN, SIGN UP AN' GET ME NINE GRAND
WOT COURSE ARE Y' GOIN' T' DO?
DUNNO... PROBABLY LAW OR MEDICINE OR SUMMAT
UNIVERSITY OF FULCHESTER
RECEPTION
ASK 'EM IF Y' CAN 'AVE IT IN FIVES, SAN... THEY'VE NEVER GOT ANY CHANGE AT THE CHINESE.
RIGHT.
RECEPTION
2 MINS LATER...
DID Y' GET IT, SAN?
DID I FUCK AS LIKE
RECEPTION
THEY SAID I DIDN'T 'AVE NO QUALIFICATIONS...
'PARENTLY, Y' NEED A GCSE T' GET IN
SO THEY DIDN'T COUGH UP?
NAH! BASTARDS.
BLOODY 'ELL... WELL IT'S BYE-BYE BAZ'S KNACKERS
AYE! SOZ 'BOUT THAT, BAZ
S'ALRIGHT, SAN. I'LL DO A BIT OF DECORATIN' FOR THAT BIRD ON ROSAMAN STREET
SHE ALWAYS PAYS CASH
GOT A GOOD JOB, 'AS SHE?
NAH! SHE SITS ON 'ER ARSE ALL DAY WATCHIN' TELLY...
...BUT SHE'S GOT LOADS OF KIDS, SEE, AN' SHE GETS A FUCKIN' FORTUNE OFF THE NASH.
SHORTLY...
GOOD MORNING. CAN I HELP YOU?
DEPT. OF SOCIAL SECURITY
AYE! I'D LIKE TO REGISTER FOR CHILD BENEFIT
OF COURSE. WHEN WAS THE BABY BORN?
OH, NOT FOR ANOTHER NINE MONTH... BAZ IS COMIN' ROUND T' SORT ME OUT TONIGHT...
...I JUST WONDERED IF I COULD 'AVE A BIT OF A SUB UP FRONT, LIKE.

ROGER MELLIE THE MAN ON THE TELLY

ANY IDEAS FOR YOUR FTV XMAS SPECIAL THIS YEAR, ROGER?
YES, TOM. IT'S CALLED LOVELY THIS CHRISTMAS...
OH!?
FTV
FTV
YES... ME SPENDING THE FESTIVE SEASON ON THE STREETS WITH THE HOMELESS.

WHAT A LOVELY IDEA, ROGER
WELL DOWN AND OUTS ARE OFTEN IGNORED...
...AND THIS TIME OF YEAR IS THE WORST IF YOU HAVEN'T GOT A ROOF OVER YOUR HEAD

I'M GOING TO BE RIGHT THERE WITH THEM, TOM... SITTING WITH THEM... TALKING TO THEM... PATTING THEIR DOGS... FINDING OUT THEIR STORIES.
WELL... THIS IS A SIDE TO YOU THAT I'VE NEVER SEEN BEFORE, ROGER.

HMM. WELL THEY'RE JUST PEOPLE LIKE ME AND YOU, TOM. THEY JUST NEED A SHOULDER TO CRY ON... SOMEONE TO HUG THEM AND TELL THEM THAT THINGS WILL BE OKAY. I'M GOING TO BRING THEM A LITTLE FESTIVE CHEER.
I'M MOVED, ROGER... HONESTLY.

IT'S GOING TO BE BITTERLY COLD OUT THERE, THOUGH, ROGER. MAKE SURE YOU KEEP WRAPPED UP WARM, WON'T YOU?

ME!?
NO... NO.. I'M NOT DOING THE OUTSIDE BROADCASTS, TOM...

EH!?.. BUT I THOUGHT YOU SAID..
FRANK!..
...HAVE YOU GOT A MINUTE?

TOM, THIS IS FRANK... HE'S GOING TO STAND IN FOR THE TRAMP SHOTS.. YOU KNOW, WHERE I'M ACTUALLY SAT WITH ALL THE FILTHY FUCKERS...
HI, MR. TOM
I GOT HIM FROM A LOOKALIKE AGENCY... £20 AN HOUR... GOOD, ISN'T HE, TOM?

HE'LL BE CATCHING THE FUCKING FLEAS WHILE I DO THE STUDIO VOICEOVERS.

JUST A THOUGHT, TOM... SHOULD WE TAKE HIM WITH US TO AFRICA NEXT TIME WE DO COMIC RELIEF?

HE CAN DO ALL THE BOLLOCKS WITH THE VILLAGERS DIGGING THEIR WELLS AND WE CAN SPEND THE DAY BY THE HOTEL POOL

Right Charlies

A FULL REVIEW of royal security has been ordered after a member of the public was able to get close enough to Prince Charles *to wank him off in the shower!*

Washing his Heir: *Prince nearly got pulled off in Palace shower.*

The unnamed intruder was able to enter Buckingham Palace unnoticed before gaining access to the Prince's inner quarters. He then managed to bypass security and entered Charles' shower cubicle undetected. The man's rounded fingers were said to have come within a pubic hair's breadth of encircling the Prince of Wales's penis, where they could have performed a slow rhythmical sex act.

Royal security personnel are concerned as to how the intruder knew what time the Prince took a shower. As a precaution, Palace protection staff have varied the Prince's body wash times. Following a review of procedures, doubles wearing false ears will now shower simultaneously in the palace's 78 other bathrooms.

According to one palace insider, security around the Prince's personal hygiene routine has been lax for some time. And there have been several breaches in the past when members of the public have come close to joining the heir to the throne in the shower.

❑ ***IN 2001,*** **two drunken Rangers fans flicked the Prince with a towel as he stepped out of the shower cubicle at Highgrove House, Gloucestershire.**

❑ ***IN 1994,*** **two men armed with a bar of Imperial Leather and a bottle of Matey lathered the Prince's back in the bath for 15 minutes before household staff raised the alarm.**

❑ ***IN 1975,*** **the young Prince was followed into a shower at Sandringham by 4 members of the IRA who turned the tap to cold and then back to very**

Buck House protection squad red-faced after shower breach

hot for a few seconds before walking around with their willies tucked between their legs, doing impressions of Princess Anne.

The head of the Royal Protection Squad, Gen. Sir Peter Billious-Attack defended palace security but admitted there were lessons to be learnt.

"Our duty is to provide high quality protection for the Prince's penis at all times, but his shower time is the weak link in the system. We had warned His Royal Highness to be vigilant, but on this occasion he had all soap in his eyes and didn't see the man's cupped palm hovering millimetres from his unit," he told reporters.

"In future we will certainly be more careful about how many members of the public we allow to wander freely around the Prince's quarters while he is bathing," he added.

TINRIBS
11-YEAR OLD TOMMY TAYLOR'S BEST PAL WAS A FANTASTIC ROBOT NAMED TINRIBS

HOORAY! WE'RE GOING ON A SCHOOL NATURE RAMBLE TODAY, TINRIBS!
HEAD MASTER
HI, I'M BARBIE. I LOVE YOU VERY MUCH.

MY WORD! THAT FARMER SEEMS A TRIFLE AGITATED.
GET AWAY FROM MY SEEDLINGS, YOU DRATTED CROWS!

SOMEONE'S PINCHED THE ARMS OFF MY SCARECROW, RENDERING IT COMPLETELY INEFFECTIVE.
I'LL NEVER FRIGHTEN AWAY THESE CROWS WITH AN ARMLESS SCARECROW.

WHAT I NEED IS SOME KIND OF STICK WITH A GLOVE ATTACHED TO EITHER END, TO REPLACE MY SCARECROW'S ARMPIECE.
MY ROBOT CHUM CAN OBLIGE YOU THERE, MR FARMER!

FIRST I USE ONE OF TINRIBS'S JAGGED SOUP TINS TO SLICE OPEN MR SNODWORTHY'S BACK AND REMOVE HIS SPINAL COLUMN
CUT CUT
YARGH!

NEXT I CUT OFF MR SNODWORTHY'S HANDS AND SCRAPE OUT THE INSIDES OF THEM USING TINRIBS'S ARMPIECE
WHIMPER

NOW WE JUST POP MR SNODWORTHY'S HOLLOWED-OUT HANDS ONTO EACH END OF HIS SPINAL COLUMN...
AND HEY PRESTO! A SUPER PAIR OF ARMS FOR YOUR SCARECROW!
WELL DONE, YOUNG MAN — YOUR REMARKABLE ROBOT HAS SAVED THE DAY!
HEAD MASTER
THREE CHEERS FOR TOMMY TAYLOR AND HIS INCREDIBLE AUTOMATED AMIGO!

GURR! I AM SICK OF EVERYONE SINGING THE PRAISES OF THAT STUPID ROBOT!
FARM
I'VE GOT TO FIND A WAY OF BLOTTING HIS COPYBOOK!

WAIT A MINUTE — THAT SIGN GIVES ME AN IDEA!
KEEP ALL DOGS ON LEASH BY ORDER
I THINK I HAVE A PLAN TO LAND THAT TIN TWERP IN DEEP TROUBLE WITH THE FARMER...
AND SHORTLY...
MISTER FARMER! COME QUICKLY!
HEAD MASTER
TINRIBS HAS LET HIS PET DOG OFF ITS LEASH, AND IT'S GONE AND KILLED ONE OF YOUR CHICKENS!

B-BUT TINRIBS HASN'T GOT A PET DOG!
OH NO? THEN WHAT DO YOU CALL THIS?!

GOOD GRACIOUS! A REMARKABLE ROBOT DOG, MADE OUT OF AN OLD ROLLER SKATE, A YOGURT POT AND AN EMPTY SQUEEZY BOTTLE!
AND IT'S CLEARLY KILLED A CHICKEN, TOO...
HEAD MASTER
SEE HOW IT'S STANDING THERE LOOKING ALL GUILTY, SURROUNDED BY FEATHERS!

IT LOOKS LIKE A CHICKEN-KILLER, ALL RIGHT!
REALLY, TAYLOR! YOUR ROBOT CHUM SHOULD HAVE KEPT HIS CYBERNETIC CANINE ON A LEASH!

RIGHT! I'M GOING TO BLAST THIS MECHANICAL MUTT'S HEAD OFF...
...AND THEN I'LL TURN THE GUN ON ITS ROBOTIC MASTER!
HEH HEH!
WAIT! DON'T SHOOT THAT ELECTRONIC DOG!
BLAM!
PUSH!
EH?
GAH! MY ARSE!

TINRIBS'S PET DOG HASN'T KILLED A CHICKEN! LOOK, THESE ARE CROW'S FEATHERS!
THE COMPUTERISED POOCH WAS MERELY RIDDING YOUR FARM OF THESE SEED-GUZZLING CROWS!

IN THAT CASE, I OWE BOTH OF THESE FANTASTIC ROBOTS A DEBT OF GRATITUDE!
DOH! FOILED AGAIN!

I WOULDN'T LEAP AROUND LIKE THAT, MR SNODWORTHY
THE BLOOD-STAINED SEAT OF YOUR TROUSERS IS ACTING LIKE A RED RAG TO MY BULL!

PITY MR SNODWORTHY'S TOO BUSY TO JOIN US FOR THIS SUPER PICNIC, TINRIBS!
BELLOW!
CASTROL GTX
ROBOT DOG
HI, I'M BARBIE. I LOVE YOU VERY MUCH.

SKIPPY
the
BUSH
KANGAROO

SHEILA BILLABONG WAS THE LUCKIEST YOUNG LADY IN AUSTRALIA. FOR SHE HAD BEFRIENDED A KANGAROO WHICH LIVED IN HER ENORMOUSLY HAIRY MUFF.

G'DAY, SKIPPY – IT SURE IS A BONZER MORNING!
TCHK TCHK TCHK!

TCHK! TCHK! TCHK!
TCHK! TCHK!
WHAT'S UP, SKIP? HAVE YA FOUND SOMETHING IN MY STOAT?

WHOY, IT'S ONE OF MY PUBIC LICE!
BUT WHAT'S THIS TANGLED ROUND THE LI'L FELLER'S LEG?

STREWTH! IT'S A TINY LITTLE SNARE!
SKREE! SKREE!
SOMEONE HAS BEEN SETTING TRAPS IN MY LADYGARDEN – BUT WHO?

IT WAS ME, YOUNG LADY!
GASP!
THOSE CRABS WILL FETCH ME. GOOD MONEY WHEN I SELL THEM TO THE BIG GENITAL PARASITE ZOOS IN EUROPE AND AMERICA!

HYAR! G'WAN, GIT INTO THAT CAGE!
SKREE! SKREE!
IT'S CRUEL TO KEEP PUBIC LICE IN CAPTIVITY – THEY SHOULD BE FREE TO ROAM AROUND MY QUIM, AS NATURE INTENDED!

HA! SOON YOU WON'T HAVE A MUFF FOR THOSE CRITTERS TO ROAM AROUND IN, MISSY!
WH – WHAT D'YOU MEAN?

I MEAN THAT YOUR MINGE IS PRIME DEVELOPMENT LAND!
AND I'M PLANNING TO BUILD A HYDRO-ELECTRIC POWER STATION RIGHT THERE IN YOUR KNICKERS!
Y- YOU CAN'T DO THAT!

OH CAN'T I? I'VE ALREADY OBTAINED THIS COMPULSORY DEPILATION ORDER, SEE?
COMPULSORY DEPILATION ORDER
WE START REMOVING YOUR PUBIC HAIR IMMEDIATELY.

C'MON BOYS – BRING IN THE INDUSTRIAL HAIR REMOVAL LASER, AND GIVE THAT BIFFER A FULL BRAZILIAN!
FAIR DINKUM, BOSS

LOOKS LOIKE THIS IS IT, SKIP!
RUMBLE!
YOUR HAIRY HOME IS ABOUT TO BE LAID BARE!

SUDDENLY SKIPPY STARTED TO LEAP UP AND DOWN IN SHEILA'S PANTS
TCHK! TCHK! TCHK!

HOWLY DOOLEY! THAT 'ROO'S KICKING UP A RIGHT OLD CLOUD OF SHORT 'N' CURLIES

WHAT ARE YER STOPPING FOR, YA USELESS BLUDGERS? GET ON WITH THE DEFORESTATION!
HANG ON A MO', COBBER – I'VE GOT A PUBE IN MY MOUTH.
PTEH! ME TOO.

GOOD ON YER, SKIPPY!
VROOM!
YOU MANAGED TO DELAY THEM JUST LONG ENOUGH FOR THE PUBIC RANGER TO GET HERE!

THIS YOUNG LADY'S GORILLA SALAD IS A PROTECTED AREA OF OUTSTANDING PUBIC GROWTH
PUBIC RANGER
SO YOU CAN TAKE YOUR DEPILATION MACHINES AND PUSH OFF!
BAH!

AND SOON THE CAPTURED PUBIC LOUSE WAS BEING RELEASED BACK INTO SHEILA'S GROWLER
I RECKON THE LI'L FELLER'S GLAD TO BE HOME, EH SKIP?
TCHK! TCHK!
SKREE! SKREE!

He put out fires~but she couldn't put out the fire in her heart that burned with the flames of passion in...

The Towering Inferno of Love

CONTINUED OVER

The following day, the street outside Mandy's house once again echoed to the sound of a fire engine's siren...
NEE!-NAR! NEE!-NAR! NEE!-NAR! NEE!-NAR!
Okay, lads. We've got a report of a chair on fire.

Stand back, Miss. Leave this to us.
I just turned my back for a moment and it went on fire.

Shortly...
There you go. It's out. Call us again if you need us.
Don't worry. I will.

The next day, Mandy dialled 999 once more...
Come on, puss...
MEOW!

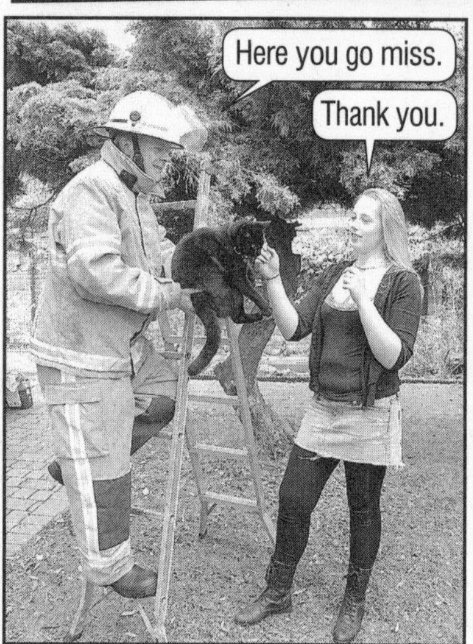
Here you go miss.
Thank you.

...and as the days went by...
RASP! RASP! RASP!
I'm so sorry, I really don't know how it happened.
Don't worry, miss. It's all in a day's work.

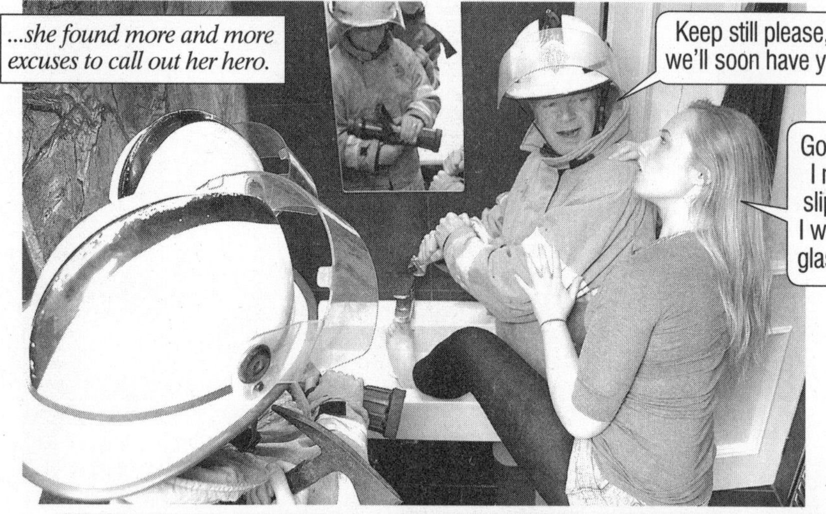
...she found more and more excuses to call out her hero.
Keep still please, miss, we'll soon have you free.
Gosh, thanks. I must have slipped when I went to get a glass of water.

Listen, miss. You've called us out a dozen times in the last week. It's getting ridiculous. What's going on?
I'm...I'm sorry...

It's just that from the day you put out my chip pan, I fell hopelessly in love with you...
...I had to see you again.

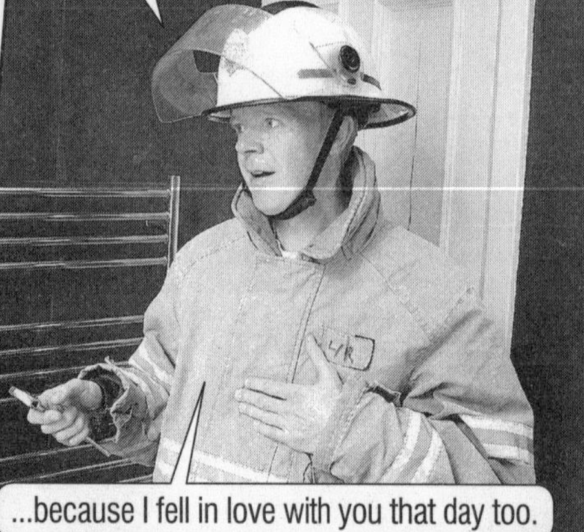
Well it would have saved a lot of fire brigade time if you had simply told me how you felt...
...because I fell in love with you that day too.

My name's Brett.
Pleased to meet you, Brett. I'm Mandy.

CONTINUED OVER

Brett spent the whole weekend in an emotional turmoil...
...and back at work on Monday, he confided in his best friend, Hank...
GREEN WATCH
Morning, Brett...
...what's wrong? You look fed up.
Oh, Hank...
...I'm so confused....
I love Mandy so much...sniff!... but she can't see beyond my uniform... sob!
There! There, Brett. Don't cry. I'm sure she does love you.
Really?...sniff!! Do you really think so, Hank?
Yes, I do...
Sniff!
...I saw the way she looked at you when you were putting her chip pan out.
Lots of girls have things for men in uniforms. There's no harm in it.
Don't throw this relationship away, Brett...
...She'll be missing you like mad. Let her have her fun with your uniform. She'll eventually come to see through it to the real you underneath.
Thanks, Hank. I'll go back to her tonight...
...in my uniform.
That's the spirit...
...anyway, come on. We were supposed to be putting that fire out at the hospital half an hour ago.
So...
Hank was right. I was making too big a deal of this. I'll give Mandy a nice surprise.
Anyone home?.. It's the fire brigade!
Oooh,Barry, you look fantastic! Promise me you'll never take your lavatory attendant's uniform off.
PHWOAR! Knickers, knackers, knockers!
LAVATORY
F.C.C PUBLIC LAVATORY DEPT.
THE END

SPOILT BASTARD
HAVE YOU DECIDED WHO'S COMING TO YOUR BIRTHDAY PARTY TOMORROW, MY LOVE?
YES! I'M INVITING ALL MY FACEBOOK FRIENDS
I'VE GOT FIVE THOUSAND OF THEM... THAT'S HOW POPULAR I AM, WOMAN.
AND I'M INVITING THEM ALL TO MY PARTY.
NO...NO, TIMMY... YOU CAN'T
DON'T YOU USE THE 'C' WORD IN FRONT OF ME...
I CAN AND I AM... YOU'RE JUST JEALOUS BECAUSE I'VE GOT 5000 FRIENDS AND YOU'VE GOT NONE!
BUT... I THOUGHT YOU WERE JUST INVITING SOME OF YOUR FRIENDS FROM SCHOOL
THEY'RE NOT MY FRIENDS. I HATE THEM... THESE ARE MY REAL CHUMS.
BUT... YOU'VE NEVER MET THEM, MY SOLDIER ... ARE YOU SURE IT'S A GOOD IDEA TO...
LOOK!
IT'S MY PARTY AND I'M GOING TO INVITE MY FACEBOOK FRIENDS. OKAY, WOMAN..? ALL OF THEM.
AND THEY'RE ALL GOING TO BRING ME A PRESENT
BUT TIMMY, MY LOVE...
...HOW AM I GOING TO CATER FOR 5000 CHILDREN?
WELL I DON'T KNOW, WOMAN. THAT'S YOUR PROBLEM...
...MY PROBLEM WILL BE TRYING TO OPEN MY PRESENTS FAST ENOUGH
BUT WHO ARE THESE PEOPLE, TIMMY?
THEY'RE MY FRIENDS
DIRTYARSE FROM BOLTON ... LIKES MOTORBIKES, DRUGS, GANG BANGS...
...DICK DIVER FROM HALIFAX... STATUS... SINGLE... LIKES: CHICKS WITH DICKS... GOODNESS ME! TIMMY, YOU CAN'T INVITE THESE PEOPLE.
facebook
LET'S SEE ... I THINK CREATING AN EVENT PAGE WOULD BE THE EASIEST WAY OF DOING IT...
'EVERYONE... IS... INVITED... TO... TIMMY'S... BIRTHDAY... PARTY... AT... 10 A.M. TOMORROW... AT... 53... RAILWAY... STREET... FULCHESTER...
TAP! TAP! TAPPITY! TAP!
NO!
...I'LL JUST PRESS ENTER TO UPDATE IT...
OH, PLEASE, TIMMY, MY LOVE! YOU DON'T KNOW THEM... THEY MIGHT NOT BE WHO THEY SAY...
...AND YOU DON'T KNOW WHAT THEY'LL BRING WITH THEM OR WHAT THEY'LL DO WHEN THEY GET HERE AND YOU HEAR SUCH TERRIBLE THINGS AND...
CLICK!!
YOU'D BETTER START GETTING THINGS READY.
NEXT DAY...
WELL, IF YOU'D TURNED AWAY ANYONE WHO DIDN'T BRING ME A PRESENT, NONE OF THIS WOULD HAVE HAPPENED, WOMAN.
I'M SORRY, TIMMY
HAPPY BIRTHDAY TIMMY
POLICE
POLICE INCIDENT
POLICE
POLICE
53
POLICE

Burrell: "I want to be Kate Middleton's 'Rock'"

Royal butler pledges loyalty to new Princess

EXCLUSIVE!

VALET OF THE DIANA-SAUCE: Pushy Burrell yesterday and (inset) Kate Middleton - who he hopes to butle for.

PRINCESS DIANA'S former butler Paul Burrell has revealed that he may return to Britain and reprise his role as official butler to a princess. And this time he's offering his services to Prince William's fiancée, KATE MIDDLETON.

After the Princess of Hearts's death, disgraced Burrell moved to the United States to begin a new career in the lucrative Lady Di memorabilia market. But the recent downturn in the economy coupled with his running out of tat rescued from Diana's London home has seen the former butler fall on hard times. And he now believes the time is right for his return to Britain.

flat

In an emotional phone call from his luxury one-roomed flat in Harlem, Diana's official rock™ denied that money was at the root of his decision to return home. Wiping away tears, he told the *News of the World*: "Diana trusted me. She confided in me in good times and bad. And I can see so much of her in her future daughter-in-law, Kate."

"It's going to be so difficult for Kate to adjust to her new life as a Royal Princess, and I want to be there for her every step of the way, like I was there for her late future mother-in-law," he continued.

"I was Diana's rock™. And now I want to be Kate's rock ™."

Burrell admitted that in doing a flit after Diana's death with a car boot full of her dresses, jewellery and pubes collected from her shower tray, he may have blotted his copybook. But he insisted he wanted to make it up to the royals and get back on good terms with them. And he believes that offering to be Ms. Middleton's personal confidante is the way forward.

treasure

"I'm not saying there will be any marital problems for Kate in the future, but if there are, I want to be there for her," he told reporters. "You don't know what life can throw at you these days."

"I know they say lightning doesn't strike twice, but if it did I would be there for Kate or her boys when she has them. An ear to listen, a shoulder to cry on," he added.

And Burrell added that he would do the job without pay!

"I feel so strongly about wanting to protect Kate, that I would be her rock™ and ask nothing in return," he told reporters. "Of course, If she wanted to show her gratitude by giving me little trinkets, keepsakes or what have you, shoes and dresses that she didn't want anymore, or pubes, then naturally I would accept them," he said.

St Edmunds

"And if she gave me lots of signed photographs of herself, but not putting 'To Paul' on them, just leaving the dedication open, then I would be honoured," he added.

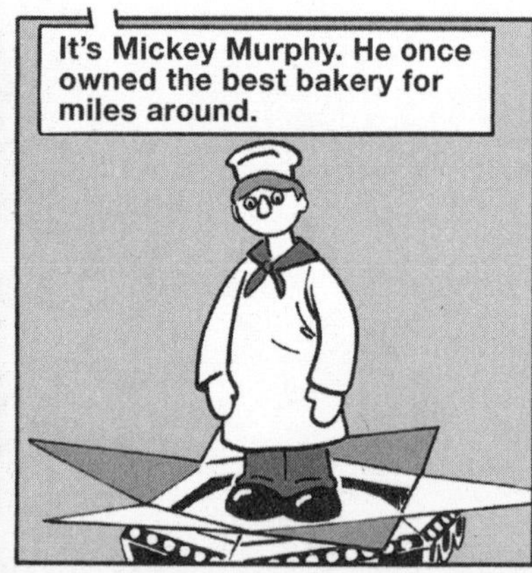

It's Mickey Murphy. He once owned the best bakery for miles around.

In 2006 a branch of Greggs opened just across the way.
GREGGS

Within two years Mickey had been driven out of business.
To Let
Bakery
Property To Let

When a job came up at Greggs Mickey thought: 'Sod it, why not?'
GREGGS
STAFF
WANTED
Apply Within

Now, instead of preparing fresh bread, cakes and pies, he just loads frozen stuff into an oven.

All his old customers queue up every day for fatty treats.

Mickey serves them politely but, deep down, never really forgave them for deserting his bakery. Most days, truth be told, he is just glad to get back into the music box. Goodbye Mickey...

BLAM! BLAM!
EIGHT! EIGHT! FUCKIN' WEK UP!
GROAN

J-JJESUSS... ME F-FFUCKIN' 'EAD... WORRISIT, LUV? WOT D'YER F-FFUCKIN' WANT?
IT'S YER DECORATIONS ON YERSHED, EIGHT.
WOT ABAHT 'EM? WOT'S UP WI' 'EM?

Y'WANT TER TEK 'EM DAHN, EIGHT. IT'S TWELFTH FUCKIN' NEYT.
EH?!

YER SHUN'T LEAVE YER CHRISMUSS DECORATIONS UP AFTEH TWELFTH NEYT... IT'S BAD LUCK...
IS THAT REYT? BAD LUCK?! BAD F-FF-FFUCKIN' LUCK IS IT?

TELL ME 'OW MY F-FFUCKIN' LUCK COULD GET ANY F-FFUCKIN' WURSE! WOT COULD POSSIBLEH GO WRONG FOH ME WOT AN'T ALREADEH WENT F-FFUCKIN' WRONG..?
...YOO F-FFUCKIN' TELL ME THAT.

A'D BE BETTEH OFF F-FFUCKIN' DEDD! ...YER SEE THAT JIMMEH SAVILE...? A F-FFUCKIN' ENVEH 'IM, ME... 'E'S DEDD - BUT 'E'S STILL GORRA BETTEH F-FFUCKIN' LIFE THAN ME.
A'M JUSST SAYIN', EIGHT, THAT'S AALL. P'RAPS YER FUCKIN' FORTUNES MIGHT IMPROVE A BIT IF YER TOOK YER FUCKIN' DECORATIONS DAHN.

CRUMP!

CHRISTMAS WITH THE BACONS

ONE DAY...
REET! I'VE BEEN WRITIN' THIS YEAR'S ROOND ROBIN LETTAH F'T' SEND OOT WI' W' CHRISTMAS CARDS
READ THE FUCKA OOT THEN, FATHA
SLOO!

AHEM... 'ERE GANS...
DEAR AALL... WORRA YEAR OF MIXED FORTUNE IT HAS BEEN 'ERE IN THE BACON HOOSEHURLD...

...IN JANUARY, FATHA TOOK FORST PRIZE OF A MEAT PLATTAH IN A RAFFLE AT THE SORSHAL CLUB...
HEH! I REMEMBAH!
SLOO!
...WHILST IN JULY, MUTHA WON TEN POOND ON THE SCRATCHIES...

BUT THERE WUZ NEE SUCH LUCK F' POOR BIFFA, WHO IN DECEMBAH SUFFERED TWO BRUKKEN LEGS, A FRACTURED HEED, CRACKED RIBS AN' LOST AALL HIS FUCKIN' TEETH.
EH!?

WHAT!?!... I FUCKIN' NEVAH!
HOO, FATHA... THIS 'UN'S CAALLIN' YEE A FUCKIN' LIAR!
IS HE, NOO?

SMACK!
OOF!

STOMP! STOMP! STOMP! STOMP! STOMP! STOMP!

BOOT! CRACK! CRACK! CRACK! BOOT!

I THINK HE'S GORRA COUPLE O' TEETH LEFT, BUT APART FROM THAT, IT'S SPOT ON, FATHA

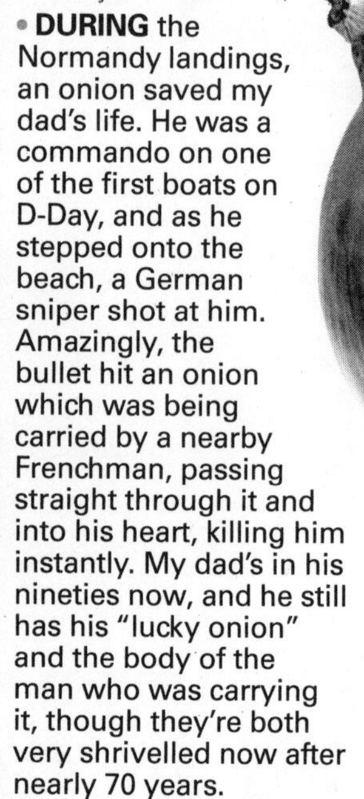

KNOW URE ONIONS

"Hi readers, short-arsed Scotch popster **MIDGE URE** here. You may know me best for being out of Ultravox and Band Aid, but here's something I bet you didn't know... I'm crazy about onions! That's right, I just can't get enough of these savoury edible bulbs. You may remember me crying in the video to my song Dancing with Tears in my Eyes, which reached number 3 in the Hit Parade. However, you may be surprised to learn that I wasn't crying because of an imminent nuclear holocaust, it was actually because I'd just been chopping up a really big onion for my dinner! Anyway, enough about me. Here's some of the best letters about onions I've received this week!"

Midge

• **DURING** the Normandy landings, an onion saved my dad's life. He was a commando on one of the first boats on D-Day, and as he stepped onto the beach, a German sniper shot at him. Amazingly, the bullet hit an onion which was being carried by a nearby Frenchman, passing straight through it and into his heart, killing him instantly. My dad's in his nineties now, and he still has his "lucky onion" and the body of the man who was carrying it, though they're both very shrivelled now after nearly 70 years.

Audrey Grenfell, Grantham

• **I COLLECT** onions, and every time I go to the supermarket I can't resist buying a few more. I've now got over 8,000 onions.

Frank Turvey, Garstang

• **I AM** a stage hypnotist, and I recently had an unusual booking to perform for the East Lancashire Onion Enthusiasts Society. As part of my act, I had to put a member of the audience into a trance, and make them eat a juicy apple whilst believing they were actually taking bites out of an onion. Something like that, anyway.

The Great Mysterio, Oldham

• **AFTER** spending many years as a consultant chiropodist, my husband changed careers and became a wholesale greengrocer, specialising in onions. Whenever he meets someone he quips that, whereas he used to work "eyeing bunions", he now spends his days "buying onions". Actually, I think he only took his new job so he could make that joke, and we've suffered a substantial cut in our income as a consequence. We've had to sell the house, and I now have to work three days a week cleaning toilets at the local greyhound track just to make ends meet. If I see any of my old neighbours from the nice area where we used to live, I have to cross the street as I'm too ashamed of my reduced circumstances to look them in the face.

Mrs Portmeirion, Ffestiniog

• **FROM** being a very small child I never liked onions, and would always leave them at the side of my plate. School dinner ladies would often try to make me eat them, but I would refuse, insisting that I didn't like them and that was that. When my mother cooked a meal, she would have to make a separate portion without onions, especially for me. Not the tiniest morsel of onion passed my lips for the best part of forty years until I got married, when my wife persuaded me to try a tiny bit of onion. She handed it to me on a fork and I tentatively took a taste, feeling certain I was going to hate it. Just as I expected, It tasted foul, and had a horrible slimy texture that made me heave.

Clixton Gyvill, Castleford

A medium-sized onion.

• **IT ALWAYS** makes me laugh when I hear football commentators refer to the goal as "the old onion bag". That's because me and my pals used to play football using a real life onion bag from the greengrocers as our net, stretched between two sticks of celery. Unfortunately, it was only about a foot wide, so nobody ever managed to score.

Frangis Marzipan, Port Sunlight

• **WHAT** a shame you don't get traditional, old-fashioned French onion sellers any more. With their berets, moustaches, bicycles and stripey jerseys, their weekly visits really used to brighten up my life. I'd always buy a few onions from them, whether I needed them or not, and then invite them inside for a nice cup of tea and a fuck.

Irene Glans, Taintbridge

• **MY LUCKY** food has always been onions. In last year's Grand National, I decided to bet £500 (an "onion" in cockney parlance) on a horse called Onion Ladder being ridden by a jockey called Spring O'Nion. Unfortunately, the horse fell at the first fence and had to be shot.

Lance Boyle, Rampton

• **I WEAR** a slice of onion round my wrist on an elastic band. Now, if anyone asks me for the time, I can tell them: "It's onion o'clock!"

Quentin Quavers, Cheese

• **I CRY** whenever I chop onions, but it's not the smell. I'm just remembering all the happy times I had with my late husband who died in tragic circumstances.

Ryvita Orotund, Gifwick

• **I THINK** there should be more scenes about onions in movies. For example, imagine how much better *Cool Hand Luke* would have been if Paul Newman had been in an onion eating contest instead of a hard-boiled egg one, or if *Dirty Harry* had thrown onions at the baddies instead of shooting them with a .44 Magnum. I also think *Star Wars* would have been better with a Death Onion instead of a Death Star.

M Commode, Brighton

• **MY LATE** wife had two glass eyes, and would often amaze visitors by chopping onions without crying. Imagine their surprise at the end of the evening when she finally revealed her little secret!

Ernest Truss, Feltcham

ONION Poetry Corner

THERE once was
a man with some
onions,
Who walked around
till he got bunions.
He got in his car,
But he didn't get far,
Because it had got
broken trunnions.

A Motion, London

O is for Often -
that's when I eat
them
N is for Never -
that's when you can
beat them
I is for Inside
they've got many
layers
O is for On
sale from veggie
purveyors
N is for Now it is
time for my tea
S is for Save a few
onions for me!

Carol Anne Duffy, London

Would you believe it about ONIONS!

YOU may not recognise the name Syd Onion, but you will when I tell you that he and fellow comic Eddie Cheese changed their names to Little and Large before rocketing to TV stardom in the 1970s and 80s!

EVERYONE knows that Draculas are repelled by garlic, but did you know that Frankensteins are allergic to onions?

WHEN the Apollo astronauts flew to the Moon, they were amazed to discover that, instead of becoming weightless in the vacuum of the lunar surface, onions in fact became ten times heavier than they were on earth. After the mission, NASA boffins were baffled when they cut the onions open to discover that they had changed into strawberries!

THE smallest onion in the world was chopped up by the world's shortest man Calvin Phillips whilst making a salad. When chopping the tiny vegetable, which was no bigger than a grain of sand, Phillips cried tears which were only visible under a microscope, and blew his nose on a handkerchief the size of a postage stamp.

ONIONS have been the subject of countless songs, such as *The Onion Song* by Marvin Gaye & Tammi Terrell and many more.

THANKS to an ancient tradition dating back to the final salad eaten by Thomas a Beckett before his death, Archbishops of Canterbury don't eat onions in case it brings bad luck. Upon his succession in 2003, the current incumbent Dr Rowan Williams decided to bring centuries of superstition to an end by eating a big bowl of fried onions at his investiture tea. However, the following week he started suffering from erectile dysfunction.

ONION is the only vegetable whose name is a palindrome, that is, it reads exactly the same forwards or backwards!

ASK A French person what they think of onions, and you will be greeted with a blank expression. That's because the French word for onions is "les oignons", which literally means "the onions".

ONION Top Tips

DON'T throw away old tennis balls. Cut in two, they can be used to store onions. Arrange them on Yorkshire puddings or an old dimpled radiator lying on its side to stop them falling over.
R Impone, Borth

RUN out of small leeks? Simply use spring onions. Or if you're making a salad and you run out of big spring onions, substitute normal-sized leeks.
R Impleach, Cyprus

USE the papery layer of skin off an onion to wrap up any Amoretti biscuits which may have accidentally come unwrapped for any reason.
Irene Pyrene, Goole

BOIL a white T-shirt in a pan filled with 4 pints of water and a dozen large, diced, red onions to make it smell of onions.
Fontella Basterd, Leverhulme

WHEN preparing food, get rid of the smell of onions by rubbing your hands on a dog dirt.
Mad Alice, Hexham

MAYORS. A string of onions sprayed gold makes an excellent substitute chain of office when yours is at the menders or stolen.
J Greenhalgh, Blackpool

AN ONION balanced on top of the cardboard tube from a roll of bathroom tissue makes an excellent tower when building a 1/200th scale model of a Russian Orthodox Cathedral.
Jissum Drupe, York

STORE valuables inside a hollowed-out onion. The bottom of the vegetable drawer in your fridge is the last place thieves will think of looking for your expensive trinkets.
Cilla Grubbins, Towcester

3MM SLICES of Spring onion with the middle bits pushed out make great "savoury Polos" for people who don't like the taste of mint but do like the taste of spring onion.
Spartacus Worms, Hereford

PROTECT your spectacles from dust when left on your bedside table overnight by cutting an onion in two and popping a half onto each lens. The onion juice can be wiped off in the morning with a soft cloth.
Lord Bragg of Wigton, London

KIDS bored on long car journeys? A pair of onions threaded onto an old pair of shoelaces makes a smashing set of "clackers" to keep them happily occupied for hours and hours.
Trampus Methley, Barnton

Your ONION Jokes

Q: *What sort of sandwiches make Winnie the Pooh cry?*
A: The ones with honey on (onion).
Winifred Tenalady, Ilfracombe

I say, I say, I say! Did you know that Shakespeare once wrote a play about a bunch of happy onions who go for a day-trip to Berkshire?
- What was it called?
The Merry Chives of Windsor!
Jimmy Carr, London

Knock Knock.
- Who's there?
Onion.
- Onion who?
Onion in? I'm here to read the meter. (Anyone in? I'm here to read the meter.)
Winifred Tenalady, Ilfracombe

Q: *What do you call a small onion?*
A: "Chive" no idea!
Tim Vine, Edinburgh

Mummy, can I have some more of this onion, please?
- No, that's shallot (that's your lot).
Winifred Tenalady, Ilfracombe

Sender: Basil, Leeds

Sender: Dave, Aberdeen

YUKON DUKE
DOG-SLEDDING CHAMPION OF THE FROZEN NORTH
and his longtime girlfriend Megan

YAAAAA! FASTER! MUSH! MUSH!!!
FOOSHH!!
JUST ANOTHER SIX DAYS TO NOME!!!

DID YOU SET THE VIDEO TO RECORD HOMES UNDER THE HAMMER?
SORRY, I FORGOT – I'M KIND OF BUSY MAKING A PERILOUS 1800 KM SOJOURN ACROSS THE BARREN SUBZERO WASTELAND OF THE ARCTIC TUNDRA.

NO, THAT'S FINE. FUNNY HOW IT'S NEVER YOUR PROGRAMMES THAT DON'T GET RECORDED.
YOU CAN JUST GO TO iPLAYER.
I DON'T LIKE WATCHING THINGS ON THE COMPUTER.
GUHHH

AND THERE'S NO NEED TO SOUND LIKE YOU'RE DYING. GIVING ME A LIFT AS FAR AS THE HAIRDRESSERS ISN'T THE END OF THE BLOODY WORLD.
IT'S NOT LIKE I DON'T DO THINGS FOR YOU.
WHTCHHHH!
MUTTER...
HYAA! MUSH!!

WHA – OMIGOD! STOP! STOP!!!
WAAAA!!! WHAT? WHAT?!?
SKREEE!!!

DID A HARNESS STRAP BREAK? DID ONE OF THE RUNNERS CRACK?!?
WHAT ARE YOU DOING TO THOSE POOR LITTLE DOGGIES!!!

HOW WOULD YOU LIKE IT IF SOMEBODY HIT YOU WITH A WHIP? EH?
COME HERE SNOOGUMS, IT'S ALL RIGHT – MUMMY WON'T LET THE BAD MAN HURT YOU.

FOR GOD'S SAKE... NOBODY'S HURTING THEM. THEY'RE SLED DOGS – THIS IS THEIR WORK.
WELL UNLIKE YOU SOME PEOPLE THINK ABOUT MORE THAN JUST WORK! DON'T YOU! YEAAAH!
UNTIE THEM SO THEY CAN PLAY FOR A BIT.

WHAT?! NO! WE'RE IN THE MIDDLE OF ALASKA! IF YOU LET THEM LOOSE THEY'LL JUST RUN AWAY AND WE'LL BE STRANDED HERE IN -40° TEMPERATURES, HUNDREDS OF KILOMETERS FROM THE NEAREST FOOD OR SHELTER!
OH DON'T EXAGGERATE.

IT'LL ONLY BE FOR FIVE MINUTES AND THEY'LL COME RIGHT BACK.
WHAT, YOU THINK THEY'LL JUST MAGICALLY COME BACK IN FIVE MINUTES?!
THEY KNOW HOW LONG FIVE MINUTES IS. DOGS ARE VERY INTELLIGENT.
WHAT?!? WHERE ARE YOU GETTING THIS FIVE MINUTES FROM? YOU'RE JUST PULLING THAT OUT OF YOUR ARSE!
HERE WE GO. ONCE AGAIN YOU'RE RIGHT AND I'M WRONG.
WELL, YES! YOU ARE WRONG! THE THING YOU'RE SAYING IS FACTUALLY NOT TRUE!
SO I'M LYING AM I?
NO, YOU JUST DON'T UNDERSTAND HOW–
OH, SO I'M STUPID! THANK YOU, THAT'S SO MUCH BETTER!

WELL WHICH IS IT... ARE YOU SAYING I'M STUPID OR A LIAR?
I'M SAYING THAT RELEASING THOSE DOGS WOULD BE A SUICIDAL ACT DOOMING US TO CERTAIN DEATH FROM HYPOTHERMIA BY NIGHTFALL!
YOU CAN'T JUST BE SUPPORTIVE CAN YOU. GOD FORBID YOU TAKE MY SIDE JUST ONCE.

BUT NO, SOON AS I OPEN MY MOUTH YOU HAVE TO JUMP IN AND PROVE ME WRONG, JUST LIKE AT JANICE AND CHRIS'S PARTY! YOU'VE GOT TO PUT ME DOWN IN FRONT OF EVERYONE!
THIS IS INSANE–
OH, SO NOW I'M CRAZY!!

WHEREAS HAVING LITTLE TOY DOCTOR WHOS ALL OVER YOUR BEDROOM – THAT'S JUST NORMAL!!
IT'S BETTER THAN EIGHT HUNDRED PAIRS OF BLOODY SHOES I NEVER EVEN WEAR!!!
WELL AT LEAST I DIDN'T SPEND A WHOLE EVENING TALKING TO SUE MACKIE!!!
NO! NO! I AM NOT HAVING THIS CONVERSATION!
COURSE NOT – 'COS I'M NOT EVEN WORTH FIVE MINUTES AM I!
I SAID NO!!!!
HOHH! I CAN'T BELIEVE YOU JUST SAID I'M NOT WORTH IT!!!
EH?!? DON'T YOU DARE!! YOU KNOW WHAT I BLOODY MEANT!!!

IT'S JUST TWO CYBERMEN AND A MORBIUS – AND WHAT ABOUT YOUR BLOODY MAGAZINES!!!
DON'T EVEN TALK TO ME.

MOTD Jimmy forging new career as rockney bassist

Hill 'Tipped to be New Dave'

BIG-CHINNED football pundit JIMMY HILL confirmed last night that he has signed up to join a re-formed CHAS & DAVE... *as the new Dave!*

The original Dave retired last year after more than three decades with the cockney knees-up band.

bass

Ex-Fulham journeyman Hill, 83, has already bought himself a guitar and signed up for a crash course in bass-playing from former Level 42 frontman Mark King.

"I'm really looking forward to going on tour with Chas and the man in little round glasses who plays the drums," Hill told his local paper *The Hurstpierpoint Prepuce*. "I can't wait to get up on stage and play all the old hits such as Gertcha, Rabbit and the Sideboard Song."

shanty

"I've already been down to Somerset House and changed my name by deed poll to Dave," added Jimmy.

Meanwhile, Hill's wife Ada has been trimming the collars off his shirts and cutting the sleeves off his jackets to turn them into waistcoats.

Hill is not the first *Match of the Day* presenter to embark on a musical career. In 1968, anchorman Kenneth Wolstenholme changed his name to Mary in order to join folk act Peter, Paul and Mary. Wolstenholme sang lead vocals in the band during a six-week residency at Batley Variety Club, while his namesake took maternity leave.

PLUCKING HILL: MOTD Jimmy set to take up bass guitar.

Garnish herb 'doubles penis length in a week,' says parsley farmer

Pass the Parsley!

A SPRIG of parsley taken with each meal will double the size of a fella's manhood in just seven days, according to a new study.

Male Garnish: Parsley packs inches on manhood, says Kepwick.

Parsley farmer Kepwick Cowesby measured his pet mouse's penis before and after adding the herb to its diet for a week, and discovered that it had grown from 2mm to 4mm long ... a whopping increase of 200%!

"If it does it for mice, it'll do it for men," Cowesby told us from his 10,000 acre Lincolnshire parsley farm. "And if it doubles your endowment in a week, just imagine what it'll do to it in a fortnight!"

roof

Now he expects demand for his produce to go through the roof as blokes clamour to take advantage of its genital-enlarging properties. He told us: "I may have to put my prices up to meet demand."

However, the study's conclusions have been met with criticism in the scientific community. Influential blogger Dr Ben Goldacre has condemned Cowesby's experimental technique as deeply flawed. He told us: "He should have used a double blind trial, with another, non-parsley-fed mouse as a control to eliminate the chance of a false positive result."

hat

"Also, it's possible he might of inadvertently skewed his results by pushing the ruler a bit further in when taking the second measurement," Goldacre continued.

"Or the mouse might of been on the bonk," he added.

NEXT DOOR'S SEXY GERBIL

THUD!

Cod Knob Pie.......

(Preparation time: 30 minutes)

INGREDIENTS

3lbs (250g) of cod penises
5 carrots (20 carrots if small)
3 pints (15ml) gravy
4lbs (10kg) pastry
3 dozen eggs

Put the cod knobs in a hot pan and move them about with a flat wooden spoon thing until they start to go a bit brown.

Meanwhile, put some flour on the table and roll out your pastry till it goes flat. If it doesn't go flat at first, put more flour on the table. When it's ready, push your pastry inside a cooking pot and carefully cut off the extra bits that flop over the side.

Now add your cod knobs, carrots, eggs and gravy, and put it into an oven for three hours.

Add salt, pepper and ketchup to taste. Delicious with mashed potatoes or pasta! Serves 2.

NEXT WEEK: *Crab Fanny Flan*

Sending a Turd to the Queen

WE'VE all sent a turd to the Queen. Posting a motion to Buckingham Palace is as much a part of British life as fish & chips, double decker buses and Test Match Special.

But have you ever stopped to wonder how your carefully packaged stool makes its way from your bathroom to her majesty's breakfast table?

Let's follow the journey of a single envelope of excrement as it travels across the country to be delivered into the monarch's hands.

8.30am Mr Smith has curled off a fine length of copper cable into a stout manila envelope. He has addressed it to the Queen at Buckingham Palace, using the correct postcode to ensure it arrives at its proper destination with the minimum of delay.

9.30am After breakfast, Mr Smith makes his way to his local post office. At the counter, the post-mistress weighs his package. The cost of sending turds through the postal system is calculated according to weight. If Mr Smith doesn't put sufficient stamps on his envelope, the Queen may be asked to make up the difference. Once the stamps are safely stuck on, Mr Smith pops it into the pillar box on the High Street.

12.30pm The pillar box is emptied three times every day. The letters, cards and packages inside are loaded into a van and taken to the sorting office.

1.30pm The local sorting office handles all the post for the region. Incoming and outgoing mail is sorted according to its destination. Whether it's Mr Smith's bowel movement heading for Buckingham Palace, a jiffy bag of diarrhoea bound for Crinkly Bottom or a parcel of dog foulage for Bono, it's all got to be consigned to its correct destination quickly and efficiently.

11.00pm Mail intended for the capital is sent by road, by air and by rail. Because the sorting office is near a main-line, Mr Smith's feeshus is put on the night train to London, where it will arrive in just a few hours.

2.30pm To save time, workers travel on the train as it speeds towards the capital, going through the mailbags and putting the letters and parcels into pigeonholes, ready to be delivered first thing in the morning.

6.30am A mere twenty-two hours after it was laid nearly three hundred miles away, the Richard the Third has nearly reached its final destination. The cheery London postman has picked it up in his bag from the station. Now he is weaving his way through the streets of the capital on his bicycle, heading for the first call on his round - Buckingham Palace.
TAXI

7.30am The envelope finally arrives in the royal quarters, where the Queen opens it using her butter knife. As she recoils in disgust from Mr Smith's bum cigar, little does her majesty pause to think about all the people who worked together to deliver it to her breakfast table.

NEXT WEEK: From Chef's Testicles to Tureen - the Story of Michael Winner's Soup.

Gok gives wires makeover

Frock guru announces new plug rules

THE government yesterday announced the latest regulations for mains electrical wiring. TV fashionista GOK WAN has chosen the stylish new palette of wiring hues, opting for a stylish set of modern pastel colours to replace the old scheme.

The latest changes have been brought in because it was thought the existing format was becoming stale and old-fashioned.

"The colour coding rules for wires in plugs hadn't been changed since 2006," said OffCable chairman Sir Frank Somebody.

TINTS

"It was time to ring the changes and embrace the new decade with a refreshing new trio of wiring tints."

"Gok was the right person to take on the task, because he's a bright spark and has a reputation for being good with colours," he added.

- ***OUT go boring, old-fashioned brown live, blue neutral and green & yellow earth.***
- ***IN come Cerise with a hint of magenta, heliotrope and peachy cream.***

At a packed press conference, Wan explained how he came to choose each of the new hues:

NOTCHR

"I looked inside a plug and I simply couldn't believe how the old colours clashed. They didn't complement one another at all," he said.

"I just looked at them, and I was like, 'No way, you've gotta go girl'," he added.

The new system was welcomed by Electricians' Union boss Derek Simpson. "My members think these new shades are to die for," he told the TUC Congress at Blackpool. "They're gorgeous. They're too, too divine."

BUTFR

The new standards come into force at midnight on June 1st. Householders will then have one month to strip out all existing wiring in their homes and replace it with three-core cable in the new colours.

MINCE CABLE: Flambouyant Gok has jazzed up plugs.

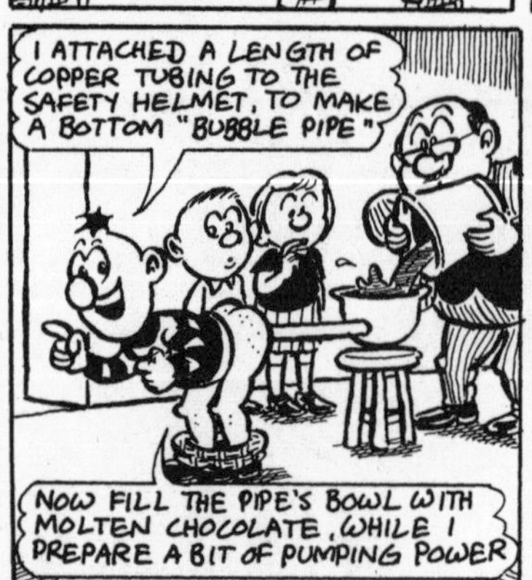

WINSTON CHURCHILL IN "HIS DARKEST HOUR"

1939
MR CHURCHILL, THE KING IS GOING TO MAKE HIS FAMOUS SPEECH TODAY, IN ORDER TO INSPIRE AND UNITE THE NATION AS WE ENTER INTO WAR.
WAR OFFICE
THE TIMES BRITAIN AT WAR WITH GERMANY
HE HAS REQUESTED THAT YOU, AS BRITAIN'S GREATEST ORATOR, SHOULD HELP HIM PREPARE HIS HISTORIC ADDRESS.

MWRAH! TELL HIS MAJESTY I SHALL COME TO THE PALACE FORTHWITH!
BLOYK GURGLE!
BRITAIN AT WAR WITH GERMANY
OOH, MY BELLY! THAT ROAST BEEF DINNER I HAD AT LUNCHTIME IS WEIGHING HEAVILY ON ME!

I'LL JUST NIP INTO THE PARLIAMENTARY LAVVY FOR A QUICK SHIT BEFORE I GO TO BUCKINGHAM PALACE
I CAN'T CONCENTRATE ON HELPING THE KING PREPARE HIS SPEECH IF I'M BUSTING FOR A CRAP!

OH DRAT! THE BOG IS OCCUPIED BY THE PRIME MINISTER NEVILLE CHAMBERLAIN

I HAVE IN MY HAND A PIECE OF PAPER...

HE'S BEEN IN THERE EVER SINCE HE ATE THAT DODGY BRATWURST IN MUNICH

MWRAH! WHY IS THERE NEVER A PUBLIC LOO AROUND WHEN YOU NEED ONE?
HOUSES OF PARLIAMENT
I'M CARRYING A DREADNOUGHT BIG ENOUGH TO SINK THE ENTIRE GERMAN U-BOAT FLEET!

THERE'S NOTHING ELSE FOR IT... MWRAH! WE WILL SHITE ON THE BEACHES!
BEACH
THERE'LL BE PLENTY OF SAND-DUNES DOWN HERE WHERE I CAN DISCREETLY UNLOAD MY BUM CIGAR

RIGHT, KNICKERS DOWN AND STAND BY FOR A D-DAY LANDING
MWRAH! ENGLAND EXPECTS EVERY MAN TO DO A GREAT BIG DUTY!

OI, NAPOLEON! YOU CAN'T DEFECATE THERE!
B-BUT THE PATROL SCOUT HAS ALREADY POKED HIS NOSE OUT OF THE FOXHOLE!

YER, WELL IF YOU DROP A LOG ONTO THAT WASHED-UP MINE, IT'LL BLOW YOUR RUDDY FOX'OLE TO KINGDOM COME!
CRIKEY!

OOH ME POOR GUTS! I HAD TO ORDER THE TROOPS TO MAKE A TACTICAL RETREAT!
MWRAH! NEVAH, IN THE FIELD OF ANAL CONFLICT, HAS SO MUCH DISCOMFORT BEEN OWED TO SUCH A MASSIVE POO!

I'LL JUST HAVE TO TRY AND MAKE IT TO BUCKINGHAM PALACE AND USE THE SHITTER THERE
BUCKINGHAM PALACE ½ MILE
WADDLE
I ONLY HOPE I GET THERE BEFORE I DROP A DEPTH CHARGE IN MY PANTS!

AND
THERE YOU ARE, CHURCHILL! I HAVE TO DELIVER MY SPEECH TO THE NATION IN A MINUTE! PERHAPS YOU CAN JUST HELP ME WITH...
BUCKINGHAM PALACE
QUACK!
NOT NOW, YOUR MAJESTY! THE BOMB BAY DOORS ARE OPEN!

THANK GOODNESS! HERE'S THE KING'S KHAZI!
HRH WC
MWRAH! I HAVE NOTHING TO OFFER BUT BLOOD, SWEAT, TEARS AND AN ENORMOUS BOWEL MOVEMENT

OH NO! THE KING'S ELDER BROTHER EDWARD VIII MUST'VE ABDICATED WITH THE THRONE!
I.O.U 1 CLUDGY toodle pip! Eddie x
WHEN HE LEFT ENGLAND IN 1936 TO MARRY MRS SIMPSON, HE TOOK THE ROYAL CHODBIN WITH HIM!

WELL I CAN'T HOLD IT IN ANY LONGER – I'VE GOT NO CHOICE...
I.O.U 1 CLUDGY toodle pip! Eddie x
I'M JUST GOING TO HAVE TO SHIT OUT OF THAT WINDOW, AND HOPE THAT NOONE NOTICES!

MWRAH! THIS IS SO UNDIGNIFIED!
IF MY REPUTATION SHOULD LAST A THOUSAND YEARS, MEN WILL STILL SAY, "THIS WAS NOT HIS FINEST HOUR"!

OUTSIDE
HUSH EVERYONE! THE KING IS ABOUT TO MAKE HIS HISTORIC SPEECH!
A-HEM!

"IN THIS GRAVE HOUR, PERHAPS THE MOST FATEFUL IN ALL OUR HISTORY..."
"..I SEND TO EVERY HOUSEHOLD OF MY PEOPLES, BOTH AT HOME AND OVERSEAS, THIS MESSAGE.."

PTTHHTTB BTHTTHP
AHHHH! WHAT A RELIEF!
GOD HELP ANYONE WHO GOT CAUGHT IN THE CROSSFIRE OF THAT LOT!

MWRAH! OH, BUGGER.
SHITTY STENCH

COCKNEY WANKER
TICK-EEETS!.. TICK-EEETS!
GERCHA LANDAN 2012 OLYMPIC TICKETS 'ERE
WOTCHA
'AVE Y' GOT A CAPPLE O' TICKETS FER THE MENS ONE 'ANDRED METRES FINAL, 'AVE YER?
LET'S 'AVE A BUTCHERS...
GAW! YOU LACKY BARSTARD... YOU'VE GOT THE LARST TWO IN THE STADIUM...
KNOCKAAHT!
OLYMPIC 2012 TICKETS OFFICIAL VENDOR ALL SEATS ALL VENUES NO VISA
...'ERE... AN' THEY'RE RIGHT ON THE FACKIN' TAPE AN' ALL... WOULD YOU ADAM AN' EVE IT?
LAVERLY JABBERLY
THERE YOU GO... BEST SEATS IN THE CAT AN' MOUSE. TWENTY BILLY THE KID T' YOU
FANKS
DON'T YOU BLINK, NAH.. THEY GO LARK SHIT OFF A FACKIN' SHAVVEL THEM JAMAICANS
TICK-EEETS! GERCHA 2012 BAILS AN' WICKETS! AFLETICS... GYMNARSTICS... CYCLIN...
OLYMPIC 2012 TICKETS OFFICIAL VENDOR ALL SEATS ALL VENUES NO VISA
...COFFIN' AN' CARSKET-BALL
ALL VENUES. ALL SEATS. BEST PRICES FROM THE MAN YOU CAN TRAST
ORWIGHT?
DON'T 'SPOSE YOU'VE GOT ANY TICKETS FER THE MENS 'ANDRED METRES FINAL, 'AVE YAH!?
LET'S 'AVE A BUTCHERS
GAW, YOU LACKY BARSTARD. YOU'VE GOT THE LARST TWO IN THE STADIUM...
KNOCKAAHT!
...RIGHT ON THE TAPE
TWENTY LOST AN' FAAAHND T' YOU, ME OLD CHINAH!
YOU SURE THESE IS LEGIT, IS YAH?
YER! ONE 'ANDRED PERCENT COPPER-BOTTOMED STRAIGHT-AP KOSHER
YER?
YER! CAM ON...
...DO AR LOOK LARK AR'D FACKIN' TURK YER, SQUIRE, EH?
NAH!.. ONLY AR 'ERD YOU COULD ONLY GET THESE OFF THE NET
WELL, YOU 'ERD FACKIN' WRONG THEN, DINCHAH?
THESE TICKETS IS GENUINE OLYMPIC SURPLASS STOCK
YOU SURE? THEY LOOK LARK FACKIN' WAFFLE TICKETS T'ME
NAH! LOOK... SEE THEM PERFORATIONS THERE...
YER
WELL, THAT'S A 'OLOGRAM, THAT IS. ...YER GUARANTEE OF GENUINE-OSITY
ORWIGHT! 'AR'L 'AVE 'EM...
DO YER TAKE VISA?
VISA?!...
FACK OFF!!!
IT'S CROSBY, STILLS AN' NASH ONLY!
FACKIN' VISAH!... NAH IF YOU DON'T WANT 'EM CHIEF, THERE'S FAAAHSANDS WOT DO, ORWIGHT!
NAH... AR WANT 'EM, AR DO
THERE YOU GO, SQUIRE. TWENTY KNICK-AH
FANK YOU VERY SCREAMIN LORD SUTCH
TICK-EEETS! OLYMPIC 2012 TICKETS! GET 'EM WHILE AR'VE GOT 'EM...
BADMINTON... FOOTBALL... 'OCKEY... 'ORSE JAMPIN'... FOUR MAN BOBSLEIGH...
'ERE...

...WOT'S GOIN' ON, THEN? YOU GOT A PERMIT T'TRADE IN THE SQUARE, 'AVE YAH?
EH?.. COURSE AR 'AVE
YER?.. LET'S 'AVE A LOOK, THEN
ORWIGHT
OLYMPIC 2012
NO VISA
...'ANG ON...
PAT! PAT! PAT! PAT!
...GAWD LAV A DACK! IT'S BEEN NICKED!
FANK GAWD YOU'RE 'ERE OFFICE-AH!
AR'D LARK TO REPAWT A FEFT!
DO WOT? YOU MAST FINK AR'M A FACKIN' IDIOT OR SAMFINK!
NAH!.. 'ONEST...
...SAM CANT'S 'AD IT AWAY WIV ME 'ERMAN'S 'ERMIT
COURSE THEY 'AVE... AN AR'M THE FACKIN'... CALIPH OF FACKIN'... BAGHDAD OR... FACKIN' SAMWHERE, IN'T AR?
NAR S'ELLIN' TICKETS IN THE SQUARE WIV-'AAHT A PERMIT IS AGAINST THE LAW-AH, INNIT?
AR DUNNO, DO AR?
WELL IT IS! AN' MR. BORIS IS GETTIN' FACKED OFF WIV TOUTIN' LITTLE TOE RAGS LARK YOU MAR SAN.
IS HE?
YER, HE FACKIN' IS!
GOIN' T' COST YOU A CAPPLE O' FAAHSAND PAAAHND IN FINES, THIS
FACK ME
YER!...
COURSE... IF YOU WAS TO BUY A CAPPLE O' TICKETS FER THE POLICEMAN'S BALL, AR FINK AR COULD LOOK THE AVVA WAY
SIGH!.. 'OW MATCH?
SAY... TWENTY 'ORSE AN' 'OUND
ME LARST TWO TICKETS THEY WERE, YOU LACKY BARSTARD
HUR! HUR! HUR!
FACKIN' ROBDOG
TICK-EEETS! GERCHA OLYMPIC 2012 TICKETS 'ERE! TICK-EEETS!
'ELLO MAR DARLINS! WOT CAN AR DO YOU FOR?
OLYMPIC 2012 TICKETS OFFICIAL VENDOR ALL SEATS ALL VENUES NO VISA
HOWDY, SIR. DO YOU HAVE TWO TICKETS FOR THE O-LYMPIC GAMES OPENING CEREMON-EE?
WE'D JUST ADORE SEEING THAT, WOULDN'T WE, HERB?
WE SURE WOULD, HONEY BUNNY
'S 'AVE A LOOK...
GAW! YOU LACKY BARSTARDS... THESE ARE THE LARST TWO!
WHY, THAT'S SWELL... ARE THEY GOOD SEATS?
GOOD SEATS..?!
...THEY'RE ONLY IN THE BLADDY ROYAL BOX, IN'T THEY... RIGHT NEXT TO 'ER MAJESTY THE QUEEN, GAWD BLESSAH!
OH, MY WORD... DID YOU HEAR THAT, HERB?.. WE'RE GOING TO SIT NEXT TO THE ENGLISH QUEEN OF GREAT BRITAIN
GEE WHIZ!
COURSE... SEATS LARK THESE DON'T CAM CHEAP
SURE, BUDDY. HOW MUCH?
FIRTY PAAHND... EACH.
OKAY... LET ME SEE... I'M NOT SURE WHICH IS WHICH WITH THIS BRITISH MONEY... GEE!
WELL, THESE PURPLE ONES IS TWOS... SEE... GOT A LITTLE '2' ON 'EM...
...SO IF 'AR TAKE FIRTY OF 'EM... THAT'S SIXTY QUID, INNIT, AN' WE'RE ALL BURKE AN' HARE
I GUESS
'AVE A NARCE DAY, NAAAH!
27TH JULY, 2012...
GO ON, HERB... SAY SOMETHING.
LEAVE IT TO ME, HONEY BUNNY...
LONDON 2012
ER
PARDON ME, LADY...
...I THINK YOU'LL FIND THAT THOSE ARE OUR SEATS... SO C'MON... SHIFT YOUR ASS.

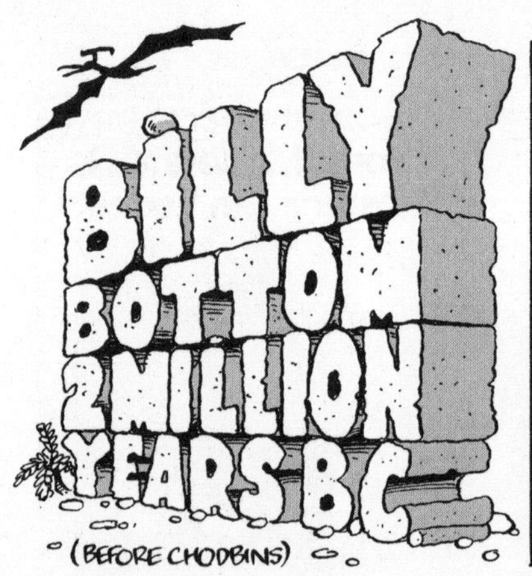
BILLY BOTTOM 2 MILLION YEARS B.C.
(BEFORE CHODBINS)

EEH! I'VE JUST 'AD FIVE SCRAMBLED BRONTOSAURUS EGGS FOR ME BREAKFAST...

...I'D BEST GO AN' PARK THE BUGGERS BEFORE I GET EGG BOUND GOOD AN' PROPER.

OOOH... SMASHIN'...
...'ERE COMES THE PACE CAR...

KNOCK! KNOCK!
WHO THE FUCK'S THAT?

AYUP, BILLY... I'M JUST OFF TO HUNT A MAMMOTH... Y'AVEN'T GOT A FLINT SPEAR HEAD I COULD 'AVE A LEND OF, 'AVE YER?
NO, I BLOODY 'AVEN'T... AN' Y'VE INTERRUPTED ME SHITE!
AN' Y' NEVER GIVE BACK ME RUDIMENTARY CHOPPIN' TOOL Y' BORROWED, NEITHER

CHEEKY FUCKIN' BASTARD...
RIGHT! WHERE WAS I?

'ERE WE GO... IT'S ON THE SLIPWAY. HNNNNNNNNG!!...
...I NAME THIS SHIP...

EXCUSE ME, SIR!... CAN I HAVE A QUICK WORD?
EH!?!
...WOT THE FUCK!?

WOT IS IT, PAL? I'M TRYIN' T'AVE A SHIT
WE'RE IN THE AREA SPREADING THE NEWS ABOUT NEANDERTHALISM...
...AND WE WONDERED IF YOU HAVE EVER THOUGHT ABOUT BECOMING A NEANDERTHAL

NO, PAL... I'M 'APPY BEING A HOMO ERECTUS
OKAY... WELL PERHAPS WE COULD LEAVE YOU ONE OF OUR LEAFLETS
AYE. CHEERS!

JESUS... I CAN'T EVEN 'AVE A SHIT IN PEACE... WOT'S THE PREHISTORIC WORLD COMIN' TO?

'ERE WE GO... IT'S NOW OR NEVER... EYES DOWN FOR A FULL HOUSE.
BILLY! BILLY!

OH, FER FUCK'S SAKE!
SLAP!
I'M TRYIN' T' DROP A FUCKIN' BIG BRONZE AGE BOLT 'ERE... CHRIST!

NO TIME FOR THAT, BILLY... THE ICE AGE IS COMING... WE'VE GOT TO LEG IT TO WARMER CLIMES... RIGHT NOW!!
BOLLOCKS T' THAT...

...I'M NOT SHIFTIN' OFF THIS FUCKIN' POT TILL I'VE DROPPED THE KIDS OFF AT THE TAR PITS...

HNNNNG! GNNNG! CHRIST... I'M PROPER BOUND UP... THIS IS GOIN' T' TAKE FOREVER

2 MILLION YEARS LATER...
HOW FASCINATING... A STONE AGE DWELLING DEEP IN THE PERMAFROST
YES... AND LOOK AT THIS, PROFESSOR...
UNIVERSITY OF FULCHESTER
...THERE ARE THE REMAINS OF A PRIMITIVE HUMANOID PRESERVED WITHIN THE ICE.

TAP! TAP!
CRASH! TINKLE!!
COUGH!
GAG! CHRIST!

BLOODY 'ELL, THAT TOOK LONG ENOUGH... STILL, BETTER OUT THAN IN, EH?
...I'D GIVE IT TEN MINUTES IF I WERE YOU, PAL.
?

Heaven Terror Alert Level Raised

ARCH ENEMIES: Bishop Williams and heavenly foe Bin Laden.

ARCHBISHOP of Canterbury Dr Rowan Williams last night announced that the Terror Alert Level in the Afterlife had been raised from "Moderate" to "Severe" following the death of Osama Bin Laden.

Bin Laden atrocity threat to paradise "real & imminent" *- Archbishop*

EXCLUSIVE

Dr Williams believes that , in the wake of his shooting last month, the late Al Qaida boss could be planning a series of atrocities in Heaven, targeting major landmarks in the mythical sky-based kingdom of God.

The Archbishop said that departed souls were now facing a real and imminent threat from the late terror chief. "The sad fact is, whilst the death of Osama Bin Laden has made the mortal world a safer place to live, it has left the hereafter facing a heightened risk of extremist outrages," he told the General Synod.

SOULS

The Archbishop urged inhabitants of the spiritual realm to be on the lookout for any suspicious behaviour. "I cannot emphasise too much the importance of celestial souls maintaining the utmost vigilance whilst going about their eternal business up on the clouds," he continued. "Ethereal beings should be on the lookout for anything that strikes them as unusual or out of the ordinary."

"If they spot a bearded angel acting suspiciously or a seraphim buying a large quantity of bleach all at once, they should immediately report what they have seen to St Peter or the nearest Archangel," he added.

ESSEXES

But even with increased security, Williams admits that it is still impossible to completely eliminate the threat posed in Heaven by a determined afterlife terrorist. And he outlined several nightmare scenarios that Bin Laden could already be planning.

"Loss of afterlife on such a scale simply doesn't bear thinking about," said Dr Williams. "And having thought about it, I'm still not really sure what happens to someone who gets killed in Heaven."

UPS

"Perhaps they go to a second Heaven, a bit higher up than the first one. Or maybe they simply end up as ghosts, haunting the clouds forever," he added.

A CHERUBIM is hijacked by a terrorist wearing a rucksack packed with Semtex, who holds a craft knife to his neck and orders him to fly at full speed into the Pearly Gates at the busiest time of day.

DEATH TOLL: 1000+

AN ANGEL joins a huge multitude to watch a concert given by the Heavenly Host. However, he is an Al Qaida sympathiser wearing exploding underpants, and they are wired to go off at the climax of the Hallelujah Chorus.

DEATH TOLL: 320-340

A FANFARE is sounded for the Lord God as he descends from on high. However, one of the heralds is actually a deceased Islamic extremist with a powerful rocket launcher concealed in his golden trumpet, which he fires into the hosanna-ing crowd.

DEATH TOLL: 70-150

IT'S MARKET day in Heaven, and the square is thronged with the souls of the departed, shopping for Ambrosia and Manna. One angel bends down as if to tighten a loose sandal strap, but he's actually a dead mad mullah who, inspired by shoe-bomber Richard Reed, has packed his footwear with explosives. And now he's lighting the fuse.

DEATH TOLL: 280-283

NOBODY gives a second glance to a golden harp which has been left under God's throne. Harps are everywhere in Heaven, so one sitting casually by the Creator's right hand doesn't attract any undue attention. But this harp contains an IUD - a home-made bomb crammed with nails, broken glass and dog dirt. As God sits down to forgive us this day our daily trespasses and lead us not into temptation... *Ka-boom!*

DEATH TOLL: 15... *including God himself.*

TONY PARSEHOLE

Why I weep for Bin Laden

SEPTEMBER 11th 2001 was a moment that will live long in the memory of all who remember that fateful day. The images of our memories of that fateful day will remain with us for years. For centuries. For decades.

The images of our memories of that fateful day will remain with us for millenniums.

And now the man who perpetrated that single most worst crime in the history of humanity is dead. Osama Bin Laden was the world's most evil man and we are well rid of him. His death is a cause for celebration.

Be in no doubt. No-one should shed a tear for this wicked devil in carnage.

But I shed a tear for him. When I heard that he had passed, I wept for Osama Bin Laden.

But I did not weep for the man he was. I wept for the man he could have been.

And I wept for the boy he once were.

And also I wept for the baby that he was before that.

Because Osama Bin Laden wasn't always a terrorist. He was once an innocent baby like me and you. Like your children. Like my children.

A newborn baby, suckling at his mother's breast.

Then later he was a toddler in shorts, taking his first steps in the big world. Crying when he grazed his knees after trying to ride his bike without stabilisers. Wide-eyed on his first day at nursery as his mum left him at the gate.

Later still he was a boy. Playing rough and tumble with his pals. Kicking a football round the park with jumpers for goalposts. Collecting stamps and painting Airfix models.

Playing conkers.

Then he was a teenager. Going to the youth club disco, naively fumbling behind the bike sheds, coughing on his first furtive cigarette.

Next he was a young man with his whole life ahead of him. Ready to take his place in the world, full of hopes, dreams, fears and love.

But somewhere along the line, Osama Bin Laden lost sight of that love.

The child within the man became overwhelmed by the man that the child had become. And in the end it cost him his life.

Osama was killed by fame. A victim of his own gilded cage of hate. A candle in the wind, snuffed out before his time by the winds of change.

He may have left us, but we'll always remember Osama Bin Laden as the People's Terrorist. The Terrorist of Hearts.

The People's Terrorist of Hearts.

And that is why I weep for Osama Bin Laden.

How many words is that? Shit, I'm still 49 short. Henry Cooper wasn't just a boxer. Our 'Enry was the People's Boxer. The Boxer of Hearts. The People's Boxer of Hearts. Still 23 to go. Ted Lowe wasn't just a snooker commentator. Our Ted was the People's Snooker Commentator. The Snooker Commentator of Hearts. The People's Snooker Commentator of there that's it. Payment terms strictly 7 days.

SAY HELLO TO WAVE BYE-BYES!

Boom time for lead coffin makers as Bin sea burial makes big splash

OSAMA Bin Laden's choice to opt for a burial at sea has set the funeral world alight. Undertakers around the globe are already reporting unprecedented demand for commital to the waves, as fashion-conscious corpses clamour to be dropped into a watery grave.

"Six foot under is SO last year," says Paris funeral stylist Alponso Giovanni. "Brine is the new soil. Being lowered into a hole is a big no-no since Bin Laden's cadaver made such a fashionable splash off the deck of the USS Carl Vinson."

WORMS

"Davy Jones's locker is THE in place for the out cold crowd," he continued. "Eaten by worms? I don't think so. O-Bin's shown the world how to bow out in style. Swimming with the fishes is the way to go, 2011-style."

And as for coffins, you can forget pine this funeral season. "Lead is this year's must-have coffin material," says Giovanni. "Wooden caskets? Hello! I don't think so."

MANGE

"If you're dead, it's got to be lead. It's simply to DIE for!"

However, the sudden rise in the popularity of maritime burial has led to a widespread lead shortage as diers clamour to secure coffins made from the fashionable dense metal.

ACT OF WARSHIP: Maritime funeral services set to be next big thing.

"Lead's flying off the shelves as quick as we can refine it," laughs Fabio di Lorenzo, chief ore extractor at the chic Milan leadworks Paco Delfonte Mining. "I've got guys working round the clock digging it up, but as soon as it comes out of the furnace it's like gone, girl."

DISTEMPER

And that means even more work for the fashionable coffin houses of Europe. Ritzy Barcelona casketouriers Enrico Palazzo recently unveiled their latest collection of couture coffins ... and surprise surprise - they're ***ALL*** lead!

Speaking at the launch of New York Funeral Week, *Vogue* interment correspondent Boris Mince insisted it's a trend that's set to continue for the foreseeable future. "If you don't want to be buried at sea, then don't die this year," he said.

Not nice to SEA you!

UNDERWATER repairs to a giant North Sea oil platform were halted last night after engineers working 500 feet beneath the surface were chased away... *by the GHOST of Osama Bin Laden!*

Divers were replacing a section of damaged footing on the Whisky Echo rig when they were surprised by a glowing apparition of the Al Qaida boss. "We recognised him because of his long beard and headdress," frogman Angus McTavish told the *Aberdeen Anus & Fissure*. "He was see-through and floating about making bubbly 'Wooo' noises."

"We tried to hide behind one of the platform legs, but he just walked straight through and continued chasing us."

"The ghost kept raising his hands up above his head and waggling his fingers," continued McTavish. "We were absolutely terrified. I could hear my teeth chattering with fear inside my big brass helmet."

BOOTS

"We tried to run away, but it was difficult because we were wearing our big, heavy deep-sea diving boots," he added.

Bin spook haunting ocean bed - report

R.I.P RIG & PANIC: Derek set to visit oil platform after ghost scare.

After their fright, the divers refused to go back into the water to finish the job unless the spook had been dealt with. Oil production was halted and rig bosses were forced to call in TV ghosthunter Derek Acorah to exorcise Bin Laden's spirit from the seabed and get the platform back on stream.

Acorah told BBC Scotland's Newsnicht programme: "In the same way that people who are buried in the earth tend to haunt graveyards, people who are buried at sea are forever doomed to roam the ocean floor looking for peace."

Now BP chiefs plan to lower Acorah and his Most Haunted co-star Yvette Fielding to the sea bed in a diving bell in an attempt to lay the restless Al Qaida man's soul to rest. The Liverpool-born medium, 67, will attempt to make psychic contact with the ghost via his Red Indian spirit guide Sam, whilst Yvette points a torch up under her chin and screams.

JOHN MENZIES

Acorah continued: "As well as the usual dangers of catching the bends or being attacked by a squid, it's also possible that I could become possessed by the spirit that I'm trying to cast out."

"If that happens, there is a danger that Bin Laden could use my body to deliver a hate-filled call to arms, appealing to viewers of UKLiving to rise up and crush the poisonous nest of devil dogs that is the West."

"Mind you, if he does that, I suspect it won't be in Arabic," he added. "It will probably come out as English with a cod-foreign accent, a bit like Bernard Bresslaw in Carry On Up the Khyber."

THE 9/11 FACTOR

THE DEATH of Al Qaida boss OSAMA BIN LADEN has left a power vacuum at the heart of the terror organisation. With their mastermind gone, the fundamentalist network will be finding it difficult to plan future outrages. The sooner a new leader is appointed, the faster they can get on with the job of bringing the infidel west to its knees.

But just who should get the job? The next figurehead must have the right blend of qualities to steer the shadowy jihadist network through the next phase of its development. The successful candidate should already have a high public profile, so who would fit the bill better than a showbiz A-lister?

We asked PR guru **MAX CLIFFORD** to suggest a few celebrities who might step into Osama's sandals. Here the silver-haired fuck-face runs through a roll call of star names to see if they have the Max Factor...

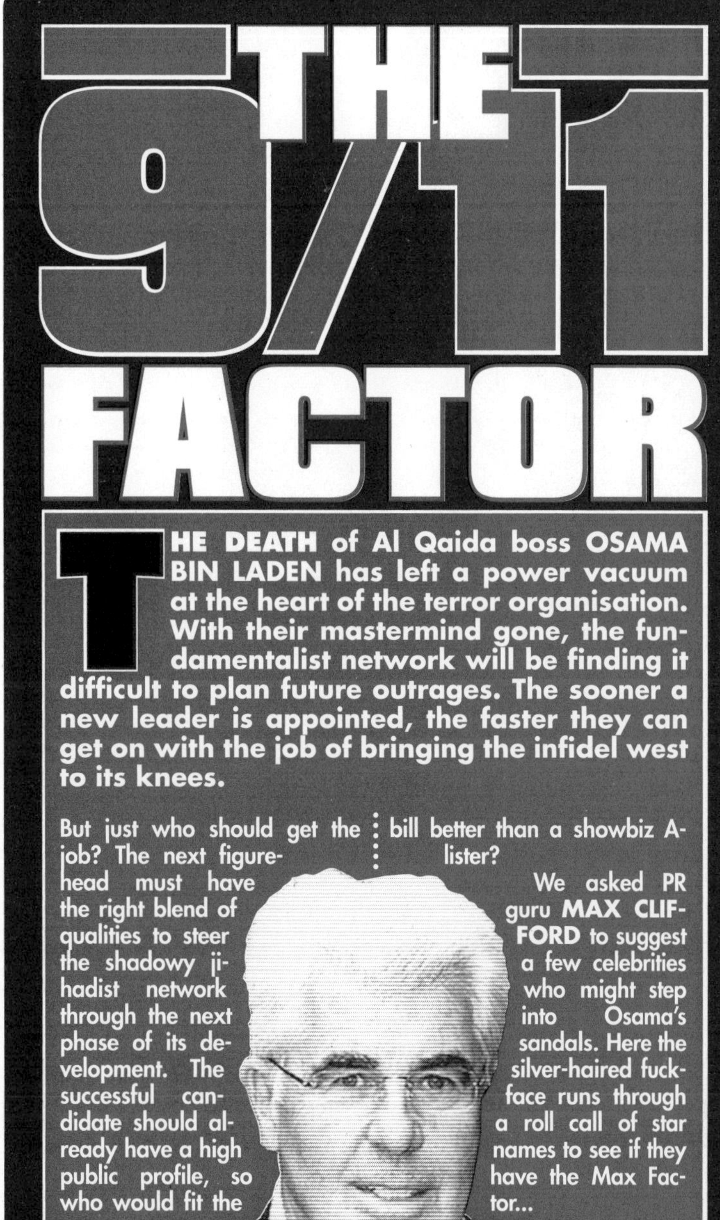

JEREMY CLARKSON.....

LOUDMOUTHED petrolhead Clarkson displays great leadership skills as he bosses round his fellow presenters on *Top Gear*, and it is likely that he would take control of a sinister global network of ruthless killers with equal ease. Just like his predecessor Bin Laden, the outspoken motormouth is unafraid to voice controversial opinions on all manner of subjects. Comfortable in front of the camera, it is easy to imagine Jezza recording word-perfect hate-filled diatribes whilst waving a Russian AK47 into the lens.

However, the 51-year-old's laddish lifestyle of smoking, booze and fast cars is unlikely to go down well with Al Qaida's fundamentalist rank and file who eschew all things western and decadent. Clarkson might not be prepared to swap his fags and Ferraris for ten years in a cave in the Tora Bora moutains of Afghanistan, wearing a long white robe and sandals.

9/11 FACTOR: 4/10

STEPHEN FRY..............

CAMBRIDGE-educated Fry has several qualities that would see him sit happily at the top of the terror organisation. As he proved when he disappeared to Belgium following lukewarm reviews for his performance in the West End play *Cell Mates*, he has an uncanny ability to go into hiding. As an ex-con, Fry is used to living in spartan surroundings and so would instantly feel at home in the draughty caves of the Khyber Pass. He also boasts an army of over 1million Twitter followers who could could be galvanised into a jihadist frenzy with 140 well-chosen characters from their leader.

However, Fry's homosexuality would not sit well with hardline Al Qaida members, and his well-documented sensitivity means he may not cope well with the epithet 'Most hated Man on the Planet'. In addition, his compulsion to message his fans 24/7 about the tedious minutiae of his life may lead him to inadvertently give away secret details of forthcoming outrages.

9/11 FACTOR: 50%

PARIS HILTON.............

AT FIRST glance, socialite hotel heiress Paris Hilton may seem an unlikely candidate to take the helm of the world's most evil terror consortium. But surprisingly, the vapid blonde bimbo does have several qualities that could stand her in good stead. Thanks to her satellite TV shows such as *The Simple Life*, *The Simple Life 2* and *Paris Hilton's My Best Friend Forever*, she already boasts a stellar world-wide profile. Also, hardline Al Qaida members have a strong aversion to women being educated, so Hilton's evident lack of intelligence and her inability to write (as evidenced by her 2004 best-seller Confessions of an Heiress), may well be seen as positive advantages. In addition, like the terror outfit, Hilton is well used to releasing grainy, home-made video footage onto the internet.

On the flip side, the 30-year-old 'It' girl is constantly being arrested for a variety of misdemeanours, an unfortunate tendency which would hamper her ability to smoothly manage a world-wide web of extremist lunatics. She also keeps a small dog in her Givenchy handbag, an unclean animal in the eyes of fundamentalists, and this could prove an insurmountable obstacle to her getting the job.

9/11 FACTOR: ★ ★ ★

BRIAN COX.................

TV BOFFIN Professor Brian Cox first rose to fame tinkling the ivories in nineties electro-synth band D:Ream, which isn't an ideal qualification for a putative atrocity-monger. However, his subsequent career as a nuclear physicist most certainly is. With access to atom bomb-making equipment, not to mention the technical know-how to put one together, mad mullah Cox and his west-hating cohorts could hold the world to ransom. And if that didn't work, the brainbox heart-throb could switch to Plan B. It is well known that Al Qaida and their Taliban chums want to blast us all back into the stone age. Cox could achieve this by reversing the polarity on the CERN Large Hadron Collider, using a stream of deadly Higgs Bosuns to rip a hole in the space/time continuum and plunge the world back into the pre-technological era of the dinosaurs.

However, it appears that the boyish egghead hasn't started shaving yet, and his inability to cultivate a Bin Laden-style beard could trip him up in his quest to take the reins of the terror network. Also, he smiles rather a lot, and his beaming, friendly face is unlikely to instill fear in the west or make an effective universal icon of evil.

9/11 FACTOR: 6.2

NOEL EDMONDS...........

AS LEADER of a global terror network, *Deal or No Deal* star Noel Edmonds would stop at nothing to impose his rigid beliefs on the people of the world. As his rise to fame and fortune proved, the ex-*Swap Shop* host is ambitious and ruthless. His habits of torturing people in gunk tanks and killing them on his Whirly Wheel challenges demonstrate Noel's scant regard for the sanctity of human life; ordinary mortals are mere pawns in Edmonds's great game of chess. And like Bin Laden, the Crinkley Bottomed TV star sports a luxurious beard, de rigeur for a credible Al Qaida leader. Noel is also a skilled pilot, and while it is unlikely that he would fly one of his own expensive helicopters into a building full of people, he is more than capable of training one of his footsoldiers, such as Mike Smith, Keith Chegwin or Mr Blobby, to do so.

The only thing counting against Edmonds is that he perhaps comes over as being a little unsympathetic. The leader of a guerilla network, no matter how evil, must be able to garner popular support from his supporters, and Edmonds's loathsome personality might unfortunately prove hard to stomach even for Al Qaida's army of merciless fanatics.

9/11 FACTOR: A-

LETTERBOCKS

Viz Comic, PO Box 841, Whitley Bay, NE26 9EQ
e-mail: letters@viz.co.uk

TOP TIPS

ALIEN abductees. Refrain from having a shit before going to bed even if you are touching cloth. That way, if you are abducted during the night, you can at least gain satisfaction from the knowledge that you have made a real mess of their anal probing equipment.
Matty, e-mail

PET OWNERS. Give your cat a treat and the encouragement to "see" more of the world by holding him in your arms and pressing his nose against things which would normally be out of his reach. Start him off on light-switches and door hinges and then move on to more complex objects like shower-heads and coving.
Alex Ferris, e-mail

CHEDDAR and Mini Cheddar cheese biscuits make tasty replacements for lost 'Spirograph' drawing wheels.
Petesk8, e-mail

WAIT UNTIL your wife has major dental surgery and then ask for a blow job. With all the anaesthetic it will feel like someone else is doing it.
Baby Dave, Derby

WOMEN. When complaining that your relationship 'doesn't have the magic it used to', bear in mind that some of the magic may have been conjured up by you giving your fella a really good seeing to at every available opportunity, rather than responding with utter indifference to all his suggestions that perhaps you might like to have sex sometime, seeing as it's been 18 sodding months without. Just saying.
C Toris e-mail

STAR LETTER

"The sun always shines on TV" sang Norwegian popsters A-ha in 1985. What absolute nonsense. I'm watching *Granada Reports* and it looks like it's pissing down.
Frank Wenzie, e-mail

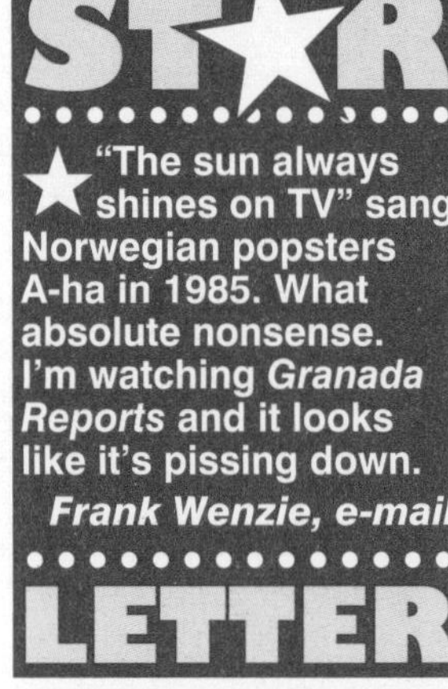

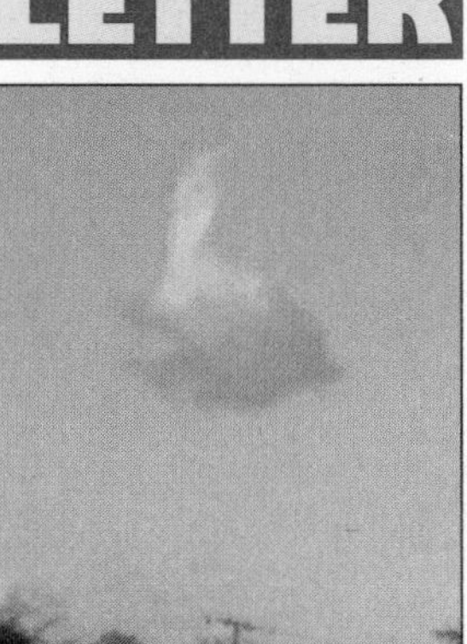

I WONDERED if you might be interested in this picture I took of a cloud which appeared for all the world to be rather rudely sticking its middle finger up at me. Do any other readers have similar photographic evidence for the regard in which Almighty God holds His creation?
Father Jennings, e-mail

GIVEN the choice between the last minute or so of *Two Pints Of Lager and a Packet of Crisps* and the latest Go Compare advert, I chose the latter. Does anyone else hate a programme this much?
Doc Bollocks, e-mail

BACK in 1974 my friend told me that Chinese ladies' fannies went sideways instead of front to back. But in 2005 Katie Melua informed us that there were 9 million bicycles in Beijing. That means either 4.5 million people in Beijing are enduring a very uncomfortable daily commute to work, or Ms Melua is a liar. I for one won't be buying any of her CDs until this whole sorry mess is cleared up.
Claude, e-mail

AT THE beginning of *The Apprentice* contestants are woken up to be told they have to be ready in 30 minutes before the car picks them up. That'd be me fucked from the start, as it takes me at least 40 minutes to have a shit in the morning.
Fat Alan, e-mail

FOR years I've been trying to shit the alphabet but can only manage the letters 'I', 'J' and occasionally 'C'. Can any of your readers do any better?
A. Scoggins, e-mail

WHILST listening to Radio 4 the other day I realised that the words "Everyone's a nazi now, everyone's a nazi" fit perfectly to the theme tune of *The Archers*. Can your readers think of any other controversial and inflammatory statements that serve as lyrics for well-known theme tunes?
Mr Smaug, Berks

UNBEKNOWN to me, every time I purchase a 'sneaky treat' from the local Tesco petrol station and use my Clubcard it records what I've bought on a database which in turn adds those items to our 'favourites' on the online shopping facility. So you can imagine my surprise when last night my wife and I did an online shop, and up popped all my secret chocolate bars, tobacco and porn mags. Thanks , Tesco. Every little didn't fucking help this time.
Ben Gingle, e-mail

I'D JUST like to confirm to my neighbours that yes, I am doing a spot of fucking gardening. That's generally what digging holes to put plants in is called. Thanks for checking though. Twats.
B Felchmarsh, e-mail

WHILST watching a BBC documentary, I learnt that Hasidic Jews aren't allowed to fart whilst wearing a hat. What a fantastic religion. I'm surprised more people haven't joined that one.
Rempton Plywood Cheam

COULD you please settle an argument between myself and my wife. She says that Adrian Chiles should grow a moustache, whereas I maintain that Richard Briers should, if he's still alive. Which of us is correct?
James Brown, Edinburgh

****SORRY Mr Brown, but you're both wrong. It is in fact Alan Titchmarsh who should grow a moustache.**

I ANNOUNCED to my 1732 Facebook friends that I was moving house last weekend and could do with a lift and not one of the fuckers turned up. Some friends they turned out to be.
Popey Mike, e-mail

BENT NOSE CORNER with *Jim Beglin*

HI, FORMER Liverpool footy star JIM BEGLIN here. I commentate for ITV and I'm famous for my catchprases "that's maybe a little harsh from the referee" and "if Tony Pulis was looking for a response then he has got it". But I also have a bit of a crooked hooter and if anything happens in the bent-nose world I'm right on it.

I often get asked to name my dream **BENT-NOSED WORLD XI**. Unfortunately FIFA rules on overseas wonky-conked players mean that I have to select players who aren't footballers and some who are even dead. But here is my fantasy team so far...

GK: That bloke off *Hi-de-Hi!*
RB: Javier Bardem **CB:**TBC **LB:**Arthur Mullard
RW: Mike Gatting **LW:**Stephen Fry
RM:TBC **CM:**Steve Bruce **LM:**TBC
CF: Mick McCarthy **CF :**Owen Wilson

Anyway, here's a round up of some wackiest bent nose news from around the world!...

• ***MUNICH, Germany*** - a man with a bent nose from birth was taken to hospital after being hit in the face by a cricket ball. When the bandages came off his nose was straight. Bet he's glad he wasn't at a softball match!

• ***BOGOTA, Colombia*** - a man entered a police station with a bent nose and a machine gun and massacred over 20 people. Let's hope he gets straightened out in the joint!

• ***HALIFAX, West Yorkshire*** - 3 people were treated for minor burns after a house fire in the town centre. One of the fireman attending the scene had a bit of a wonky nose. Hope it didn't put him out (of joint)!

That's all for now, bent-nose fans!

I COULD understand that footballer taking out a "super injunction" if he had been caught shagging someone like Gail out of *Coronation Street* instead of Imogen from *Big Brother*. If it was me shagging Imogen, I would want everyone to know about it.

John Cohen, e-mail

I RECENTLY saw an advert for the Dettol No-Touch hand wash system. The selling point was that you don't need to touch the bottle for the liquid to come out, and thus avoid contact with any germs which may be on the dispenser. Thank heavens for Dettol - God forbid you should touch something with germs on it immediately prior to washing your hands.

Michael Trippett, e-mail

UP THE ARSE CORNER

Sender: Andy Cross, Perth, Australia

Sender: Andrew Glazebrook, e-mail

WE WERE watching a tribute to Chopin in Beijing on Euronews in Cyprus when who should pop up but Mrs Brady as a modern sculpture. Do we get a fiver, pencil stub, what have you?

Robert Brew & Jane Aiken, Cyprus

YESTERDAY, whilst I was waiting at the checkout of Sainsbury's in Truro, the lady in front of me put three bottles of cheap lager, two packets of Tenna Lady incontinence pads and a tube of Anusol haemorrhoid cream on the conveyer belt. Have any of your readers seen a more stark and revealing basket of shopping than that?

Nick Lyon, e-mail

I RECENTLY saw a picture of the Bay City Rollers at a Silver Jubilee street party that must be THE most 1970s photo there is. Unless, of course, you've got a picture of, ooh, I don't know, a Womble talking to an Oxo cube, say.

Clive Inskip, Wrightford

**WHAT, like this one, Clive?*

ON A recent holiday I accidentally left my copy of *Viz* on the plane on my way out. When I got home I bought a new copy to finish reading it. It's only now I realise I'd already read the good bits on the plane and so I feel quite ripped off. It is quite a cynical ploy to hide extra costs like this from innocent holidaymakers and I will not be booking with Thomas Cook again.

Matt Hart, e-mail

COULD any of your readers tell me if the world ended on May 21st as I live in Birkenhead and quite frankly it's very difficult to tell.

Stephen Porter Birkenhead

WITH reference to Mr Plywood's letter *(facing page)*, Jewish women must keep their heads covered with a hat at all times when in the synagogue, so what happens if they need to pass wind during the service? It seems that God has them over a barrel.

Aiken Drum, London

CAN ANY of your clever Dick readers tell me why I have to learn Japanese in karate lessons? I came for a fight, I'm not ordering fucking lunch.

S Nipple, e-mail

JUDGING by how much he shit himself at the word 'surprise' on his birthday. It's hard to believe my grandad fought in any war, let alone survived it.

Aaron Delays, e-mail

HOW about a jigsaw of that bloke kissing that bird's arse?

Iain McKellan, e-mail

'IT'S NOT about the money, we don't need your money, it's not about the price tag, we just want to make the world dance' sings Jessie J. This being the case, can she explain why one of her concert tickets cost £54.99 plus £5.20 postage fee?

David Milner, Durham

MY WIFE recently won this trophy at the our local darts awards night. Have any other readers (or their wives) received such a lame award?

Bonnag Coole, e-mail

CELEBRITY SWEARS

No. 8,342: ***David Coleman***

AUNTIE DEPRESSANT

SHE'S NOT WELL, YOU KNOW...

HI AUNTIE! WE THOUGHT WE'D COME VISIT YOU!
OOH! THAT'S NICE!

MAKE YOURSELF COMFY. I'LL JUST FINISH UP IN THE KITCHEN.
OKAY!

SHE'S BEEN AN AWFULLY LONG TIME. D'YOU THINK SHE'S ALRIGHT? DAD SAYS SHE HASN'T BEEN HERSELF LATELY.
I BET SHE'S BAKING COOKIES AGAIN!
YAY! COOKIES! LET'S GO SEE

TOP TIPS

FOOL people into thinking that you used to have a tail by cutting a large hole in the seat of your trousers.

Sam B, e-mail

STICK your fingers in both ears and simultaneously push them in and out rapidly to recreate the opening of 'Silver Machine'. Hey presto, an instant Hawkwind classic wherever you go, and no need for an expensive iPod.

T D Charles, e-mail

JUSTIFY drinking alone by surfing Facebook at the same time. Hey Presto! You're now a social drinker!

Sari Simpson, e-mail

LION tamers. Add extra excitement to placing your head in a lion's mouth by first putting a fruit pastille on its tongue.

Pud, Leeds

DRINKERS. Avoid waking your other half when you come home inebriated by, over the course of the night, individually wrapping up all the coins in your pocket one by one in toilet paper and securing with an elastic band. This will eliminate any noise when they inevitably fall from your pockets whilst getting into bed. You may also want to mark the denomination on each one with a black felt pen to save unwrapping them all again whilst looking for your taxi fare.

T. Dogshit, e-mail

SAVE space in your freezer by storing frozen peas in the holes in potato waffles.

Richard Vaughan, e-mail

MIXING gin with tomato ketchup makes an acceptable emergency Bloody Mary.

Tom Christy, e-mail

TIMES Online readers. Save yourself £1 per day by simply going to thesun.co.uk and reading everything in a received pronunciation accent.

Mjr Cuntingdon Smythe e-mail

SHEP'S INCH HIGH BANJO BAND
SHRUNK TO THE SIZE OF ANTS BY A METEOR EMITTING STRANGE COSMIC RAYS...
...SHEP'S BANJO BOYS NEVERTHELESS CONTINUED TO TOUR THE WORKING MEN'S CLUBS OF THE NORTH OF ENGLAND, PLAYING THEIR BLEND OF TRAD JAZZ AND RAGTIME.

ONE EVENING.
GOT EVERYTHING FOR THE SHOW AT THE SHIPLEY WMC, SHEP?
NOT HALF, BILL. I'M LOOKING FORWARD TO IT.

TAXI'S HERE, BOYS.
GREAT.

COME ON, LADS. HE'S PROBABLY GOT THE METER RUNNING ALREADY.
HOLD ON A MO...WHERE'S KEN?
HE SAID HE WAS GOING TO HAVE A BATH BEFORE THE SHOW.

HELP! HELP!
UH-OH! SOUNDS LIKE KEN'S IN TROUBLE.

HELP!
GLUB!...
HELP!
QUICK, BOYS. CLIMB THE TOWEL!

HEEEELP!
OH NO! HE'S BEING SUCKED DOWN THE PLUG HOLE!
COME ON! ONTO THE SOAP DISH.

SO.
JUST A BIT CLOSER, JOE. I'M NEARLY THERE...

GODDIM!
HOORAY!

BY HECK, THAT WERE CLOSE. THANK YOU, BOYS.
NO PROBLEM, KEN...
...NOW COME ON, WE'VE GOT A TAXI WAITING.

FIVE MINUTES LATER.
EVERYBODY GOT THEIR INSTRUMENTS?
YOU BET YER BOOTS, SHEP.

SUDDENLY.
SCREEEE!
LOOK OUT! SPIDER!
ARRRRGH!!

DON'T MISS NEXT WEEK'S THRILLING EPISODE, WHEN THE BANJO BOYS GET CAUGHT IN A SPIDER'S WEB AND THEN CHASED BY A WASP.

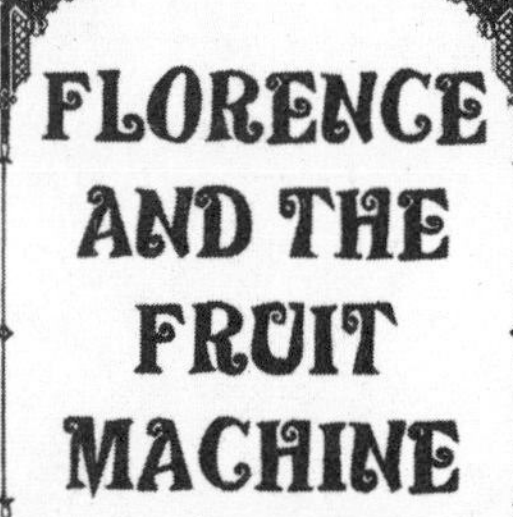
FLORENCE
AND THE
FRUIT
MACHINE

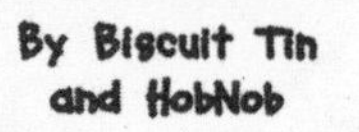
By Biscuit Tin
and HobNob

BRITISH ARMY FIELD HOSPITAL, CRIMEA 1855.
NURSE, COULD YOU MOVE ME PLEASE? MY BEDSORES ARE CAUSING ME GREAT PAIN.

OF COURSE PRIVATE ASPINALL, JUST ONE THING THOUGH - I COULDN'T TAP YOU FOR A COUPLE OF POUND COINS?
SIGH, NOT AGAIN! TOP DRAWER, AND YOU STILL OWE ME FOUR FROM LAST WEEK.

CHEERS ASPINALL. RIGHT ... PAY OUT YA BASTARD.
Pots'o'Dosh
HEY! WHAT ABOUT MY BEDSORES!
NURSE! A BEDPAN PLEASE!

FOR FUCKSAKE WOMAN A BEDPAN! I'M TOUCHING CLOTH HERE!
HEY CARTWRIGHT, WHILE YOU'RE DOWN THERE - WHAT'S COMING NEXT ON THAT THIRD REEL? - I'VE GOT TWO NUDGES HERE ...

ER, I DUNNO, CHERRIES I THINK.
RIGHT, GIVE US A COUPLE OF COINS - I'M GOOD FOR IT - PAYDAY FRIDAY.

PAH! FUCKING MACHINE - NEVER PAYS OUT. CHERRIES INDEED!
WHINE!!!

HENNESSEY, WAKE UP! GOT ANY POUND COINS? I'LL PAY YOU BACK TUESDAY.
GROAN! EVERY... FUCKING... NIGHT!

HEY EVANS, WHAT THE FUCK ARE YOU DOING? THAT'S FOR STAFF ONLY, GET BACK TO BED!
OH NURSE PLEASE, JUST A LITTLE LIGHT RELIEF TO EASE THE MELANCHOLY.
Pots'o'Dosh

JACKPOT! I CAN'T BELIEVE MY LUCK!
YOU SPAWNY BASTARD EVANS, I'VE BEEN FEEDING THAT FUCKER ALL WEEK!
K-CHING
K-CHING
K-CHING
SKRRSH

THAT'S MY FUCKING MONEY - YOU WERE TOLD - STAFF ONLY!
I WON IT FAIR AND SQUARE! ... AAARGH!!!

HAND IT OVER YA CRIPPLE!
NIGHTINGALE! YOU ARE A DISGRACE TO YOUR PROFESSION!

CONSIDER YOURSELF DISMISSED - I WILL LOOK AFTER THESE MEN NOW!
YOU'RE WELCOME TO THEM! BUNCH OF TIGHT ARSES ANYWAY!
HURRAH!
GOOD RIDDANCE!

AS FOR THIS, WE SHALL SELL IT ON AND PURCHASE MACHINERY MORE APPROPRIATE TO A FIELD HOSPITAL'S NEEDS.
Pots'o'Dosh

AW, BASTARD! JUST 500 OFF MY HIGHEST SCORE THERE -
HENNESSY ... ANY POUND COINS?
DANCE YOURSELF DIZZY
NURSE! A BEDPAN!

THE BACONS

MUTHA FATHA BIFFA

LONG VEHICLE
NATIONAL BLOOD TRANSFUSION SERVICE

HOO, NORSE! THE BAIRN 'ERE WANTS T' GIVE BLOOD
OKAY. IF YOU TAKE A SEAT I'LL BE OVER WITH THE NEEDLE SHORTLY.
NEEDLE!?!

FORGERRIT... HE'S GORRA PHURBIA ABOOT NEEDLES. HE'S SHIT SCARED O' THE FUCKAZ!
HAD ON A MINUTE, FATHA. MEBBEZ THERES A WAY......

WHISPAH! WHISPAH! FUCKIN' WHISPAH!
GOOD IDEA, MUTHA.

SLAM!
OOOF!

SLAM! SLAM! SLAM! SLAM! SLAM! SLAM!

BIFFA IS A CUNT

SLAM! SLAM! SLAM! SLAM! M! SLAM!

THERE Y' GAN...THERE MUST BE A COUPLE O' PINTS THERE, EASY.
WHERE D' WE GAN FER W' TEA AN' BISCUITS?
FUCKIN' GROAN!

Vanished Rocker Richey: Here I am!

INVISIBLE MANIC: Street Preacher Richey disappeared without trace in 1995.

MANIC Street Preachers fans were celebrating last night after missing band member RICHEY MANIC finally turned up... ***down the back of his own sofa!***

The hard-living guitarist vanished in 1995, when he was presumed to have committed suicide by jumping off the Severn Bridge. But he was yesterday sensationally discovered alive and well in his Cardiff home.

sofa

His wife, Ada Manic, told us: "I was reaching down behind the sofa cushions, looking for the telly remote, when I felt something moving. I pulled it out and saw it was an arm."

Missing Manic turns up after 16 years

"I recognised it as Richey's, because it still had the scars on it from when he carved '4 Real' on it with a razor blade," she continued.

"I pulled a bit harder and the rest of him popped out. He was covered in fluff, coins and sweet wrappers, but he looked none the worse for his mammoth ordeal."

"After sixteen years of eating crumbs and cat hair, Richey was absolutely spitting feathers," said Mrs Manic. "But after a nice cup of tea and some heroin, he soon cheered up."

sogud

The guitarist explained that he fallen down the back of the sofa in 1995 whilst plumping the cushions. He had apparently been shouting for help for sixteen years, but his wife hadn't been able to hear him for the telly.

PUFF PANT! THIS IS HARD WORK
YOU'RE IN THE WRONG GEAR.

It's a Three-Way Tache C

BALL v KNUTT v

IT'S THE topic that's splitting the country in three. In pubs, clubs and fertility clinics from Land's End to John O'Groats, there's only one question on everybody's lips: ***Who's the best curly-haired, moustachioed Bobby?***

Is it Oldham-born funnyman BOBBY BALL, with his catchphrase "Rock on Tommy", northern actor BOBBY KNUTT, or is it test-tube baby pioneer fanny mechanic BOBBY WINSTON?

Well now it's time to find out once and for all, as Ball, Knutt and Winston they go moustachioed curly head to head to head.

BOBBY BALL		BOBBY KNUTT	
DOUBLE ACT			
EX-WELDER Bobby first shot to fame in the seventies as part of double-act Cannon & Ball with straightman pal Tommy. Their comedy partnership has kept them at the top of the showbiz tree ever since, with a sparkling career including a poorly-received remake of Will Hay's film *Ask a Policeman*, their own comic strip in the now-defunct *Look-in* magazine and a comedy routine which was edited out of an episode of *Bruce Forsyth's Big Night* in 1978.	9	**IT'S A** lacklustre start for the Sheffield-born journeyman actor, who has ploughed a lonely furrow throughout his showbusiness career. An early attempt to form a double-act with Sir Adrian Boult came to nothing, when the eminent orchestral conductor turned down the chance to earn £10 a night touring the working men's clubs of South Yorkshire in favour of a permanent post at the LSO. Knutt's search for a straightman called Tommy Raisins is ongoing.	3
BORN IN OLDHAM-NESS			
BOBBY was born in Oldham on January 28th 1944, so you might expect him to get full marks in this round. However, as a devout Christian, Ball has been born again, and he was in leafy Lytham St Annes when it happened, over 40 miles from Oldham town centre.	4	**WITH** his flat cap and even flatter vowels, it's no surprise to find out that Knutt is Yorkshire born and bred. But his birthplace of Sheffield in the heart of the White Rose county is a mere 27-mile stone's throw from Oldham, earning him a middling score in this round.	6
BEING NAMED AFTER A TES			
COMIC Bobby's surname of Ball is also a synonym for a testicle, making this a plum round for the 5'4" Lancashire lad.	9	**ACTOR** Bobby's surname of Knutt is also a synonym for a testicle, making this a plum round for the 5'8" Yorkshire lad.	8
PRODUCT ENDORSEMEN			
IN 2008 Ball, alongside his comedy partner Tommy Cannon, became the face of Safestyle UK uPVC windows. In doing so, he joined a glittering roster of A-listers who have also held the prestigious post, including Frank Sidebottom, Reg Holdsworth, Cheryl Baker and Britain's largest man Barry Austin.	6	**ALTHOUGH** he has not lent his face to any high profile advertising campaigns, Bobby's distinctive voice is familiar to television viewers as that of "The Gaffer" from the Tetley tea-folk- the best-loved animated characters in British advertising. After them fucking meerkats that go "Simples".	8
HONOURS			
IN 1983 Cannon & Ball were named Variety Club Showbusiness Personalities of the Year, so it's full marks for Bobby in this round. Unfortunately, however, his comedy partner Tommy Cannon is entitled to 50% of those marks, so he walks away with a poor score of 5.	5	**ACCORDING** to his agent's website, Bobby has won "many awards for his style of humour". Unfortunately, it doesn't say which awards these are or name any of them, but they're obviously very numerous and probably extremely prestigious too. So we're honouring Bobby with a high score in this round.	8
NOT PLAYING GOD			
AS A devout born-again Christian, Ball is too scared of God's wrathful vengeance to play Him. Bobby prefers to spend his time saying prayers and singing hymns in an attempt to appease his jealous and angry creator, lest he be smoted down and rented in twain by the bad-tempered, judgemental deity he loves.	7	**ALTHOUGH** Knutt played Albert Dingle in *Emmerdale* and mechanic Ron Sykes in *Coronation Street*, he has never played God in a soap or, indeed, in any production. The closest he came to playing the Almighty was when he was cast as His messenger the Archangel Gabriel in a primary school nativity play in 1951.	6
HOW DID THEY DO?			
BALL 40		**KNUTT 39**	

THERE'S strictly Ball-room only on the winner's podium. Arch-rivals Knutt and Winston are left trailing in his wake as bra bounce all the way to the top of the curly-haired, moustachioed Bobby billboard. *Rock on Bobby!* NEXT WEEK: It's Fawlty v

a!

WINSTON

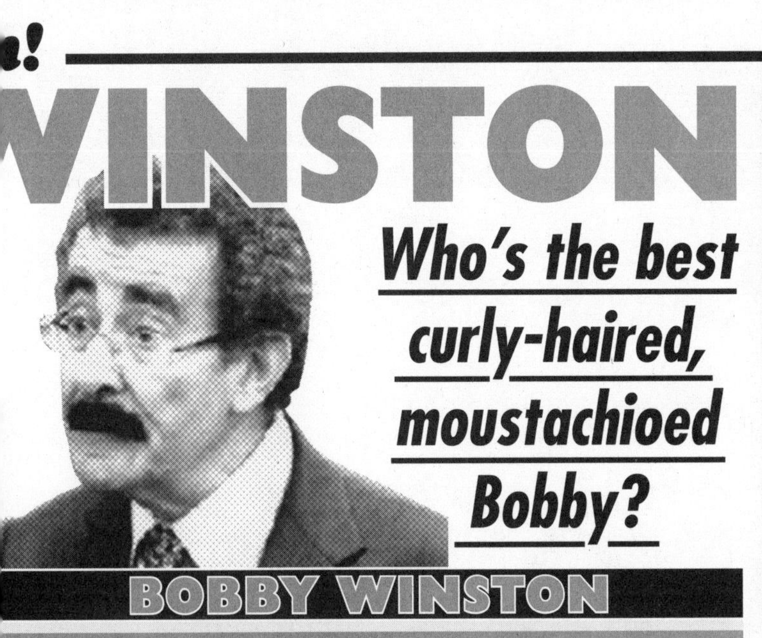

Who's the best curly-haired, moustachioed Bobby?

BOBBY WINSTON

WINSTON first came to prominence as half of the in-vitro fertilisation double-act Winston & Steptoe, with his side-kick Professor Tommy Steptoe. The pair made headlines in 1978 when their pioneering work resulted in the birth of the world's first test-tube baby Louise Brown. However, they split up soon afterwards when Steptoe wanted to research obstetric laparoscopy whilst Winston decided to pursue a solo career in autologous endometrial co-culture. **8**

BOFFIN Bobby would doubtless like us to think he was born in Oldham, but he can't pull the wool over our eyes, as he was actually born in London! In fact, it is Professor Brian Cox who can actually lay claim to being the only telly egghead to hail from the Lancashire town. **5**

.E

SCIENTIST Bobby's surname of Winston is not also a synonym for a testicle, making this not a plum round for the 5'11" London lad. **6**

AS A renowned scientist, Winston is careful to only lend his name to high quality products that he really believes in - such as garage doors, automatic sun awnings and classy online bingo websites. So when he endorses St Ivel Omega 3 brain-boost milk, you know that it really will make your kids more intelligent. **10**

DOCTOR, Professor, Lord, Royal Society Michael Faraday Prize, BMA Gold Badge... these are just a few of the many myriads of honours and awards that have been heaped upon Robert Winston during his glittering career in science, medicine and the media. It's full marks in this round. **10**

WINSTON plays God every day from 9 till 5 in his test-tube baby laboratory, tampering with the very fabric of life itself and meddling with the forces of nature. "People said I was mad, they said I was insane. But the fools are laughing no more. Behold my creation. It lives! It lives!" he told a press conference following the birth of Louise Brown in 1978. **0**

WINSTON 39

:ing Lancashire funnyman Ball proves he's got what it takes to

v Hume: Who's the barmiest Basil?

Hip-Hoppiness!

AFTER nearly 60 years in showbiz, veteran comic KEN DODD is set to re-launch himself... ***as a RAPPER!***

New image for Knotty Ash Ken

The buck-toothed funnyman plans to ditch his family-friendly image and become hip-hop artist **K-DODDY**, complete with bling, guns and a troupe of scantily-clad "bitches" shaking their jam-booties to ear-splitting bass sounds.

● **OUT** ***will go his trademark tickling sticks, Diddy Men and "What a lovely day, missus!" motto.***

● **IN** ***will come Uzi machine guns, Diddy Hos and a brand new catchphrase - "How discommuthafuckinockerated I am".***

Dodd's hardcore new show, *K-Doddy - Straight Outta Knotty Ash,* is set to shock the funnyman's faithful fans, who flock to see his act at provincial venues up and down the country.

theatre

Retired Burnley dinnerlady Ada Colostomy-Bag, 88, who has seen the comic perform his over fifty times, says she won't be buying tickets when the tour reaches her local theatre.

profit

She told us: "Ken Dodd used to be a byword for family entertainment. His act was good clean fun, with no jokes for all the family and no smut or bad language."

temperature

"But I'll be blowed if I'm going to pay good money to see him going on about effing the police and calling everyone a mother-effing cocksucker," she added.

SNOOP DODD: *Ken's set for new career as hardcore rap star.*

THERE'S A BIG DRAUGHT COMING THROUGH THAT WINDOW.

SID the SEXIST

For the first time, the very best of David James's classic howlers and gaffes brought together in one fantastic DVD box set...

OVER 50 HOURS OF FARCE

David James's "FOR FUCK'S SAKE LADS!" COLLECTION

Builds week by week into a 10 DVD collection of Callamity James's most famous goofs and blunders, all followed by him blaming somebody else. Highlights include...

- ***BOOTING** the ball angrily upfield...*
- ***SITTING** on his arse looking pissed off...*
- ***POINTING** at parts of the penalty area and shouting...*
- ***PICKING** the ball out the back of the net while shaking his head and muttering to himself...*
- ***SHOUTING** 'for fuck's sake lads, who was supposed to be marking him?' at defenders...*

...and MANY MORE!

David James's "FOR FUCK'S SAKE LADS!" volume 1 · volume 2 · volume 3 · volume 4 · 18

The first volume of this collection at the FANTASTIC introductory* price of just

£1.99 Ask your Newsagent to reserve a copy **NOW!**

**Subsequent volume numbers 2 to 9 priced at £7.99. Volume 10 priced at £159.99 which we fully expect enough anal retentives to shell out for in order to keep their collection complete.*

"After the lord mayor's show, whatever that means"
- Mark Lawrenson

"Indecision is final"
- Alan Hanson

"Keystone cops"
- Lee Dixon

"Hillarious!"
- Robert Green

"Woeful"
- Alan Green

PARENTAL ADVISORY EXPLICIT CONTENT

PRAISE THE LORD! IT'S IVAN JELICAL

IVAN'S CHURCH IS STAGING A PROTEST
ODEUM
BE UNDER NO ILLUSIONS, LADIES AND GENTLEMEN...
SHOWING TODAY
HARRY POTTER AND THE MAGIC CAKE
MAGIC IS EVIL
Harry Potter = Satanism
THIS FILM IS THE TOOL OF SATAN!

HARRY POTTER IS PRESENTED AS BEING A HARMLESS FANTASY, A BIT OF INNOCENT FUN FOR CHILDREN... BUT HOW HARMLESS IS IT?
Satanism
DON'T MAKE EYE CONTACT WITH THEM, JOSHUA.

THESE FILMS PORTRAY THE PRACTICE OF MAGIC AND SORCERY – AND THE BIBLE IS ABSOLUTELY CLEAR ON THIS SUBJECT...
GOD TELLS US TO SHUN THE OCCULT, FOR IT IS A DOORWAY TO THE POWERS OF DARKNESS.

"LET NO ONE BE FOUND AMONG YOU WHO PRACTICES DIVINATION OR SORCERY, ENGAGES IN WITCHCRAFT OR CASTS SPELLS..."
"ANYONE WHO DOES THESE THINGS IS DETESTABLE TO THE LORD." DEUTERONOMY CHAPTER 18 VERSES 10-12.

BUT HARRY POTTER IS JUST MAKE-BELIEVE... HOW IS IT HARMFUL?
Harry Potter = Satanism
SERIOUSLY, I DON'T UNDERSTAND WHAT YOU'RE OBJECTING TO.

LET ME ANSWER HIS QUESTIONS, PASTOR BROWN – FOR HE SEEKS AFTER THE TRUTH.
YES. GO FORTH AND ENLIGHTEN HIM, BROTHER IVAN.

UM, WOULD YOU MIND NOT STANDING QUITE SO CLOSE
OK, MY QUESTION FOR YOU IS THIS...

"AND JESUS SAID UNTO THEM: I WILL ASK YOU A QUESTION". MARK, CHAPTER 11 VERSE 29
RIGHT, YEAH, SO I JUST WANTED TO ASK...
"ASK AND IT WILL BE GIVEN YOU; SEEK, AND YE SHALL FIND". MATTHEW 7 VERSE 7.

RIGHT, WHATEVER, BUT WHAT I DON'T UNDERSTAND IS...
"THEY HAVE NOT KNOWN NOR UNDERSTOOD: FOR HE HATH SHUT THEIR EYES THAT THEY CANNOT SEE, AND THEIR HEARTS THAT THEY CANNOT UNDERSTAND". ISIAH 44;18

LOOK, ARE YOU GONNA HEAR ME OUT, OR WHAT?
"HE WHO HATH EARS TO HEAR, LET HIM HEAR." LUKE 14 VERSE 35.
WILL YOU JUST SHUT UP A MINUTE?
"AND JEREMIAH COMMANDED BARUCH, SAYING, I AM SHUT UP; I CANNOT GO INTO THE HOUSE OF THE LORD". JEREMIAH 36:5

OH FORGET IT! I MAY AS WELL BE TALKING TO A BRICK WALL!
"THEREFORE I WILL CRY OUT TO ALL MOAB, FOR THE MEN OF THE BRICK WALL WHO MOURN". JEREMIAH 48:31

YOU'RE COMPLETELY BLOODY CUCKOO, YOU ARE!

"AND THESE SHALL YOU HOLD IN ABOMINATION: THE OWL, AND THE NIGHTHAWK, AND THE CUCKOO, AND THE HAWK AFTER HIS KIND." LEVITICUS 11:16.

WELL DONE, BROTHER IVAN! YOU HAVE LIGHTED A LAMP OF UNDERSTANDING IN HIS SOUL!
LET US PRAISE GOD, FOR ANOTHER LOST SHEEP HAS BEEN SHOWN THE WAY TO THE BOSOM OF CHRIST!

PRAISE HIM! HALLELUYAH!

SHORTLY
= Satan
HARRY POTTER
HARRY POTTER NOT ONLY GLORIFIES WITCHCRAFT – IT PROMOTES THE SIN OF HOMOSEXUALISM, AS WELL!

ONE OF THE CHARACTERS IN THIS FILM, A WIZARD NAMED BUMBLEVORT, IS AN UNASHAMED SODOMITE!
EXPLICIT SCENES SHOW HIM ENGAGING IN THE ACT OF ANAL INTERCOURSE!

THERE ISN'T A WIZARD CALLED BUMBLEVORT IN HARRY POTTER!
I DON'T BELIEVE YOU'VE EVEN SEEN ANY OF THE FILMS. I'VE READ ALL THE BOOKS.

THEN YOUR SOUL IS IN MORTAL PERIL, YOUNG LADY!
Harry Potter = Satanism
FOR YOU HAVE POISONED YOUR MIND WITH THE LUCIFERAN / SODOMITICAL PROPAGANDA OF THE WHORE OF BABYLON!

BIFF!
OOF!
NO ONE CALLS MY PRINCESS A WHORE!

LATER
FULCHESTER EVANGELICAL BAPTIST CHURCH
BRETHREN AND SISTREN: I REGRET THAT TODAY'S DEMONSTRATION AGAINST THE FORCES OF EVIL WAS NOT A COMPLETE SUCCESS.

I HAVE PRAYED FOR GUIDANCE – AND GOD TOLD ME THAT WE SHOULD ACTUALLY WATCH ONE OF THESE BLASPHEMOUS FILMS!
GASP!
THUS MAY WE BE BETTER INFORMED ABOUT THE WILES OF THE ANTICHRIST

BUT PASTOR BROWN – SURELY HARRY POTTER IS FULL OF HOMO-SATANIC PROPAGANDA!
DO NOT BE AFRAID, BROTHER IVAN....

THE DEVIL'S LURES MAY ENSNARE THE WEAK – BUT WE ARE STRONG IN OUR FAITH.
Harry Potter
FILLED WITH THE POWER OF CHRIST, WE WILL NOT BE BEGUILED BY SATAN'S LIES.

TEN MINUTES INTO THE FILM –
FULCHESTER gay church of Satan
PRAISE BE TO SATAN, OUR LORD AND MASTER!
ALL WORSHIP BEELZEBUB, PRINCE OF DARKNESS!

A Faceful of Fist

Dirty Harry Clint's punch sound nabbed in raid

THE NOISE that is made when someone gets punched in the face by CLINT EASTWOOD is among several sounds stolen after a break-in at a Hollywood audio archive. Bosses at Paramount Studios have been left in a panic as the sounds were stored on a C-90 cassette which had not been backed up.

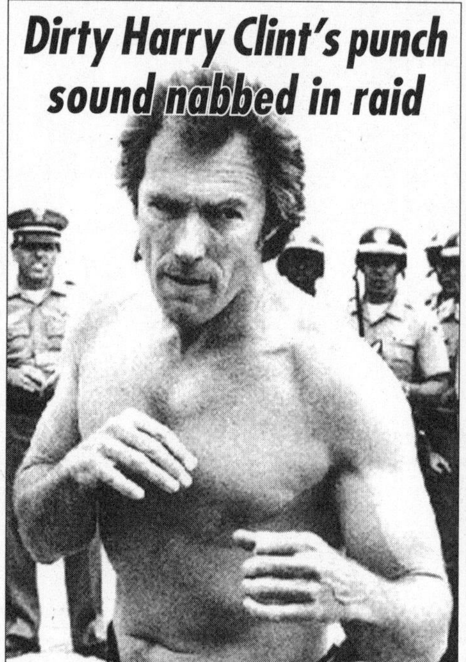

The thieves are thought to have deliberately targeted the noises, possibly stealing them to order for a customer in the far east where there is a booming market for american film sound effects. And it is now feared that the sound of Eastwood lamping someone square in the face could be lost forever, played only in private to satisfy the whim of a rich Japanese businessman.

worth

"I don't know how much that noise was worth, but it doesn't matter anyway. It's simply irreplaceable," said studio chief Hymen T. Oysterburger. "It sounds like someone hitting an oven-ready chicken with a 12-inch ruler, but no one knows how it was really made. It is lost forever," he added.

Other sound effects stolen in the break-in are reported to include:

- ***THE SCREECH of a police car as it rounds the bend in the 1970s***
- ***THE SOUND Sylvester Stallone makes when he gets hit***
- ***THE SOUND of bullets ricocheting off wood in a wild west town***

With no back up available, studio bosses called in Eastwood, 72, to record the ACTUAL sound of him hitting someone in the face. The *Fistful of Dollars* actor spent two days hitting Manuel Gomez, a studio parking lot attendant, square in the face whilst sound technicians recorded the effect on state-of-the-art equipment. But according to one insider, the results were disappointing.

"Clint must have smacked the guy about fifteen hundred times," he told us. "The techies worked on it for hours, playing with the levels, tweaking this and tweaking that. They did their darndest, but all they could get was a dull thud," he said.

hill

The sound has accompanied all Eastwood's punches to the face since 1964 and the actor admits the theft could mark the end of an era.

"I used to love the reassuring hollow thwack when I punched someone in the face in my films. I don't think anything, not even a real smack in the kisser could measure up," he said, extremely slowly, stopping to light a cigar and squinting quizzically into the sun.

MAN WITH NO PUNCH SOUND: Eastwood yesterday

BEN TAKES A POP AT FIFA

Ben Volpiere-Pierrot yesterday and (inset) in his exceptionally brief heyday in 1986.

Curiosity frontman to bring committee 'Down to Earth' with single re-release

ENGLAND'S failure to land the 2018 World Cup was a national embarrassment. Despite being the bookies' favourite, the Three Lions bid secured only 2 votes at last December's FIFA meeting, with Russia taking the prize of hosting the world famous tournament.

But former Curiosity Killed the Cat frontman Ben Volpiere-Pierrot is not so much embarrassed as angry. So angry in fact, he is relaunching his 1986 smash hit *Straight Back Down to Earth* in protest.

FIFA FOE FUN: Sepp Blatter.

And rather than advocating the dismantling of FIFA or a boycott of future world cups, the beret-wearing ex-frontman is suggesting a passive revolution based around his record that will hopefully make FIFA think twice about its controversial actions.

SHED

"This song will be the official 2018 bid failure single," Volpiere-Pierrot told a sparsely-attended press conference in his garden shed. "And if there is one thing that is sure to send a message that will resonate through FIFA's corridors that we are angry about their decision, then it's a slab of lightweight but catchy eighties blue-eyed white boy funk soul," he added.

"And my bandy-legged dancing would also offer Britain a sobering but yet strangely toe-tapping acceptance that while we may not host the World Cup, we can still relaunch a struggling career or two," he told a reporter.

JOHNNY

Volpiere-Pierrot, now 45, admits that he has been waiting 24 years for an appropriate news item to provide him with a tenuous excuse to rerelease the track.

"The first chance we had was the Challenger Shuttle disaster, but we missed it by 6 months," he said. "And Lady Diana's funeral would have been a spectacular way to mark the 11th anniversary of our number three hit, but Elton John bagged that one."

BLOB

But Volpiere-Pierrot believes that this time round the song will reach the coveted Number One spot, and probably stay there for longer than Bryan Adams's *Everything I Do* did. And he is asking internet users and music fans to back his campaign to ram the message home to FIFA.

"Perhaps if one of these computer whizzes puts together some kind of online petition on Facebooks or the Twitter asking us play a protest concert with Johnny Hates Jazz and Living in a Box for example, that would certainly make Sep Blatter and his cronies sit up and take notice," he said.

ROGER MELLIE

THE MAN ON THE TELLY

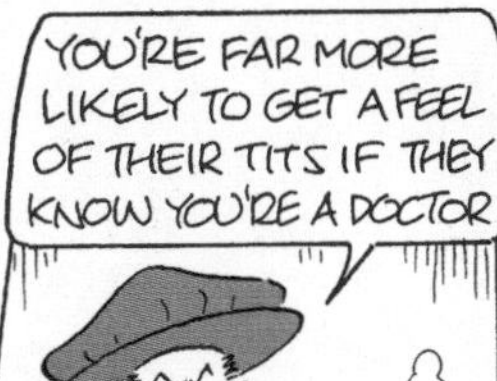

PARTY C

CHARLIE SHEEN hit the headlines recently when his crazy lifestyle of party excess finally caught up with him. The tabloids have been filled with lurid tales of the *Two and a Half Men* star's hedonistic behaviour. But Sheen is just the latest in a long line of Hollywood bad boys - and girls - whose careers have spiralled out of control thanks to their insatiable appetite for partying.

And one man who has seen at first hand the wild exploits of the cinema celebrities is their official party organiser. For ten years **PARSLOW FLINT** has been the go-to guy when the Tinseltown stars want to let their hair down.

Doncaster-born Flint began his working life as a children's entertainer, but soon left to seek his fortune in Beverly Hills. He has since thrown celebrity-studded bashes for a catalogue of stars that reads like an A to Z of silver screen royalty.

But after his dizzying decade in the fast lane, Flint has finally decided it's time to step off the high octane fame merry-go-round. Now back in Doncaster, he is set to lift the beans and spill the lid on what goes on in the US movie capital once the cameras stop rolling.

EXCESS ALL AREAS: Doncaster-born Flint (right) saw stars partying at close range.

Tinseltown fixer blows lid on celebs' partying excesses

"Sure, the Hollywood stars work hard, but once the director calls "Cut!", they like to party even harder," he told us. "And when I say party, I mean party with a capital 'p'!"

Harry star Clint liked to play dirty

"**THE FIRST BASH THAT I** organised was a birthday party for *Dirty Harry* star Clint Eastwood. Everyone who was anyone was there at his ranch in Carmel - Charlton Heston, Dennis Hopper, Meryl Streep ... the guest list read like a *Who's Who* of motion picture A-listers. I had never been so close to so many of my movie idols, and I was in complete awe of them. But I had a job to do, and to get the party off with a swing I had organised a game of musical chairs.

Everyone was up for it, because the prize was one of those things where you put an iron-filings beard on a face using a magnet.

The game started pretty well. *When Harry Met Sally* star Meg Ryan was out first, and as the number of chairs went down she was quickly followed by Marlon Brando, Henry Fonda and Donald Sutherland. It was all very good-natured, but as we got down to the last few chairs, the mood altered and became a little more competitive.

The last two in were Robert De Niro, and the birthday boy Clint. I started the music for the final time and the pair started circling round the single remaining chair.

But Clint wasn't playing fair. He was running round the back of the chair, pushing De Niro out of the way, and then really slowing down round the front, hovering his bottom over the seat for as long as he could, all the while watching my hand on the volume control like a hawk.

When I eventually turned the music down, De Niro was at the front, but Clint barged him out of the way and sat down. There was a bit of a scuffle, but Eastwood sat tight, gripping the underneath of the chair as tightly as he could.

I always thought Clint was good, but I saw a bad and an ugly side to him that day. Just like his character *Dirty Harry*, he bent the rules any any which way he could to avoid losing.

As I left the party, clutching a fistful of dollars I had been paid for my services, I thought I had seen the worst Hollywood had to offer. The next ten years would show how wrong I was."

ENTRAL!

Fatal Attraction left Douglas green at gills

"**IN MY TIME, I'VE FOUND** that there is usually one person at a party who is hellbent on spoiling things for the rest. And I'm afraid I would have to put *Basic Instinct* star Michael Douglas in that category.

I had been asked to organise a wrap party at Sharon Stone's house to celebrate the end of filming for *Basic Instinct*. It was my job to make my way up and down the table with a jug of orange squash, making sure that all the celebrity guests had something to drink.

When I got to Michael Douglas, I noticed that he had piled his paper plate high with cakes, chocolate biscuits and buns. I suggested that he ought to have a few sandwiches before making a start on his dessert.

In a family paper like this, I can't tell you what the *Falling Down* star said in reply, suffice to say it turned the air blue and ended with the word "cocksucker".

If it was up to me, I would have washed his mouth out with soap. But this was Hollywood, where a big name like Douglas can call the shots.

In *Wall Street*, his character Gordon Gekko famously said "Greed is good", and from where I was standing it looked like he was determined to live up to that slogan.

For the next hour, I watched Douglas stuffing his Oscar-winning face with trifle, blancmange and bowl after bowl of jelly with custard.

It came as no surprise when he eventually stood up and announced that he was feeling poorly, before being sick all down his front.

Five minutes later, when his dimpled-chin *Spartacus* star dad Kirk Douglas arrived to take him home, Michael was sitting in his vest and pants, looking very sorry for himself and clutching a bin-bag containing his shirt and trousers.

From the expression on Douglas Senior's face, it was clear that the *Romancing the Stone* actor was in for a proper roasting as he drove him home in his stretch limo."

Mr Sheen cleaned up on party treats

"**THEY SAY THERE'S NO** honour among thieves, but during my years in Tinseltown, it often seemed to me like there was no honour among the stars either.

I'll never forget one party I was roped in to arrange. It was a big do at Cybil Shepherd's house to celebrate her series *Moonlighting* winning three Emmies at the Golden Globes, and the guest list read like a star-studded *Who's Who* of TV A-to-Zs.

The party went pretty well; I made some balloon animals and then organised a game of What Time is it, Mister Wolf?, which was won by Al Pacino.

At the end of the afternoon, as the guests lined up to leave, I stood by the door and got ready to present each of them with a party bag containing a pencil-end monster, a box of Poppets and a slice of cake wrapped in a napkin.

First in line was Charlie Sheen. He thanked me politely for his gift and left. I thought no more about it and carried on handing out party bags to the rest of the guests, including Wesley Snipes, Sylvester Stallone and Scarlet Johansson.

Suddenly, standing in front of me with his hand out, I was surprised to see Charlie Sheen again. The greedy so-and-so must have ran round the side of the house, back in through the patio doors and re-joined the line!

I told him I was sure he'd already had his bag, but he looked me straight in the eye and told me I must be mistaken.

I knew Sheen was a good actor after seeing him in *Foodfight!*, *Scary Movie 3* and *Scary Movie 4*, but his performance on this occasion was so convincing I even began to doubt my own memory.

I had no choice but to hand him a second party bag. However, it turned out I had been right after all, for at the end of the party, I was one party bag short and so Shelley Duvall had to go without.

The Oscar-nominated star of *Popeye*, *The Shining* and *Annie Hall* had to fight back the tears as I apologised that there had been a mix-up with the number of party bags.

In truth, I knew there had been no such mistake and I hadn't messed up.

Unable to control his demons, Sheen had taken twice as many party bags as he was entitled to. Looking back now, it's clear that he had already pressed the self destruct button and his behaviour had started to spiral out of control."

SINCE stepping off the Tinseltown rollercoaster and returning to the UK, Parslow has been attempting to re-launch his career as a party entertainer in his native Doncaster. But he hit a setback last week after pleading guilty to a minor offence at his local magistrates court.

He was placed on the sex offenders register, and banned from going within 200 yards of any primary school in South Yorkshire for the next three years. "There was a misunderstanding over an innocent game at a child's party I was organising," Parslow told us.

"It involved the kiddies reaching into my pocket and trying to identify various sorts of sweets. To cut a long story short, there was some confusion over the rules and one of the mums got the police involved. It was all very unfortunate," he added.

NEXT WEEK: Parslow remembers how Kevin Costner weed himself after drinking loads of lemonade at the *Waterworld* Premiere party, despite his wife Sigourney Weaver asking him repeatedly if he needed the toilet.

Letterbocks

Viz Comic
P.O. Box 841
Whitley Bay
NE26 9EQ
letters@viz.co.uk

STAR LETTER

MY R.E. teacher told me that in times of sadness, the Bible was something positive to draw on. So I did Jesus with a big willy.

Ed O'Meara e-mail

I CAN never decide whether I like Genghis Khan or not. On the one hand he butchered an estimated 40million people from China to Hungary, but on the other he is credited with developing a system of reliable tax collection.

Algernon Bedford, e-mail

POLITICIANS should be made to wear a Magic Crystal of Truth around their necks all the time that would glow green when they tell the truth and red when they lie. I know they don't exist, but surely scientists could invent one. They can put a man on the Moon for heaven's sake.

Hector Boron, Leeds

AS A Heterosexual man, there is nowhere I can go and have a chance of fucking Beyonce or Kylie Minogue. If I was Homosexual, I would have a chance of fucking George Michael if I turned up at Hampstead Heath late on. Where's the justice?

Rev. Ian Craggs, e-mail

IN THE unlikely event that the girl band *The Saturdays* came round demanding a portion while my wife was out, I'm not sure which order I would do them in. I think I'd probably just play it by ear.

Big Dave, e-mail

I WONDER what people are going to do after the year 9999, because all forms have four boxes to put the date in, and the year 10,000 will have five digits. They will all have to be re-designed. I am aware that the problem is a long way off, but there is no point leaving things until the last minute.

Ada Rubidium, Luton

WHENEVER I feel down I always think of East 17's Brian Harvey, running over his own head whilst being sick out of a car after eating 4 baked potatoes. Always cheers me right up.

Theo, e-mail

ARE you still doing Jimmy Carr spotting? If so, I spotted his head for sale at the side of the road in Ashton in Makerfield. Do I win £5?

Al Kay, Wigan

YOU wouldn't believe the poor customer service I received from WH Smith in my dream last night. I won't be shopping there again.

Christina Martin, e-mail

I'VE only got one leg, and whenever I buy a pair of shoes I always have to throw one away. Why don't shops sell shoes individually for half price? People with two legs would then pay the same price for their shoes as they always do and one-legged people would be able to buy only the shoes they need.

Frank Cadmium, Torquay

PS. It would also benefit people with three legs who at the moment, I would imagine, are forced to buy two pairs of shoes and discard one.

"WE'RE all in this together" said the Government, trying to keep the nation's spirits up in these straightened times. Well we certainly weren't in the Royal Box at Wimbledon together with Chancellor George Osborne and the Governor of The Bank of England. On a work day.

D Coster, e-mail

HAVING just knocked over a full cup of coffee, I used kitchen roll to clean up. Can I respectfully suggest that the "Juan Sheet" character in the advert change his name to Arfur Roll?

Gail Smith, e-mail

CONVINCE colleagues you're Andy Murray by bringing your mum and girlfriend to work with you.

Sexton Hardcastle, Berlin

WEDNESDAY night 5-a-side footy players. Avoid playing in the same team as someone with the same name as you. Alternatively, don't be upset when, in order to identify you from your namesake, you are refered to as 'Fat Paul', to pick a name entirely at random.

Grant Cunningham, e-mail

SUPERMARKETS. Don't throw away your rotten, misshapen and undersized fruit. Re-label it as 'Fairtrade' then double the price.

Peter Britton, e-mail

CATS. Annoy your owner by being the reason they don't take their dream job in America then scratch the fuck out of the new leather chair they bought themselves as a consolation.

Clive Seatbelt, e-mail

MAKE your neighbours think they live next to Michael Jackson by chasing a monkey round your garden with your hair on fire.

Tam Dale, e-mail

RECREATE the joys of camping by turning your oven on full heat then lying on the kitchen floor on lots of stones while inside a bin liner, and filling your living room with dogshit.

Matt Skillz, e-mail

ZOO keepers – Provide added entertainment for your visitors by running round with a rifle and a panicked expression, asking people if they saw "which way it went".

Mike Tatham, e-mail

SMEAR excrement around the rim of your vacuum cleaner's wand for a clean and efficient alternative to fly-paper.

Stevno Bruise, e-mail

COACH drivers. The painted white line down the centre of country lanes is a convenient indicator of one's safest position on the roadway. It is not your source of motive power like in Scalextric.

TD Charles, e-mail

WHISTLE blowers. Guarantee anonymity by only ever using a dog whistle.

Stoner Smurf, e-mail

ON A recent visit to Switzerland I was delighted to find this notice politely telling visitors what not to do, including warning against letting their dogs shit all over the place. Nothing unusual about that, but it's the look of sheer bloody minded anger in the dog's face as he delivers his motion that tickles me. I wonder if any other readers have pictures of other such cartoon animals straining for a crap that could beat this? I very much doubt it.

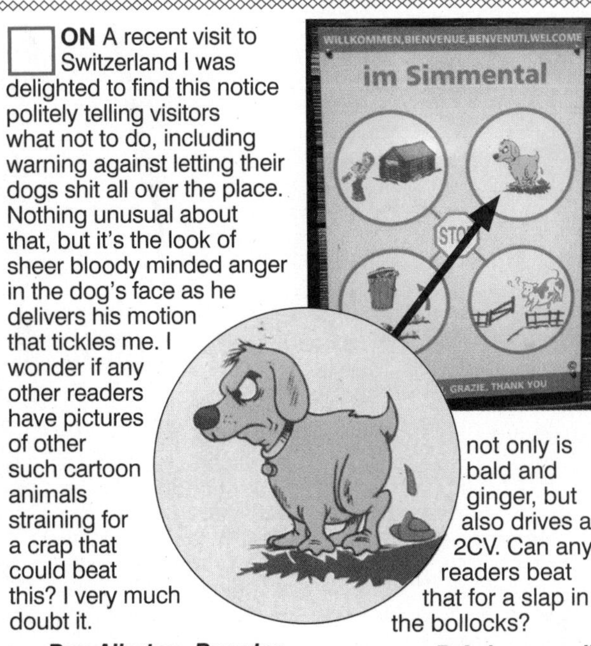

Roy Allerton, Bywater

DO ANY of your readers know what happens to the tennis balls that the young ladies of Wimbledon have been storing up their knickers for 3 hours? It looks to me like they just belt them off into the crowd which seems a criminal waste.

S Nurgle, e-mail

MY MISSUS had an affair with a man who not only is bald and ginger, but also drives a 2CV. Can any readers beat that for a slap in the bollocks?

B Ache, e-mail

IN THE name of equality, isn't it about time we had a picture of a bird kissing that bloke's arse?

Katrina Mullin, e-mail

** SHAME on you, Ms Mullin. Your reduction of men to mere objects of a woman's pleasure is sexist and highly offensive, and has no place in a family magazine like Viz.*

Man dies after docs dismiss symptoms as 'sniffles'

Victim: Mr Artfield in happier times.

THE FAMILY of a Luton man who died just hours after being sent home by his GP are seeking compensation from the local health authority.

Peplow Artfield went to Dr Dee Dynbych complaining of a runny nose, sneezing and aching limbs, but his symptoms were brushed aside as "a mild case of the sniffles." However, before he got home, the 56-year-old grandfather of three was dead.

wife

His wife told reporters: "We feel badly let down. Doctor Dynbych has got a lot of questions to answer."

"It beggars belief that she could tell my husband he had a simple cold when in reality, he had just hours left to live," she added.

fly

It appears that after leaving the surgery, Mr Artfield returned home with the intention of having a Lem-sip and going to bed. However, as he made his way across the busy A361, he was run over by a steamroller, killing him instantly.

Dr Dynbych has since been suspended on full pay, pending a BMA inquiry into her conduct.

nuggets

Mr Artfield's son Peplow Jr., 41, confirmed that the family were seeking compensation for their loss. "Our dad paid his stamps all his life. He deserved better than this," he said. "No amount of money will bring him back, but a large amount of money will definitely cheer us up quite a bit."

TEA Q&A with the AB of C out of the C of E

Dear AB of C

MY doctor recently told me that I only have 6 months to live, and now I'm worried that there won't be any tea to drink when I get up to Heaven.

Yootha Marmalade
Braintree

• Don't worry Mrs Marmalade. I can assure you that there's plenty of tea in Heaven. In fact, on arrival at the Pearly Gates you will be given a cup of tea that never runs out and never goes cold. Imagine that. An endless cuppa for all eterni-"tea"!

Dear AB of C

DO they use tea bags or loose tea in Heaven? Only I don't really like teabags because you can taste the paper.

Charlie Potatoes
Clerkenwell

• This was the subject of a meeting of the General Synod in 2003, and we decided by 12 votes to 8 that it's definitely loose tea that you get in Heaven. They have tea bags in Hell and they always burst so the sinners get all leaves in their mouths for ever. Satan sometimes also leaves the bag in the cup and there's no sugar. Not only that, the milk is on the turn even though you can't smell it, so there's floaters in your tea.

Dear AB of C

I HAVE always tried to live a good life. I go to church each Sunday, I do a lot for charity and I've never touched myself "under the bridge". Yet whilst pouring myself a cuppa at a cafe yesterday, the tea ran down the underside of the spout and went in the saucer, making the sugar sachet all wet. The man at the next table looked like a paedophile, yet his teapot poured perfectly. How could a just God have allowed such a situation to occur?

Emily Vergin, Chastebury

• We can't see into the mind of the Lord. The Bible tells us that He moves in mysterious ways His wonders to perform, so He may simply of been testing your faith when He caused the tea to go all down the underside of the spout. Or He may of been punishing you for a sin that you committed at some time during your life, possibly when you were a very small child. Remember, He sees all and He's been watching your every action from the moment you were conceived. It's even possible that God was visiting His wrath upon you for a sin committed by one of your ancestors, perhaps nothing more than a fleeting, impure thought. For it is written in the Good Book that The Lord shall visit the sins of the fathers upon the children of the evildoers, wreaking his vengeance upon them even unto the eighth generation.

Dear AB of C

WITH reference to my previous letter *(above)*, I like the idea of a never-ending cup of tea in Heaven. However, tea always goes right through me, and I'm worried that I'm going to be spending more time sat on the toilet spending tuppence than at the Lord's right hand.

Yootha Marmalade,
Braintree

• Don't worry, Mrs Marmalade. I'm sure that God has a plan. Remember that Heaven is paradise, and everything there is perfect, so perhaps you'll only have to go for one big wee a day, rather than lots of little ones. Or you might be able to just pull up your angel's frock and "go" whilst you're sitting on a cloud, and it'll turn into a rainbow.

Dear AB of C

I ONLY drink tea out of my favourite mug. It's got "World's Best Grandad" on it, and I want to take it to Heaven with me when I pass on. I'm planning to get cremated, and although the undertaker thinks my mug should survive the heat, he says it will probably get smashed in the machine they use to grind the ashes up at the crematorium. Is there any way I could take my mug with me to the hereafter in one piece, do you think?

Albert Pleurisy, Leeds

• I don't think it would be safe to take a real cup into Heaven, as it could easily slip off a cloud during an unguarded moment and hit somebody down on the earth. But even though your favourite mug may not survive your cremation, I am quite certain that its spirit will be waiting for you in paradise when you get there, good as new. Any chips or cracks in the pot will have been fixed, thanks to the infinite grace of the Lord.

Dear AB of C

A FEW months ago, I put the radio on and made myself a cup of tea. As I took my first sip, the news came on about the terrible tsunami in Japan, which had killed tens of thousands of innocent people. How could a loving God allow so much suffering to occur on such a vast scale?

Perkin Bootle, Everton

• Bother! I was just going to answer that question in a succinct and convincing manner, only my secretary has just told me that the ecclesiastical milliner has arrived to measure my head for a new Archbishop's hat.

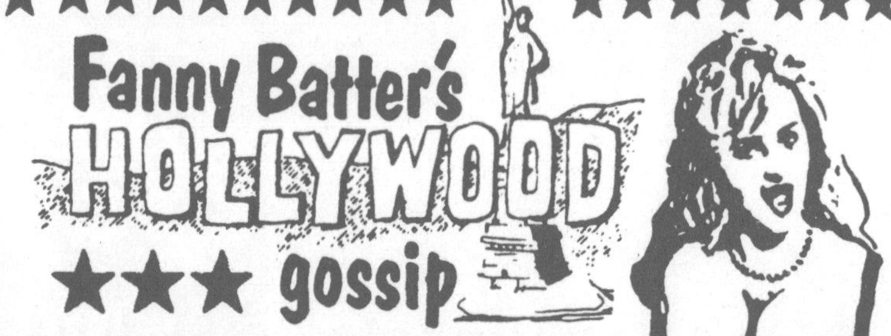

ALL THE BUZZ FROM SUNSET STRIP TO TINSELTOWN... *AND BACK!*

FILMING of the latest *Pirates of the Caribbean* blockbuster ground to a halt yesterday ... and all because *Jack Sparrow* star **JOHNNY DEPP** had made himself sick on sweets! According to my on-set spies, the 47-year-old heart-throb actor had been forced to prepare his own packed lunch after mum *Cleopatra* sex-pot **LIZ TAYLOR** woke up dead of congestive heart failure in her 2,800-bedroom Bel-Air mansion.

Half-way through the morning, Depp proudly showed the contents of his *Power Rangers* lunch-box to co-star **KEIRA KNIGHTLEY**, who confided in pals **COURTNEY COX** and **BRIAN GLOVER** what was inside. "There were no sandwiches or fruit in there, just sweets," Knightley is believed to have said. "It was crammed with Mars Bars, Topics, Caramacs and Curly-Wurlies!"

Sweet-toothed Johnny then proceeded to munch his way through his entire stash in one sitting, before announcing to director **JOEL SCHUMACHER** that he had a tummy ache. Shortly afterwards, Beverly Hills GP to the stars **Dr DOOGLAS HOWSER MD** confirmed studio bosses' worst fears when he advised *Edward Scissorhands* star Depp to take the rest of the day off filming, costing Paramount Studios a cool $20 million in lost production time.

A little bird tells me the new movie has been dogged with bad luck. Filming was held up for three weeks when co-star **IAN McSHANE** was injured in a stunt. Word on the street is the former *Lovejoy* actor had built a ramp out of pallets and breeze-blocks on some waste ground near his San Diego beachfront apartment, and was intending to jump over close pals **JOHN MALCOVICH**, **CHRISTOPHER WALKEN** and **FRANK THORNTON** on his new BMX. But the *Deadwood* star misjudged the leap and came a cropper, landing on his chin in some nettles.

Will this film ever get finished? Watch this space, me hearties!

TINSELTOWN'S buzzin' with rumours that *Batman* star **CHRISTIAN BALE** got out of bed to go for a wee in the middle of the night this week ... and put his slippers on the wrong feet! Word is, the *American Psycho* actor took a couple of steps and even reached the landing of his $500billion Laurel Canyon condo before he spotted his goof.

Luckily, the rest of the wee went without a hitch, and Bale woke up in the morning with no recollection of what had happened. But that hasn't stopped late night chat-show kings **JAY LENO** and **DAVID LETTERMAN** making merry at *Terminator* star Bale's slipper slip-up. "I hear Christian Bale can't tell his left foot from his right foot. Perhaps he ought to borrow some galoshes from Jimmy Cricket!" joked Leno on his top-rated NBC show whilst somebody played a drum-roll.

So are the whispers true? One thing's for sure, you won't get an answer from Bale, who remained tight-lipped on the red carpet outside Grauman's Chinese Theatre at the premiere for *Predator vs Police Academy*. "I'm not saying anything," he winked. But he later tweeted a cryptic message to his 40 trillion followers: "out buyin nu slippaz lol".

Whatever could he mean by that? You heard it here first!

KEEP IT to yourself, but the word on Sunset Boulevard is that *Tomb Raider* star **ANGELINA JOLIE** has a new number one destination for her number twos! Angelina, 36, was so impressed with the toilets in her 7-star hotel on a recent jaunt to the United Arab Emirates, that she's refusing to "go" anywhere else!

What was it about the luxury throne in the $50million-a-night Burj al Arab ensuite that so captivated the Lara Croft actress? Was it the solid gold seat, studded with Koh-i-Noor diamonds, the alabaster cistern - complete with platinum ball-cock - or the mink Luton? Angelina's keeping shtum.

But whatever it is, it's got the *Changeling* star hopping on a 747 at LAX every morning, regular as clockwork, arriving in Dubai mid-afternoon with the turtle's head and checking into her luxury penthouse suite just in time to pinch one off. After wiping, the *Beowolf* star flushes, washes her hands and then flies home to hubby **BRAD PITT**, arriving jet-lagged back at the couple's $400billion San Fernando ranch in time to go straight to bed!

Surely it's only a matter of time before Angelina's dizzying toilet routine starts top take a toll on her marriage to hunky *Fight Club* star Brad. Let's hope it doesn't drive him back into the arms of ex-squeeze **JENNIFER ANISTON**, who's now a free agent following the death of her snooker-commentating hubby "Whispering" **TED LOWE**.

Fanny x x

Fanny's BATTER BITS

WICKED WHISPERS FROM THE TINSELTOWN GRAPEVINE

WHICH *ageless Queen of the screen puts down her peach-like complexion to the fact that she moisturises her face every morning with rhinoceros spunk ... courtesy of her local zoo? I can't tell you who the Prime Suspect is, or this Dame would take me to "Helen" back!*

WHO *is the veteran Hollywood star who recently checked himself into an exclusive Bel Air ass clinic in a bid to cure his addiction to sticking cacti up his brown-eye? He's trying to cure his prickly habit any which way he can, but at a million bucks a night, it looks like it's going to cost him a Fistful of Dollars!*

WHICH *A-list songstress is presently being wooed by a filthy hobo? The star has been spotted sharing a romantic, brazier-lit dinner of discarded Big Mac & Fries with the flea-ridden tramp and his dog, before retiring to his cardboard box in a railway arch for a night of torrid passion. I can't identify this Funny Girl for legal reasons, but pals say Barbra's definitely a Woman in Love!*

IN THE WORLD OF THE FUTURE THERE IS ONLY ONE LAW – AND THAT IS THE LAW OF..

THE BOTTOM INSPECTORS

HERE ARE THE LATEST BOTTOM CRIME STATISTICS, OBERBOTTOMFUHRER.
MINISTRY OF BOTTOM INSPECTION

HM. THERE APPEARS TO BE A SIGNIFICANT INCREASE IN THE SMUGGLING OF CONTRABAND ANUSOL.
WIPE
YES, OBERBOTTOMFUHRER...

EVER SINCE THE PROHIBITION ACT OUTLAWED THE USE OF PILE OINTMENT LAST YEAR, THE BLACK MARKET TRADE HAS GROWN DRAMATICALLY.
IT IS SOLD IN ILLICIT CLUBS KNOWN AS "CHEEKEASIES" WHICH CATER FOR THOSE WHO HAVE CRIMINAL BUMCLEFT AFFLICTIONS.

I WANT THESE CLUBS LOCATED AND SHUT DOWN. EVERY SINGLE ONE OF THEM.
WE MUST SEND A CLEAR MESSAGE TO THOSE WHO FLOUT THE LAW PROHIBITING HAEMORRHOID CREAM...

RECTAL IMPERFECTIONS ARE AN OFFENCE AGAINST THE BOTTOMREICH, AND PERPETRATORS WILL BE PUNISHED SEVERELY.
OBI
WE WILL SQUEEZE THEM TILL THEY POP!

LATER, ACROSS TOWN
I SAY CHARLES, HOW MUCH FURTHER TO THIS PLACE?
SHH! WE'RE NEARLY THERE

KNOCK KNOCK!
NOW KEEP QUIET – I NEED TO GIVE THE PASSWORD

SHUNK!
HOW HANGS THE FRUIT TONIGHT?
THE GRAPES ARE HANGING LOW.

GOOD EVENING SIR – NICE TO SEE YOU AGAIN.
RELIEF FROM PILES
MOE'S CHEEKEASY
THANKS TED. THESE PEOPLE ARE MY GUESTS.

FOUR SHOTS OF PREPARATION H WITH GERMALOID SUPPOSITORY CHASERS, PLEASE MOE.
RIGHT AWAY, SIR
COTTON BUDS
ANUSOL
OH, AND I'D BETTER HAVE A SAVLON ANTISEPTIC WIPE FOR THE SPOT ON MY BARSE.

THIS IS A MARVELLOUS PLACE, CHARLES – BUT I MUST JUST USE THE LOO.
YOU'LL LOVE IT IN THERE, VERONICA – THERE'S MOISTENED TOILET PAPER WITH ALOE VERA!
GOSH! HOW DECADENT!

LET'S SIT OVER HERE
LOOK! INFLATABLE INNER TUBES ON EVERY SEAT! I'D FORGOTTEN SUCH COMFORT EXISTED!

YES, THIS IS A PLACE IN WHICH ONE CAN RELAX, BEYOND THE CONSTRAINTS OF BOTTOM LAW...
A PLACE WHERE, JUST FOR A LITTLE WHILE, OUR BUTTOCKS CAN FEEL FREE.

SUDDENLY
CRASH
THIS IS A RAID!
OH MY GOD – IT'S THE B-MEN!

THIS IS AN ILLEGAL GATHERING. YOU ARE ALL UNDER ARREST.
I WONDER HOW THEY FOUND OUT ABOUT THIS PLACE? WE WERE ALL SO DISCREET!

A SIMPLE PHONE CALL WHEN I WAS IN THE LOO WAS ALL IT TOOK.
VERONICA! YOU TIPPED OFF THE BOTTOM INSPECTORS! BUT WHY?

YOUR MISTAKE WAS TO BRING AN UNDERCOVER AGENT ALONG TO YOUR DEN OF BOTTOM INIQUITY.
OBI
SWEET JESUS! SHE WAS AN O.B.I. BUM MOLE ALL THE TIME!

PUT THEM ALL INTO THE BOT MARIAS – THE BOTTOM CORRECTION CAMP AWAITS!
IN THE WORLD OF THE FUTURE, THERE IS NO SANCTUARY FOR THOSE WHO DEFY THE LAW OF THE BOTTOM INSPECTORS!

Have Your Say!

November's news of Prince William's forthcoming marriage to Kate Middleton brought joy to an otherwise gloomy United Kingdom. Rising unemployment, economic uncertainty and the threat of terrorism were instantly forgotten as the country rejoiced in the glorious announcement. Our bulging royal wedding postbag reflects the nation's euphoric reaction to the marriage of the Millennium...

WHEN the news that William was to get married came on the radio, I was so overjoyed that I had an orgasm on the spot. When I told my husband the news I had another one, and so did he... in his trousers. It was especially marvellous as he hasn't been able to achieve an erection of any sort for over 25 years. We're both in our 80s and think the Royal Family is lovely.

Edna Bolshevik, Cardiff

I'M unemployed and I've just taken out a 2500% APR QuickQuids loan in order to pay off some of the interest on an outstanding debt to Ocean Finance. My money woes have left me worried sick, not sleeping and suffering from panic attacks, alopecia and depression. But I instantly forgot all my troubles the moment I heard that Prince William was to marry the lovely Kate. I wish the happy couple all the luck in the world.

Reg Plywood, Widnes

WHILST out shopping I had somehow become trapped in the mechanism of an escalator and was suffering excruciating agony as the gears tore at my lower body. But when I overheard the paramedics that were rescuing me talking about the forthcoming royal wedding, I was so overjoyed that I forgot all about my plight. Although I lost both of my legs and most of my genitals in the machinery, that heartwarming piece of news made it the best day of my life.

Lobworth Ludd, Brighton

I'M SORRY to be a party pooper, but I don't think that Miss Middleton is of a high enough class to marry our future king. Her mother and father may be rich, but they run a business, for heaven's sake. Prince William should marry somebody whose parents are extremely wealthy but don't do anything, like Prince Charles did.

Hector Lowestoft, Tring

IT IS wonderful news that William has finally popped the question to his long-term sweetheart Kate Middleton. I only hope that no photographs of Chris Tarrant pulling up her bikini top and exposing her breasts appear in the gutter press to tarnish this magical day for the happy couple.

Hector Tring, Lowestoft

KATE Middleton might be marrying the heir to the throne, but she will never take the place of her predecessor Lady Diana in my heart. Well, not unless she gets photographed legs akimbo, wearing a thin dress and with her back to the sun so you can see her box. If she does that, the dirty cow gets my vote.

Sexton Caseworth, Throatsbridge

ACTUALLY, on second thoughts I rather hope that pictures of Chris Tarrant pulling up Kate's bikini top DO appear in the press. They look like a cracking pair of jubblies.

Hector Tring, Lowestoft

IT WOULD be a shame if Kate's old flames decided to spoil the happy couple's special day by blabbing sordid details about past relationships to the tabloids. To prevent this happening, perhaps MI5 should quietly round up all her ex-boyfriends and "deal with them", no questions asked.

Mrs Gateau, Jedburgh

WILLIAM is a very lucky young man. Kate will be a beautiful bride, and one day she will make a wonderful Queen. Let's hope the marriage doesn't turn sour so they have to kill her off like they did with Lady Di.

G Knollington, Fleetwood

I AM concerned that Kate's parents sell things for a living, and that these tradesmen's genes may be passed down to any children that she and Wills may have. Our country will be a laughing stock around the world if its future princes and princesses decide to work on a market stall or set up a burger van in a layby.

Rev J Foucault, Truro

SOME people say that William shouldn't marry Kate Middleton because she is a commoner, but they obviously haven't seen the woman who lives round the corner from my brother in Huddersfield. She goes to the newsagents in her dressing gown, gobs in the street and they say she sucks off the rent man in her back yard. Now that's common.

Gary Scrote, Wakefield

I BET Kate Middleton's dad wishes he'd of gone down the bookies when his daughter was born and put a tenner on her one day becoming the Queen. They would of given him odds of 500/1 easy, and he'd of had ten grand in his back bin as soon as the present Queen and Prince Charles died. The fact that he probably didn't do must of have taken the shine off the happy news of the engagement.

J McCririck, Bed

WILLIAM has picked himself a young and beautiful bride, just like his father Prince Charles did all those years ago. Let's hope Wills hasn't followed his dad's example by also getting himself a fugly piece on the side to empty his nuts up.

Audrey Fforbes-Hamilton, Surbiton

I AM an ardent republican, and when I saw on the news about the forthcoming royal wedding, I was so incensed that I put my foot through my TV and sent Buckingham Palace the bill. However, the Queen wrote back saying that due to cutbacks, she can only replace my 8-year-old set on a like-for-like basis whereas I would have preferred a large, modern flatscreen with surround sound.

Walter Bookbinder, Newcastle

Beverley Craven's ROYAL WEDDING NEWSROUND

✱ **KEEPERS** at London Zoo had their own special reason to celebrate the forthcoming royal marriage. For on the same day Buckingham Palace announced the engagement, the zoo's giant panda Gin-gin gave birth to two cubs. The successful delivery is the culmination of a six-year-long endangered species breeding programme involving other pandas from zoos and safari parks around the world. Delighted staff decided to name the new arrivals William and Kate in honour of the double celebration. The cubs have now been gassed, stuffed and mounted, and will be presented to the happy couple as a memento of their special day.

✱ *WILLS and Kate's reception will see the baking of a mammoth wedding cake, big enough to provide a slice for each and every one of the hundreds of honoured guests. But the cake will have to go some way before it equals the size of the world's largest ever wedding cake. When the billionaire Emir of Abu Dhabi recently got married, his chefs created a cake that was over five hundred miles high. The towering confection contained enough flour to fill fourteen thousand Wembley Stadiums, over six million tons of raisins, and was coated with enough icing to cover the whole of Belgium to a depth of twenty feet.*

✱ **THE royal couple will make their way to Westminster Abbey in the Coach of State, originally built for Queen Victoria's Coronation in 1838. The carriage, which will be drawn on its journey from Buckingham Palace by eight white horses, is made of solid Welsh gold which is three times as expensive as any other sort of gold. The liveried coachmen who will attend the couple on their journey have had their tongues surgically removed to prevent them repeating any gossip they may hear during the two-mile trip. Before they have a chance to write something down, their fingers will be crushed in a special vice at the Tower of London.**

✱ *THE choice of Westminster Abbey to stage the wedding surprised royal watchers, who had previously tipped St Paul's Cathedral as first choice location for the historic service. In actual fact, several different venues submitted bids to host the marriage, and the abbey was only chosen at the end of a lengthy assessment process carried out by Buckingham Palace officials. Other venues that tendered unsuccessful bids included Canterbury Cathedral, Emmanuel Church in West Hampstead, the Chapel Royal at St James's Palace, St George's Chapel in Windsor Castle and the Sands Centre, Carlisle.*

✱ **CONSTITUTIONAL experts insist that special care has to be taken to ensure that the matrimonial vows taken by the royal couple during the service are correctly worded. At her wedding in July 1981, nerves famously got the better of William's late mother Lady Diana Spencer, causing her to get the order of her husband's Christian names (Charles Philip Arthur George) muddled up. And at her 1960 marriage to Anthony Armstrong Jones, a clearly drunk Princess Margaret made such a hash of her vows that she accidentally got married to US entertainer Sammy Davis Junior.**

✱ *ACCORDING to media analysts, the wedding of Prince William and Kate Middleton is set to be the biggest television event of the Millennium, with an estimated six hundred thousand trillion billion people around the world switching on to watch the happy couple make their vows on April 29th. The previous record viewing figure for a TV broadcast was way back in 2004, when a global audience of twenty-six thousand million billion million tuned in to watch Hannah Gordon introduce a special celebrity edition of Channel 4's Watercolour Challenge, featuring Dave Lee Travis, Lembit Opik, Germaine Greer and Phil 'The Power' Taylor.*

✱ **WATER companies around the country are gearing up for an unprecedented sudden surge in demand at the end of the royal wedding service, when millions of telly viewers all round the country switch off their sets and get up to make a cup of tea. "There is a real risk that every reservoir in Britain could be drained bone dry in a matter of seconds," warns Guardian environment expert George Monbiot. "And when all those kettles boil simultaneously three minutes later, enough steam will be released into the atmosphere to completely block out the sun, causing a mini ice age which will destroy the human race. We are standing at the edge of an abyss."**

✱ *OF course, the thing that literally everyone in the world is waiting to see is Kate's dress. When the blushing bride steps from her golden coach outside Westminster Abbey and the viewing public gets its first glimpse of her frock it will be the most exciting moment since records began. However, Palace officials are privately said to be petrified at the possibility of a bird doing a shit on the dress on live television. As a result, in the weeks leading up to the wedding, millions of the unemployed will be recruited to climb up London's trees in order to hammer a small cork up the anus of every bird in the capital.*

✱ **ARCHBISHOP of Canterbury Rowan Williams is set to officiate at William and Kate's forthcoming nuptials, and he is already making preparations for the most important marriage service of his career. Dr Williams is famous for his bushy eyebrows, which he teases up at the sides because he thinks it makes him look a bit like an owl and therefore wise. A Lambeth Palace spokesman told us: "The Archbishop is determined to look even more ludicrous than usual for this royal wedding, so he's having two enormous eyebrow merkins specially weaved out of baboon pubes."**

INSURANCE ~ SCAMMERS 4U

WHO ARE WE?

Insurance-scammers4U is a nationwide network of corrupt personal injury lawyers, deceitful insurance companies, dodgy mechanics, dishonest doctors and bent coppers who are largely unaccountable and are collectively on the take in order to supplement their already generous incomes. And because we operate with impunity we can offer you ***100% no-win no-fee*** compensation and slowly drag the country down into the gutter!

"I was waiting a junction thinking about how I was going to pay off my credit card, when suddenly it came to me! I know, I'll rear-end the car in front of me at the next roundabout!"

"And thanks to insurance-scammers4U, I got 100% of the compensation, whilst all the other drivers' premiums skyrocketed!

HOW IT WORKS

1. You have a crash & contact your car insurance company

HUGE payouts for the most spurious or even nonexistent injuries!

2. The insurer refers you to a personal injury lawyer

3. The personal injury lawyer tells you that you have whiplash and he rings a doctor

4. The G.P. signs off a medical form that says you have 'mild whiplash'

5. You get £4K! A policeman laughs about it all!

Call now & get a FREE neck collar worth £20!

YOU HAVE NOTHING TO LOSE!

"I was on the verge on bankruptcy until I heard about this 'rear-ending the car in front of you at a junction' scheme. Within 2 weeks I got my own my neck brace, and after a month I received £3,000 !" ***Mrs. B, Essex***

INSURANCE~SCAMMERS 4U

Aldridge Prior HE'S A HOPELESS LIAR

NO I'M NOT
AND THAT'S THE GOD'S HONEST TRUTH.

DING DONG!

EEH, HELLO ALDRIDGE, PET. I HAVEN'T SEEN YOU FOR AGES.
YEAH, I MOVED TO AMERICA MUM. I LIVE IN HOLLYWOOD ACTUALLY. BEVERLEY HILLS

I GOT A JOB AS CLINT EASTWOOD'S PERSONAL BODYGUARD. THE PAY ISN'T BAD, FOUR GRAND A WEEK. NO, FIVE.
SIX.
THAT SOUNDS GOOD, LOVE. DID YOU FIND THAT AT THE JOB CENTRE?

NO, I WAS WALKING DOWN THE STREET AND THESE TEN BLOKES TRIED TO MUG ME, SO I USED KUNG FU ON THEM. I BECAME A BLACK BELT WHEN I WAS WITH THE SAS, YOU SEE.
ANYWAY, CLINT EASTWOOD WAS PASSING AND SAW THE WHOLE THING. HE HIRED ME AS HIS BODYGUARD ON THE SPOT.

I'VE GOT TO KNOW ALL THE BIG HOLLYWOOD STARS. CHARLES BRONSON, STEPHEN SPIELBERG...
EEH, FANCY!
YOU KNOW THAT DOCTOR WITH THE BEARD OUT OF HOLBY CITY? HE'S MY NEXT DOOR NEIGHBOUR IN BEVERLEY HILLS.

OH, THAT REMINDS ME. I NEED TO BOOK A TAXI TO TAKE ME UP THE HOSPITAL TOMORROW MORNING.
I'VE GOT AN APPOINTMENT TO SEE THE SPECIALIST ABOUT MY BAD KNEE AT 9 O'CLOCK.
DON'T BOTHER WITH A TAXI, MUM. I'LL GIVE YOU A LIFT TO THE HOSPITAL IN MY NEW CAR.
IT'S A MERCEDES MCLAREN SLR, WORTH FOUR HUNDRED GRAND. I WON IT OFF BRUCE DICKINSON OUT OF IRON MAIDEN IN A POKER GAME.

TA, LOVE. MY APPOINTMENT'S AT NINE, SO WE NEED TO LEAVE HERE BY HALF EIGHT.
NO PROBLEM, MUM. I'LL BE HERE AT 8.15 ON THE DOT.

NEXT MORNING, 8.40 AM
ALDRIDGE, WHERE ARE YOU? YOU'RE LATE!
YOU'RE SUPPOSED TO BE TAKING ME TO HOSPITAL IN YOUR NEW CAR, REMEMBER?

YEAH, I'M STUCK IN TRAFFIC. A LORRY JACK-KNIFED ON THE RING ROAD AND THERE'S A TWO MILE TAILBACK.
FIST OF FURY
BUT DON'T WORRY, I KNOW A SHORT CUT. I'LL BE THERE IN FIVE MINUTES.

TWENTY MINUTES LATER
TSK.

ALDRIDGE, IF YOU CAN'T GIVE ME A LIFT JUST SAY SO, AND I'LL CALL A TAXI.
I'M RUNNING LATE AS IT IS.

NO, THERE'S NO NEED FOR A TAXI. I'LL BE PICKING YOU UP IN TWO MINUTES.
FIST OF FURY
NOEL EDMONDS IS GIVING ME A LIFT IN HIS HELICOPTER. HE'LL GET US TO THE HOSPITAL IN NO TIME.

NOEL EDMONDS?
YEAH, HE'S A GOOD MATE OF MINE. I'M IN THE HELICOPTER WITH NOEL RIGHT NOW. AND BONO OUT OF U2.
WE'LL BE LANDING IN THE STREET OUTSIDE YOUR HOUSE IN THIRTY SECONDS

2
HOBBLE HOBBLE HOBBLE

AN HOUR LATER
FUME!

EVENTUALLY
PUT PUT PUT PUT PUT

ALDRIDGE, I'M OVER AN HOUR LATE FOR MY APPOINTMENT! WHAT HAPPENED?
WHERE'S NOEL EDMONDS AND HIS HELICOPTER?

OH YEAH, BEING IN A HELICOPTER WAS GIVING ME FLASHBACKS TO VIETNAM, SO I HAD TO GET OUT. BUT YOU CAN RIDE ON THE BACK OF MY SCOOTER, INSTEAD.
I CAN'T GO ON THAT THING WITH MY BAD KNEE!

OK, I'LL GIVE PRINCE WILLIAM A CALL. HE'LL ARRANGE FOR A HARRIER JUMP JET TO TAKE YOU UP THE HOSPITAL. ME AND HIM ARE GOOD FRIENDS.
YOU KNOW THAT KATE MIDDLETON WHO HE'S MARRYING? SHE'S MY SECOND COUSIN.

JUST FORGET IT, ALDRIDGE!
NO, REALLY... SHE WAS IN MY CLASS AT PRIMARY SCHOOL...
I'M GOING TO RING A TAXI.

HELLO, AARDVARK CABS? HOW SOON CAN I HAVE A TAXI AT NUMBER TWO, FULCHESTER CRESCENT?
FIVE MINUTES? YES, THAT'LL BE FINE, THANK YOU.

THERE! THE TAXI WILL BE HERE IN FIVE MINUTES.
I SHOULD'VE DONE THAT IN THE FIRST PLACE.

HALF AN HOUR LATER
OH FOR GOODNESS SAKE, WHERE IS THIS TAXI?!
IT'S TWENTY-FIVE MINUTES LATE! I'LL GIVE THEM A RING.

YEAH, YOUR DRIVER'S GOT STUCK IN TRAFFIC. WELL, IT WAS A FLAT TYRE ACTUALLY. THE BIG END WENT.
TAXI
AARDVARK CABS
BUT HE'LL BE WITH YOU IN TWO MINUTES. HE'S JUST PULLING INTO YOUR STREET NOW...

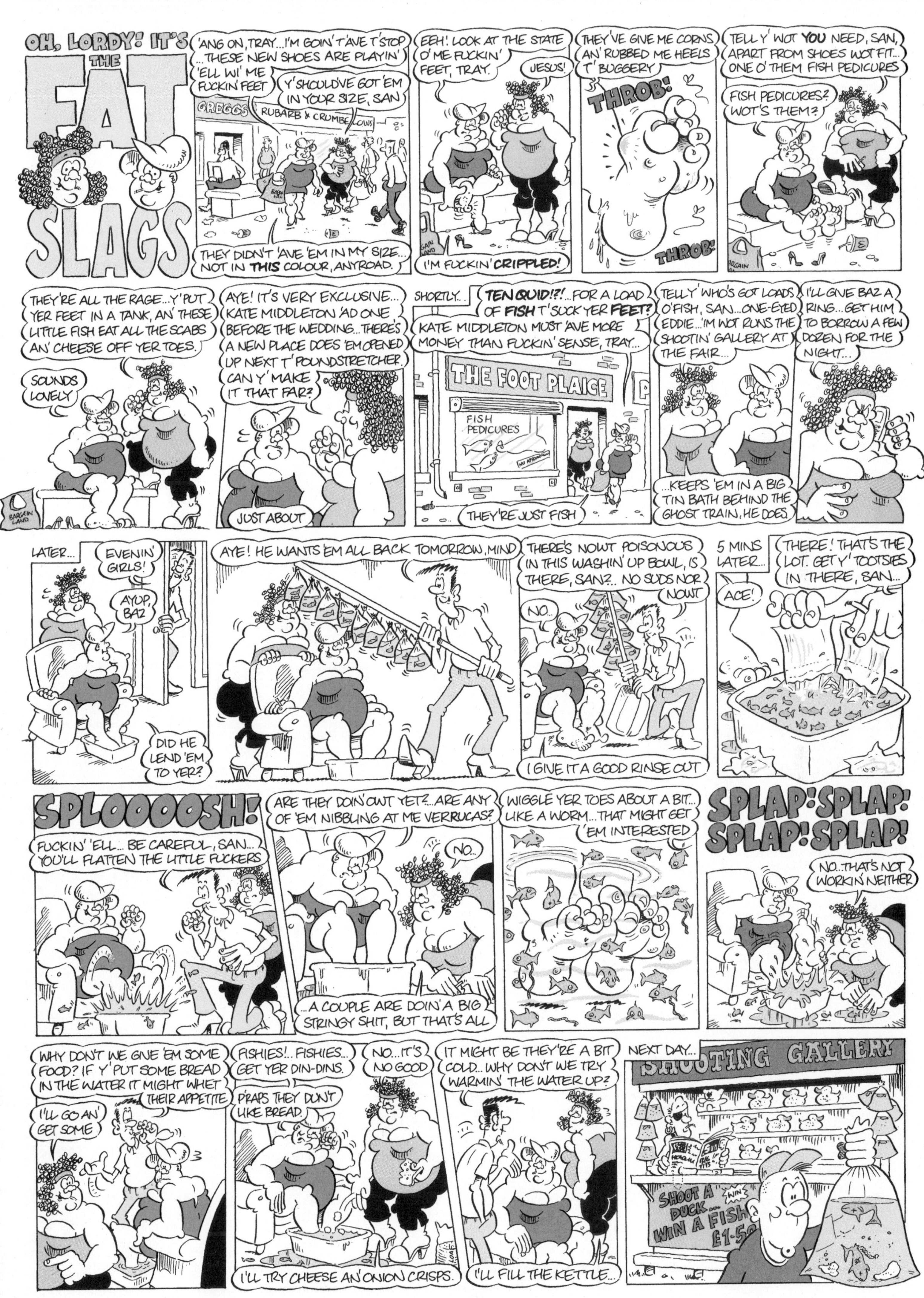
OH, LORDY! IT'S THE FAT SLAGS
'ANG ON, TRAY... I'M GOIN' T'AVE T'STOP ...THESE NEW SHOES ARE PLAYIN' 'ELL WI' ME FUCKIN' FEET
Y' SHOULD'VE GOT 'EM IN YOUR SIZE, SAN
GREGGS
RUBARB & CRUMBLE
THEY DIDN'T 'AVE 'EM IN MY SIZE... NOT IN THIS COLOUR, ANYROAD.
EEH! LOOK AT THE STATE O' ME FUCKIN' FEET, TRAY.
JESUS!
I'M FUCKIN' CRIPPLED!
THEY'VE GIVE ME CORNS AN' RUBBED ME HEELS T' BUGGERY
THROB!
THROB!
TELL Y' WOT YOU NEED, SAN, APART FROM SHOES WOT FIT... ONE O' THEM FISH PEDICURES
FISH PEDICURES? WOT'S THEM?
THEY'RE ALL THE RAGE... Y' PUT YER FEET IN A TANK, AN' THESE LITTLE FISH EAT ALL THE SCABS AN' CHEESE OFF YER TOES.
SOUNDS LOVELY
AYE! IT'S VERY EXCLUSIVE... KATE MIDDLETON 'AD ONE BEFORE THE WEDDING... THERE'S A NEW PLACE DOES 'EM OPENED UP NEXT T' POUNDSTRETCHER. CAN Y' MAKE IT THAT FAR?
JUST ABOUT
SHORTLY...
TEN QUID!?!... FOR A LOAD OF FISH T' SUCK YER FEET?
KATE MIDDLETON MUST 'AVE MORE MONEY THAN FUCKIN' SENSE, TRAY...
THE FOOT PLAICE
FISH PEDICURES
THEY'RE JUST FISH
TELL Y' WHO'S GOT LOADS O' FISH, SAN... ONE-EYED EDDIE... 'IM WOT RUNS THE SHOOTIN' GALLERY AT THE FAIR...
...KEEPS 'EM IN A BIG TIN BATH BEHIND THE GHOST TRAIN, HE DOES.
I'LL GIVE BAZ A RING... GET HIM TO BORROW A FEW DOZEN FOR THE NIGHT...
LATER...
EVENIN' GIRLS!
AYUP, BAZ
DID HE LEND 'EM TO YER?
AYE! HE WANTS 'EM ALL BACK TOMORROW, MIND
THERE'S NOWT POISONOUS IN THIS WASHIN' UP BOWL, IS THERE, SAN?.. NO SUDS NOR NOWT
NO..
I GIVE IT A GOOD RINSE OUT
5 MINS LATER...
ACE!
THERE! THAT'S THE LOT. GET Y' TOOTSIES IN THERE, SAN...
SPLOOOOOSH!
FUCKIN' 'ELL... BE CAREFUL, SAN... YOU'LL FLATTEN THE LITTLE FUCKERS
ARE THEY DOIN' OWT YET?.. ARE ANY OF 'EM NIBBLING AT ME VERRUCAS?
NO..
...A COUPLE ARE DOIN' A BIG STRINGY SHIT, BUT THAT'S ALL
WIGGLE YER TOES ABOUT A BIT... LIKE A WORM... THAT MIGHT GET 'EM INTERESTED
SPLAP! SPLAP! SPLAP! SPLAP!
NO... THAT'S NOT WORKIN' NEITHER
WHY DON'T WE GIVE 'EM SOME FOOD? IF Y' PUT SOME BREAD IN THE WATER IT MIGHT WHET THEIR APPETITE
I'LL GO AN' GET SOME
FISHIES!.. FISHIES... GET YER DIN-DINS.
NO... IT'S NO GOOD
P'RAPS THEY DON'T LIKE BREAD.
I'LL TRY CHEESE AN' ONION CRISPS.
IT MIGHT BE THEY'RE A BIT COLD... WHY DON'T WE TRY WARMIN' THE WATER UP?
I'LL FILL THE KETTLE...
NEXT DAY...
SHOOTING GALLERY
SHOOT A DUCK... WIN A FISH £1-50

BLACKPOOL GEARS UP FOR MELTDOWN

IT SEEMS like there's a new nuclear disaster every week. A day rarely goes by without an atomic power station going into meltdown somewhere around the world. Whether it's Chernobyl, Five Mile Island or Fuckyshima, the list goes on and on.

And with the fallout from these disasters spreading round the earth's atmosphere at the speed of light, radioactive contamination is no longer just a problem for the people living near the affected sites. We're all at risk from radioactivity and the dangers it brings, and the British Isles is no exception.

But one UK borough is determined that this summer is not going to turn into a nuclear winter. The seaside resort of Blackpool is ready and waiting for anything the world's exploding fast breeder reactors can throw at it. And Lord Mayor Don Clapham had this message for the forthcoming atomic holocaust: "Bring it on! We're not going to let death-rays stop our visitors catching the sun's rays along the Golden Mile."

In the wake of the Japanese Fuckyshima power plant meltdown, the Lancashire town's council called an emergency meeting to draw up a 10-point plan to safeguard residents and visitors from nuclear Armageddon.

FISSION CHIPS: Blackpool's seaside traditions are safe from radiation, says Mayor.

Lancashire sunspot set to become radiation hotspot. "Bring it on!" says Mayor.

THAT 10-POINT PLAN IN FULL

1 **THE WINTER Gardens to be re-named the Nuclear Winter Gardens, with a re-opening ceremony performed by the Lady Mayoress in a lead suit.**

2 *TO LIMIT daily exposure time to harmful Gamma radiation, boarding house guests to be evicted an hour later and allowed back in an hour earlier than usual.*

3 **THE PUNCH and Judy booth on the South Pier will be replaced with a 40 ft thick reinforced concrete bunker, to be painted in red and yellow stripes to allay panic.**

4 *A NEW, limited edition ice cream cone to be introduced - a Strontium 99 with Uranium 100s & 1000s, competitively priced at just £1.49 for the duration of the emergency.*

5 **HOUSEHOLDS in Blackpool and Fleetwood will be issued with a new, bright yellow wheelie bin for radioactive waste only. This would sit alongside the current green recycling and brown garden waste bins.**

6 *BIN COLLECTION rotas would be ammended accordingly from the current fortnightly arrangement to once every three weeks, with the yellow bins being emptied every third Thursday.*

7 **THE COUNCIL would impose a £50 fine for disposing of atomic waste in the wrong bin.**

8 *A CHARGE of £25 would be levied on anyone putting the yellow bin out on the wrong day, although an official warning letter would be issued before any penalty was imposed.*

9 **A POSTER campaign featuring a cartoon yellow wheelie bin called "Ned the Atomic Dustbin" - to be designed by the Mayor's son - will remind residents that the new bins must be left with their handles facing outwards, their lids fully closed and not obstructing pathways.**

10 *ANY DINOSAUR eggs presently on display in the town Museum will be placed in a secure box in the stock room. This is in order to prevent stray atomic rays causing them to hatch into Godzillas, which could go on the rampage and eat Blackpool Tower.*

But what concerned Planning Committee members most was the prospect of an increase in the number of mutants in Blackpool. The Mayor explained: "We've all seen the films where there's a nuclear disaster and the human population is reduced to a race of hideously deformed creatures living underground in the drains."

"As a council, it's difficult to plan for, as it is impossible to anticipate what sort of outlandish mutations might happen to Blackpool's residents and holidaymakers."

"But whether it's simply a man with lumpy skin, a woman with three tits or a dog with its owner's face, they're all welcome to join in the fun in the fallout in Britain's premier holiday destination," Councillor Clapham added.

with Naylor Hammond BSc.

MOST people think that atomic power is dangerous, but it's exactly the same as the power you have in your home. Just like mains electricity, it can be used for boiling the kettle, making toast and running your television set. The only difference is, it's made in a circular, rather than a normal-shaped power station. Radioactive fuel is made out of isotopes, which are put into rods by men wearing rubber gloves and goggles. These are then dipped in water to keep them cool, a bit like a biscuit being dunked in your tea. But instead of crumbs falling into the bottom of your cup, electricity comes off the rods. It is 240 volts and comes in three different wires, earth, neutral and live - 80 volts in each wire. Nuclear power also comes in three different sorts of amps - 3, 5 and 13, depending on what sort of plug it comes out of.

Bye for now!

Naylor Hammond BSc

Giant insects set to take over the world by 2020, says scientist

It's a Bug's Life

A BOFFIN from Britain's leading university says that nuclear fallout from the Japanese quake has already set in motion an unstoppable chain of events that will lead to giant insects ruling the earth within the decade.

The head of entomology at Oxford University predicts that radioactive dust from the Fuckyshima meltdown will cause cockroaches to grow up to nine feet tall, allowing them to over-run the planet by 2020.

HEINZ

What's more, says Heinz Ravioli, there's nothing we can do to stop it.

"Nothing can now be done to prevent a plague of giant bugs taking over the world. Our puny human weapons will have no effect against their bulletproof carapaces," he warned. "Their giant pincers will snip a tank in half as if it were naught but a flimsy twig. Our atomic bombs will merely make them stronger."

TEEN

"But be in no doubt, in the forthcoming insect wars, the living shall envy the dead. For the insensate oblivion of the grave shall seem sweet compared to the living torment which awaits those who survive"

"For those who perish - men, women and children - shall be carried back to the cockroaches' lair, and there they shall be bound inside coccoons as strong as steel rope," continued Professor Ravioli. "Their grisly fate? Only this - for their still-warm flesh to become a living larder for the next generation of our cockroach overlords."

GONE THE BUSES: Giant cockroaches will destroy all traces of human civilisation, says Dr Ravioli.

BRONZE

"Imagine the agony, as the hungry pupae twist and writhe within, their ravenous jaws chewing their way through the yet conscious innards of their host, stretching and distorting the skin from within. Then, after six months of inconceivable pain, the maggots will burst forth, finally bringing the sweet release of death to the human whose body has nourished them," he told an Oxford primary school's year 4 nature club.

A-List X-Men!

Celebrity superpowers scenario set to come true

JUST like in the comic book adventures of the X-Men, scientists believe that leaked radiation from Fuckyshima could alter the genetic structure of our DNA, causing us to develop super-human powers.

X-Ray vision, telekinesis, the ability to freeze things by pointing at them... all of these powers could one day become commonplace if the meltdown at the Japanese atom plant isn't brought under control.

But how will this scenario affect our favourite TV stars? We asked a selection of showbiz celebs which superpowers they would like, how they would use them and what they would be called.

JONATHAN ROSS..............

"I'D call myself Captain Elastic, and I'd have infinitely stretchy limbs to enable me to feel up women from the comfort of my own living room," said the chat show king. "I'd make my arm go all thin and poke it out through the letterbox, and then stick it up the skirt of any bird I fancied anywhere in the world, and have a bit of a grope of her bum and fanny."

JIMMY KRANKIE.............

"IT'D be fandabidozi to be invisible. I'd use my superpower to hide from my husband Ian when he's going to give me a slippering for getting up to mischief," said the septuagenarian Scotch ladyboy. "Then, while he couldn't see me, I'd shoot him up the bum with my catapult. Hee-hee! I wouldnae need a costume, neither. I'd call myself The Invisible Boy, or possibly The Invisible Elderly Lady."

RACHEL ALLEN................

"I'D like microwave vision, so I could cook things just by looking at them," said the TV cook. "That way, I'd never have to clean out my oven again. I'm not sure quite how I would regulate the power. Perhaps I'd look with one eye if I only wanted to defrost something, or glare really hard if I was roasting a ham. I'd have a cape and a black visor to stop me burning my friends and family. And I'd probably call myself Therm-O-Woman, or something like that."

NOEL EDMONDS...............

"I'D like the ability to control the minds of everybody in the world," said the sinister whirly wheeler-dealer. "The whole earth's population would be nothing more than my puppets, dancing with mute obedience to my every whim. I'd call myself Noel Edmonds."

Tragic death of TV alcoholic

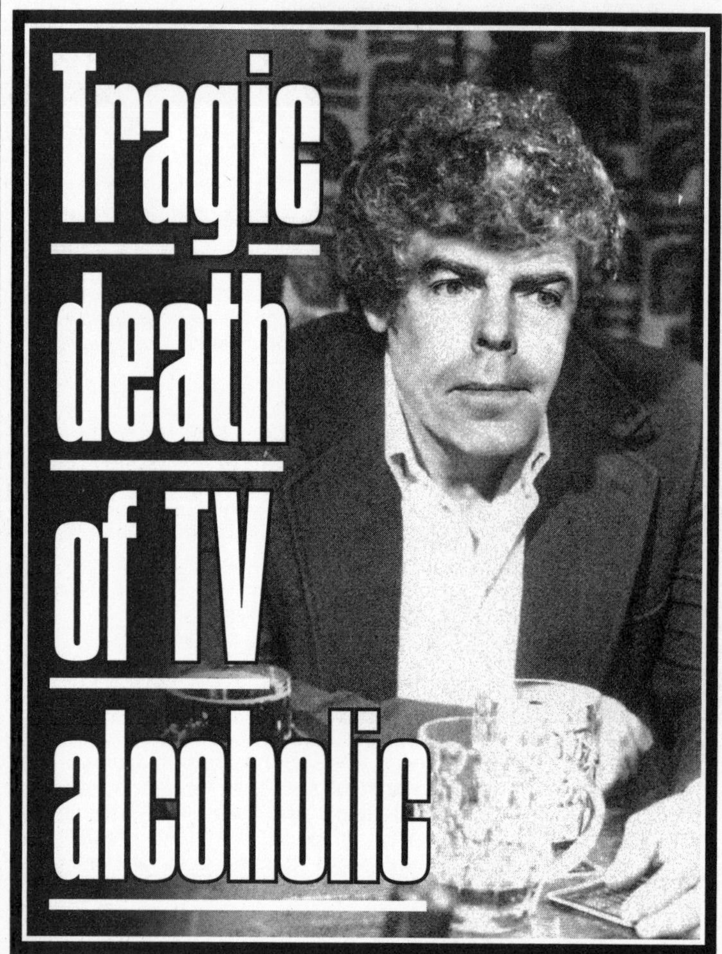

THE broadcasting industry yesterday paid tribute to TV alcoholic PETER WENLOVE who died last week, a victim of his addiction to TV drinking.

By our ARTS CORRESPONDENT
OLIVER REED standing on a table with his belt undone

Wenlove started TV drinking socially, cradling the occasional wine glass filled with cranberry juice by an untouched dinner, or enjoying a relaxing glass of water with a slice of lemon in it at the TV pub after a hard day's TV work. But his TV drinking soon got out of control. By the end, according to sources, he was downing up to ***TWENTY*** pint glasses full of cold tea every night.

FACE DOWN

TV friends became concerned for his safety when a firebar was seen burning a short distance in front of some tea towels in his kitchen. And in June, a much younger man of approximately Wenlove's height and build, wearing his clothes, was hit by a car before landing face down in the road.

TV business rival Trent Dominic remembers meeting Wenlove at his TV office. "He was under a lot of TV stress, staring out of the window at a faint painting of the street, as if looking for answers," he says.

"He downed tumbler after tumbler of apple juice with ice cubes in the bottom. I mean, I'm a fairly heavy TV drinker, but I couldn't keep up. I'd need to go to the toilet. But of course, we never do."

BUM FLUFF

Wenlove's TV family were by his bedside at the end, as were two small white rectangles and some information about when *Emmerdale* would be on.

TV doctors said he died from an excess of hushed medical dialogue leading to over-complications and a series of close-ups of a machine beeping more and more slowly.

As a mark of respect, there was two seconds' silence and then the theme music.

SID the SEXIST

'ERE'S THE DRINKS, LADS...
The DOCKER'S FIST
THE DOCKERS FIST

GET ON THE OOTSIDE O' THEMS.
NECTAH!

BOB WUZ JUST TELLIN' US HE'S SEEN A BLURK ON THE INTERNET WOT COULD SUCK HIS AIRN COCK.
OH AYE? BIG FELLA, WAS HE?

NAH. THAT'S THE THING, SID. HE WUZ SMAALLER THAN YEE!
HO!HO!
CHEEKY BASTAAD.

IT'S NOWT T'DEE WI' THE LENGTH O' YER URLD FELLA, SID.
AYE. BUT YUZ'VE HEV T'BE CANNY SUPPLE, THOUGH BUT.
NAH MAN. ANYONE CAN DEE IT, THEY RECKON.

THAT RON JEREMY OFF THE SCUD FILLUMS... HE CAN DEE IT... AN' HE LOOKS LIKE HE'S EXPECTIN' FUCKIN' TWINS!
WELL 'OW COMES, THEN?

WELL IT'S AALL IN THE TECHNIQUE, MAN.
AYE...

...MATE O'MINE'S BROTHER'S A ORTHOPAEDIC SORGEON, AN' HE SEZ THAT THE HUMAN SKELLINGTON IS FAR MORE FLEXIBLE THAN YUZ'D IMAGINE...

HE TELLT US HOW T'DEE IT...

WOT YUZ'VE GOT T'DEE IS RURL UP INTO A GEET BAALL, THE SMAALLER THE BETTAH... THEN YUZ HEV TO TWIST TO THE LEFT...

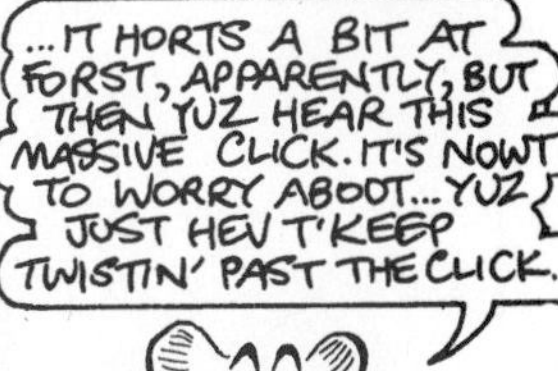

...IT HORTS A BIT AT FORST, APPARENTLY, BUT THEN YUZ HEAR THIS MASSIVE CLICK. IT'S NOWT TO WORRY ABOUT... YUZ JUST HEV T'KEEP TWISTIN' PAST THE CLICK...

...THEN, WHEN YUZ'VE DONE THAT, YER LIFT YER REET LEG UP... AND BINGUR!
YER CHOPPAH'S REET IN FRONT OF Y'MOOTH..!

...AALL READY FORRA THORTY-FAWA-AN'-A-HAWFAH!
WELL I CANNAT SEE WHY ANYBODY WOULD WANT T'DEE THAT.
AYE. IT'S A BIT FUCKIN' PORVEY, IF Y'ASK ME.

AYE. AN' IT'S TECHNICALLY FUCKIN' HURMURSEXUAL, AN' AALL.
AYE. IT'S FUCKIN' SAD, THAT. TRYIN' T'NOSH YUZ AIRN DOBBAH.
TOO REET.

IF Y'CANNAT GET A LASS T'SUCK YER COCK, IT SHOULD STAY FUCKIN' UN-SUCKED, THAT'S WOT I RECKON, SID.
AYE, BAZ.

...WELL I DIVVEN'T HEV ANY TROUBLE IN THAT DEPARTMENT, LADS!
ME NEETHAH.
AYE.

NEXT NIGHT..
The DOCKER'S FIST
'ERE'S THE DRINKS, LADS...
NECTAH!

HEY, WOT A COINCIDENCE... AALL OF W'FAALLIN' DOON THE STAIRS AFTAH TRIPPIN' ON W' LITTLE BROTHERS' RURLER SKATES, EH..?
AYE.. WOT'S THE FUCKIN' ODDS O' THAT, EH?
SHUFFLE SHUFFLE
THOOSAND T'ONE.

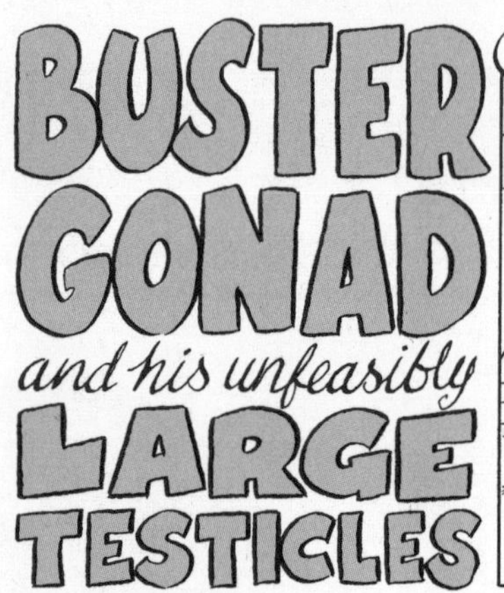
BUSTER GONAD
and his unfeasibly
LARGE TESTICLES

HI, READERS. I'VE GOT A JOB AT SEALAND MARINE PARK...
...IT'LL BE A PRETTY SHORT CARTOON THIS WEEK, AS I DOUBT I'LL GET INTO ANY JAMS OR SCRAPES HERE
SEA LAND
PENGUINS

MORNING, GONAD. FIRST JOB OF THE DAY IS TO MUCK OUT THE OCTOPUS ENCLOSURE
YES, MR. GRIMSDALE
SEA LAND
MANAGER

SO...
...AND HERE WE HAVE THE EX-TREMELY RARE POLYNESIAN PINK HAIRY OCTOPUS...
AND THE UNUSUAL THING ABOUT THIS SPECIES IS THAT THEY MATE ONLY ONCE IN THEIR LIFE AND THEN IMMEDIATELY DIE...
OCTOPUS ECOLOGY LECTURE TODAY 10·00 o'clock

...THEIR TENTACLES GRAB HOLD OF THEIR PREY WITH AMAZING STRENGTH
SEA LAND
OCTOPUS ECOLOGY LECTURE TODAY 10·00

...AND ONCE IN THEIR GRASP, THERE IS LITTLE ANYTHING CAN DO TO SHAKE THEM OFF

YEEOW! MY PLUBBLELUBBLELUBBLELUMBS!
HUMP! HUMP! HUMP! HUMP! HUMP! HUMP!
SEA LAND
!?

HUMP! HUMP! HUMP! HUMP!
FRING!

BAH! THIS OCTOPUS HAS BANGED ITSELF TO DEATH ON YOUR NUTS, YOUNG MAN... DO YOU KNOW HOW MUCH POLYNESIAN PINK HAIRY OCTOPUSES COST!?
ER...NO.
£100
...AND IT'S COMING OUT OF YOUR WAGES, GONAD

SHORTLY...
THE SEA URCHIN NEEDS SOME MEDICAL TREATMENT...SO I'M HOLDING IT STILL WHILE THE VET SHOOTS IT WITH A TRANQUILISER DART.
READY?
DOLPHINS
ROCK POOL
VET
YES...

...HANG ON... AREN'T YOU COMING IN THE WATER TOO?
NO NEED...

...THE DART IS COMP-UTER GUIDED. ALL I HAVE TO DO IS SET THE RIGHT ANIMAL ON THIS DIAL, HERE
LOBSTER
WHALE
SEAL
EEL
URCHIN
CRAB
FISH
SHARK
CLICK!
...LIKE SO...

...AND WHEN I PULL THE TRIGGER, THE DART WILL HOME IN ON THE PINKEST, ROUNDEST, SPINIEST THING IN THE POOL

PLAP!
GAAAA!!

10 MINS LATER...
SO...ASLEEP ON DUTY, EH, GONAD?...I'M DOCKING YOU AN HOUR'S PAY FOR THAT, BOY
ZZZZZZZ!

NOW GET BACK TO WORK IMMEDIATELY, YOU BIG BOLLOCKED BUFFOON!
PUNT!
SEA LAND
YES, MR. GRIMSDALE

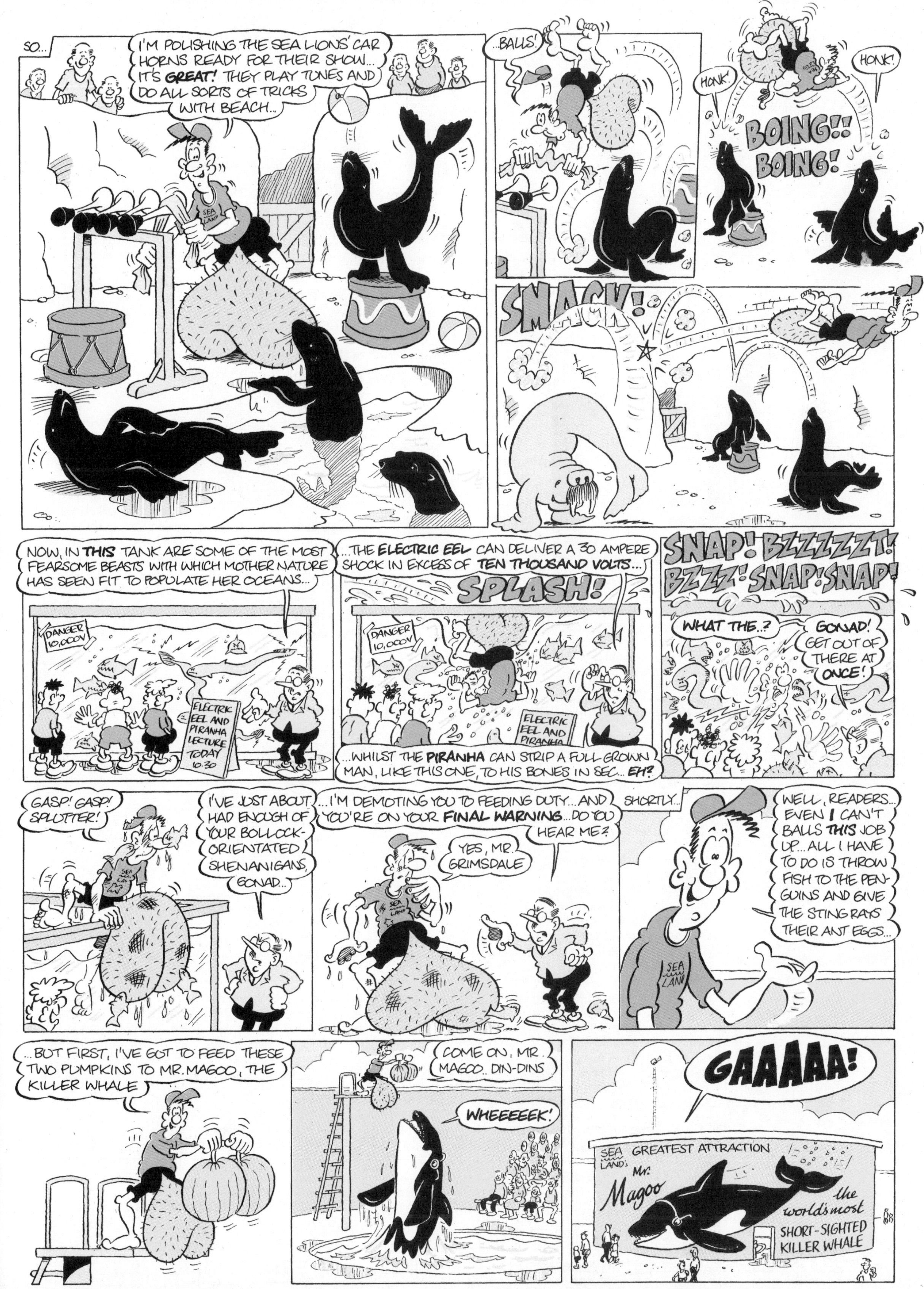
SO...
I'M POLISHING THE SEA LIONS' CAR HORNS READY FOR THEIR SHOW... IT'S GREAT! THEY PLAY TUNES AND DO ALL SORTS OF TRICKS WITH BEACH...
...BALLS!
HONK!
HONK!
BOING!! BOING!
SMACK!
NOW, IN THIS TANK ARE SOME OF THE MOST FEARSOME BEASTS WITH WHICH MOTHER NATURE HAS SEEN FIT TO POPULATE HER OCEANS...
DANGER 10,000V
ELECTRIC EEL AND PIRANHA LECTURE TODAY 10:30
...THE ELECTRIC EEL CAN DELIVER A 30 AMPERE SHOCK IN EXCESS OF TEN THOUSAND VOLTS...
SPLASH!
DANGER 10,000V
ELECTRIC EEL AND PIRANHA
...WHILST THE PIRANHA CAN STRIP A FULL GROWN MAN, LIKE THIS ONE, TO HIS BONES IN SEC... EH?
SNAP! BZZZZZT! BZZ! SNAP! SNAP!
WHAT THE..?
GONAD! GET OUT OF THERE AT ONCE!
GASP! GASP! SPLUTTER!
I'VE JUST ABOUT HAD ENOUGH OF YOUR BOLLOCK-ORIENTATED SHENANIGANS, GONAD...
...I'M DEMOTING YOU TO FEEDING DUTY... AND YOU'RE ON YOUR FINAL WARNING... DO YOU HEAR ME?
YES, MR. GRIMSDALE
SHORTLY...
WELL, READERS... EVEN I CAN'T BALLS THIS JOB UP... ALL I HAVE TO DO IS THROW FISH TO THE PENGUINS AND GIVE THE STING RAYS THEIR ANT EGGS...
...BUT FIRST, I'VE GOT TO FEED THESE TWO PUMPKINS TO MR. MAGOO, THE KILLER WHALE
COME ON, MR. MAGOO.. DIN-DINS
WHEEEEEK!
GAAAAA!
SEA LAND'S GREATEST ATTRACTION
Mr. Magoo the world's most SHORT-SIGHTED KILLER WHALE

LETTERBOCKS

Viz Comic, PO Box 841
Whitley Bay NE26 9EQ
e-mail: letters@viz.co.uk

STAR LETTER

★ **I RECENTLY** bought a bag of crisps that was clear in pointing out that I should eat fruit and veg as part of a balanced diet. When I bought a bag of apples however, they had sloppily forgotten to advise me to eat crisps as well. Come on fruit growers, play your part in helping promote balance and end obesity.

Chingford Rob, Chingford

THE Tivo advert says that I can record 3 shows that are on at the same time. That's all well and good but there haven't been 3 good things on at the same time since about 1995.

Christina Martin, e-mail

I THINK £3.20 is far too high a price for your publication. Times are hard after all. I flicked through issue 209 and felt it was worth about £2.40. As such from now on I will be stealing every 4th issue. The first one I plan to steal is issue 211, so you might want to increase the price of this issue a few pence to cover the cost to yourselves.

Jonathan Wacey, e-mail

I READ in *The Sun* about the curse of the '27 Club' for pop stars. Amy Winehouse died at 27 just like Jim Morrison, Kurt Cobain, Jimi Hendrix and many others. Do any of your readers know how old Jedward are?

Rob Frazer, e-mail

I CAN'T help feeling that snooker would be a lot more entertaining if the players screamed every time they hit the ball like them women tennis players do.

Tim Rusling, e-mail

THEY say that when you drop a piece of toast it always lands butter side down. Well mine doesn't as I always have margarine. Let's see the PC loonies work that out.

Richard Hawkins, e-mail

IS IT true that if you did a shit on the moon it would not deteriorate as it would here on earth and go all white and crispy? And if you visited your bum cigar years later it would still stink just as much? Perhaps one of your readers has been to the moon and might know the answer.

Tommy Blue, e-mail

** WELL, readers. Are YOU one of the 12 people who have been to the moon? perhaps you got caught short on the lunar surface and had to drop your payload. And then perhaps you went back on a subsequent Apollo mission and saw what it looked like. Write and let us know at the usual address and mark your envelope "I've done a shit on the moon." There's a crisp tenner for the first Apollo astronaut we hear from.*

ON A recent episode of BBC's *Fake or Fortune*, Fiona Bruce was horrified to discover the extent of the Nazis' looting of art treasures during the second world war. Frankly, nicking a few paintings to stick on Goebbels's office wall seems like small potatoes compared to some of the other shenanigans they got up to.

Hampton Laidlaw Finsbury

ME AND my brother are dead ringers for the Chuckle Brothers, and we thought we might make a few quid as lookalikes, opening supermarkets and the like. However, we can't find any job that the actual Chuckle Brothers aren't prepared to do themselves. And they're cheaper.

Roland Butter, Camden

I SPOTTED a vicar on a bike this morning. However, I was disappointed to see that he was speeding along on a racing bike, wearing cycling shorts and a helmet. Quite frankly, if vicars aren't going to wobble along on an old fashioned bike wearing a full black cassock and cycle clips, then I'd rather they walk.

Hector Goode, Cheam

IN LESBIAN porn, why is it that one woman can seduce another by feigning she is being a good listener followed by a few minutes of hair touching and kissing before going for her tits and fanny. If a bloke were to do that he would be accused of taking advantage and would probably get a call from the police. It's one rule for a normal bloke and another for a Hungarian Honey with pert titties, a shaven thatch and long blond hair wearing a red or black matching bra and G-string set.

Boss Hogg, e-mail

Cat Launches Perfume

EXCLUSIVE!

LOLA, the cat that was put in a wheelie bin by that woman, yesterday launched her new fragrance at a glitzy party in London's West End.

A spokesman for Lola said the 4-year-old tabby was excited to have got the chance to put her name to a signature scent, which combines notes of jasmine, saffron and sandalwood with honeysuckle highlights.

"Lola has spent her life pulling sparrows apart, pissing up the curtains and licking her own arse, so she seized upon her sudden internet fame as an opportunity to make her mark in the glamorous world of exclusive perfumery," he said.

Miaow - Un Parfum de Lola, is set to hit the stores in the Autumn, priced from £315 for a really little bottle in a great big fancy box.

Top Tips

MOTORISTS. Save a fortune on expensive repair bills by simply turning your radio full blast whenever your engine makes a funny noise.

S Poole, Bushey

MEN. Recreate the thrill of being a male stripper at a hen party by repeatedly shouting "Off! Off! Off! Off!" to yourself in a high pitched voice whenever you undress for bed.

Bobby Harrison, e-mail

BLEND parmesan cheese, basil, olive oil, and hay. Hey presto! Hay pesto.

Edd Almond, e-mail

ACTORS. Increase your chances of appearing in a Richard Curtis film by being Hugh Grant or Colin Firth.

John Cohen, e-mail

TOURISTS. Save money on expensive City Sightseeing tours by simply driving behind the bus with your windows down.

Michael Kayll, e-mail

KIDS. Confuse cuddly toys by acting like their best friend in the world for 8 years then suddenly deciding overnight to give them to a charity shop.

Scruffy the Lion, e-mail

HAIRDRESSERS. Next time a dentist arrives for an appointment, make sure you keep him waiting at least 35 minutes. Then just trim one side of his head and tell him he'll have to return two weeks later to finish the job.

John Jinks, e-mail

SEAN Connery. When playing an Egyptian in Highlander or an Irishman in The Untouchables, have a vague stab at the accent for about 5 minutes, then revert back to Scottish.

John Cohen, e-mail

ACTORS. Create the magic of appearing at this year's Edinburgh Festival from the comfort of your own home by shouting in an empty room for an hour each day and flushing £5000 down your toilet.

Martin Miller, e-mail

GENTLEMEN. If your wife won't let you have the lights on during intimacy, simply don a pair of night-vision goggles. You get to see everything and she won't know you're wearing them.

Rob Cottam, e-mail

CYCLISTS. Tie a paint brush loaded with yellow

HAS anybody seen a shitter celebrtity endorsement than this one for Turtle Mats?

Renton Clubcard Totnes

"Turtle Mats are brilliant!"
Sir Ranulph Fiennes, explorer

THIS morning I awoke to find that a fox had chewed my outdoor pipe lagging, ripped it off and taken a shit on it. Well, I assume it was a fox. It could plausibly be one of the neighbour's kids.

Christina Martin, e-mail

MY LOCAL Tesco petrol station is having a 'family fun day' this Sunday. I must admit that of all the places to take the family to have some fun, a petrol station was never top of my list. Then again maybe access to bags of charcoal and thousands of gallons of fuel may make things interesting.

Fluff Freeman, e-mail

ON page 94, Mr Smaug asks readers for controversial statements to serve as lyrics to popular theme tunes. Well, I have lately taken to singing to the theme of *EastEnders* - "I support the I.R.A, get the fucking Brits out of our island." I'm not particularly Republican, neither am I Irish truth be told. I just like the way the words bounce along with the melody.

Jim Sadler, Wales

THE ABDOMINAL SNOWMAN
COME ON THEN... HIT ME... HARD AS YOU LIKE..

UP THE ARSE CORNER

Barney Tolsh e-mail

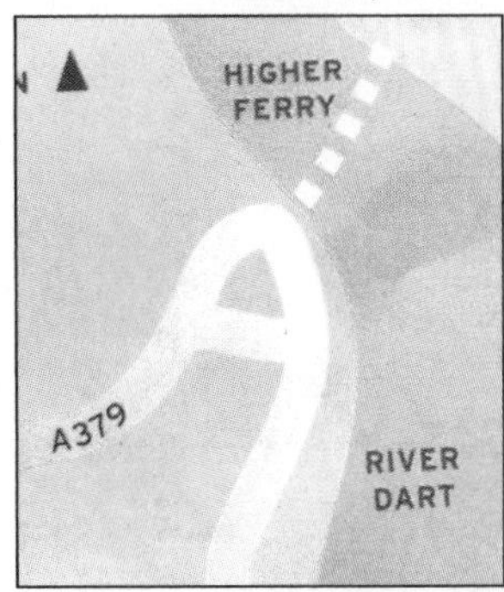

Kerin McEwing e-mail

I'D give the River Dart a miss until the A379's finished with it, if I were you.

@slowpokesam, e-mail

IN HIS song *Thriller*, Michael Jackson sang 'They will possess you, unless you change that number on your dial'. Well, come the zombie apocalypse, I fail to see how my going ex-directory will protect me. Unless they're extremely well organised zombies and plan on ringing first to check if I'm in.

Andy Mansh, e-mail

Queen Takes the Biscuit!

ELIZABETH II may be the longest-reigning British monarch of the century, but her Diamond Jubilee year of 2012 could see her lay claim to an even more impressive crown. For to celebrate her sixty glorious years on the throne, her majesty aims to break the world record for eating Jaffa Cakes.

To seize the title, the Queen will have to chomp her way through nearly 200 of the orange-filled biscuits in 10 minutes. It's a tall order, but one that the 85-year-old royal feels she's more than equal to.

record

A Palace spokesman told us: "The Queen is determined to smash the record and is practising hard every day to perfect her technique, which involves dunking the Jaffa Cakes in water to soften them, before stuffing them in her mouth five at a time and swallowing them without chewing."

of sport

The attempt will be shown live on Dutch cable TV show *Dat is Te Gek!*, which features members of the public attempting outlandish feats. Host Pik van der Valk told us: "It's really great that your Queen is coming on the show next year, and we're expecting big viewing figures for her shot at the record."

Max jaffa: H.M. has biscuit title in sights

Right royal record bid for jubilee year

But constitutional expert Lord St John of Fawsley was less enthusiastic. "I know that a modern royal family has to be seen to be in touch with its subjects, and that sometimes this means indulging in activities that they might not normally countenance, but this plan seems to me to be beyond the pale," he told Radio 4's Eddie Mair.

"The prospect of her majesty appearing on some foreign gameshow, covered in crumbs and frantically shovelling fistfuls of biscuits into her chocolate-smeared mouth for the amusement of a baying studio audience ill befits the high station in which she was placed by the grace of God," he added.

domination

The present eating record is held by *Downton Abbey* writer Sir Julian Fellowes, who managed to scoff 194 Jaffa cakes in 10 minutes on the Spanish variety show *¡Adelante!* in 2004.

paint to the end of your right hand handlebar. This will mark any car that passes too close and allow the police to easily identify the offenders.

Frank Bugle, e-mail

DAILY MAIL reporters. Run a story on your website about how appalling it is that a pervy landlord installed hidden cameras to spy on unsuspecting teenage students. Then follow it with a "showbiz" story about Miley Cyrus wearing a bikini, illustrated with lots of photos of her in the bikini, taken from a long way away without her knowledge.

Nicko, Australia

SMOKERS. Save money by exhaling into a balloon when enjoying a cigarette. Tie the balloon when full and at a later date it can be untied and slowly deflated into your mouth for a free tobacco fix.

Les Ewan, e-mail

RIOTERS. Wear at top hat and shout "Buller! Buller! Buller!" whilst causing criminal damage to prevent the Prime Minister, the Lord Mayor of London and the Chancellor of the Exchequer from criticising your actions.

T Thorn, Hexham

LOCAL council reducing the frequency of your rubbish collection? Simply start a rumour that you are going out with Pippa Middleton and tabloid journalists will empty your bins on a daily basis.

Hector Thorne, Hexham

DENTAL floss makes an ideal noose for depressed ants wishing to hang themselves from the branches of a bonsai tree.

Hasto, e-mail

BASTARDS. Convince your neighbour that he has developed tinnitus by hanging a wind chime in your garden where he can't see it.

Darryl Lane, e-mail

CALCULATE your body weight by standing on your scales wearing your shoes, note the weight, x. Then weigh one of your shoes and note the weight y. Your bodyweight, w, is then given by the equation $w=x-2y$.

Carrie Thortersen, e-mail

I've got a Stephen Fry!!!
YOUNG BILLY JONES WAS THE LUCKIEST BOY IN BARNTON... FOR HIS PET WAS NONE OTHER THAN BANANA-NOSED BONK-BAN POLYMATH STEPHEN FRY...

ONE DAY...
COME ON, BOY. LET'S GO FOR A WALK IN THE PARK SO YOU CAN DO YOUR BUSINESS.
MMNEEYEH!
STEPHEN

SO...
WOAH! SLOW DOWN, BOY!
MMNEEYEH!

DO YOU WANT THE iPHONE, STEPHEN?.. DO YOU WANT THE iPHONE, BOY, EH?
MMNEEYEH!

FETCH!
MMNEEYAH! MMNEEYAH! MMNEEYAH!
MMNEEYAH! MMNEEYAH! MMNEEYAH! MMNEEYAH!

HA! HA! FOOLED YOU!
!?

TWITTER! TWITTER! TWEET! TWEET! TWITTER!

300 MILES AWAY...
WOW! STEPHEN'S GONE FOR WALKIES IN THE PARK... I'LL TWITTER HIM BACK STRAIGHT AWAY
... HOPE... YOU... ENJOY... YOUR... WALKIES... STEPHEN

COME ON, BOY, LET'S GO AND CHASE THE DUCKS ON THE BOATING LAKE
MMNEEYAH! MMNEEYAH!
OI, YOU!!

CAN'T YOU BLOODY WELL READ?..
... OUT THE PARK, BOTH OF YOU!
FOOTLIGHTS ALUMNI MUST BE KEPT ON A LEAD BY ORDER

COME ON, STEPHEN. WE KNOW WHERE WE'RE NOT WANTED
MMNEEYAH!
LET'S GO HOME. YOU CAN HELP ME WITH MY LATIN HOMEWORK

SUDDENLY...
CRUMBS... IT'S ROBBIE COLTRANE. HE MIGHT TAKE EXCEPTION TO YOUR HARSH CRITICISM OF HIM IN YOUR LATEST AUTOBIOGRAPHY
BEWARE OF THE ROBBIE COLTRANE
WE'D BETTER TIPTOE PAST.

SHHH! DON'T WAKE HIM UP, BOY... HE LOOKS LIKE A VICIOUS BRUTE.
ROBBIE
ROBBIE

TWEET! TWEET!
OCH!?
MMNEEYAH!
ROBBIE

LEAP!
OCH! OCH! OCH!

BIFF!
OCH! OCH!
MMNEEYAH!
SOCK!
STOP IT! NO... NO!
THUMP!
STOP!.. BAD GLASWEGIAN

SHORTLY...
I DON'T WANT TO BE CRITICAL, STEPHEN, BUT I DON'T THINK YOU PUT UP A VERY IMPRESSIVE SHOW IN THAT FIGHT...

DON'T GET ME WRONG... I KNOW YOU DID YOUR BEST, BUT... DON'T TAKE THIS PERSONALLY... I FELT YOU JUST DIDN'T... SPARKLE...
COME ON, BOY. LET'S GO HOME.

NEXT MORNING...
STEPHEN... WALKIES!

STEPHEN..!?!
STEPHEN

BELGIUM

STUDENT GRANT

Power to t

Sacked window cleaner spills bea

SECRETARY Gill Snow recently found herself made redundant after 40 years working for evergreen singer CLIFF RICHARDS. But she's not the only member of the Peter Pan of Pop's inner circle to be given the push. For window cleaner CLIXTON WYVIS was shocked to be told his services were no longer required after nearly three weeks' loyal service at the 70-year-old bachelor boy's Weybridge mansion.

The shock of his dismissal caused the 36-year-old Wyvis to enter a spiral of self destructive behaviour. And speaking to us nearly a week later, he is clearly still bitter about the treatment he received from Richards.

"I'll never forget the day I got the push," he says. "I had gone up my ladder to clean Cliff's bedroom window as usual, when I realised I had forgotten to fetch my bucket. It was a long way down, so I thought it would be quicker to just go in the house and get a bucket."

BUCKET

"I didn't think Cliff would mind, so I forced the catch and climbed into his room. Once inside, I started going through his drawers looking for a bucket, but I couldn't find one."

"I found some brand new silk shirts that I thought would make good chamois leathers, and I put them in my pocket. I fully intended to return them once I had finished cleaning the windows."

POTATOES

"I looked through all the drawers and under the bed, but I couldn't find a bucket anywhere. Then, while I was going through his wardrobe, one of Richards's minders came in the room and grabbed me by the collar."

"He saw me and put two and two together to make five. I got no chance to explain myself as I was dragged out of the house, marched down the drive and thrown off the premises."

"I was left in no doubt that my window cleaning services would no longer be required. Never mind a golden handshake, I never even got my wages for that week," says Wyvis.

Now, in the wake of the shabby treatment he has received from the Christian singer, Wyvis is set to EXPOSE the secret world he was privy to behind the electrified gates of Cliff's exclusive Bachelor Boy pad.

PARKY

"I've seen a side of Richards that would turn his fans' hair white, if it wasn't already white," he says. And now, in a series of public lectures, Wyvis is poised to expose the shadowy double life of the squeaky clean singer.

Cliff's Dolls Certainly Weren't Living

ON his first day working for Cliff, Clixton noticed that one of the rungs on his ladder was a bit loose. With a lot of windows to clean, he decided to look in the star's garage for some tools to mend it.

"The door was locked, so I broke a pane of glass and opened it from the inside. I took a selection of power tools and hid them under a bush so I could return for them after dark, fully intending to replace them once I had fixed my ladder."

"While I was in there having a last look round for any other tools I might need, I noticed a bicycle pump lying on a bench. True, there was a mountain bike in the garage, but its tyres were both completely flat. Cliff clearly wasn't using his pump on that."

"There was only one possible explanation - that Richards maintains a harem of inflatable love dolls, probably in a special sex room concealed behind a sliding panel in his mansion."

"What goes on in that orgy chamber beggars belief, as the Peter Pan of popshots uses the bike pump to top up his buxom, latex lovers in between sordid bouts of rubbery rumpy-pumpy. And one thing's for sure, *the leathery lothario's legions of loyal fans would be sickened to see how their supposedly celibate hero really gets his kicks.*"

We're All Smuggling on a Summer Holiday

THE clean-living star famously eschews the typical trappings of rock'n'roll excess, professing to prefer a game of tennis and a cup of tea to a bong full of heroin and a bottle of Jack Daniel's.

But while Cliff may not indulge in drugs himself, sacked window cleaner Wyvis believes the whiter-than-white singer is involved in the narcotics trade in other, more sinister ways.

"It was payday and I went round to collect my money. I'd done all the windows, front, back, top and bottom, so I felt I'd earned every penny of my seven pound fifty."

"I knocked on the door, but there was no answer. Peering through the letterbox, I could see his coat hanging on the end of the bannisters, and I guessed that his wallet was probably in the pocket. I knew Richards was upstairs recording a duet with Kiki Dee, and I didn't want to interrupt his creative flow, and I thought that he wouldn't mind if I took the money myself."

"The door was locked, but luckily I had a jemmy with me and I was soon inside. I found his wallet, but unfortunately he didn't have the exact money in it. So I took a fifty pound note and two twenties from it, fully intending to bring Richards his eighty-two pound fifty change back the next day."

"However, whilst going through the wallet, I became suspicious when I noticed that there were no rubber johnnies in it. Every man keeps a few rubber johnnies in his wallet, so I got to wondering what the famously-celibate Richards had used his for."

"To my mind, there was only one possible explanation. He was muling drugs to and from his holiday home in Barbados, wrapping blocks of hash, wobbly eggs and Es in rubber johnnies and pushing up his bottom."

"I had often wondered how, despite not having had a Number One hit since 1999, Cliff managed to maintain all the trappings of a millionaire lifestyle well into the 21st century. And now the answer was staring me in the face."

"I somehow think the Queen might have had second thoughts about giving Cliff a knighthood if she'd known about the evil trade that keeps him living in the lap of luxury."

MOVE IT: **Richards gave Clixton his marching orders.**

he P45

bout Peter Pan of Pop

WHAT A PANE: Window cleaner Wyvis got his cards from Cliff.

Goodbye Cliff, Hello Samantha

DURING the second week of his job, a chance visit to he singer's rivate athroom ed Wyvis to sobering iscovery bout his mployer's rivate life.

"I was half vay through oing the onservatory vindows when saw Cliff rive off for his norning tennis esson. I needed wee, but I idn't want to se the outside oilet in the rounds in case was broken, o I decided to use one in Richards's n suite next to his bedroom."

"The house was locked, but one f the conservatory windows had een left half open and I thought I night be able to squeeze through. fter a bit of a struggle I was in the ouse."

"I ran up to Cliff's third floor edroom, let myself into the athroom and had my wee. I'd plashed a bit on the seat, so I ecided to look round for a face annel to wipe up after myself. However, in the cupboard over the narble basin, I found something hat turned my stomach - a box of orn plasters."

"From looking for a sponge in his loset earlier that week I was aware hat Cliff only wore soft, hand-nade loafers. I knew they were xtremely comfortable, as I had orrowed a few pairs the previous ay when I had accidentally come o work without any shoes on, fully ntending to return them. They vere not the sort of footwear that vould give anyone corns."

"There was only one reason, and one reason alone, that Cliff would have had corn plasters in his bathroom cabinet. He was routinely dressing up in women's clothing, and the plasters were to stop his bright red six-inch stilettos from chafing his heels as he paraded up and down the room, dressed like a French prostitute, complete with black lace basque, split pencil skirt, crotchless knickers, fishnet stockings and suspenders."

"Frankly, if the crowd who famously joined Cliff in an impromptu singalong of his hit Congratulations on Wimbledon's Centre Court could have seen him getting his kinky transvestite kicks, I doubt they would have raised their voices with quite so much gusto."

RICHARDS may not have recorded the song Puppy Love, but if he had done instead of Donny Osmond, it would have been eerily fitting to describe the next discovery that Wyvis made about his secretive employer.

"I had accidentally dropped my chamois leather on the front path as I knocked off one evening. When I arrived for work the next morning it had gone, and it occurred to me that Cliff might have picked it up and locked it in the glove box of his Rolls-Royce for safe-keeping."

"As luck would have it, I happened to have a length of stiff wire with me, so I poked it down the side of the car window and used it to pop the central locking. Once inside the car, I opened the glove-box and started sorting through the contents."

"Sadly, there was no sign of my chamois, but there were a few CDs of some of my favourite bands which I was sure Cliff wouldn't mind me borrowing, so I put them in my pocket."

"Since I didn't have anything to play them on, I took the CD player as well, carefully prising it out of the dashboard so as to cause as little damage as possible. I had every intention of replacing it, so I left all the wires hanging out so they could be easily re-connected the next day."

"But what I found next sickened me to the pit of my stomach. For hidden in the central console was a pair of reading glasses and a road atlas of the British Isles. Innocent enough items individually, sure, but put together they could point to only one conclusion."

"Richards was clearly putting the glasses on in order to pore over the maps, finding directions to notorious dogging sites throughout Great Britain. Driving there in his roller, he'd park up and peer in through the steamed-up windows of nearby cars, masturbating in his trousers whilst watching anonymous couples having sex."

"Clean-cut Richards famously came second in the 1968 Eurovision Song Contest when his song received 28 votes. *But if that competition's judges had seen the Cliff I knew - the one who got his perverted jollies frantically pulling himself off in a seedy layby - I'm sure they would have given him "nil points" instead."*

THROUGHOUT August, September and October, Clixton Wyvis will be delivering a series of extended, open air public lectures about Cliff Richard on the Egham Bypass, followed by an informal Q&A session on the bench in front of Accessorize in the Arndale Centre.

TOP DOGGING

Al Fresco sex site given 'Gold Flag' status

JUST 5 years after being branded shambolic, one of Britain's best loved dogging sites has now been awarded Gold Flag status by government inspectors.

Last week the secluded lay-by on the A508 in Northamptonshire was found to meet the highest European standards for impromptu outdoor sex venues. And it marks an amazing turnaround for the previously failing dogging location.

In 2006, an unannounced visit by a team inspectors revealed a culture of neglect at the site, with spent condoms strewn across the floor, poor natural light and picnic tables used for gang bangs covered in bird droppings. Most worrying of all, inspectors highlighted loose, sharp pieces of wood that could cause injury to fannies and knackers.

site

Following the 2006 report, dogging site manager Barry Collymore tendered his resignation. His replacement, Phil Mitchell immediately set about an ambitious programme of renovation. Last night he accepted the Gold Flag award in a ceremony at Northampton Town Hall.

"Just to let you know, I'm not that bloke off of EastEnders who was apparently into dogging," he told local digitaries. "I just happen to have the same name as him."

heering

"Anyway, our aim was to create a flagship dogging area where middle aged men could come and watch some housewife getting banged in the back of a Citroen Picasso by her boss, without them standing on broken glass or stinging their bell ends in nettles when they go to finish themselves off in the bushes," he added.

The renovation of the lay-by took 2 years and was achieved with the help of local community groups.

"Seriously, I'm not that fellow who fixes cars in Albert Square, you know, the one who allegedly went dogging in his camper van," Mitchell continued.

"It's just a coincidence, honest. Anyway the whole community pulled together to help create a dogging site to be proud of, and this award is really for them," he said.

Mitchell, who claims never to have acted in a BBC soap opera thanked everyone who helped in the project. But he singled out members of the Northampton WI for particular praise.

tutch

"They worked really hard, making tea and baking cakes for the volunteers. The even mucked in scrubbing jizz stains off the tree bark," he said.

"And the results are stunning. There is parking space for 5 vehicles with mattresses in the back and the picnic tables have smooth finished edges, perfect for safely pulling a train on a bored 50 year old nominal ledger clerk," he added.

PORKING SPACE: ***Phil Mitchell, manager of the A508 layby which has earned a coveted Gold Flag status.***

Fall of the Allardyce

Hammers' Big E for Big Sam

WEST HAM UNITED have issued an apology to Sam Allardyce after the former manager was sacked SEVEN times by the club in 6 months - despite never having been employed by them.

The former Blackburn Rovers manager was enjoying a relaxing break between sackings when he first received a letter from the Board of Directors at West Ham, thanking him for his efforts at the club and dispensing with his services.

The former Newcastle United chief assumed it was merely a clerical error and thought nothing of it, but over the following months several more letters arrived, all terminating his contract at Upton Park.

exercise

A spokesman for the London-based club blamed the letters to the sometime Bolton Wanderers manager on an administrative slip during a staff training excercise.

"Sacking Sam Allardyce is something that every football club must be prepared for. It is part of West Ham's disaster management strategy," he told reporters at a press conference. "We routinely run through his imaginary dismissal once a month, so that when we eventually come to do it for real it won't be a problem."

However, the exercises are so realistic that administrative staff at the club never know whether they are sacking the former Notts County manager for real or not. As a result, one-time manager of Limerick FC Allardyce continually receives dismissal letters from the West Ham board.

notices

The letters are usually followed up by a phone call telling the erstwhile West Brom assistant that his sacking was just an exercise and not to be alarmed. But the constant practice dismissals are taking their toll on the ex-Blackpool chief.

"It's terrible," said former Preston North End caretaker manager Allardyce. "I can't plan anything or take holidays because I am in constant fear of the sack from West Ham, even though I am not currently employed."

knife

But despite the mistake, the West Ham directors defended their stance. A spokesman told reporters: "We make no apologies for our actions in repeatedly sacking Sam Allardyce every month."

"If it inconveniences one ex-manager, then it's a small price to pay for making sure the correct processes are followed in the event that Sam Allardyce is employed and then very likely dismissed by our club a few months later," he added.

WEST HAM AND EX: Former manager Allardyce has had non-existent contract repeatedly terminated.

WEST HAM UNITED

ELTON JOHN'S TARMAC CON

SIR ELTON IS IN CONCERT..
THIS NUMBER IS FROM MY LATEST ALBUM AND IT'S CALLED "NEVER TOO OLD TO HOLD SOMEBODY"

IT'S A SONG THAT'S REALLY SPECIAL TO ME
BECAUSE Y'KNOW, I REALLY BELIEVE THAT ELDERLY PEOPLE HAVE SUCH A LOT TO OFFER US...

SHORTLY
..LIKE THE CASH THEY'VE GOT STASHED UNDER THEIR MATTRESSES, FOR INSTANCE!
GRAND THEATRE
ARTISTES ENTRANCE
C'MON DAVE, LET'S GO AND SCAM SOME SENIOR CITIZENS.

HELP ME GET THE TAR BOILER ONTO THE TRUCK.
WE GONNA BE TARMACING SOME OLD FOLKS DRIVEWAYS, ELTON?

THAT'S RIGHT — BUT FIRST WE NEED TO GET HOLD OF A VITAL BIT OF EQUIPMENT.
SLOW DOWN AS WE PASS THESE ROADWORKS, DAVID.

WE'LL JUST "BORROW" A COUNCIL-ISSUE WORKMAN'S JACKET..
GRAB
HEH HEH! NOTHING REASSURES THE CRUMBLIES LIKE THE SIGHT OF A BONA FIDE "MAN FROM THE COUNCIL".

AND
THAT OLD DEAR LOOKS LIKE AN EASY TOUCH
STAND BY TO FLEECE HER FOR HER PENSION

'SCUSE ME MISSUS, WE'RE FROM THE COUNCIL ROADS DEPARTMENT.
OH YES?
WE'VE BEEN TARMACING THE MAIN ROAD UP BY THE ROUNDABOUT

ANYWAY, WE'VE GOT A BIT OF TARMAC LEFT OVER, SO WE CAN DO YOUR DRIVEWAY IF YOU WANT.
ROADS DEPT
CALL IT A HUNDRED QUID.

WELL... I DON'T KNOW...
THIS OLD DRIVEWAY'S LOOKING WELL ROPEY. COST YOU A FORTUNE, NORMALLY.

WELL I...
RIGHT, THAT'S SETTLED THEN. WE'LL START WORK STRAIGHT AWAY.
MILK AND FOUR SUGARS FOR ME, LOVE.

THAT'S IT DAVE, JUST SPREAD A THIN COATING OVER THE OLD DRIVE
IT'LL CRUMBLE OFF IN A FEW DAYS BUT WE'LL BE LONG GONE BY THEN.

ELTON, YOU'RE LAYING THE TARMAC OVER THE LAWN!
CORRECT! WE'VE GOT TO MAXIMISE THE SURFACE AREA OF THE NEW DRIVE. YOU'LL SEE WHY IN A MINUTE.

SHORTLY,
THERE YOU GO LOVE, ALL FINISHED.
ERM..THANK YOU. A HUNDRED POUNDS, WASN'T IT?

THAT'S RIGHT LOVE, A HUNDRED QUID PER SQUARE YARD.
WHAT? BUT—
NOW, YOUR DRIVEWAY IS... LET'S SEE... TEN FOOT BY TWELVE, WHICH IS JUST OVER THIRTEEN SQUARE YARDS...

I'LL ROUND IT DOWN TO THIRTEEN HUNDRED POUND. TELL YOU WHAT, MAKE IT A GRAND FOR CASH.
BUT I CAN'T AFFORD... I THOUGHT YOU MEANT A HUNDRED POUNDS ALTOGETHER...

NOW COME ON LADY, YOU MADE A VERBAL CONTRACT. THAT'S LEGALLY BINDING, THAT IS!
OH DEAR, I'LL JUST HAVE TO BORROW THE MONEY OFF MY SON...

BERT WORKS FOR THE COUNCIL TOO, YOU KNOW...
ROADS DEPT
OH LOOK! HERE HE COMES NOW!
EH?

HEY MUM, YOU WON'T BELIEVE THIS...
SOME THIEVING BUGGER NICKED MY JACKET TODAY...

HANG ABOUT — THIS IS MY JACKET!
OO-ER!

AND WHAT THE BLEEDING 'ELL HAVE YOU DONE TO MY MUM'S DRIVEWAY?
RUN FOR IT, DAVID!

COME BACK 'ERE, YOU LITTLE SCROTE!
YIPES!

THAT'S FUNNY — BERT'S COUNCIL JACKET HAS DISAPPEARED AGAIN.
HE PUT IT ON THIS WALL JUST A MOMENT AGO.

'SCUSE ME MISSUS, WE'RE FROM THE COUNCIL ROADS DEPARTMENT...
RAY CHARLES
TARMAC
"FIX THE ROAD, JACK, AND DONTCHA COME BACK NO MORE, NO MORE, NO MORE, NO MORE..."

Mrs Brady Old Lady

COO-EE! DOLLY! IT'S ME... ADA!

...THE DOOR WAS OPEN SO I LET MESELF IN...!
I'M IN THE FRONT ROOM, ADA..!

JUST COME TO SEE IF YOU HAD A NICE TIME STEPPING OUT LAST NIGHT WITH MR. PLAXTON, DOLLY...
OOH, I DID ADA. I HAD A SMASHING EVENING. WHAT A LOVELY MAN.

A REAL GENTLEMAN, HE IS... VERY CLEAN. NONE OF THAT SMUTTY TALK, ADA.
GOOD. I CAN'T BE DOING WITH ALL THIS EFFIN' AND JEFFIN', DOLLY...

WHERE DID YOU MEET HIM..?
AT MR BANNERJEE'S BOWEL CLINIC, ADA. WE WAS BOTH THERE WITH OUR ANII.
HOW ROMANTIC.

IT WAS. I WERE HAVING A SESSILE RECTAL GROWTH LANCED...
ANOTHER!? EEH! YOU'RE A MARTYR TO THEM POLYPS OF YOURS, DOLLY.

...MR. PLAXTON WAS HAVING AN IMPACTED FEESHEE SYRINGED.
THAT'S NICE.
AYE. HE WAS TELLING ME, HE'S GOT A VERY WEAK PERISTALSIS, ADA...
...WEAK AS A KITTEN HIS COLONIC TRACT.
EEH.
...FINDS IT HARD TO GET HIS FECULANT MOVING.
TSK

ANYWAY, WE GOT CHATTING OVER A BARIUM MEAL AND HE ASKED ME OUT BECAUSE HIS WIFE'S DEAD.
THAT'S NICE, DOLLY. WHERE DID HE TAKE YOU?

WE WENT TO THE REX, ADA, TO THE TEA-DANCE. LOVELY TIME, WE HAD...
OOH, FANCY.
...THEN HE BROUGHT ME HOME IN HIS ROVER.

EEH, MY SIDNEY HAD A ROVER WHEN WE WAS FIRST COURTING, DOLLY. HE USED TO PICK ME UP FROM ME MAM'S IN IT AND WE'D GO AND PARK DOWN LOVERS' LANE...

...THEN HE'D EFF ME ON THE BACK SEAT, DOLLY. VERY NICE SEATS IT HAD DID THAT CAR... LEATHER, THEY WERE...
SLOOP!
...AND JEFF IN ME HAIR...

ARE YOU GOING TO SEE HIM AGAIN, DOLLY..?
WELL, HE'S STILL 'ERE, ADA... HE SPENT THE NIGHT.

EEH! DOROTHY EARNSHAW! I NEVER HAD YOU DOWN FOR A SCARLET WOMAN.
NO, ADA. WE DIDN'T GET UP TO ANY FUNNY BUSINESS...

... MR PLAXTON WENT TO DO A DUTY IN THE DOWNSTAIRS EXCUSE-ME HALF WAY THROUGH MIDSOMER MURDERS AND I'VE NOT SEEN HIDE NOR HAIR OF HIM SINCE.

EEH, THAT'S A LONG TIME TO BE TRYING TO STOOL... WE'D BEST GO AND SEE IF HE'S ALRIGHT...

SO...
COO-EE! MR PLAXTON! ARE YOU ALRIGHT IN THERE..? WOULD YOU LIKE A NICE CUP OF TEA WHILE YOU'RE TRYING..?
...OR A SLICE OF PARKIN?

HE'S NOT ANSWERING, ADA...
HELLO..? MR PLAXTON... MR. PLAXTON..!

OH DEAR...
HE DUN'T LOOK TOO GOOD, ADA...

NO DOLLY... I THINK HE'S GONE... 'APPEN HE'S PASSED OVER WHILST EVACUATING.
EEH.

CONTINUED OVER...

I ROLL OUT ME PASTRY ON THAT TABLE, ADA, IT DUN'T SEEM VERY HYGIENIC TO BE LAYING MR. PLAXTON'S CORPSE OUT ON IT.
JUST GIVE IT A RUB DOWN AFTER I'M DONE, DOLLY...

BIT OF BORAX AND YOU'LL BE ABLE TO EAT YOUR DINNER OFF THIS TABLE, YOU WILL.
HNNG!

OOH, NO, NO.. I'VE GOT ME STANDARDS, ADA. I'LL HAVE TO PUT SOME PAPER DOWN UNDER HIM.
TSK... WELL, IF YOU WANT...
AYE.

I'LL USE THE TELEGRAPH IT SEEMS A BIT MORE RESPECTFUL THAN THE YELLOW FREE-ADS.

HUPP!
THERE... THAT'S BETTER.

NOW WHAT DO WE DO, ADA..?
WE HAVE TO PUT TWO COINS ON HIS EYES TO PAY THE FERRYMAN, DOLLY...
DO WE..?
OOH YES...

...OTHERWISE HE'LL BE STUCK AT THE RIVER STYX, DOLLY, POISED BETWEEN PLATITUDE AND LIMBO FOR ALL ETERNITY.
OOH DEAR...
...POOR MR. PLAXTON.

HAVE YOU GOT ANY COINS, DOLLY?
WELL, I'VE GOT SOME POUNDS, BUT HE'S NOT HAVING THEM, ADA. I NEED 'EM FOR THE METER.

MY SISTER USED TO PUT TEA BAGS ON HER EYES...
AYE, BUT THAT WAS FOR THE BAGS UNDER 'EM, DOLLY. NOT BECAUSE SHE WERE DEAD.
SHE'S DEAD NOW, THOUGH.

I'VE GOT SOME OF THEM ROUND TEA BAGS, ADA... WILL THEY DO..?
AYE... WELL... BEGGARS CAN'T BE CHOOSERS, I SUPPOSE...

TELL YOU WHAT - I'LL MAKE US A CUPPA WITH 'EM FIRST, SO AS NOT TO WASTE 'EM.
GOOD IDEA.
TEA

I'LL ARRANGE MR. PLAXTON INTO AN ATTITUDE OF TRANQUIL REPOSE WHILE IT'S BREWING, DOLLY.
SMASHING.

5 MINUTES LATER...
THERE YOU GO, DOLLY. HE'S READY TO MEET HIS MAKER.
EEH, ADA..! YOU'VE DONE A BEAUTIFUL JOB. HE REALLY LOOKS AT PEACE.
YOU'VE GOT A GIFT FOR IT, ADA... A GIFT.

ROGUE HACK CHAT

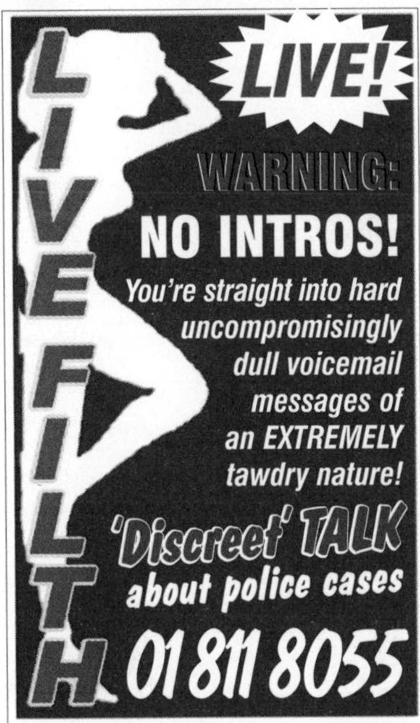

TWO'S COMPANY

ROGUE HACK-TALK

01 811 8055 +pin 171

WARNING:

HACK-TALK contains material of an extremely ILLICIT NATURE. Low-moralled OVER 18s only!

All lines owned by NEWS INTERNATIONAL, in co-operation with The Metropolitan Police. Calls can cost your job. All charges can lead to a custodial sentence & terminate in prison.

ALTERNATIVE DIETING

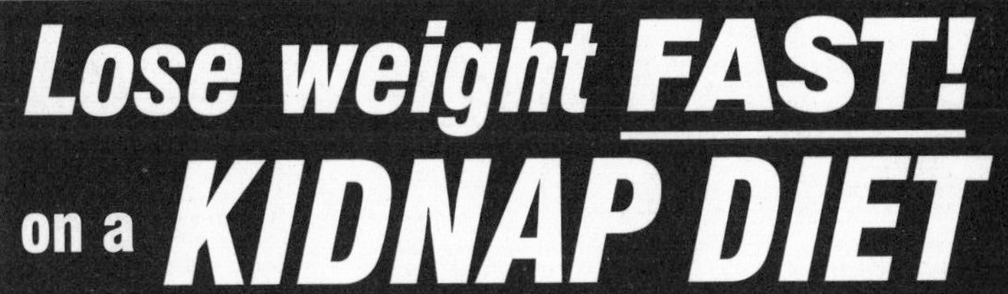

"I was chained to a radiator in Beirut and given half a cup of delicious rice a day. I lost FIVE stone in just THREE years!" Mrs B, Essex.

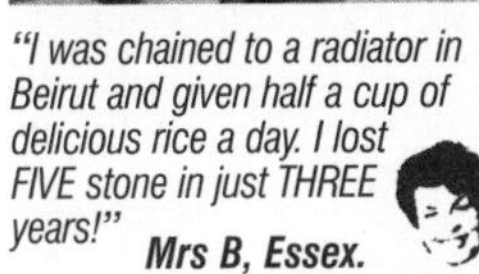

"I did it... and so can YOU!"

Terry Waite

Check online for our special offers and last minute deals at WWW.KIDNAP-DIETS.COM

(a member of ABTA - the Association of British Travel Abductions)

A New Year. A New YOU!

BOOKING NOW FOR 2011!

Drop a dress size when you choose from these exotic locations...

- **Beirut Abduction** *(the original package - still the best!)*
- **Baghdad Hostage** *(includes free orange jumpsuits)*
- **Libyan Stand-Off** *(optional tent meeting with Colonel Gaddaffi & Tony Blair)*
- **Somalian Desert Trek** *(reckless yachting holiday not provided)*
- **Bogota Drug Ransom** *(may include several failed rescue attempts)*
- **Khmer Rouge Jungle March** *(includes 18 months work in a commune)*
- **North Korean Border Snatch** *(minimum term of 5 years)*

Look how much you can lose!

Location	Duration of Kidnap		
	3 mnths	12 mnths	36 mnths
Beirut	12lb	2st	3st
Baghdad	1st	2st	3st
Bogota	10lb	1st	2st
Mogadishu	2st	3st	4st

WEIGHT LOSS: *Typical weight loss when chained to a radiator for an average of 6 months. Requires willpower.*

SUICIDAL SYD
~He's Always Trying to Pop His Cork

HULLO READERS! LONG TIME NO SEE! YOU ALRIGHT?
AS GOOD AS CAN BE EXPECTED I SUPPOSE.
READER'S VOICE
COOL! I'M A REALLY HAPPY BUNNY THESE DAYS AND OPTIMISTIC ABOUT LIFE.

I DON'T LET THE WORLD'S PROBLEMS GET ME DOWN ANY MORE. I'VE DECIDED THAT, SURE, THINGS ARE BAD BUT YOU JUST HAVE TO BE POSITIVE.
IT'S THE ONLY WAY TO BE!

NEWSAGENT
CRISIS IN MIDDLE EAST
NATURAL DISASTERS ON INCREASE
YEP, THAT'S BAD, BUT TERRIBLE EVENTS OFTEN UNITE THE COMMUNITY. ONE JUST HAS TO PUT A POSITIVE SPIN ON THINGS!

WHAAAT?! OH JESUS CHRIST! HOW CAN ONE OF ITV'S FLAGSHIP SHOWS SURVIVE WITHOUT ITS GURU?
SIMON COWELL MIGHT NOT DO X-FACTOR THIS YEAR PERHAPS

IF THE X-FACTOR GOES DOWN THE PAN THAT'S MY SATURDAY NIGHTS STUFFED!
GLOOM
I'M SO DEPRESSED I THINK I'LL KILL MYSELF.

AND SO...
HO HO! I'VE TIED MY TESTICLES TO THE BACK OF THE LOCAL BOY RACER'S CAR. THE SPEED IN WHICH THE YOB DRIVES OFF WILL RIP MY SCROTUM FROM MY BODY LIKE NO ONE'S BUSINESS!
I'M LIKELY TO DIE OF SHOCK INSTANTANEOUSLY.

SORRY SYD, BUT THAT CAR'S GOING NOWHERE. THE LOCAL ARTS COUNCIL HAVE DETERMINED IT'S A PIECE OF STREET ART AND HAVE GIVEN ME A WEDGE OF NOTES FOR IT, WHICH I'LL NO DOUBT SPEND ON A DIFFERENT FORM OF "SPEED". CHORTLE!
TCHAA! JUST MY LUCK!

SOON...
THERE HAVE BEEN REPORTS OF A PUMA STALKING THESE WOODS, SO I'VE COVERED MYSELF WITH SAUSAGES AND PORK CHOPS TO LURE IT OUT.
ANY MOMENT NOW THE PUMA WILL LUNGE AT ME AND RIP MY GIZZARDS OUT. WHAT A WAY TO GO!

CHUCKLE! I KNOW WHAT YOU'RE THINKING READERS. THE "BIG CAT" WILL PROBABLY TURN OUT TO BE A FOX AS USUAL. HOWEVER, EVEN A BITE FROM A FOX COULD LEAD TO BLOOD POISONING.
FINGERS CROSSED, I COULD STILL BE DEAD BY TOMORROW.

BAH! IT'S NOT A PUMA OR A FOX. IT'S JUST MADONNA STROLLING THROUGH HER OLD COUNTRY ESTATE WHILST WEARING THAT BLACK FURRY THING SHE HAD ON AT THE OSCARS.
AND SAY WHAT YOU LIKE ABOUT HER BUT SHE'S NO CANNIBAL.

HMMM... PERHAPS ALL IS NOT LOST! I COULD FASHION THESE SAUSAGES INTO A NOOSE AND HANG MYSELF FROM THAT TREE! JOB DONE!

RRUMMBLE!
SMAAASH!
AW NO! WHAT'S GOING ON?

SORRY SYD, BUT THIS ENTIRE AREA IS BEING FLATTENED TO MAKE WAY FOR THE HIGH SPEED RAIL NETWORK.
NNNGH! DONKEY'S BOLLOCKS! HOW'S A MAN EXPECTED TO TOP HIMSELF THESE DAYS?

HMM... HANG ON... HIGH SPEED RAIL NETWORK YOU SAY?
THAT'S CORRECT. WE PLAN TO BE OPERATING BY THE YEAR 2030.

RIGHT. I'M TAKING TO MY BED AND I DON'T WANT TO BE DISTURBED.
Syd's House

YEARS LATER~
WELL, IT HASN'T BEEN EASY LOCKED IN MY BEDROOM MAINTAINING A CONSTANTLY DEPRESSED STATE FOR 19 YEARS BUT HERE I AM, STILL SUICIDAL IN 2030!

NOW ALL I HAVE TO DO IS WAIT FOR THE NEXT 250 MPH TRAIN AND I'LL BE MINCEMEAT.

SORRY SYD, BUT BY THE TIME THE RAIL NETWORK WAS COMPLETED EVERYONE HAD MADE THE SWITCH TO TRAVELLING BY JETPACK! TRAINS ARE OBSOLETE NOW.
GAHH!

MIND YOU, THIS IS THE FUTURE WE ALWAYS DREAMED OF! PERHAPS LIFE ISN'T SO BAD AFTER ALL.
YES, IT'S LIKE LIVING IN A SCIENCE-FICTION WONDERLAND.

FANTASTIC! WHAT WAS I THINKING? LIFE IS FOR THE LIVING AND I CAN'T WAIT TO SEE WHAT MODERN SURPRISES THIS WORLD HAS WAITING FOR ME.

YES, JUST WATCH OUT FOR THE INTELLIGENT APES ON HORSEBA... OH TOO LATE.
BLAM!
VIZ 204
LEW STRINGER..

mr. LOGIC

HE'S AN ACUTE LOCALISED BODILY SMART IN THE RECTAL AREA.

WITH A CORE TEMPERATURE OF 13·6 MILLION DEGREES KELVIN AND PRESSURE SUFFICIENT TO FUSE HYDROGEN INTO HELIUM AT A RATE OF 620 MILLION TONS A SECOND, I DOUBT THAT THE INTERIOR OF A YELLOW DWARF STAR WOULD BE AN ENVIRONMENT CONDUCIVE TO REPOSE...

NO. I DIDN'T MEAN...

...FURTHERMORE, THE 186 MILLION MILE ROUND TRIP THROUGH VAST FIELDS OF LETHAL ELECTROMAGNETIC RADIATION AND CORONAL EJECTION MATTER WOULD, I SUGGEST, PROVE SOMEWHAT IMPRACTICAL.

OKAY. HOW ABOUT A WEEK ON A BEACH SOMEWHERE?

AN HOUR LATER...

...SO THAT'S 168 CONSECUTIVE 60 MINUTE INTEGERS OF WHICH PERIODS - OR ANY SUBSET THEREOF - YOU MAY SPEND AS MANY OR AS FEW AS YOU WISH WITHIN THE HOTEL - WHEREIN YOU WILL BE FURNISHED WITH THE USE OF A BED THROUGHOUT THE DURATION OF YOUR STAY...

...AND FURTHERMORE PROVIDED WITH LIMITED ACCESS TO SUCH COMESTIBLE ITEMS AS ARE AVAILABLE BETWEEN THE HOURS OF 7 AND 9 am (LOCAL TIME) IN THE DESIGNATED DINING AREA, AND NOMINALLY UNLIMITED QUANTITIES OF SUCH PROVENDER AS IS MADE AVAILABLE BY THE HOTEL PROPRIETORS BETWEEN THE HOURS OF 8 AND 10 pm (LOCAL TIME...)

LETTERBOCKS

Viz Comic, PO Box 841, Whitley Bay, NE26 9EQ
e-mail: letters@viz.co.uk

STAR LETTER

★ **DIDN'T** George Michael and Sir Elton John make better music when everyone presumed they were heterosexual and you actually believed they were singing at women? Come on all you gay pop stars, get back in the closet and set the charts alight once again.

Stephen Usher, e-mail

THOSE meerkats can stick thier stuffed toys up their arses. I've yet to see a better stuffed toy and I challenge *Viz* readers to top this filthy little bastard. Maybe someone has a knitting pattern for felching giraffes or some ducks doing Belgian Biscuit perhaps?

Airdre Onion, Airdre

DOES anyone know where they keep the syrup at Sainsburys?

Rob Frazer, e-mail

TO THE bloke on his fourth pint of cider, complaining loudly about all the 'cunts eating breakfast' in my local Wetherspoons. It was 8.30am.

Brian McWitty, e-mail

I WENT to a zoo recently, and I must admit that I was rather surprised at how small the chipmunks were. I know nothing about them, and I had a preconception that they were about the size of a rabbit, and to find out that they were only slightly larger than a mouse came as quite a disappointment. Have any of your readers been similarly disallusioned by the size of an animal?

Tiptoes Glendinning e-mail

MY HUSBAND used to love the taste of blue cheese. But after suffering a bang on the head one day he could no longer taste it. In fact he couldn't taste anything, as it was a falling piano that hit his head and it killed him instantly.

Ada Wiffles, Luton

WHAT is the point in having zebra crossings on the continent when the drivers don't know what they are for? They just give pedestrians a false sense of security. Come on foreign governments, tell your drivers what zebra crossings are for or stop painting the bloody things on your roads.

Rosemary Flatbread e-mail

I AM a greengrocer, and the other day a customer took me to task over one of my signs. I had written *Cherry Tom's 40p/lb*. The complainant said that the apsotrophe in Tom's was superfluous, as the function of the *s* was to indicate the plural of Tom, and not to make it posessive. He said that as it stood, it appered that someone called Cherry Tom owned 40p/lb, which was completely nonsensical. I had to laugh, however, since rather than denote a plural, the apostrophe served to indicate an ommission of letters, as in *can't* and *shouldn't*, as I was unable to spell tomatoes.

George Sheldon, Nottingham

TOP TIPS

JAM makers. Don't buy preserving jars from Lakeland Kitchens at £6.99 per dozen. Simply buy 12 jars of Morrison's own brand curry sauce at 9p a go and tip the rancid muck down the toilet.

Irene Greengage, Hull

BORED of listening to your favourite CD? Then simply scratch it to fuck with a compass to give it a new gabba techno edge.

Stephanie Greystokes e-mail

SCATTERING half a teaspoon of dried chilli flakes over a cut grapefruit half and leaving it overnight in the fridge will make the grapefruit taste of chilli. So don't do it.

Robert Canning, e-mail

ENGLAND rugby team. Strike terror into the All-Blacks by performing a Morris dance in response to their Haka. Similarly, the Irish team should perform the Riverdance.

Chris Higson, e-mail

SINGLE men. When expecting female company at home, be sure to leave a carefully-placed tape measure in view with the tape pulled out to 9-and-a-half inches.

Jimmy Boogaloo, e-mail

Grammar, We Love You

YOUR grammar queries answered by **Prof. Ingledew Botterill, MA** (Oxon)

Dear Prof. Botterill,

I'M HAVING friends round for dinner next week and I plan to bring out a cheese board after the meal. There will be about five different types of cheese, but I'm not sure what the plural of cheese is. Do I invite everyone to help themselves to the cheese, the cheeses, or even the cheesii?

Rosemary Flatbread, Pinner

Prof. Botterill says...

There has been much debate over the years as to what the plural of cheese is. Many academics say that cheese, like sheep, is the same in the singular form as the plural, whereas others say that an s must be added as a suffix. So in much the way that 'barge' becomes 'barges', then cheese becomes cheeses. However, it is far from certain which is correct. To ensure you avoid making a grammatical *faux pas*, it would probably best if you serve each cheese one at a time.

Dear Prof. Botterill,

WHAT ARE the rules on using colons and semi-colons? Under what circumstances should I use a one as opposed to the other?

Tarbuck Thrush, Gravesend

Prof. Botterill says...

The colon is used at the end of a sentence along with a left or right parenthesis which denotes either the grave or light mood of the sentence. The semi-colon should only be used in conjunction with the right parenthesis to lend a tone of irony to the sentence or statement it suffixes. Under no circumstances should the semi-colon be followed by a left parenthesis as this renders the sentence that preceedes it ironically miserable, an utterly meaningless concept.

PASTYBATION LINES

Calls cost 99p/pasty and terminate in the oven.

WARNING: Includes scorching, molten-hot fillings that could burn your gob.

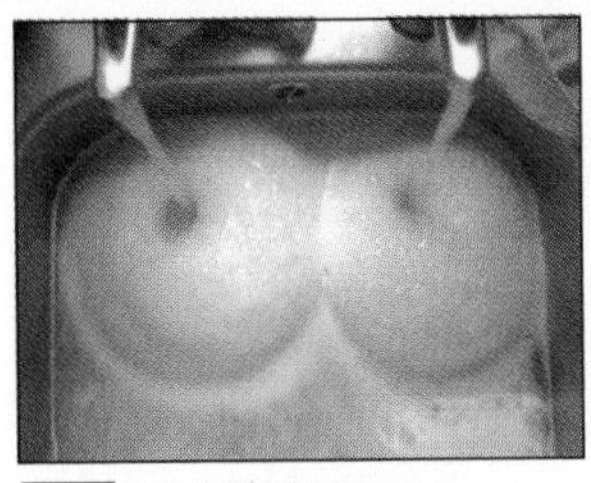

ANYONE fancy a soapy tit wank?

Errington182, e-mail

WHY does Nick Clegg always look so fucking miserable? If I got upwards of 100 grand to go "Yes, Dave" five times a day I'd be pretty chuffed.

Mike Morris, e-mail

IN Australia they have bookies in pubs. Bye.

Dirk Fwow, Heathrow

HONESTLY, I'm such a silly sausage! The other day, I spent ages looking for my glasses that I'd had just a minute before. I was getting more and more frustrated as I went from room to room, looking for my specs in places I'd already checked. I couldn't understand why my wife was laughing at me. Then I realised... they were stuck up my arse!

Ernest Marples, Penge

SHALLOW GRAVE
MY FAVOURITE ARTIST IS THOMAS KINKADE, THE PAINTER OF LIGHT
RIP

AM I the only one developing an unhealthy crush on Christina Martin? In my mind she is a slim, attractive, 30-something who loves fine dining and wears chic clothes. But I have a horrible feeling she is a short, fat northern lass with a penchant for kebabs and whose wardrobe is dominated by jeans, trainers and replica football tops.

Mike Tatham, Dundee

** WOAH there, Mr Tatham. Your comments are sexist and offensive and have no place in a family magazine like Viz. We have met Ms Martin and the fact that she's a bit of a cracker has no bearing on our decision to publish her correspondence. Her letters are published solely on their merit and your comments about her possible physical appearance belittle the bird's efforts.*

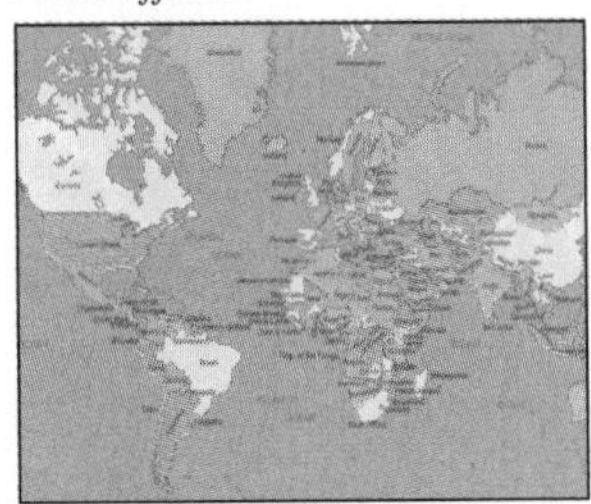

MY husband and I have a large map of the world on the kitchen wall. Throughout our marriage, we have stuck a pin in every place we have visited. However, we always holiday in the same place, Filey, so there is just one pin in it. We did book a week in Bridlington one year, but we got worried we might not like it, so we cancelled and went to Filey again instead.

Glenda Clitworth Primrose Valley

ANY chance of a photo of that bloke kissing Christina Martin's arse?

K Bander, e-mail

Have Your Say...

In the latest **PLANET OF THE APES** film, an experimental Alzheimer's treatment being tested on chimpanzees causes them to become super-intelligent and rebel against mankind. We went on the street to find out what **YOU** thought about chimps taking the reins of power...

I'M NOT sure that a world run by chimps would be a good thing. Perhaps it would be best if scientists stuck with testing things on mice in the future. That way, the worst that could happen would be they might rise up and steal all the cheese.

Mrs Urethra Armchair, Pyles

I DON'T like chimpanzees. Quite frankly, I do not care for their unpleasant bottoms, their gums or their excitable attitude. They were alright in the PG Tips adverts, riding tandems and moving pianos, but I'm not going to pay good money to see them at the zoo or in a film.

Clifford Prepuce, Glans

I AGREE with the previous writer. You simply don't know where you stand with chimps. Honestly, one minute they're running round in dungarees, drinking out the spout of a teapot, the next they're biting some poor woman's face off.

Areola McFlurry, Halford St Mary

SCIENTISTS such as Richard Dawkins would have us believe that we share 99% of our DNA with chimpanzees. Well, perhaps Mr Dawkins eats bananas with his feet and spends his day throwing his faeces at passers-by, whilst screeching and masturbating, but I can assure you I do not. Please do not try to drag us all down to your level, Mr Dawkins.

Gerald Perineum, Taint

LIKE Edgar Rice Burroughs's famous character Tarzan, my parents were killed in a light aircraft crash in the Belgian Congo when I was a baby. Rescued from the wreckage by a kindly chimpanzee, I was raised by apes, and eventually rose to become their King. It was an exciting life; I spent my days riding around on elephants, wrestling crocodiles and stabbing leopards. Unlike Tarzan, however, after being rescued and returned to civilisation following twenty years in the jungle, I didn't inherit a title and a large country estate, and I now work as a mobile wheelie bin cleaner in the Wolverhampton area.

T Umgawa, Tipton

I AM an anthropological zoologist, and I am presently involved in a Harvard University project which involves teaching a chimpanzee to communicate through the medium of sign language. Our experimental subject, Bongo, shows a truly amazing innate ability to pick up words and after two years of intensive instruction is able to clearly convey his thoughts and feelings to me and my team. However, all he ever says is either that he fancies a wank or he's thinking of throwing some of his shit at someone.

Dr Jane Foodhall, Cambridge, Mass.

SINCE early childhood, I have been fascinated by the idea of breeding a human/chimpanzee hybrid. Such a mongrel, combining as it would the intelligence of *Homo sapiens* with the strength and agility of *Pan troglodites* would certainly be a force to be reckoned with. I presently work in the canteen at Knowsley Safari Park, so access to monkeys isn't a problem. But what I want to know is, should I bang a female chimpanzee to get it pregnant, or should I get one of the males to do my missus? What do your readers think?

Reg Hollis, Liverpool

WITH reference to Mr Hollis's letter above, my mother is a cleaner at Whipsnade Zoo, and during the seventies she got pregnant off one of the monkeys. I was very excited about about my new hairy sister, but it wasn't a big success. In the end, I think my dad let it go in the woods. It ran up a tree and we never saw it again.

Denis Piercing, Huntingdon

HOW come monkeys are all hairy, yet they have pink arses with no hair on, whilst I'm as bald as a coot and I've got a big hairy arse? Perhaps Charles Darwin could explain that!

Rev. J Foucault, Truro

WOMEN. When arguing with your boyfriend that you are the more logical of the species, do not then go and buy clothes that do up round the back.

Phillip Smith, e-mail

TV WATCHERS. If there is a person in a celebrity version of a TV show who you don't recognise at all, they are from Hollyoaks.

Christina Martin, e-mail

A SLICE of soft white bread makes an ideal 'memory foam' mattress for your pet hamster.

Dave Clackerbag, e-mail

HAVE fun with American tourists by asking where they are from, then pretending you've never heard of it. Extra fun can be had by asking "Is that near Canada/Mexico?"

Teamy Teamy, e-mail

24 DAYS before the clocks go back an hour, start putting your clock back an hour every night. That way you not only get an extra hour in bed for nearly a month, but you also gain a whole day. Or should that be 23 days before? Or 25? I can't do the maths.

Colin Smith, e-mail

CIGARETTE manufacturers. Increase sales by featuring pictures of large-breasted women on your packets rather than photos of diseased lungs and hideous neck cancers.

Chubby O'Toole, e-mail

WEARING an iPod whilst making love to your wife will block out her complaints for doing so.

Paul Townend, e-mail

FAT MEN. Next time you sit next to a swimming pool on a flimsy white patio chair, ensure that the camcorder is rolling. There could be 250 notes in it for you.

Bernard Pork, e-mail

WHEN visiting Thailand, avoid getting tricked into taking a Ladyboy back to your hotel by first asking them to throw a tennis ball over-arm.

Grant Warner, New Zealand

CONVINCE your downstairs neighbours that you have a new subwoofer by simply stamping on the floor in time with the music you're listening to.

Chris Kelly, email

FOOTBALL fans. Recreate the magic and excitement of transfer deadline day by sitting in your work canteen until one minute before closing, then buying a pot noodle for £25.

Mighty Red Barney, e-mail

WALKERS. Use the phrase 'take on fluids' instead of 'drink water' to make it sound like you're conducting a fucking military expedition instead of going for a walk in some hills.

D Cooper, e-mail

FINBARR SAUNDERS AND HIS DOUBLE ENTENDRES
FNARR! FNARR!
GOSH! FINBARR! COME OVER HERE AND HAVE A LOOK AT MR GIMLET'S BIG HAIRY SACK..!
IT'S FULL TO BURSTING, MRS SAUNDERS.
CHARF! CHARF!
YOD! YOD!
WUB! WUB!
SNERP! SNERP!
F-NUT! F-NUT!
AG! AG!
IT'S SPRING, SO THESE NUTS ARE SO HEAVY THAT MY BALL-BAG IS HANGING DOWN BETWEEN MY KNEES.
CHUFF! CHUFF!
SPAD! SPAD!
K-YOK! K-YOK!
...IT'S A BUMPER ISSUE AND I'VE GOT SEVERAL OF THEM TO DELIVER, YOU SEE.
Nuts
J. Ball & Co Newsagents High St. Fulchester
I DIDN'T REALISE YOU STILL DID A PAPER-ROUND, MR. GIMLET.
OH YES. I'VE GOT QUITE A LONG ONE.
FOO! FOO!
YURP! YURP!
...HERE IS YOUR GUARDIAN, MRS. SAUNDERS.
GOODNESS ME - IT'S NOT NEARLY AS BIG AS I REMEMBER IT, MR GIMLET.
QUONK! QUONK!
NIP! NIP!
STOT! STOT!
FNARR! FNARR!
PEB! PEB!
INDEED. THE GUARDIAN IS NOW PUBLISHED IN THE SO-CALLED "BERLINER" FORMAT. IT'S MUCH SMALLER AND FLOPPIER THAN IT USED TO BE A FEW YEARS AGO...
CLAB! CLAB!
SNUP! SNUP!
...HOWEVER, THE WEEKEND EDITION IS BULKED OUT WITH A VARIETY OF SUPPLEMENTS AND A COLOUR MAGAZINE...
...SO IT STILL GETS QUITE THICK ONCE A WEEK ON SATURDAY MORNING.
JIB! JIB!
WOOF! WOOF!
HUT! HUT!
NARF! NARF!
SO MUCH SO THAT I SOMETIMES HAVE A STRUGGLE TO SQUEEZE IT BETWEEN THE FLAPS OF YOUR BOX, MRS. SAUNDERS.
SPOOT! SPOOT!
JOP! JOP!
SAUNDERS
NI! NI!
YOU COULD ALWAYS POP IT THROUGH THE FRONT DOOR.
PERHAPS. BUT THERE'S NO WAY I COULD PUSH A BROADSHEET - SUCH AS THIS FINANCIAL TIMES - THROUGH THAT RUSTY LETTERBOX OF YOURS.
I SUPPOSE YOU'RE RIGHT, MR GIMLET. AT YOUR AGE THERE'S A RISK YOU COULD PUT YOUR BACK OUT TRYING TO STUFF A BIG PINK 'UN INSIDE MY DRIED-UP OLD SLOT.
NARR! NARR!
BURB! BURB!
K-FURN! K-FURN!
SPA! SPA!
K-WOOAR! K-WOOAR!
YIKK! YIKK!
SPOM! SPOM!
NOOP! NOOP!
CHUD! CHUD!
GARP! GARP!
FRAFT! FRAFT!
TUB! TUB!
GROMP! GROMP!
NODGE! NODGE!
HAMBLE! HAMBLE!
FUNF! FUNF!
ITMA! ITMA!
CRUNN! CRUNN!
PONK! PONK!
TWIB! TWIB!
FLUMP! FLUMP!
BLOON! BLOON!
SPO! SPO!
CHEB! CHEB!
THRUMP! THRUMP!
DOOB! DOOB!
FNUK! FNUK!
LOL! LOL!
AROOGA! AROOGA!
NGGF! NGGF!
OB! OB!
LUD! LUD!
GAG! GAG!
TURF! TURF!
GNONK! GNONK!
OF COURSE, I'M A QUALIFIED SPINAL OSTEOPATH, MR. GIMLET, SO I COULD EASILY FIX A DISLOCATED VERTEBRA.
SAUNDE
SPLENDID! WOULD IT BE A PERMANENT CURE?
...NOT NECESSARILY MR GIMLET.
IF YOUR BONE DID MOMENTARILY POP OUT, I'D JUST THUMB IT BACK IN AGAIN...
COME TO THINK OF IT, I DO FEEL A LITTLE BIT STIFF AT THE MOMENT...
...MY FULL LOAD IS WEIGHING ME DOWN SOMEWHAT...
OOH! ME BACK! AAARGH! I THINK I MUST'VE JUST SLIPPED A DISC, MRS SAUNDERS!
OOOH! AAARGH!
ERM...HERE - YOU'D BETTER FINISH OFF MY PAPER-ROUND, FINBARR, I'M GOING OFF WITH YOUR MOTHER SO SHE CAN PUT ME RIGHT INSIDE...
SO...
OOH!... UH-UH!
UH-UH-UH...
...YESS!
YOU'RE NOT THE USUAL PAPER LAD. WHERE'S MR GIMLET?
HE'S GOT A BAD BACK SO HE CAN'T COME.
YOU COULD'VE FOOLED ME, FINBARR. FROM THE SOUND OF IT, HE'S JUST SHOT HIS WAD UP YOUR MAM'S TWAT.

Bear Grylls Has Ate Ray Mears

~ Reuters

SURVIVALIST BEAR GRYLLS last night confessed to having ate his TV rival RAY MEARS.

Ex-SAS man Grylls, 37, was filming an episode of his top-rated Discovery Channel show in woodland outside Milton Keynes when he came across ITV bushcraft expert Mears foraging for nuts and berries in a copse.

BEAR NECESSITIES: Jungle survivalist Grylls consumed Mears alive.

"It was about one in the afternoon and I was feeling a bit peckish," Grylls told the *Flitwick Glans & Argus*. "I was about five miles from the hotel where I was staying. Over rough ground, that was more than an hour's walk, and the hot buffet closed at two."

MEAT

"When you're out in the wilds and you don't know where your next meal is coming from, you have to seize every eating opportunity with both hands," continued Grylls. "Ray was a big lad with enough meat on him to keep me going till tea-time."

"I used all my Black Ops training to sneak up behind him and wrestle him to the ground. Killing, butchering and cooking him would just have wasted energy, so I just ate him alive," he added.

VOUCHER

Grylls later made Mears's skin into an inflatable raft on which he crossed the River Lovat in order to get to the Kentucky Fried Chicken in Stoke Hammond.

What's in a Name?

ASK ANYONE who their favourite television personality is and about 4% will answer MYLEEN CLARSE. The glamorous 33-year-old classically-trained musician is seldom off our screens, whether she's co-hosting *Pop Star to Opera Star*, flogging us shampoo in the advert breaks, or soaping her tits under an Australian waterfall. But how much do we really know about this glamorous 33-year-old classically-trained musician? Once again, the answer is all in the name...

M is for MAMMARY GLANDS

WHEN she appeared on ITV's *I'm A Celebrity, Get Me Out of Here!*, Myleen's firm breasts hit the headlines as she donned a revealing bikini to shower under a jungle waterfall. 10 million viewers tuned in every night to watch rivulets of water cascading over her voluptuous curves and down her cleavage. But Myleen is more than just a beautiful body. She is also a successful babywear entrepreneur in her own right.

Y is for YELLOW

MYLEEN'S favourite colour is yellow, and it features heavily in her signature range of fashion baby clothes for the 0 to 5s. "I like yellow because it's a joyful colour," she told *Heat* magazine's Boyd Pointless. "It's a refreshing change from traditional gender-stereotyping hues such as blue and pink. It doesn't say 'I'm a boy' or 'I'm a girl'. Yellow says 'I'm a baby, and I'm free to be whoever I want to be!' It's also good because spew and piss don't show up on it," she added.

L is for LEGS

MYLEEN'S shapely pins are the talk of the showbiz world, but they're not just there for the fellas to look at. Classically-trained musician Myleen also uses them for walking around on and operating the pedals on her grand piano when she's playing Brahms, Beethoven and Mozart. She's recognised as one of the world's greatest pianists, knowing all the notes of the piano off by heart and many scales.

E is for EGYPTOLOGY

AS A mummy herself, Myleen is very interested in mummies. "I love the way the Egyptians dressed their corpses in all bandages," she told Channel 5's *The Wright Stuff*. But despite her passion for ancient Pharaohs, Clarse avoids going to see them in museums, for fear that their curses may come true on her.

E is for EGGS

CLARSE loves eggs, scoffing up to four dozen king-size hens' eggs each day. But get this, she doesn't like the yolks or the whites. She only eats the shells!

N is for NIPPLES

MYLEEN boasts two nipples, one in the middle of each breast. When she posed for *Loaded* magazine in a series of skimpy outfits, lucky readers got tantalisingly close to getting a glimpse of them on a number of occasions. However, it would be wrong to think of Clarse as merely a sex object. For she is also a talented television presenter who has fronted a succession of top-rated shows on the box, such as *Escape from Scorpion Island* and many more.

C is for CHARITY

MYLEEN does an awful lot for charity, though she doesn't like to talk about it except on her website. Whilst the average Briton supports a couple of charities at most, just some of the worthy causes Clarse lists on her website total eight. That makes big-hearted Myleen 400% more compassionate than the rest of us!

L is for LOVELY

LOVELY is the only adjective which can adequately describe Myleen's hair. Her luxuriant locks first came to prominence when Clarse won through the heats of ITV search-for-a-star show *Pop Idol* to become a member of pop band S Club 7. Her lustrous tresses have since been seen thousands of times on shampoo adverts, lottery programmes and a variety of other assorted low-rent telly shows.

A is for ARSE

MYLEEN is the owner of the most bootylicious rear in the whole of showbusiness. Although she's careful to keep it out of sight under a dress or inside a skimpy bikini, all red-blooded males spend hours each day fantasising about what it it might look like in the flesh. But they would do well to remember there's more to Miss Clarse than her pert little derriere. She's also a child-rearing expert, hosting her own series of informative web videos on the subject of parenthood.

R is for RACISM

CLARSE abhors racism in all its forms. Although she was born in England, her father is half Austrian and her mother is Filipino, making her three-quarters foreign. "I simply can't be doing with racism," she told *Steeplejack Monthly*. And she had this message for anyone considering becoming a racist: "You're out of order, simple as. End of."

S is for SHOWPAN

MYLEEN'S favourite composer is Showpan. As a classically-trained musician, she makes short work of his symphonies, sonatas and concertos. "I can play them all with both hands," she told *Classic FM* magazine. But music-lovers would do well to remember that there is more to Clarse than her virtuoso skills at the keyboard. She's also got a smashing pair of tits. And a fanny.

E is for ELEPHANTS

CLARSE loves elephants... but only African ones. "I can't stand Indian elephants," she told Radio 4's *Desert Island Discs*. "With that stupid lump on top of their heads and their slightly smaller ears, they really get my goat. As far as I'm concerned, the quicker them big grey fuckers get poached into extinction, the better."

NEXT WEEK: WHAT'S IN A NAME? - MR T.

Celebrity DR DOLITTLE for a DAY

WE ALL dream of being able to talk to the animals like Dr Dolittle. Even celebrities spend most of their day imagining what it would be like to converse with other species. We asked a few stars what animals they would speak to and what they would say to them if they were…

DR DOLITTLE FOR A DAY!

WALT DISNEY
Dead animator

I'M just a head in a fridge these days, and boy is it cold in here. If I could talk to the animals, I think I'd ask some penguins the secret of keeping warm at the North Pole. Those little flightless critters slide about on their bellies and swim in sub-zero water, and they don't even shiver. Meanwhile my nose is constantly blue and I'm as cold as a witch's tit.

NICK HANCOCK
Sort of comedian

I'M a mad keen fisherman, but I'd hate to think that pulling fish out of a river using a hook in the side of their mouth was in any way cruel. So I think I'd talk to some river fish, perhaps a gudgeon or a perch, and I'd ask them if it hurt to have a barbed piece of metal stuck through their lip. However, they only have a memory span of four seconds, so unless they had been caught three seconds before our conversation, they wouldn't remember.

PAUL McCARTNEY
Ex Quarrymen lead guitarist

I LOVE animals that much that I don't eat them. If I could talk to any animals, I think I would go down to a farm and chat with some of the cows that were ready for slaughter. I'll tell them what a bummer it was that they were about to be killed and eaten, and if it was left to me I'd leave them alone to live wild in the fields. I think that would cheer them up a bit.

BONO
Twat

I REALLY don't know which animal I would choose to speak to. There are over a million animal species on earth and they would all love the privilege of being in my presence and telling me how marvellous they think I am and how much they would like to thank me for saving the planet. So to choose one over every other would be unfair. But I'd probably choose meerkats, because I love them in the adverts.

HM THE QUEEN
Queen

I REALLY like honey and so I would love to talk to the bees that made it. I would chat with a few selected worker bees and drones first, asking them what they did, how long they had been doing it and did they enjoy it. Then I'd meet the queen of the hive and chat to her. Both being queens ruling over a large number of subjects we would have lots in common and lots to talk about. We would probably talk about how difficult our jobs were but how well we did them.

JAMIE OLIVER
Another twat

A NO brainer, I'd talk to hippopotami. I'd tell those big boys that they wouldn't be so chunky if they had a proper diet. I'd give them a few tips on some proper pukka nosh that they could knock up from fresh ingredients found by the river's edge in Africa. Bish Bash Bosh.

BRIAN BLESSED
Shouty crackers actor

I WOULDN'T TALK TO THE ANIMALS. I'D SHOUT AT THEM! I'D PROBABLY GO TO A LION AND CHALLENGE HIM TO A SHOUTING CONTEST. THEN I'D GO AND FIND SOME WHALES WHOSE VOICE CAN REACH 188 DECIBELS AND BE HEARD OVER 1000 MILES AWAY, AND I'D SHOUT THEM INTO A COCKED HAT.

RUSSELL BRAND
3rd twat on the list

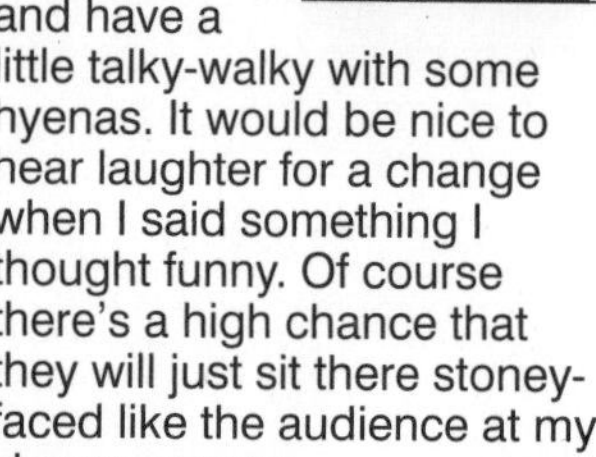

THAT'S easy-weasy! I would go and have a little talky-walky with some hyenas. It would be nice to hear laughter for a change when I said something I thought funny. Of course there's a high chance that they will just sit there stoney-faced like the audience at my showy-wowwy.

JOE SWASH
Nonentity

IF I were Dr Dolittle for a day I'd get straight down to the zoo and have a bit of an old chinwag with some elephants. These creatures are famed for never forgetting anything, so they might be able to tell me who the fuck I am and what I've been in.

JOHNNY FARTPANTS

I DON'T KNOW, JOHNNY! WE'VE TRIED EVERYTHING TO CURE YOU OF YOUR HORRENDOUS ANAL EMISSIONS...
FULCHESTER CLARION
SORRY DAD.
...ACUPUNCTURE, HYPNOSIS, DIETING — NOTHING SEEMS TO IMPROVE YOUR NOXIOUS GUTS.

HANG ON — WHAT'S THIS?
CAT UP TREE SHOCK
ADVERTISMENT
COME SWIMMING with DOLPHINS!
CURES
• DEPRESSION
• STRESS
• ROTTEN GUTS
IT'S GREAT
AQUARIUM
HMM! ITS A LONG SHOT — BUT WORTH A TRY!

SO, AT THE AQUARIUM..
IN YOU GET, JOHNNY — LET'S SEE IF THE SOOTHING PROXIMITY OF THESE GENTLE DOLPHINS WILL CALM YOUR RAMBUNCTIOUS ARSE.

WOW! GLUB! THAT PLAYFUL DOLPHIN HAS SPLASHED ME AND MADE ME SWALLOW A HUGE MOUTHFUL OF WATER!
SPLOOSH!

MEANWHILE OUTSIDE
OH DEAR, I'VE ACCIDENTALLY FILLED THE AQUARIUM WITH CABBAGE WATER INSTEAD OF NORMAL WATER!
AQUARIUM
WATER IN
SHORT-SIGHTED OPERATIVE
AH, WELL, I DON'T SUPPOSE IT'LL DO THE DOLPHINS ANY HARM.

CRUMBS — IT FEELS LIKE THERE'S A STORM A-BREWING IN MY BOTTOM
RUMBLE

BLOYK!
YOIKS! THAT ONE WAS LIKE AN EGGY DEPTH CHARGE!

YOU YOUNG VANDAL! YOUR UNDERWATER CHUFF HAS KILLED ALL OUR DOLPHINS!
RANCID STENCH
OOPS!

THIS AFTERNOON'S DOLPHIN SHOW IS DUE TO START IN A FEW MINUTES, TOO!
FULCHESTER AQUARIUM
DOLPHIN SHOW DAILY
THERE'S ONLY ONE THING FOR IT, JOHNNY...

QUACK!
HO! HO!
SPROUTS
MY A-QUACK-TIC DISPLAY HAS TURNED OUT TO BE A GUFFTASTIC SUCCESS, READERS!

T-WRECK!

***ON THE SHELF:* Lonely Marc now spends days in drab urn. And (inset) in happier times.**

POSTERS of glam-rocker MARC BOLAN once adorned the bedroom walls of countless teenage fans. With his cork-screw hair, tight trousers and flawless complexion, the T-Rex frontman was the pin-up boy of the seventies.

Years take toll on 20th Century Boy Bolan

But the young girls who worshipped the drop-dead gorgeous chart-topper three decades ago would be hard-pressed to recognise their idol now.

fantasy

Gone are the androgynous good looks, mischief-filled eyes and high cheek-bones that once marked him out as a fantasy boyfriend for millions of screaming teeny-boppers. For Bolan is now almost unrecognisable as the star who set millions of hearts a-flutter in 1977.

Reduced to a small pile of dust, the singer who once kept the nation dancing to an endless succession of hits now prefers to spend his time well away from the public gaze, locked in a one-room urn on his mother's mantelpiece.

traffic

Whereas Marc's pop contemporaries, such as David Bowie and Elton John have worn their years well, these days Bolan is grey and powdery, weighing less than a bag of sugar. And whilst he would have stopped traffic in his heyday, the singer now barely merits a second glance from visitors to his mother''s front room, where he spends his days propping up the gas bill - a shadow of his former self.

blind faith

"I barely recognised him, he looked so different," said home help Janice Coxbank. "I really fancied him in the seventies, but he's really let himself go."

"It's sad, really," she added.

And fellow T-Rex member Mickey Finn was equally upset by how Bolan has ended up. "He's a really nice guy, and it's is really shocking to see him in this state," he said from his worm-ridden coffin in London's plush Highgate cemetery.

GILBERT RATCHET

CURSED FIVERS 'CAUSING PILES'

Are jinxed banknotes responsible for haemorrhoids epidemic?

A MYSTERIOUS nation-wide outbreak of piles is being blamed on a batch of five pound notes which were accidentally printed using cursed ink.

People who have come into contact with the rogue fivers, which all feature the image of 19th century social reformer Elizabeth Fry, have reported painfully swollen rectal blood vessels, anal bleeding and discomfort whilst passing stools.

people

The epidemic has affected people from all walks of life all over the country:

● ***A MECHANIC** from Mansfield, who received one of the notes in his change at a fish & chip shop, later developed galloping piles, which he had never had before.*

● ***A SCHOOL** dinner lady in Fife suffered anal swellings after being handed two of the jinxed notes in her wage packet.*

● ***A NATIONALLY-known** Welsh newsreader's piles ruptured whilst he was on air, after he picked up one of the rogue notes off the floor of the BBC lavatories.*

● ***A CORNISH** tractor driver had to spend a week off work sitting on a rubber ring after exchanging five pound coins for one of the notes from a friend who needed change for a parking meter.*

A spokesman for the Royal Mint admitted that the rogue batch of fivers had been printed using hexed ink.

He told us: "We had a rush order come in for a load of fivers, and as we'd ran out of blue ink, we bought some in cheap off the internet."

"Unfortunately, we didn't realise there was a curse on it, as the ink factory had been built on the site of medieval piles hospital."

sixty-two

"The bad news is, anyone who touches them will get Chalfonts something rotten. But the good news is, they're still legal tender," he added.

BUM DEAL: Mansfield man got haemorrhoids from fiver in change.

+ TELL-TALE SIGNS +++ TELL-TALE SIGNS +

Portrait of Elizabeth Fry
❑ Yes ❑ No

Serial number between 1099883345 - 234986457
❑ Yes ❑ No

Searing pain in the rectum when defecating
❑ Yes ❑ No

Searing pain in the rectum when standing up
❑ Yes ❑ No

Searing pain in the rectum when sitting down
❑ Yes ❑ No

Have YOU got one of the rogue fivers?

If you ticked "Yes" to any of these questions, then your bank note is definitely from the hexed batch.

Viz vicar vows to beat fiver curse

THE JINXED FIVERS have brought untold suffering to anii up and down the country.

Doctors' surgeries have been swamped by patients complaining of grape-like rectal excrescences, and manufacturers of popular piles treatments such as Preparation H and Anusol have been forced to recruit extra staff to cope with increased demand for their products.

But one man who has vowed to lift the haemorrhoid hex is Viz vicar the Rev. Bickerton Normanby.

He told us: "The only thing more powerful than piles is the love of the Lord God Jesus Christ."

And he made this promise to afflicted *Viz* readers: "I can lift the curse off your fivers by invoking the Holy Spirit to cast the demon Michael Miles out of each and every note."

"Simply send in as many fivers as you can find to Viz, PO Box 841, Whitley Bay, NE26 9EQ, and I will do the rest," he told us. "You may also like to send in any tenners or twenties that have been in contact with them in your wallet, as this curse can be very contagious."

"Unfortunately, the exorcism service is so powerful that it results in the destruction of the note, so unfortunately I am unable to return any of your money," Rev. Normanby added.

20 THINGS YOU NEVER KNEW ABOUT... HALLOWEEN

WOOOOOO! It's the spookiest night of the year. At full moon on October 31st, all the ghosties, goolies, long-legged beasties and things that go bump in the night rise from their graves to walk amongst the living. And if you hear a knock at your door, may the Lord have mercy on your soul, because chances are it's either a denizen of the netherworld, a flesh-hungry zombie or a teenager demanding a pound not to push dog dirt through your letterbox. But how much do you really know about this ancient pagan festival? When did it start? What's it all about? When's it going to fucking stop? It's time to bar your windows, pull your chair closer to the fire and prepare to have your blood chilled by twenty spine-tingling facts about Halloween.

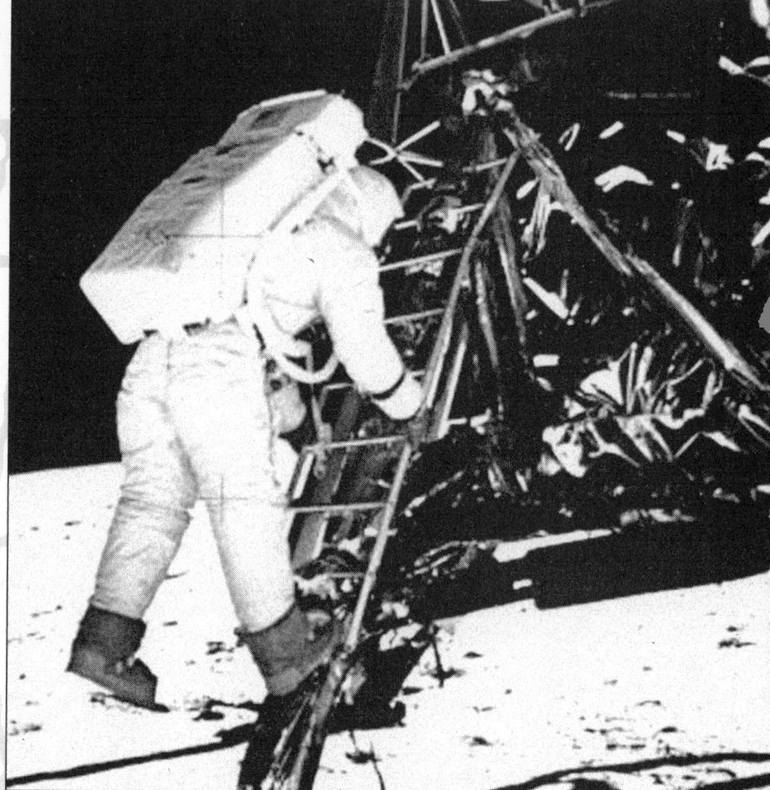

1 The name "Halloween" is a corruption of the words "Haribos Evening", named after the better-than-nothing cheap sweets which are traditionally given out on October 31st.

2 The practice of trick-or-treating is usually associated with children, but according to royal biographer Gyles Brandreth, the Queen's mum the Queen Mum used to enjoy the custom well into old age. At Halloween, residents of the Balmoral estate were accustomed to answering the door to the ancient brown-toothed royal, dressed as a Frankenstein and demanding sweets and money. If they refused to play along, the fun-loving centenarian would instruct her loyal footman Backstairs Billy to push corgi excreta through their letterbox.

3 Halloween has been the subject of many top-rated movies, such as *Halloween*, *Halloween II*, *Halloween III* and *Halloween IV: The Klumps*.

4 It's not just on Earth that people enjoy Halloween ... it has even been celebrated on the Moon! In 1969, Apollo spacemen Pete Conrad and Al Bean found themselves on the lunar surface as night fell on October 31st. Surprised by a knock on the door of their capsule, they opened it to find command module pilot Richard Gordon holding a torch under his chin and demanding sweets. When the two astronauts refused to hand over any Haribos to their colleague, the disgruntled trick-or-treater pushed a specially-developed dog dirt pill through the letterbox of their moon lander and left a big scratch down the side of their lunar rover with a sonic screwdriver.

5 It's well known that ghosts can walk through walls, but you probably didn't realise that paper stops them in their tracks. This means that Japan, where all the houses are made of paper, is the most unhaunted country on earth.

6 Since everything in Australia is the opposite of what we have in Britain, Halloween for folks down under falls in late Spring - a week *after* their Bonfire Night! Likewise, Aussies celebrate the witching hour at twelve noon instead of midnight, when frightened children walk the streets, knocking on strangers' doors and offering them Haribos.

7 Amazingly, scientists have also observed the practice of trick-or-treating amongst many other species. For example, on October 31st each year, termites of the genus *Dictyoptera* leave their mounds and call on neighbouring termite colonies, where they demand a special sweet fungus called *termitomycus*. If no mould is forthcoming, they use their prehensile maxillae to push ant droppings through the door.

8 Perhaps the most rubbish ghost of all is the Holy Ghost, which is the ghost of Our Lord Jesus Christ. It hasn't got its head under its arm, it doesn't drag a load of chains up the stairs and waggle the knob on your bedroom door, and it doesn't lob tea-cups round in the kitchen. It doesn't even wander the dark corridors of a stately home, wailing in an ethereal voice whilst endlessly trying to wash blood from its hands. Instead of haunting something, the Holy Ghost dwells in people's hearts and sits at God's right hand, whatever the fuck that means.

9 58-year-old Draylon Taint III is the USA's most prolific trick-or-treater. Every Halloween, Mr Taint calls on every house in his hometown of Carbondale, Illinois. During a marathon 24-hour session, he knocks on an estimated 26,000 front doors, collects 750kg of Haribos, throws up to 520 dozen eggs at houses and pushes more than a ton of dog dirt through people's letterboxes.

10 What could be more frightening than a ghost? The answer is... TWO ghosts! In fact, boffins studying fear reactions at the University of Copenhagen recently concluded that the scariest combination of spooks was two ghosts, a Dracula and three Frankensteins.

10½ In second place was a werewolf, four mummies and a Creature from the Black Lagoon.

11 Rationing restrictions meant that trick-or-treaters were unable to obtain eggs for the duration of WWII. As a result, between 1939 and 1945, small boys were forced to throw powdered eggs at houses where the occupants had failed to hand over enough sweets or money. The real eggs were all shipped out to the soldiers at the front, so they could throw them on Halloween in a bid to boost morale.

12 A householder in Leeds received one of the most terrifying trick-or-treat calls on Halloween in 1987. On answering a ring on her doorbell, Iris Dunnock found not a group of toddlers half-heartedly dressed as witches, but a genuine ghost stood on her doorstep demanding a pound! The spectre was the restless spirit of a trick-or-treater who had been killed at that very spot 100 years previously. Petrified Mrs Dunnock slammed the door in the spook's face. Moments later, he pushed a see-through dog-dirt through her letterbox.

13 The custom of Halloween dates back to 1184, when Pope Lucius III issued a papal edict demanding a tithe from all members of the Catholic church. Monks in frightening masks were sent out on October 31st each year, with orders to collect a handful of Haribos from each household. Any heretics who resisted their demands were summarily excommunicated from the church and had their bins knocked over.

14 According to the British Association of Clothing Manufacturers, demand for clean underpants reaches a peak on November 1st. That's because an estimated 1 in 5 of the adult population has pappered their trolleys the previous evening on account of all the ghosts and skeletons.

15 On October 31st 1582, the old-fashioned Julian calendar was abandoned in favour of the Gregorian calendar. However, the mismatch between the two dating systems led to a shortfall of just over a week, and it was decided to repeat October 31st eight times on the trot before November 1st. The resulting festival of trick-or-treating led to hugely increased profits for Poundstretcher, as demand for Haribos soared.

16 The most lavish treats ever bestowed on trick-or-treaters were given out on Halloween 1946 by American oil billionaire John Paul Getty. The generous tycoon filled a bowl with Koh-i-noor diamonds the size of hens' eggs, and encouraged local youngsters to dip into it when they called round.

17 French Palaeontologists working in the Lascaux Caves have discovered what they believe to be the earliest evidence of trick-or-treating amongst hominids. Primitive wall paintings seem to show Neanderthal children in Frankenstein masks pushing dinosaur turds through the letterbox of an old Cro-Magnon lady's cave.

18 In 1988, readers of TV Times voted Halloween pumpkins the third most frightening raggedy-mouthed, orange-faced thing, after Clyde the monkey out of *Every Which Way But Loose* and *Wish You Were Here* presenter Judith Chalmers.

19 On Halloween 1984, Indian Prime Minister Indira Gandhi answered a knock at the door, expecting to find local youngsters trick-or-treating. Instead, she found two heavily-armed assassins who shot her dead and fled, after cheekily helping themselves to two handfuls of Haribos!

20 The world's tiniest ghost is the restless spirit of the world's smallest man Calvin Philips, which is said to haunt a doll's house in Salem State Toy Museum, Massachusetts USA. Philips was tragically killed there on Halloween 1932, when he was crushed under a marble during a game of Ker-Plunk. As he floats up and down the 8" high stairs, dragging a chain made of paperclips, the miniature spectre emits "Woooo"s which are so high-pitched that they can only be heard by bats.

Rub'n'tug shop receives top prize from plain English campaign

GETTING THEIR MASSAGE ACROSS

EXCLUSIVE!

PULLING IT OFF: The Salford knocking shop that managed to earn plain English award.

A MANCHESTER THAI MASSAGE parlour has been bestowed with a Plain English Gold Award following a surprise visit by a local inspector.

Madame Lai Lai's massage Emporium in Salford was commended for its "clear and concise wording that leaves its clientele under no confusion as to the services on offer".

A sign over the door reading "Will wank you off for £50 on the pretence that you are having a massage. Blow jobs and shagging available for more of your money" particularly impressed the inspector, who praised the establishment for the "clarity and directness of their message".

Clacton Purves from the Plain English Campaign has spent the past 23 years inspecting over 300 rub'n'tug shops around Britain. And this is the first time the pressure group's top award has been given to such an institution.

annoys

"Nothing annoys people more than overcomplicated language, jargon and ambiguity," said Purves. "The Inland Revenue and Local Councils in particular are notorious for the confusing wording on their forms and official correspondence."

"However, in my experience massage parlours are one of the worst culprits," he added.

Purves claims that many of the establishments he has visited have ambiguous and vague business descriptions which could confuse customers and lead to embarrassing situations. And as an undercover punter, he has had his fair share of bad experiences.

toys

"I remember going into one establishment in Leeds pretending to be an obese middle-aged pervert with a bad back and a hard on," he told the Salford & Eccles Clarinet.

"I was asked to lay on a bed naked while a topless woman covered me in oil and gave me a perfunctory shoulder rub. She then skirted around my penis, occasionally brushing it and smiling at me, before cupping my nuts and asking if I wanted a 'sensual massage'."

"As a consumer, I wasn't sure what services were on offer. For someone who is hard of hearing or unable to pick up on body language and simple suggestion, this could be a real issue," he continued.

case

"I pointed out to the proprietor that she was in breach of the consumer code and that she fell short of the high standards of the Plain English Campaign," said Purves.

"I explained to her that what she should have said was 'Do you want wanking off now sir? It's £20'," he continued. "At that point, she called for security and I was beaten within an inch of my life."

When contacted, a spokesman for the Plain English Campaign claimed to have no record of employing anyone by the name of Clacton Purves.

JOHNNY FARTPANTS

Drunken bakers

When's last time we had a drink for Christmas?
I don't know.

A proper Christmas drink.
Shut up the shop.
And had a drink.

Yesterday?
No, not just drinking...

Like that time we all went down the Hare and Bear.
When?

You, me and the gaffer.
Not me pal.
Maybe you and him.

Could have been...
Perhaps you still had the wife.

Remember you fighting with a carol singer once and the boss trying to break it up.

Yeah, that was then.
Silly old bitch bawling right in my earhole...

Was that the Christmas your missus fucked off?

No.
It *was* a Christmas though, wasn't it?

Yes.
Thought so.
You was in a right fucking state.

Christmas fucking Eve.
Kid an' all.

Pubs cost a bastard mint.
Nah, we'll slip a few half bottles in to top us off...

BUSTER GONAD & his UNFEASIBLY LARGE TESTICLES

MY SISTER IS GETTING MARRIED TOMORROW, SO I'M SPLASHING OUT ON A BESPOKE WHISTLE & FLUTE
DOES SIR DRESS TO THE LEFT OR TO THE RIGHT?

WELL, USUALLY STICKING OUT THE FRONT IN A WHEELBARROW
?

SEVENTEEN INCHES, MR PRICE...
SEVENTEEN INCHES, MR BEAL...
...NOW IF SIR WOULD STRETCH OUT HIS ARMS SO AS MR. BEAL CAN MEASURE SIR FOR SIR'S JACKET.

WHALLOP!

SHORTLY...
I'M AFRAID SIR'S KNACKERS FRACTURED MR. BEAL'S SKULL. BUT NOT TO WORRY... I'M SURE WE CAN FIND SIR A NICE 'OFF-THE-PEG' SUIT.
PRICE & BEAL.

NEXT DAY...
DID YOU REMEMBER TO BRING ALONG THE CONFETTI, BUSTER?
CRUMBS!! I KNEW I'D FORGOTTEN SOMETHING

OH, BUSTER, YOU BIG BOLLOCKED BUFFOON... I CAN'T TRUST YOU TO DO ANYTHING

JUST WAIT HERE, MUM... I'LL GO AND FETCH IT

I'LL SCRATCH MY NUTS AND COLLECT SOME POD SCURF... NOBODY WILL KNOW THE DIFFERENCE... HEH! HEH!
SKRIT! SKRIT! SKRIT!

HMM! CONFETTI ISN'T WHAT IT USED TO BE... IT USED TO BE SHAPED LIKE BELLS AND HORSE SHOES. THIS JUST LOOKS LIKE DANDRUFF
PTHOO!
PTHA!
... WITH CURLY HAIRS IN IT

AT THE RECEPTION
LOOK, BUSTER. YOUR SISTER IS GOING TO CUT THE CAKE

GET A PHOTO FOR ME, WOULD YOU?
YES, MUM
FLUM!

HERE GOES...
HUNH!?!
YANK!

R-R-RI-IP!!
SPLAT!

BAH! HOW AM I GOING TO GET A PHOTOGRAPH OF ME CUTTING THE CAKE WHEN IT'S ALL OVER THE FLOOR?.. YOU AND YOUR STUPID BALLS.
OOER!

WAIT! I'VE GOT AN IDEA!

OKAY... SAY CHEESE AND GET READY TO PLUNGE THE KNIFE IN...
AFTER THREE...

ONE... TWO... THREE...
GAAAA!

WHO SCARES WINS

GULF WAR hardman Andy McNabb was last night being comforted by friends after suffering what he called "the most terrifying experience of my life" when he became trapped... *on a Ghost Train!*

EXCLUSIVE

SAS Man's Fairground Horror

The fearless *Bravo Two-Zero* author, whose best-selling book charted his experiences behind enemy lines as a member of Britain's elite commando unit, was on a Special Forces works outing to Mablethorpe when colleagues dared him to go on the Spooky House ride alone. However, his carriage suffered an electrical malfunction and McNabb spent 20 minutes stuck inside the seafront attraction.

agent

Management at Sketchley's Funfair called in engineers to fix the problem and release the highly-decorated former Black Ops agent. By the time he was finally brought out, it is estimated that McNabb had been subjected to ***TEN TIMES*** the amount of terror experienced by a typical visitor to the £1 attraction.

Onlookers described McNabb as looking white as a sheet when he emerged from the Ghost Train. "He was in a dreadful state," said Ada Cobnutt, who was visiting the funfair with her son. "His hair was stood right up on end, his teeth were chattering and his knees were knocking together, making a castanet noise."

service

"I can't imagine what he must have gone through in there," she added.

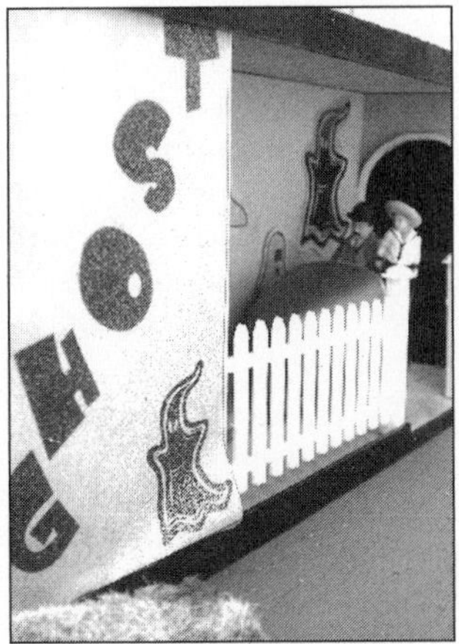

***BRITISH WAIL:** The ghost train that broke down.*

McNabb, 53, later spoke about his harrowing ordeal on a local radio phone-in programme. "It was horrible," he told Sutton-on-Sea 203's *Alan Twatt After Midnight*. "The lights kept flashing on and off and there was a Dracula in a coffin. Every fifteen seconds, the lid opened, he sat up and some laughter came out of a loudspeaker."

"I was absolutely petrified," he added.

During his twenty-minute nightmare, the *Who Dares Wins* toughnut was also subjected to

- ***COBWEBS** and rubber spiders*
- ***PLASTIC** skeletons daubed with fluorescent paint*
- ***BITS OF** string touching his face and making him jump*
- ***A LOUD** whistle going off behind a bit of plywood*

"There was a notice on the wall that said: 'In case of breakdown do not leave your car', but let me tell you, I was going nowhere," continued McNabb.

"I was literally paralysed with fear."

squirrel

"During my time in the SAS, I was chained to a wall by Saddam's Imperial Guards, had my fingernails pulled out with pliers and had 10,000 volts put through my scrotum. I never batted an eyelid during all those experiences and more, but those twenty minutes of sheer terror in the Spooky House ghost train will haunt me forever."

And the hard-as-nails author confided that the traumatic episode has left him mentally scarred.

He told Twatt: "I find it very difficult to sleep at night. After brushing my teeth each night, I drive 350 miles to my parents' house in Eastbourne so I can go in their bed."

"And I make them leave the light on and make sure the wardrobe door is shut in case there is a Frankenstein in there," he added.

***GOING COMMANDO:** Ghost train scared pants off of McNabb (right).*

Scottish Woman: "I've not seen *THAT* photo"

EXCLUSIVE

A WOMAN on the Isle of Mull last night admitted that she had not seen that photograph of *DEBBIE MCGEE*.

Agnes McTavish, a retired weaver on the remote Scottish island, revealed that she had yet to see that photograph of Debbie McGee during an interview with her local newspaper.

appendix

"I've only been off the island once in my life," she told the *Mull Intelligencer & Argus*. "That was for an appendix operation when I was five, so the opportunity to see that photograph of Debbie McGee has never really arisen."

preface

"I have seen that film of Steve Davis though," she added. "To be honest, I thought it went on a bit."

***NEVER A MULL MOMENT:** Agnes hasn't seen <u>that</u> photo.*

Letterbocks

WHAT a shame about Colonel Gaddafi. He always seemed like a nice man when he came on the television. He reminded me a bit of that Maradona only taller. Mind you I never had any time for him, on account of he cheated in that football game. I hope those Libyan rebels are ruddy proud of themselves.

Mrs Joyce Grimaldi Oswestry

WITH reference to Mrs Grimaldi's letter *(above)*, me and my husband always preferred Saddam Hussein to Colonel Gaddafi. He had a cheeky twinkle in his eye that put us in mind of a young Alfred Marx. We were very sorry to see him getting hanged on YouTube.

Mrs Doreen Lymeswold Salisbury

I WATCHED with horror the mobile phone footage of the crowds leaping about and shouting next to Colonel Gaddafi's body. I only hope that when our own dear Queen passes on, the British people behave with a little bit more decorum than the Libyans, 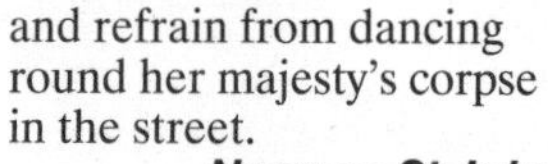 and refrain from dancing round her majesty's corpse in the street.

Norman St.John-Ambulance, Yeovil

Traditional Toy Obscured on Grounds of Political Correctness

IT SEEMS that every day the news reports somebody famous who has died. Yet you never hear about non-famous people dying. It seems to me that being famous might be bad for your health.

Edna Crentin, Luton

PENGUINS are my favourite animals. With their black and white plumage, I often think they'd make very smart waiters in a restaurant! However, when they shit, their arse goes off like a shotgun and it stinks of rotten fish, which might put the diners off their food a bit.

Antonia Soper, Slimbridge

WE'VE got a pond in the garden, only it's very deep and the water's quite murky so it's often quite difficult to see the fish swimming about in it. To solve the problem, my husband tied a different coloured ping-pong ball onto each fish, attached with a length of string through a hole punched in its dorsal fin with a pencil. Now we can see where each fish is at any time.

Iolanthe Jism, Chinbury

VIZ COMIC
PO Box 841
Whitley Bay
NE26 9EQ
letters@viz.co.uk

STAR LETTER

THESE aliens ought to abduct a few British farmers and probe their anuses instead of just the Mexican ones they do at the moment. With their national diet of chili beans, Jalapeno peppers and Tabasco sauce, the blistered Mexican ringpiece is hardly a good yardstick by which to judge the human race.

Gerald Joskin Boston Spa

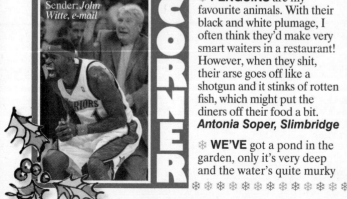

THERE'S something very very nasty going wrong with my private parts, but I'm not going to go to the GP with it. That's because my doctor's a lady, and she'll no doubt be too busy thinking about knitting patterns, shoes or recipes to give me a proper diagnosis.

Frank Gleet Discharge-upon-Thames

I AGREE with Mr Gleet *(above)*. I've been haemorrhaging blood and pus from my anus for nearly three months now, because I'd rather put up with my symptoms than listen to my female GP yattering on about who's going out with who on *Emmerdale Farm*. This country ought to recruit some proper male physicians with their minds on the job, so that these lady "doctors" can go back to being nurses, where their dolly daydreams can't hurt anybody.

Rex Fissure, Bacup

I SPOTTED this in my street. Now I don't know if this is meant to be charming, ironic or a threat for midget burglars. You decide.

Steve Usher, e-mail

ANY TIME I'm a bit glum I can always think back to that amusing anecdote of my mate John being chased by a badger. I recommend it, works every time. So that's John and a badger okay? Excellent.

James Lewis, e-mail

I THINK we were all pleased that the Saudi authorities overturned the planned barbaric lashing of a woman caught driving. However, the law is the law and justice must seen to be done. Therefore it would be a nice touch if say, a Royal Princess could be filmed spanking the naughty young woman with her bare hand, admonishing her at the same time. If they were both naked so much the better, as this would show the Saudis are not all fuddy duddies when it comes to women covering up.

Sheik Yahbooti, e-mail

OLAY keep claiming they fight the 7 signs of ageing. Does that include becoming more right wing? Because that's the really problematic one.

Christina Martin, e-mail

UP THE ARSE CORNER

Sender: *John Witte, e-mail*

TOP TIPS

MISERS. Save money by buying Wilkinsons own brand anti-perspirant, which also doubles for fly spray, judging by the smell.

Josso John, e-mail

CANADIAN Tourists. Make sure no-one mistakes you for an American by putting Canadian flag badges on every item of clothing you own.

Teamy Teamy, e-mail

EMBARRASSING Bodies presenters. Include one or two mundane medical cases in your programme to avoid any comparison with a Victorian freak show.

Gerry Paton, e-mail

A CAT covered in vaseline with its ears pinned back makes an ideal domesticated pet otter.

Alex Upchuck, e-mail

AN iPod nano taped to a house brick makes an ideal early 1980s-style 'Walkman' for nostalgic portable music fans.

Craig Scott, e-mail

A SPREADEAGLED mouse tied to a small kite makes an ideal pet bat on a lead.

Alex Upchuck, e-mail

NUDISTS. Stay warm this winter by wrapping yourself in cling film.

Joseph Hoben, e-mail

SLIGHTLY overweight women. Look and feel like you are Kate Moss by moving to Worksop.

Simon Burdett, e-mail

I HAVE to go to the Blackburn/Burnley area and I have an old OS map from 1984. Can any reader tell me if it's worth buying a new one or has the Blackpool/ Burnley area not changed much in the last 27 years?

Mr Muddy, e-mail

ON A recent episode of *Saturday Kitchen*, actor and musician Martin Kemp talked glowingly about his upcoming movie that he revealed he had also written. It dawned on me that I will never, ever watch this film and I found this very reassuring. In a world threatened by cyber-terrorism and economic instability, can any other readers think of a time when they were so content?

Bruntacus, Manchester

I WAS playing rugby last week, and brought an opposing player to the ground by diving on him, and holding his legs until he fell over, to the delight of my team and the spectating crowd. However yesterday while playing a game of football, I did exactly the same thing and got sent off. Typical. It's just one set of rules for rugby, and another set of rules for football.

Justin Brett, e-mail

I HATE it when tramps walk up to you asking for cash. It immediately puts you on the wrong foot. I feel much more sympathy for tramps who are lying down on the ground, totally destitute. If they have pissed themselves or they are near a dog shit, so much the better. I'm not giving my hard-earned cash away to one of these upright 'posh' tramps.

Ben Margerison, e-mail

I BELIEVE a lot of conflict in the Wild West could have been avoided completely if cowboy architects had just made their towns big enough for everyone.

Dodge City Pete
Dodge City

WHO'S that cunt off *Minute to Win it*? Not Joe Swash, the other cunt.

Malcome Middleton
e-mail

**WELL readers, do YOU know who that cunt is? Perhaps he's that arsehole off that thing on the telly. Or maybe he's that twat in that programme on Sky1. Write in and tell us, but don't mark your envelope 'I know who that cunt is'.*

MY MATE Phil knows the exact time he was born. I don't even remember seeing a clock, and anyway I couldn't even tell the time till I was about seven. Do you think he was some sort of child genius?

Kev Plankton, e-mail

I SEE from recent stories in the press that as well as an arse, Pippa 'Buns' Middleton also has a face. And quite a good one at that. So now I find myself in a quandry as to where I'd like to drain my spuds first - buns or chin. Until the great day comes and I actually have the decision to make, I'll guess I'll have to settle for whatever picture I can find in *OK!* magazine.

Dazzla, Warrington

WHY IS it acceptable for horses to shit in the street and not me? I'm the one who pays council tax.

Tommy C, Bristol

AS requested, here's a photo of my dog balancing a tangerine on his head.

Eddo75, e-mail

LOOK OUT! LOOK OUT! Viz's Mr Moneybags IS ABOUT!

ALL THROUGH the month of December, we're going to be doing our bit to bring a bit of festive cheer to cash-strapped *Viz* readers. We've sent our secret millionaire MR MONEYBAGS on a mystery tour around the UK, and he'll be handing out crisp tenners to any reader who spots him.

And he's aiming to make your Christmas £10 jollier!

Keep your eyes peeled for Mr Moneybags. He could be anywhere... in a pub, at the dog track or in a betting shop. He's easy to recognise - he's 5'10" to 6'4", weighs between 15 and 20 stone and has a distinctive shaved head and neck tattoos.

trousers

If you think you've found Mr Moneybags whilst out and about, walk up behind him and pat the back pocket of his trousers whilst saying the words: ***"I fancy a bit of what's in there"***.

pliers

If it's Mr Moneybags, he'll take out his wallet and hand you a crisp ten-pound note. But if you've been unlucky and it's not him, don't despair. Simply keep looking for him. *Remember - you can have as many goes as you want.*

Christmas Wooly-Pully Ethical Dilemmas

Your jumper-knitting moral queries answered by Archbishop of Canterbury Dr Rowan Williams

Dear A.B. of C.

I'M KNITTING a jumper for Christmas for my nephew, but the thing is he's only got one arm. What I want to know is, should I knit both arms, even though one of them won't get used, or should I just do one arm and sew the other side up? I don't want to cause any offence, but equally I don't want to waste any wool.

Audrey Trumplet, Bunting

KNITTING a one-armed sweater might look like you are cruelly drawing attention to your nephew's disability, whilst leaving an empty sleeve flapping about might also prove embarrassing for him. Why not knit both arms on the jumper, then stuff the empty one with rolled-up newspaper, and also knit him a nice pink wooly hand to go on the end? The Bible tells us that on Judgement Day we will all be restored to full health, so when your nephew gets to the Pearly Gates and his missing arm grows back he will be able to take the newspaper out, remove the pink hand and wear the jumper as normal.

Dear A.B. of C.

I'M KNITTING a jumper for Christmas for my teenage grandson. The only problem is, I think he might be one of these "gays" that they've got these days, and it's left me with a bit of a problem. Should I knit him a nice blue jumper with a racing car on the front, or since he may be one of them, do you think he'd prefer a nice pink one with all flowers on it and frilly lace round the collar and cuffs?

Ada Scrotum, Denby Dale

THIS IS a tricky one, Mrs Scrotum. I think, after much thought and prayer, I can say definitively that there is no simple answer to this problem. You should ask God to guide your needles and knit what is in your heart.

Dear A.B. of C.

I USUALLY knit a jumper for Christmas for my son-in-law Derek. However this year, he was convicted of being the infamous Tipton Cannibal Murderer and sentenced to life in prison. In court, it was revealed that he had killed and eaten at least 15 people, including my daughter. My problem is, I'm not sure what initials to knit on the front of the sweater: "DP" for Derek Plywood or "TTCM" for The Tipton Cannibal Murderer.

Mrs Shitstern
Wolverhampton

THE ONLY name that God recognises is the name that you were Christened with (except for people like Cliff Richards, who is much better known by his stage name than his real name). I would say that if your son-in-law intends to pray to the Lord for forgiveness, and happens to be in a jumper with his nickname on it at the time - wearing it almost like a badge of honour - God might take quite a dim view of that.

DURING World War 2, they brought in rationing because they said the soldiers needed all the egg, knicker elastic and bananas at the front. But we've been at war in the Middle East for the best part of ten years now and yet there's still plenty of eggs, knicker elastic and bananas in the shops. If you ask me, Churchill was trying to pull a fast one. Mind you, I never trusted him as his eyes were too close together. I preferred Hitler.

Mrs Stroke
Jissolm-upon-Thames

Hitler Youth
VILL YOU GO IN BIN SHOP FOR ME?

OOR
FRANKIE

AT THE BOYLE HOOSEHOLD
JIST LOOK AT A' THESE COMPLAINTS I'VE RECEIVED ABOOT YER TASTELESS JOKES, FRANKIE!
SORRY PAW.
YE CANNAE OPEN YER MOOTH WITHOOT CAUSIN' OFFENCE WITH YER NEAR-THE-KNUCKLE COMMENTS!

MIND YE KEEP OOT OF ANY MORE CONTROVERSY, FRANKIE...
OR I'LL SLIPPER YER AIRSE!
GULP! OK PAW

PAW WAS AFFY CROSS – I'LL HAVE TAE TURN OVER A NEW LEAF
FRAE NOO ON, I'LL MAKE NAE MUIR OFFENSIVE REMARKS!

FRANKIE, HERE'S A POOND IF YE FETCH ME A TIN OF BITUMEN FRAE YON HARDWARE STORE
HARDW
I NEED IT TAE TAR MA SHED ROOF.
OKAY, MR MCHEGGIE.

A TIN O' BITUMEN FER MR MCHEGGIE, PLEASE – HIS SHED ROOF NEEDS TAE BE RE-TARRED.
EH? SPEAK OOT! HIS SHED ROOF NEEDS TAE BE WHIT?

RE-TARRED! RE-TARRED!
GASP! FRANKIE BOYLE!

I SUPPOSE YE THINK CALLIN' AULD GEORGE A RETARD IS BEIN' "REFRESHINGLY UN-PC" DAE YE?
EH?
WELL I FIND THAT KIND O' LANGUAGE MICHTY OFFENSIVE!

I'LL BE TELLIN' YER PAW ON YE, YE ENVELOPE-PUSHIN' YOUNG WHELP!
B-BUT I WISNAE... OCH! WHIT'S THE USE?

AH WEEL, AT LEAST I'VE STILL GOT MA POOND.
LOLLIES
McLUIGI'S
ICES
I'LL USE IT TAE BUY AN ICE CREAM.

SORRY IT'S A WEE BIT MIS-SHAPEN – MA MACHINE'S ON THE BLINK!
HO HO! WHIT A FUNNY LOOKING RASPBERRY RIPPLE!

SO! YE FIND MA DISABILITY AMUSING, DAE YE FRANKIE?
HUH?
I TEK MUCKLE OFFENCE AT BEIN' CALLED A RASPBERRY RIPPLE, YE CHEEKY PUP!

YE AND YER NAE-HAULDS-BARRED HUMOUR! I'LL BE TELLIN' YER FAITHER!
BUT I DIDNAE MEAN... OCH, I'D BEST JIST LEAVE!

SHORTLY
SWEET
CONF
OPEN
I SPENT MA POOND ON A BIG BAG OF PENNY CHEWS, INSTEAD.

AW NAW! THE BAG'S SPLIT!
ACH, THIS IS TURRIBLE – THERE'S CHEWS EVERYWHERE!

WHIT DAE YE MEAN BY COMPLAINING ABOOT THERE BEING JEWS EVERYWHERE?!
HUNH? B-BUT RABBI MURDOCH...
THAT'S YER IDEA OF "EDGY COMEDY", IS IT?

WAIT TILL I TELL YER PAW, YE ANTI-SEMITIC YOUNG RIP!
JINGS! I'D BETTER SCARPER!

CRIVVENS! I'VE FALLEN INTAE WEE JOANNIE'S DOLLY'S PRAM!

HELP MA BOAB! NOO JOANNIE'S DUG IS ATTACKIN' MA TROOSERS!
YIP YIP grrr grrr
GIT AFF ME, YE MUTT! G'WAN, BEAT IT!

BEAT IT... JIST BEAT IT!
WISHT! WID YE LOOK AT YOUNG FRANKIE DAEIN' A MICHAEL JACKSON IMPERSONATION!

AYE – SINGIN' JACKSON'S HIT SONG 'BEAT IT' WHILST PRETENDING TAE HUMP A BABBY IN A PRAM!
EH?
PAEDOPHILE JOKES NOO IS IT, FRANKIE? OCH, YE DINNAE KEN WHEN TAE STOP.

YER FAITHER WILL NO' BE PLEASED WHEN WE TELL HIM!
JINGS! I'M IN FER A PROPER SLIPPERIN' WHEN I GET HAME!

HOWEVER, AT THE HOOSE
FRANKIE, THIS GENTLEMAN WANTS TAE SPEAK WITH YE.
HE'S AN EXECUTIVE PRODUCER FER CHANNEL 4.

YER SHOCKING AND OOTRAGEOUS BEHAVIOUR IS THE TALK OF THE TOON, FRANKIE.
HOW WOULD YE LIKE YER AIN PRIMETIME TELEVISION SERIES?

AND...
...HERE'S ANITHER ONE: HOW MANY WANKING PAEDOPHILES DOES IT TAKE TER CHANGE A SPASTIC JEW'S LIGHTBULB UP THE QUEEN'S DRIED-UP AULD FADGE?
FRANKIE'S LAUGH SHOW
SONY DVD
HO HO! HE'S AFFY FUNNY!
RADIO RENTALS
TV AND VIDEO
AYE – YE KEN YE SHOULDNAE LAUGH, BUT YE CANNAE HELP IT!

ROGER MELLIE
THE MAN ON THE TELLY

HOW ARE THE PROGRAMME IDEAS COMING ON, ROGER?
SLOWLY... GOT A BIT OF WRITERS BLOCK, TOM

WELL YOU'D BETTER THINK QUICK... YOU'VE GOT THE MEETING WITH THE COMMISSIONING EDITOR OF ITV TOMORROW
I KNOW, TOM
WHAT HAVE YOU SO FAR?

LET'S SEE... FRY'S TURKISH DELIGHT
WHAT'S THAT ABOOT?
I DON'T FUCKING KNOW, TOM...

...STEPHEN FRY TRAVELS ROUND TURKEY IN A...A... MICROLIGHT OR SOMETHING
ERM...NO...

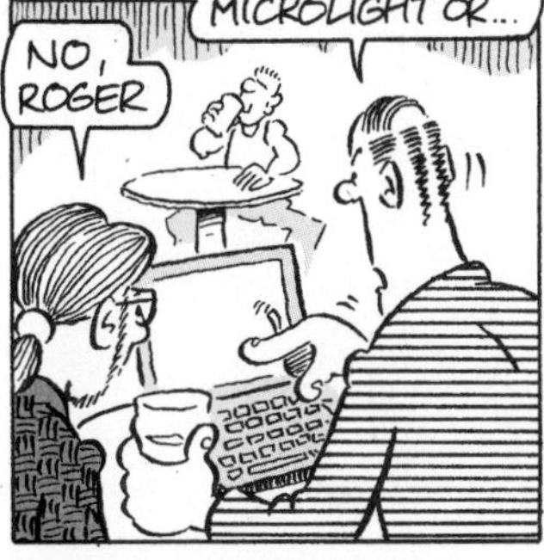
CLUNES'S TURKISH DELIGHT? MARTIN CLUNES TRAVELS ROUND TURKEY IN A...A MICROLIGHT OR...
NO, ROGER

CLUNES'S WALLOONS... MARTIN CLUNES TRAVELS ROUND BELGIUM IN A...A...
OH, I DUNNO...
...IN A FUCKING SUBMARINE, TOM
NO, ROGER. THE SCHEDULES ARE CLOGGED UP WITH CELEBRITY TRAVELOGUES
JOANNA LUMLEY... BILLY CONNOLLY... TREVOR MACDONALD... THEY'RE ALL AT IT
CLUNES'S MACAROONS... MARTIN CLUNES HAS GOT THREE DAYS TO SET UP A BAKERY AND WIN A CAKE COMPETITION...
HEAR ME OUT, TOM...
I DON'T THINK SO ROGER...
...THE JUDGE IS ARRIVING IN 45 MINUTES AND ALL HIS BAKING TRAYS ARE FUCKED... IT'S GOT PERIL, TOM... THEY LOVE PERIL IN THEIR SHOWS

CUE A DRAMATIC PIANO CHORD AND WE'RE INTO THE SHIT BREAK
NO...NO...NO!
YOU CAN'T JUST TAKE AN EXISTING FORMAT AND TWEAK IT... YOU HAVE TO THINK OUTSIDE THE BOX, ROGER... THINK ORIGINAL

NEXT DAY...
MR. WANKSTAIN WILL SEE YOU NOW, MR MELLIE
ITV
THANKS, LOVE
GOOD LUCK, ROGER

AH, ROGER. COME IN, COME IN. HAVE A SEAT, WILL YOU?...
STRAIGHT DOWN TO BUSINESS, EH?
NOW, I'VE BEEN LOOKING THROUGH YOUR IDEAS...

...BLACK GOLD... THE STORY OF OIL... WHAT'S THAT?
IT'S A DOCUMENTARY...
...AN EXPOSÉ OF HOW THE FUEL COMPANIES CALL THE SHOTS ON GOVERNMENTS

HMM! WHAT ABOUT THIS?... MY GRANNY USED TO SAY.
THAT'S A FUN SCIENCE SHOW
IT TESTS OLD WIVES TALES IN THE LABORATORY

THE FANTASTIC VOYAGE?
A JOURNEY INSIDE THE HUMAN BODY USING CGI AND NANO TECHNOLOGY
WOW!.. THAT SOUNDS ABSOLUTELY FASCINATING.

WELL, ROGER... I HAVE TO SAY THAT THESE IDEAS OF YOURS ARE HIGHLY ORIGINAL. HIGHLY ORIGINAL INDEED
THANKS

AND UNFORTUNATELY THAT'S THE PROBLEM, ROGER.
HUNH!?
YOU SEE, WE'RE LOOKING FOR TRIED AND TESTED FORMULAE. SHOWS THAT TAKE EXISTING FORMATS AND GIVE THEM A BIT OF A TWEAK

...I DON'T KNOW... ER... GORDON RAMSAY'S TOILETS FROM HELL FOR INSTANCE... OR CELEBRITY TRAVELOGUES... ROBSON GREEN'S GREENLAND... ALI BONGO IN THE CONGO... OH, NO, HE'S DEAD ISN'T HE?
HOW ABOUT SOMETHING WITH MARTIN CLUNES WHERE HE HAS TO BAKE SOMETHING...

HE'LL HAVE TO BAKE IT AGAINST THE CLOCK, MIND... WITHOUT A CLIFFHANGER EVERY TEN MINUTES THE VIEWERS ALL TURN OFF...
...SO YOU GO AWAY AND HAVE ANOTHER THINK, EH, ROGER?...

...BUT REMEMBER, THE DEADLINE FOR PROGRAMME SUBMISSIONS IS IN 3 HOURS
CHUNG!

WITH THE DEADLINE LOOMING, ROGER HAS GOT JUST 3 HOURS TO COME UP WITH A NEW SHOW... BUT THINGS ARE ABOUT TO GET WORSE...
COMING UP...
OH BLEEP THE BLEEP BATTERY ON MY LAP TOP IS BLEEEP DEAD!
JOIN US AFTER THE BREAK.

WELL, I HAVE TO HAND IT TO YOU, ROGER. I NEVER THOUGHT THEY'D GO FOR 'ROGER'S T.V. SHOW FORMAT PITCH NIGHTMARE'
NEVER UNDERESTIMATE THE STUPIDITY OF THE VIEWER, TOM...
ROGER'S TV SHOW FORMAT PITCH NIGHTMARE
END OF PART TWO
...AND THERE'S NO POINT FEEDING PIGS CHERRIES WHEN THEY'RE HAPPY WITH SHIT

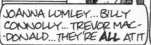

BIFFA
LOVE
HATE
BACON

AND NOW ON BBC 1, THE BLUE PLANET...
GEDDIN'... I FUCKIN' LOVE NATURE PRURGRAMMES, ME... HEH!

HOO, SON... D'Y' FANCY STARTIN' A BIT RIOT AN' DEE A BIT LOOTIN' AN THAT?
EH?... AYE... I'LL GET MESEL A GEET BIG FUCKIN' TELLY
CHAMPION

OUTSIDE
RIOT!
WOT'LL WUZ SMASH UP FORST, FATHA?
DON'T MATTAH, SON... OWT!

LET'S TORN THIS FUCKIN' CAR AWA F' STARTAZ!

THU
HNNG!
THUMP

KRUMP!

HEH! HEH!... WOT A FANTAKKA SIGHT, EH BIFFA, SON?
AYE!
HAD ON FATHA...

...WUZ'VE JUST TORCHED W' AAN FUCKIN' CAR
HEY! WE FUCKIN' HEV AN' AALL
AYE! W' DINVEN'T WANT T' GAN SHITTIN' ON W' AAN DOORSTEP. ...LET'S GAN TORCH THE TOON!
BACON5

TWO AN' A BAIRN T' THE FUCKIN' TOON, PAL
NEWCASTLE 32
BUS STOP
ARRIVAL

SHORTLY...
NICE THINGS
THOMPSON'S

HOO, FATHA! LET'S LOOT THIS FUCKAH
GOOD IDEA MUTHA
DIXONS
WUZ'LL NEED SUMMAT HEAVY FO' T' HOY THROUGH THE WINDEE, MIND

'ERE'S SUMMAT, MUTHA.
PUFF!! PANT!!

JUST THE FUCKIN' JOB, THAT

CLUNK!

DIXONS
CRASH!
52 INCH

LOOK AT THAT, MUTHA...THE FUCKIN' DOOR WAZ URPEN AALL ALONG
Y' FUCKIN' PAIR O' CUNTS, YUZ
OFF YER ARSE, SON...
...WUZ'RE WASTIN' VALUABLE LOOTIN' TIME

REET... I'M GANNA GET MESEL' A **GEET BIG FUCK OFF** TELLY FO'T' WATCH THE BLOO PLANAT

THIS 'UN'LL DEE... HEH!
HEY! YOU PUT THAT BACK
72 INCH!!

HOO, MUTHA... WUZ'VE GOT W'SELLS A HEV-A-GAN-HEE-RUR
HEV WUZ, NOO?.. WELL PRAPS HE'D LIKE T' HEV A GAN ON MY FUCKIN' **BOOT!**

PUNT!
HOO, SON... DIVVEN'T FORGET T' LOOT YERSEL AN EXTENDED WARRANTY IN CASE THE FUCKER BREAKS DOON
GOOD IDEA, FATHA
72 INCH

REET. LET'S GAN T' ARGOS AN' FOOTLOCKAH F' SOME WATCHES AN' TRAINAZ
DIXONS

NEXT DAY...
LOOK AT THE SIZE O' **THAT** FUCKAH, READAZ...
...I FUCKIN' **LOVE** LOOTIN', ME

THUMP!! BANG!! CRASH!!
EH?.. WOT THE FUCK..!?

HOO!.. KEEP THE FUCKIN' NOISE DOON, YOUS TWOS...
I'M TRYIN' T' WATCH THE FUCKIN' BLOO PLANAT
TUG!
BIFFA'S ROOM FUCK OFF

WUZ'RE ON ANOTHER ORGY O' DESTRUCTION, SON... IT'S LIKE A FUCKIN' **DRUG**, MAN.
SMASH THE FEDS
LET'S LOOT THE FUCKIN BAIRN'S ROOM, FATHA!
RIP!!

WHACK!

ANARCHY! ANARCHY!
FUCKIN' BASTAADS

WE ALL love to get drunk and photocopy our arses at the office Christmas party. It's a festive tradition that is as much a part of the holiday season as mulled wine, carol singers and the yule log crackling merrily in your grate. But have you ever stopped to wonder where this time-honoured custom comes from? Join us now on a fascinating trip through history, as we take a look at...

Photocopying your arse at the office Christmas party through the ages

LASCAUX, FRANCE, 55,000 BC. A stone age Neanderthal, drunk on crudely-fermented tree-fern wine at a festival to celebrate the winter solstice, smears woad on his buttocks and presses them against a series of stone tablets, to the ribald amusement of his fellow revellers.

PALESTINE, 33AD. Jesus throws a combined Christmas and birthday party and invites his twelve-strong staff of disciples. After turning a chalice of water into lager, which he then drinks, Christ sits on several A4-sized squares of linen. Miraculously, each one develops a mysterious image in negative of his bottom. After the crucifixion, the apostles distribute the buttock shrouds to the four corners of the known world, where they remain to this day as objects of veneration and raucous hilarity.

1451, MAINZ, GERMANY. Prior to the invention of printing, multiple pictures of arses at Christmas parties have to be laboriously illuminated by monks using quills, with a single image often taking taking several weeks to complete. However, the development of Johannes Gutenberg's press in the 15th Century speeds up the process considerably. Whilst drunk at his office Christmas party, Herr Gutenberg drops his trousers, climbs onto his printing machine and runs off over 200 impressions of his backside. The next morning, a chastened, embarrassed and hung-over Gutenberg is forced to call on all his employees in an attempt to retrieve the offending prints.

1851, LONDON. The morning after a grand Christmas party thrown by Queen Victoria, a cleaner sets about clearing up dozens of sepia photolithographs of the monarch's buttocks which are pinned up all around the State reception rooms at Buckingham Palace. However, there are to be no more office parties during Victoria's reign as, during the revelries, the angry royal has been not been amused to catch her beloved Prince Albert behind a filing cabinet, getting his cloth tit off Florence Nightingale.

2011, HOUSTON, TEXAS. These days, thanks to advances in technology, you don't even have to be present at the office party in order to photocopy your arse! Here, high above the earth in the weightless vacuum of space, a Shuttle astronaut drops his spacesuit trousers and sits on the lens of the Hubble Space telescope. The images are beamed digitally 250,000 miles to NASA Mission Control, where the NASA Christmas bash is in full swing, and 150 copies of his buttocks are instantly printed out by the computer console.

NEXT WEEK: Banging a bird from accounts in the stationery cupboard at the office Christmas party whilst semi-erect through the ages

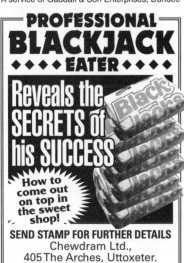

Top Gear Conman GUILTY

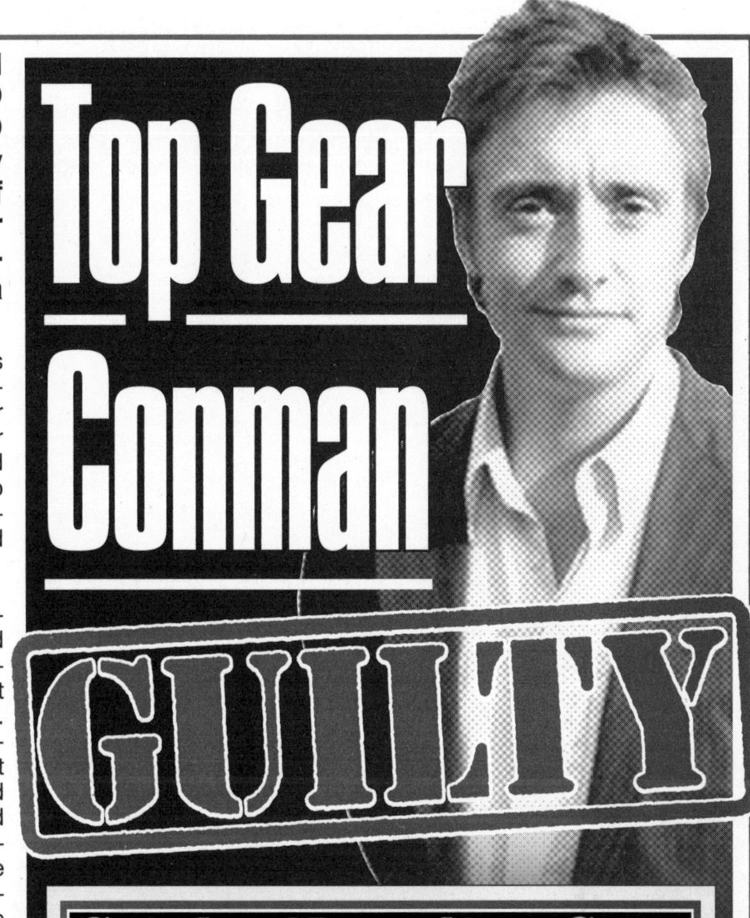

TV petrolhead RICHARD HAMMOND was yesterday found guilty of obtaining money under false pretences after faking his own survival in a rocket car accident.

The *Top Gear* presenter, 41, was killed when he crashed a high-powered jet car during a stunt for the popular Sunday night motor show in 2006. But a court heard yesterday how he pretended to be alive after the accident, claiming over £1million in wages and expenses from the BBC.

A *Top Gear* spokesman yesterday said that everyone involved in the programme felt betrayed. "We all believed that Richard had survived the accident," he told reporters outside Streatham Crown Court. "To find out that he's been pulling the wool over our eyes for five years is disappointing to say the least."

Hoaxer Hamster faces music for car crash scam

salary

Hammond, 4'1", managed the deception so well that even close family members didn't suspect he had perished in the 300mph dragster smash at Elvington Airfield in Yorkshire. Known to fans around the world by his nickname 'The Hamster', the presenter continued to bank his salary between 2006 and 2011, turning up at the BBC every day to present the top-rated show alongside co-hosts Jeremy Clarkson and James May.

"He gave every appearance of being alive," said a BBC source. "But it was all an act. How could he lie to us like that, letting us think that he wasn't dead?"

kebbege

Hammond's body stood impassively in the dock as the Judge passed sentence. In his summing up, Mr Justice Easter-Island told Hammond: "You have betrayed the trust of the public and of your colleagues. Only the fact that you have been dead for the last five years has saved you from a lengthy custodial sentence."

The late Hammond declined to comment as he was whisked away from the court in a police hearse to Basingstoke crematorium where he was reduced to ashes and put in a vase.

Catch a Frauding Star

RICHARD Hammond is not the first celebrity to be caught out conning the great British public. Here is a checklist of shame, counting down the top 5 showbiz scammers...

In 1995, *Gladiators* star **WOLF** claimed £280 in incapacity benefit after he accidentally drove a friend's moped off Beachy Head, cricking his neck and leaving himself with severely restricted movement. However, after receiving a tip-off, DSS officers spotted him on television, fighting with a pugil stick, running up a travelator and hurtling round a combat arena in an atlas-sphere.

Newsreader HUW EDWARDS **was disciplined by BBC bosses after a series of fraudulent e-mails were traced to his computer in the *10 O'Clock News* studio. For six months, the Welsh anchorman had been posing as a Nigerian businessman with a large sum of money to invest. He had targeted gullible internet users, promising them large sums of cash once a hefty 'set up fee' had been paid.**

At Christmas 2009, That's Life host **ESTHER RANTZEN** set up a free gift-wrapping service in a tent in the *Blue Peter* garden at BBC Television Centre. Stars and production staff alike left expensive gifts to be wrapped by the toothy presenter. However, unseen in the tent, Rantzen was working a scam - removing expensive i-pods, perfumes and watches from their boxes and replacing them with a similar weight of soil. By the time the fraud was discovered on Christmas morning, Rantzen had fled the BBC and was miles away, trying to get elected as MP for Luton.

Boggle-eyed astronomer PATRICK MOORE **and grinning boffin** BRIAN COX **were hauled over the coals for running a 'Find the Lady' scam in *EastEnders*' Albert Square market. Professor Cox would pose as an ordinary passer-by and win £5 off Moore in what would appear to be a simple card game. However, when others tried their luck and wagered their cash, *The Sky at Night* host would win every time. By the time security chased the pair off the set, the egghead conmen had scammed nearly £400 from the cast of the popular soap.**

In 2009, **RUSSELL BRAND** turned up at the BBC claiming he was a comedian. He talked his way into Broadcasting House and conned the elderly Director General into giving him tens of thousands of pounds in return for shoddy and unfunny radio programmes. When listeners finally discovered the extent of his fraud, Brand was challenged by the Corporation, but by that time he had fled to America.

OH, XMAS! IT'S THE
FAT SLAGS
XMAS DAY...
YOU SURE THAT TURKEY WAS ALRIGHT, TRAY? ME GUTS IS AWFUL...
...I'M FARTIN' LIKE FUCKIN' THUNDER
ME AN' ALL
QUACK!
I THOUGHT Y'SAID IT WERE FREE RANGE
NO... I SAID IT WERE FREE...
BRAAP!
...DAVE FOUND IT IN A BIN OUT BACK OF ICELAND LAST WEEK
HONK!
IT 'ADN'T BEEN THERE LONG... IT WERE ONLY HALF DEFROSTED
WELL IT'S WRECKED MY FUCKIN' GUTS...
...I'M DROPPIN' SOME EVIL FUCKIN' FARTS 'ERE, I AM
ANYROAD, WOT'S WI' THE STOCKINGS AN' THE BALCON-ETTE BRA, SAN?
QUACK!
I'M GOIN' T' GIVE ME-SELF T' BAZ AS AN EROTIC CHRISTMAS PRESSIE
TOOT!
BRAAP!
FUCK! I NEARLY FOLLOWED THROUGH ON THAT ONE
LISTEN... I'M GOIN' T' GET IN THIS BOX, AN' YOU CAN WRAP ME UP AN THEN GO AN' GET BAZ OUT THE PUB...
PIP!
...THEN WHEN HE UNDOES THE SELLOTAPE I JUMP OUT AN' SHOUT 'MERRY CHRISTMAS' AN LET 'IM 'AVE 'IS WICKED WAY
PARP!
SQUOONK!
DO IT UP PROPER, TRAY... I DON'T WANT 'IM T' GUESS WOT HE'S GEDDIN.
RIGHT... GO AN' FETCH 'IM TRAY... AN' DON'T BE LONG. IT'S A BIT CLOSTRA IN 'ERE
BLAP!
CHRIST
SHORTLY...
SO HERE IT IS, MERRY CHRISTMAS, EVERYBODY'S HAVING FUN...
'ERE, BAZ... SAN'S GOT Y'A PRESSIE F' CHRISTMAS... SHE WANTS Y'T' COME BACK T' OURS AN' OPEN IT
'AS SHE?...
AH, THAT'S NICE... LISTEN, D'Y'FANCY A QUICK DRINK BEFOR WE GO, TRAY?
GO ON THEN, BAZ
JUST A QUICK 'ON MIND
PIP!
SAME AGAIN, IS IT, DAVE?
AYE
4 HOURS LATER...
...SO HE'S WANKIN' AWAY, AN' THE CAT COMES IN AN' STARTS LICKIN' HIS HELMET... AN' HE THINKS TO 'IMSELF... "WELL, WHY NOT?"
NA-AA
PIP!
FUCKIN' CAT!
HEH! DIRTY GET!
EEH, BAZ... LOOK AT THE TIME. I TOLD SAN I'D ONLY BE TEN MINUTES.
EEH, DON'T FRET.
...I'M NOT IN ANY RUSH TO UNDO A PAIR O' FUCKIN' SOCKS, TRAY.
NO, IT'S NOT SOCKS, BAZ
EH? WOT IS IT, THEN?
DOG HAMMER
I CAN'T TELL Y'... IT'S A S'PRISE. BUT SHE'S WENT TO A LOT OF TROUBLE
HONK!

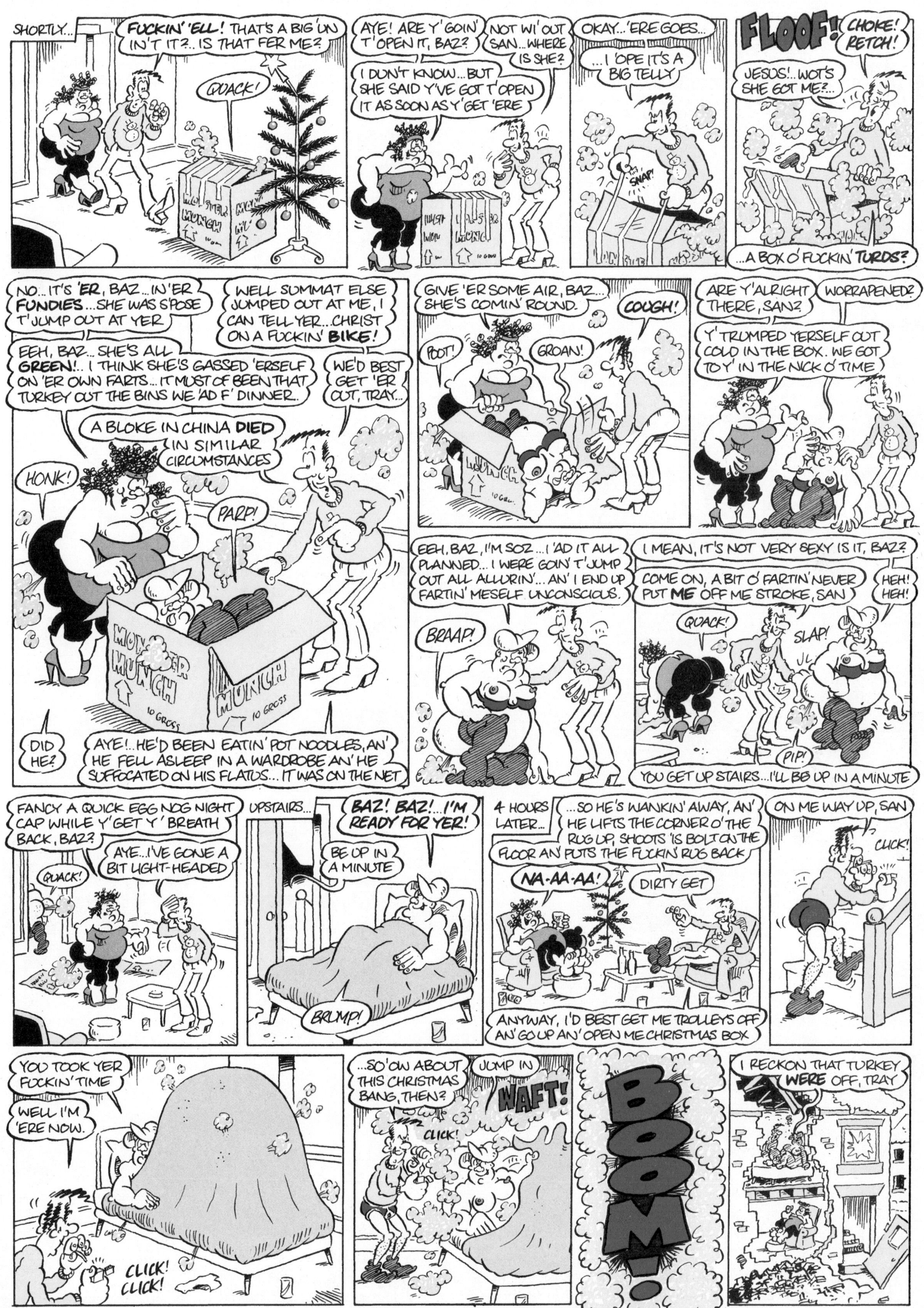
SHORTLY...
FUCKIN' 'ELL! THAT'S A BIG 'UN IN'T IT?.. IS THAT FER ME?
QUACK!
AYE! ARE Y' GOIN' T' OPEN IT, BAZ?
NOT WI' OUT SAN... WHERE IS SHE?
I DUN'T KNOW... BUT SHE SAID Y'VE GOT T' OPEN IT AS SOON AS Y' GET 'ERE
OKAY... 'ERE GOES...
...I 'OPE IT'S A BIG TELLY
SNAP!
FLOOF!
CHOKE! RETCH!
JESUS!... WOT'S SHE GOT ME?...
...A BOX O' FUCKIN' TURDS?
NO... IT'S 'ER, BAZ... IN 'ER FUNDIES... SHE WAS S'POSE T' JUMP OUT AT YER
WELL SUMMAT ELSE JUMPED OUT AT ME, I CAN TELL YER... CHRIST ON A FUCKIN' BIKE!
EEH, BAZ... SHE'S ALL GREEN!.. I THINK SHE'S GASSED 'ERSELF ON 'ER OWN FARTS... IT MUST OF BEEN THAT TURKEY OUT THE BINS WE 'AD F' DINNER..
WE'D BEST GET 'ER OUT, TRAY...
A BLOKE IN CHINA DIED IN SIMILAR CIRCUMSTANCES
HONK!
PARP!
DID HE?
AYE!.. HE'D BEEN EATIN' POT NOODLES, AN' HE FELL ASLEEP IN A WARDROBE AN' HE SUFFOCATED ON HIS FLATUS... IT WAS ON THE NET
GIVE 'ER SOME AIR, BAZ... SHE'S COMIN' ROUND.
COUGH!
POOT!
GROAN!
ARE Y' ALRIGHT THERE, SAN?
WORRAPENED?
Y' TRUMPED YERSELF OUT COLD IN THE BOX. WE GOT TO Y' IN THE NICK O' TIME
EEH, BAZ, I'M SOZ... I 'AD IT ALL PLANNED... I WERE GOIN' T' JUMP OUT ALL ALLURIN'... AN' I END UP FARTIN' MESELF UNCONSCIOUS.
BRAAP!
I MEAN, IT'S NOT VERY SEXY IS IT, BAZ?
COME ON, A BIT O' FARTIN' NEVER PUT ME OFF ME STROKE, SAN
HEH! HEH!
QUACK!
SLAP!
PIP!
YOU GET UP STAIRS... I'LL BE UP IN A MINUTE
FANCY A QUICK EGG NOG NIGHT CAP WHILE Y' GET Y' BREATH BACK, BAZ?
AYE... I'VE GONE A BIT LIGHT-HEADED
QUACK!
UPSTAIRS...
BAZ! BAZ!... I'M READY FOR YER!
BE UP IN A MINUTE
BRUMP!
4 HOURS LATER...
...SO HE'S WANKIN' AWAY, AN' HE LIFTS THE CORNER O' THE RUG UP, SHOOTS 'IS BOLT ON THE FLOOR AN' PUTS THE FUCKIN' RUG BACK
NA-AA-AA!
DIRTY GET
ANYWAY, I'D BEST GET ME TROLLEYS OFF AN' GO UP AN' OPEN ME CHRISTMAS BOX
ON ME WAY UP, SAN
CLICK!
YOU TOOK YER FUCKIN' TIME
WELL I'M 'ERE NOW.
CLICK! CLICK!
...SO 'OW ABOUT THIS CHRISTMAS BANG, THEN?
JUMP IN
WAFT!
CLICK!
BOOM!
I RECKON THAT TURKEY WERE OFF, TRAY

RICHARD LITTLEJOHN IS... GOING TO HELL IN A HANDCART

TCHOH! ACCORDING TO THIS STORY I'VE JUST MADE UP, THE HEALTH NAZIS ARE TELLING ME THAT EATING MORE THAN 2 BACON SARNIES A WEEK IS BAD FOR MY **HEART**, NOW... TALK ABOUT THE NANNY STATE...
CLICK!.. ...CLICK!...
DEAR, OH DEAR, OH DEAR

WELL MY OLD MAN DIDN'T DIE IN TWO WORLD WARS SO SOME BARMY BRUSSELS BUREACRATS COULD STOP ME HAVING A GOOD OLD-FASHIONED BRITISH BACON BUTTY WHENEVER I LIKE...
HERE YOU GO, MR LITTLEJOHN.
OH, NO... NO HAMPSTEAD GUARDIANISTAS ARE G
TO DICTATE WHAT **I** HAVE FOR BREKKY... NO SIR

STROLL ON... I THOUGHT THE ROAD TO HELL WAS PAVED WITH GOOD INTENTIONS... FEELS LIKE IT'S NOT BLOODY WELL PAVED AT **ALL!**
'SPOSE IT'S TOO MUCH TO ASK THE LOCAL HELL COUNCIL TO FILL THESE **POT HOLES** IN...

...PROBABLY BLOWN ALL THE RATEPAYERS' CASH ON MUSLIM DROP-IN CENTRES, BLACKS ONLY SWIMMING POOLS AND BOOKS ON LESBIANISM FOR THE LIBRARIES.
...I THOUGHT I'D HEARD IT ALL!

RICHARD WILLIAM LITTLEJOHN ... **BEHOLD!!**... THE RIVER STYX DO YOU HAVE THE COINS TO PAY THE FERRYMAN?

...AS FOR THE COINS, I'VE ONLY GOT **STERLING!** I DARE SAY IT'S ONLY **EUROS** HERE IN THE PEOPLES REPUBLIC OF HELLISTAN... TCHOH!..
EUROS!!..
AND HERE'S ME THINKING **WE** WON THE WAR!

HERE WE GO... NO DOUBT I'LL HAVE TO WEAR A HI-VIZ JACKET AND HARD HAT TO GET ON THIS THING... AND SIGN A BLOODY DISCLAIMER FOR GOOD MEASURE...
...IT'S THE 'ELF AND SAFETY COMPENSATION CULTURE' GONE MAD, I TELL YOU...CAH!!

HONESTLY... IF YO DIDN'T LAUGH, YOU'D CRY.

NOT THAT PETROL PRICES BOTHER **THIS LOT**... I BET THEY'RE **ALL** ON DISABILITY BENEFITS... COINING IT IN FOR BEING DEAD.
SHIT
JAB!!
PULL THE OTHER ONE, IT'S GOT BELLS ON... THEY'RE NO MORE DEAD THAN I AM

RICHARD WILLIAM LITTLEJOHN... FOR YOUR WICKED LIFE, YOU SHALL BE CHAINED TO A HOT ROCK AND YOUR LIVER SHALL BE PECKED OUT BY A GRYPHON... FOR ALL ETERNITY.
EH? CALL THAT A PUNISHMENT?... HELL'S MORE LIKE A HOLIDAY CAMP THESE DAYS...

AND I DARE SAY THE TRENDY ANIMAL RIGHTS LOONIES WILL BE ON TO YOU FOR CRUELTY TO GRYPHONS, IF YOU PLEASE
PUNISHMENT, MY ARSE... SL ON THE WRIST, MORE LIKE